FRESH
FROM
THE
GARDEN

OTHER BOOKS BY PERLA MEYERS

The Seasonal Kitchen

The Peasant Kitchen

From Market to Kitchen

Burpee's American Harvest Cookbooks: The Spring Garden

Burpee's American Harvest Cookbooks: The Early Summer Garden

Perla Meyers' Art of Seasonal Cooking

Spur of the Moment Cook

FRESH FROM THE GARDEN

Cooking and Gardening Throughout the Seasons
with 250 Recipes

PERLA MEYERS

CLARKSON POTTER/PUBLISHERS
NEW YORK

To my son Claude, who gives me so much joy.

CLARKSON N. POTTER, POTTER, and colophon are trademarks of Clarkson N. Potter, Inc.

Some of the recipes in this book were previously published in *Burpee's American Harvest Cookbooks:
The Spring Garden* (1988) and *Burpee's American Harvest Cookbooks: The Early Summer Garden* (1988).

Printed in the United States of America
Design by Margaret Hinders

Library of Congress Cataloging-in-Publication Data
Meyers, Perla
Fresh from the garden : cooking and gardening throughout the seasons with 250 recipes /
by Perla Meyers. — 1st ed.
Includes index.
I. Cookery (Vegetables) 2. Vegetable gardening. I. Title.
TX801.M492 1996
641.6'5—dc20 96-3269
ISBN 0-517-59357-2
10 9 8 7 6 5 4 3 2 1
First Edition

ACKNOWLEDGMENTS

Many wonderful and generous gardeners and cooks helped me with this book, but I was particularly influenced in my pursuit of perfect freshness by my maternal grandmother, my mother, and my late father. They taught me the everlasting value, appreciation of true seasonality, and joys of a kitchen garden.

A word of thanks to my editor, Pam Krauss, whose effort and faith in my work made this book possible. To my agent, Michael Cohn, who worked closely with me from beginning to end with much patience. To Debra Aleksinas for her help in shaping the introductory material.

And last, I wish to thank the many cookshops and wonderful students who have taken my classes throughout the country. Their encouragement has fueled my continued enthusiasm for my love of food and for cooking *Fresh from the Garden*.

CONTENTS

INTRODUCTION

All my hurts my garden spade can heal.

RALPH WALDO EMERSON

MORE THAN TWENTY YEARS HAVE PASSED SINCE I WROTE MY FIRST book, *The Seasonal Kitchen.* It represented a celebration of the seasons at a time when most Americans still thought that canned and frozen were just as good as fresh. Of course, I was at a distinct advantage on the freshness front, having grown up in Mediterranean Europe with a vegetable garden just outside the kitchen door. It surprised me no end that Americans, with their diversity of climates and soil hospitable to a truly spectacular variety of vegetables as well as fruits, had moved so far away from the concept of kitchen gardening, and in turn lost touch with the natural rhythms and bounties of the seasons.

Certainly for me, finding a way to once again experience the pleasures of cooking and eating vegetables only minutes out of the garden was a priority. As soon as the opportunity presented itself, I started a small vegetable garden of my own. My husband and I had just bought a small farmhouse in Connecticut, and we immediately searched for the sunniest spot in which to work our spade. Our soil had never been farmed, and we spent endless hours removing stones and tree roots, breaking up the lumps of clay-like earth, and trying to find a way to water the newly prepared garden patch.

I started the basics, the tomatoes, cucumbers, lettuce, and peas, and as the garden grew, so did my very assortment of vegetables and herbs. I stocked up on seed catalogs and eventually added some sorrel—a vegetable that to this day is difficult to find unless you grow it yourself—fava beans, and French string beans, working from memories of my Mediterranean childhood garden in an effort to re-create those days of bountiful harvest.

Admittedly, all did not come easy. Despite my efforts, my soil resisted, as did the Northeast climate. I was soon to be reminded I was in Connecticut, not in Barcelona, that the sun was not going to be shining for eight months of the year and that I would be forced to give up on some of my most treasured vegetables. At times, I almost despaired. Seed catalogs listed only a basic selection with mostly hybrid varieties seemingly developed for cooks and farmers more concerned with appearance, size, and shipping qualities than taste. Fortunately, all this has since changed, and with the advent of small seed companies it is now possible to grow and harvest a wonderful range of greens, tubers, vegetables, and fruits.

Tasting even those first, sometimes disappointing, specimens reaffirmed my belief that fresh and seasonal were the two most important bywords for any cook; as I continued to garden, and cook, and garden some more, the concept for *The Seasonal Kitchen* began to take shape. I felt that Americans needed to be reminded of the wonders of the kitchen garden—that there was something extraordinary just beyond the conventional American grocery store aisles with their pretty, but often out-of-season and mostly tasteless, produce. I knew instinctively that people would respond to the variety and immediacy seasonal produce brings to any menu, transforming even the simplest of dishes into an infinite spectrum of flavors.

Today, we are finally recognizing that vegetables deserve our full attention. When assessing the cuisines of the Mediterranean, Europe, and the Middle East that have become so very fashionable in recent years, it is the vegetable preparations of these countries that are the most exciting and the most memorable. The stuffed vegetables of Turkey, the vegetable paellas of Spain, the classic vegetable fricassees of southern France, not to mention the myriad noodle and rice dishes of Italy, all marry our favorite grains and pasta shapes with an endless variety of seasonal produce.

And along with the pleasures of the table, Americans are also warming to the inherent satisfactions of growing their own vegetables, the unique joys that come from placing a platter of thickly sliced tomatoes from one's own garden on the table, or from preserving pints of corn relish and pickled onions to bring back the scents and warmth of the garden plot all winter long. For me, gardening is a passion rooted in my small plot of the earth. The planting, weeding, and, finally, harvesting truly fuel the soul. As my father once said, "Once you have had the luxury of your own garden, it is hard to imagine life without it."

A kitchen garden needn't be large to offer up enough fresh lettuce, beans, squash, and tomatoes to happily feed a family from just weeks after the last frost right up to full winter. And even the weekend gardener can ensure a generous harvest by choosing untemperamental vegetables that don't need daily weeding or monitoring. If you have the time, the space, and the energy—for, make no mistake, gardening can be back-breaking, if rewarding, labor—I urge you to try even a few plants, perhaps several of your favorite herbs, a few pepper and tomato plants, or perhaps more exotic choices like asparagus or snap peas. Once you've sampled your first harvest, there'll be no turning back.

Even if your thumb is resolutely black, however, thanks to the tradition of the farm markets and roadside stands that seem to be proliferating throughout the country, even non-gardeners now have access to freshness at its best and most flavorful. True, this seasonal access to garden-fresh produce is only available a few months out of the year, and of course, it varies from region to region. Unfortunately, many so-called farm stands buy much of the produce they carry from the same suppliers as the local supermarket does, and often they even charge more for it. It is really up to you to know what vegetables are in season and to be on the lookout for what appears to have been grown locally, or at least on the same coast.

If we truly care about taste, it is important that we support our local farmers by being willing to pay the somewhat higher prices in return for the cream of the crop. After all, it is thanks to these dedicated people that we can enjoy true flavor without putting in the labor that a kitchen garden demands. I, too, understand the need for convenience, especially for the working cook whose shopping is limited to a once-a-week stop at a supermarket. Still, you need not settle for tired, wilted, and bruised vegetables and unripe fruit. Once you recognize true freshness you are bound to become hooked on flavor, as I am. You may never again want to settle for second best. Why not build your cooking repertoire around what is truly seasonal rather than around produce that has been shipped from 3,000 miles away?

Yes, we have prolonged seasons during which many of our vegetables are less than perfect, in which flavor is lost through long cold storage and transportation. But that gives us all the more reason to take advantage when the harvesting season is in our backyards, or down the road a bit, and give the vegetables of the season a chance to shine on their own. Believe me, they will never let you down.

This book is a celebration of these jewels of nature. It will surely convince you of what my father used to say whenever he came into the kitchen with a bowl or basket of whatever crop he had just picked, often chewing on a soil-covered radish or carrot: "Fresh is good, fresh and seasonal is better, and fresh from the garden is best."

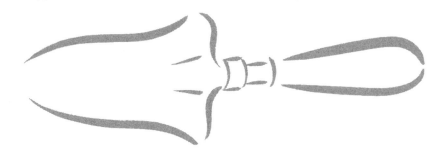

The first day of spring is one thing, and the first spring day is another.
The difference between them is sometimes as great as a month.

CHINESE PROVERB

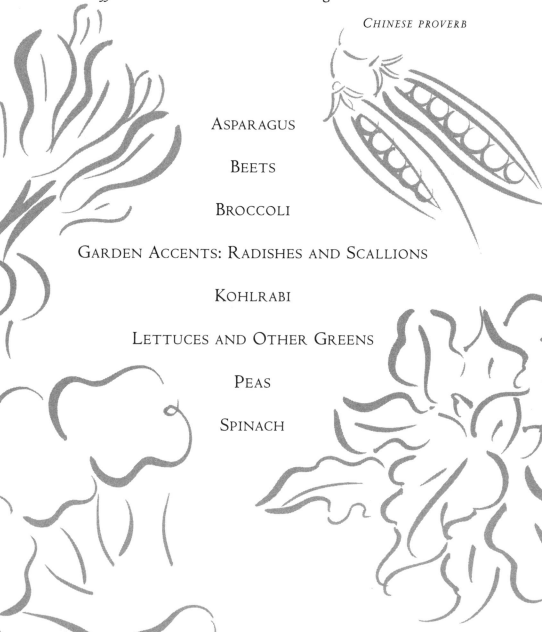

ASPARAGUS

BEETS

BROCCOLI

GARDEN ACCENTS: RADISHES AND SCALLIONS

KOHLRABI

LETTUCES AND OTHER GREENS

PEAS

SPINACH

Spring means many different

things to many people. To my grandmother, spring meant "apron greens," which

would grow wild in the meadows near our house. She had a keen eye for spotting

very young dandelion greens just at the right stage and would drop the young

shoots into her large apron. We would often go together into the fields and I still

remember seeing the smile on her face. She knew her greens and would relish the

thought of these spring gems tossed into a sweet Viennese lemon and honey

dressing or added at the last moment to a full-bodied consommé.

For my father, spring meant going after fresh morel mushrooms, which he loved. He especially liked teaching me how to spot these lovely, mild, and unique mushrooms. My mother's mind was set on the vegetables and herbs of her youth in Austria that were unavailable in Barcelona: dill, kohlrabi, beets, and mâche lettuce were tops on her list, and she was pretty single-minded about getting these into the garden and onto the table.

For many Americans, and especially American gardeners, spring brings with it a sense of fervent anticipation to those of us who cannot wait to return to the garden. I envision tiny, delicate leaves of lettuce, feathery tops of carrots, and baby pea shoots while I wait for the last signs of frost to disappear.

Spring also tests your patience. I am usually prepared weeks before the garden is ready for planting, since I have already spent weekends roaming through my favorite garden centers, eyeing and mentally selecting too many seedlings, including the many annual flowers I like to intersperse among my vegetables. I can't resist the temptation of one more "new" variety of tomato or bug-resistant cucumber plant, nor can I pass up an enticing perennial for yet another border that I know will take more time and effort than I can honestly give it as a weekend gardener.

As I bundle up and go trudging off into the garden in early spring, there is still a nip in the air and the wind is less than gentle. But my hands ache for the touch of the warm soil, and I am ready for the sight of the greens and yellows that dominate a spring garden. Every New England gardener knows that you can easily be tricked by Mother Nature, as a brilliant, sunny day in early spring can easily be followed by a blanket of snow the next. Still, it's difficult to resist the intoxicating smell of the moist soil, and my euphoric mood is not dampened by the relative shortness of the Northeast spring. Instead, I challenge it—I try to get my lettuces, peas, and radishes, spinach and kohlrabi into the garden and on into the kitchen as quickly as possible. Spring is about this kind of exuberance, about feeling that you can accomplish everything. The days are longer, the evenings warmer, and the energy just seems to flow.

This is when the first green vegetables sprout forth from the long-barren dirt, a sign of good things to follow and a tease to the palate. They start the juices flowing for the fresh, crisp, earthy taste we have yearned for during the long winter months. Every spring vegetable is a star. Fresh, crisp, tender lettuce, curly or headed, red or green, is something not to be found at the local supermarket, and those who experience it from garden to table can never quite appreciate its store-bought cousins in the same way again. And if May could be named for a vegetable, it would be known as asparagus month. Who can resist this incredible vegetable, be it in a soup, risotto, or pasta or simply cooked and served with a brown butter?

The farm stands, dormant through the winter months, once again begin to sprout along the roadsides. What a joy to see that abundance of produce so early in the season. Of course, I get carried away, buying too much and then facing all that good food wondering what in the world I am going to do with it. But so what? How bad can a plateful of young greens be tossed in a simple shallot and mustard dressing? Or a perfect dish of tiny peas?

While the calendar month may read the same all around the country, spring is at a different stage depending on climate. At a time when New Englanders are limited to the slim pickings of early spring—the first sugar snaps, or tender rhubarb—Californians or Floridians, for instance, have long been enjoying the fruit of their labor. I admit I feel a pang of envy when I think of those states where the U PICK signs call our attention to fertile fields of juicy ripe strawberries and where you see people lugging large baskets brimming with peppers, tomatoes, and giant spring onions fresh off the farm stands.

But whichever region of the country you call home, there is magic in the spring garden. For me, it still recalls the many companionable hours I spent planting with my father. I loved making the tiny holes, dropping the seeds carefully, and covering them gently with the loose soil. At night, I would imagine that I could hear the radishes grow, and even before breakfast I would tiptoe through the rows to see what, if anything, had happened during the night. Once I spotted the pinkish-red top of a radish I would set my mind to eat it as soon as it was ready, which often was too early. Still, nothing that anyone could buy fresh at the market is ever as pleasurable as those first pickings of spring.

ASPARAGUS

NOT SO VERY LONG AGO, THE ARRIVAL OF FRESH ASPARAGUS AT THE markets was a true harbinger of spring. Suddenly, in mid-March, there they were—first pencil thin, then fat and juicy looking. Then, long before you tired of them, asparagus would again disappear, not to return for another nine months.

Today, things are quite different. Asparagus is shipped to greengrocers and supermarkets from thousands of miles away and their season has been lengthened to an average of six months. In fact, this elegant vegetable has become so ubiquitous that few cooks or gardeners know how much better it tastes when the stalks are cut fresh from the garden.

When I was growing up, the asparagus season was celebrated with some reverence. Asparagus was considered a delicacy and received undivided attention as an appetizer accompanied by a well-flavored hollandaise, a mustard sauce, or a lemon mayonnaise. The asparagus we enjoyed then was snow white, a result of blanching—a gardening method by which the entire stalks are covered with soil to shield them from the sun and prevent the photosynthesis that leads to the development of green pigment.

Few spring vegetables lend themselves to as many exciting preparations as asparagus. One of the most delicious soups I know of is an intensely flavored asparagus soup, and both hot and cold pasta dishes work beautifully with this vegetable. It is delicious sautéed with peas and diced ham (see page 72) or pickled (page 10).

At the same time, asparagus, more than other vegetables, has the "presence" to stand alone as an appetizer with little adornment other than melted butter. The Italian style of topping a plateful of cooked asparagus with fried eggs is an outstanding way to enjoy this delectable vegetable; I often serve it as a light main course along with crusty bread and some sweet butter. Although I rarely serve asparagus as a side dish, I do find that it makes a wonderful accompaniment to broiled salmon or poached or sautéed scallops.

Generally, asparagus needs little or no garnishing, but it can take a more assertive sauce, such as the Emerald Mayonnaise on page 9. Asparagus that has been blanched in advance can be reheated by gently braising it in a little butter with a touch of fresh herbs, which creates a little light sauce.

How to prepare asparagus as well as how to cook it have been matters of controversy. Some purists claim that asparagus spears should be snapped off where they break naturally and then need little or no peeling. I prefer to cut off one to one and a half inches from the bottom of the stalks and then peel them halfway up with a vegetable peeler or a small sharp knife. This method allows you to enjoy the entire stalk and makes for more even cooking.

Rather than steam asparagus, I generally prefer to cook it in plenty of boiling salted water until just done. I tie the spears into small bundles of even size, leaving two to three spears loose for testing. And I must confess that I disapprove of the currently fashionable method of serving asparagus still on the crunchy side. The spears should be cooked through—certainly not overcooked or waterlogged, but also not left raw. Once cooked, asparagus should be spread on a single or double layer of paper towels and left to cool.

STORAGE

It is best to cook asparagus the same day you pick it or buy it. I usually blanch the entire batch and serve it hot one day and chilled the next. However, asparagus should keep well up to four or five days refrigerated in a plastic bag. When it has been cooked ahead of time and refrigerated, it is best to bring asparagus back to room temperature since the cold kills the subtle taste of the delicious spears.

To freeze asparagus, snap about two inches off the stalks, separate the stalks according to thickness and then blanch in boiling water, counting two minutes for the thin stalks and three to four minutes for medium ones. If you prefer, the stalks may also be steamed, which usually takes a minute or two longer.

GARDENING

Asparagus, unlike most vegetables, is a hardy perennial. Though you should not expect to reap significant harvests for at least two years, once they are established, asparagus plants can remain productive for fifteen to twenty years.

I prefer to plant one-year-old roots (available by mail-order and other sources), which become productive two years after planting, rather than sow seeds, which require an additional year. In either case planting must be done in very early spring. It will be worth your while to put extra care into preparing the soil since you literally will be laying the groundwork for years of productivity to come. Asparagus roots usually are planted in two-foot-wide trenches; a ten-foot-long trench yields about five pounds of spears each spring. Carefully follow the planting directions that accompany your roots, and be sure to incorporate lots of well-rooted manure or compost into the soil. Resist the temptation to cut any spears at all the first year, or more than just a few the second. This way plants will direct optimal energy toward developing strong, permanent root systems.

Established asparagus plants require little fuss. Each spring, use a vegetable fertilizer before growth begins. Be generous with water, especially while the fern-like top growth is developing; the heavier the top growth in summer, the better the yields the following spring. A three-inch layer of straw applied to asparagus beds as a mulch will help retain soil moisture and produce stalks that are cleaner and less in need of peeling.

Soup of Asparagus and Spring Onions

Like most vegetable soups, this one tastes best the day after it is made. You may eliminate the cream, but believe me, a touch of the real stuff does make a difference. If you want to go real "fancy," sprinkle each serving with a bit of julienned smoked salmon and serve the soup with some crusty black bread on the side.

1. Melt the butter in a heavy 3-quart casserole over low heat. Add the scallions together with a couple tablespoons of the broth and simmer, covered, until tender.

2. Add the flour and cook, stirring constantly, for 1 to 2 minutes without browning. Add the remaining chicken broth all at once and whisk until well blended. Add the asparagus stalks, season with salt and pepper, and simmer, partially covered, for 30 minutes.

3. Strain the soup and return the broth to the casserole. Puree the vegetables in a food processor until smooth. Add the pureed vegetables to the broth and whisk until well blended.

4. Add the asparagus tips and cream and simmer until the tips are just tender. Taste and correct the seasoning. Serve the soup hot or at room temperature, garnished with a sprinkling of fresh dill or chives, if desired.

SERVES 6

4 tablespoons (½ stick) unsalted butter
16 medium scallions, trimmed of 3 inches of greens and finely minced (about 2 cups)
6 cups chicken broth, preferably homemade (page 360)
3 tablespoons all-purpose flour
I pound asparagus, tips reserved, stalks peeled, and cut into 1-inch pieces
Salt and freshly ground white pepper
⅓ cup heavy cream
Optional: 2 tablespoons finely minced fresh dill or chives

Fricassee of Asparagus with Bitter Greens

2 tablespoons olive oil

1¼ pounds asparagus, trimmed, peeled, and cut into ½ by 1½-inch matchsticks

1 tablespoon unsalted butter

2 large Belgian endives, cored and cut into a ½-inch julienne

½ to ⅔ cup chicken broth, preferably homemade (page 360)

2½ cups stemmed arugula

1 large garlic clove, peeled and finely minced

Salt and freshly ground black pepper

There is definitely an etiquette governing the eating of asparagus that dictates it should be eaten by itself with a minimum of fussy preparation. But recently I have found that it is fun to treat asparagus in a more contemporary way, teaming it with wilted greens in this simple and vibrantly colored fricassee. Serve the fricassee as a starter followed by a risotto or a seasonal pasta dish.

1. In a large nonstick skillet, heat the oil over medium heat. Add the asparagus and cook, stirring constantly, until lightly browned.

2. Add the butter to the skillet together with the endives and ½ cup of broth and cook until the endives have wilted, about 2 to 3 minutes. If the juices run dry, add the remaining broth. Add the arugula and garlic, season with salt and pepper, and cook, stirring constantly, until the arugula has wilted and the juices have evaporated. Serve hot.

SERVES 4

Asparagus in Emerald Mayonnaise with Marinated Shrimp

An emerald mayonnaise is simply one of those addictive sauces that enhances just about every food it is served with. It is good with poached or grilled salmon or steamed artichokes, or served as a dip, but it is absolutely the perfect accompaniment to cooked asparagus. For an interesting variation omit the shrimp and wrap three or four cooked stalks in a thin slice of smoked salmon or mild, good-quality prosciutto.

1. In a saucepan, steam the spinach in the water that clings to its leaves, stirring just until wilted. Cool slightly, then squeeze out as much moisture as possible and coarsely chop.

2. Combine the spinach, scallions, parsley, garlic, and anchovies in a food processor or blender. Add the crème fraîche or sour cream, mayonnaise, and lemon juice and process until smooth. Season with salt and a large grinding of black pepper and chill for 4 to 6 hours or overnight.

3. Combine the shrimp and Provençal Vinaigrette in a small bowl and marinate for 30 minutes at room temperature.

4. To serve, place the cooked asparagus on a platter in an even layer and spoon the sauce over the spears. Place the shrimp in a decorative pattern on top of the sauce. Garnish with the chives and the sieved egg, if using, and serve slightly chilled.

S E R V E S 6

THE MAYONNAISE

2 cups tightly packed fresh spinach leaves, well rinsed
3 tablespoons minced scallions
3 tablespoons minced fresh parsley
2 large garlic cloves, peeled and crushed
4 flat anchovy fillets, drained
½ cup Crème Fraîche (page 358) or sour cream
1 cup mayonnaise, preferably homemade (page 362)
Juice of 1 large lemon
Salt and freshly ground black pepper

12 to 18 cooked shrimp
4 tablespoons Provençal Vinaigrette (page 359)
1½ pounds asparagus, peeled, trimmed, and left whole, steamed (see page 11)

GARNISH

2 tablespoons finely minced fresh chives
Optional: 1 hard-boiled egg, peeled and sieved

Ginger-Pickled Asparagus

1 pound asparagus, trimmed,
   stalks peeled and cut into
   1½-inch pieces
1 cup rice wine vinegar
½ cup sugar
½ teaspoon salt
3 ¼-inch slices fresh ginger,
   peeled

I made my first batch of pickled asparagus on a whim, but it has been such a hit among family and friends that it is now one of my pantry staples. If you do not plan to can the pickles (see Note), be sure to keep them refrigerated. Serve these crispy spears as a side dish to a hamburger, a tuna burger, lamb kebabs, or a nicely grilled ham and cheese sandwich.

1. Place the asparagus in a mixing bowl and set aside.

2. Combine the vinegar, sugar, salt, and ginger in a medium saucepan and bring slowly to a boil. Stir until the sugar has dissolved. Pour the hot syrup over the asparagus and let cool completely.

3. Pack the asparagus in a pint jar, add the liquid (including the ginger), cover tightly, and refrigerate for 24 hours before serving. The asparagus will keep for up to 6 weeks in the refrigerator.

MAKES 1 PINT

NOTE: This recipe can easily be doubled or even tripled, and may also be canned in sterilized jars. In this case, pack the asparagus into the jars and immediately process the jars for 10 minutes. Cool, check lids, and store in a cool place.

Creamy Risotto with Asparagus, Lemon, and Chives

An asparagus risotto nicely enriched with a touch of butter and plenty of freshly grated Parmesan is one of spring's signature dishes throughout Italy. Now you will find versions of this seasonal classic at top restaurants on both sides of the Atlantic. Making your own risotto takes a little time but it is most satisfying. Serve the risotto as a starter or as a weeknight main course together with a salad or a plateful of Classic Spinach alla Catalane (page 81).

1. Place the asparagus in a vegetable steamer, set over simmering water, and steam, covered, until just tender, about 5 minutes. Set aside.

2. In a small bowl, combine the lemon juice and cream, whisk until well blended, and set aside.

3. In a heavy 3½-quart casserole, melt the butter over medium heat. Add the onion and cook until soft but not browned. Add the rice and stir to coat it well with the butter. Add 2 cups of the broth and season with salt and pepper. Reduce heat to very low, cover the casserole tightly, and simmer for 10 minutes.

4. Raise the heat to medium and uncover the casserole. Stirring the rice constantly, add the remaining broth ¼ cup at a time, until each addition has been absorbed, for the next 10 minutes; you may not need all of the remaining broth. The rice should be tender on the outside but still chewy on the inside.

5. Add the reserved cream mixture together with the asparagus, chives, and Parmesan and just heat through. Taste and correct the seasoning, stir in the optional butter for enrichment and serve at once in deep soup bowls, garnished with additional Parmesan and a large grinding of black pepper.

SERVES 4 TO 5

12 asparagus spears, trimmed, peeled, and cut into ½-inch pieces
2 tablespoons fresh lemon juice
¼ cup heavy cream
2 tablespoons unsalted butter
1 medium onion, peeled and finely minced
1¼ cups Italian rice, preferably Arborio
3½ to 4 cups chicken broth, preferably homemade (page 360)
Salt and freshly ground black pepper
3 to 4 tablespoons finely minced fresh chives
¼ cup freshly grated Parmesan cheese
Optional: 2 tablespoons unsalted butter for enrichment

GARNISH
Freshly grated Parmesan cheese

BEETS

FOR ANYONE WHO HAS EVER STROLLED THROUGH A SATURDAY MORNING market in the hill towns of Provence, the sight of perfectly shaped baked beets glistening in the sun is hard to forget. There they are deep rich red, and ready to use without further preparation.

Unfortunately, the French and Italian custom of selling cooked beets has not been adopted by American markets, so we have to plan ahead. But fresh beets are worth the somewhat lengthy cooking time, for this is a vegetable that can practically double as a fruit. Full of flavor, naturally sweet, and with a color so unique and beautiful, beets stand in a class by themselves among other root crops.

Because beets like moisture and cool temperature, they are even more popular in northern climates than in this country. In Scandinavia, cooks have created wonderful dishes with beets as the key ingredient, often combining them with apples and a sweet lemon dressing. Throughout northern and central Europe a beet, herring, and potato salad is popular in both restaurants and homes.

Store-bought beets tend to be large and past their prime, rendering them tough, woody, and extremely slow to cook. But when homegrown and cooked fresh, beets are deliciously sweet, slightly crisp, and good hot or cold. Beets do work best in certain combinations—particularly with other vegetables such as cucumbers, new potatoes, and cabbage—and with crisp salad greens. Because of their assertive color, which tends to bleed, beets should be used with ingredients and vegetables that look attractive with a tinge of red.

Growing your own beets is extremely rewarding. I have tried varieties that are rarely available commercially and now grow the apricot-colored beet, which is even sweeter than the red beet and does not bleed. It is quite attractive sautéed either with a sprinkling of minced dill or as a garnish for a mixed green salad tossed in a sweet honey and lemon dressing. The golden roots are especially good when picked young as "baby" beets, and the greens are better for cooking than those of the red varieties. Use the greens for a quick stir-fry or stew them gently in a touch of butter with a light enrichment of sour cream and a sprinkling of dill.

Other fine varieties include Cylindra, a cylindrical beet that is perfect for slicing; Lutz Green Leaf; Winter Keeper, an all-purpose beet the roots of which store exceptionally well; and Little Ball, a natural baby or miniature beet. Of course, any beet picked quite young can serve as a "baby." Use the little jewel-like roots for pickling whole or as a garnish to a roast duck or a sweet-and-sour beet sauce. Except for borschts, in which beets must be grated raw, all red beets should be cooked unpeeled with as much as an inch of their tops left on.

Although they take even longer to cook than boiled beets, baked beets retain more crispness than beets cooked in water. Tiny garden-fresh beets can be steamed, but I usually prefer to cook them in lightly salted boiling water and test them for doneness with the tip of a sharp knife. Once cooked and cooled, the skins will slip right off and the beets are ready to use in flavorful salads and soups and as a hot vegetable enhanced by a sprinkling of herbs.

It is well worth pickling your own beets if you have a garden surplus. Even though pickled beets are readily available, I find that my own have a better texture—and they are fun to make and can be served the very next day. Serve with boiled beef, boiled smoked tongue, roast loin of pork, or roast beef with a side dish of horseradish cream.

STORAGE

Beets can be stored successfully in the refrigerator for up to two weeks. Remove their greens, leaving one inch of the tops attached, and then place the roots in a perforated plastic bag. Cooked beets will keep for four or five days. Although they may start to shrivel, their flavor will not be affected. To prepare beets for freezing, cook them unpeeled and with an inch of their tops attached, until tender. Slip off the skins and pack them whole, sliced, or cubed in well-sealed plastic bags. They keep for four to six months.

GARDENING

The faster beets grow the better they generally taste, so I spend some time conditioning the earth to create the rich, loose loam in which they flourish. Once planted in the right stuff, beets go on their merry way with little attention from the gardener. I start sowing seeds in early spring, as soon as the ground is workable, and continue sowing at three-week intervals, stopping two months before the expected arrival of fall frost. Then I have a season-long supply of young and tender roots. Because plants are hardy enough to withstand light frost, harvesting can continue far into autumn.

Beets are particularly sensitive to acidic soil, so be sure to dig in some ground limestone if the pH level is below 6.0. Before sowing, spade or rototill the bed to a depth of at least eight inches, raking away any stones.

Open a seed packet of beets and what you see are "seedballs," each of which contains several seeds. Clusters of seedlings will arise from the planted seedballs, and you should promptly thin out all but the strongest seedlings from each cluster. Provide enough water during hot spells to keep beet foliage from wilting. Without plenty of water, the roots will become tough.

HARVESTING

Beets are ready to be picked seven to eight weeks after sowing. It is best not to delay because if left in the ground the roots become tough and woody. I check for size by pushing aside some soil by hand. If the root tops are two inches or more across, I pull them up. Do not use a trowel or other sharp tool since beet skins puncture easily, ruining the root.

Beet and Cucumber Salad in a Sweet Mustard Vinaigrette

Here is a refreshing and delicious salad that makes a nice addition to the picnic basket or the hors d'oeuvre table. You can vary it by adding some diced boiled potatoes and serving the salad on a bed of crisp Belgian endives.

1. Combine the lemon juice, sugar, mustard, dill, and scallions in a serving bowl. Add the oil in a slow stream, whisking constantly until smooth and creamy. Season with salt and pepper.

2. Add the beets, cucumbers, and cheese to the vinaigrette and toss gently. Chill for 4 to 6 hours before serving. Serve slightly chilled, accompanied by thinly sliced pumpernickel bread.

SERVES 4 TO 5

Juice of 1 large lemon
2 teaspoons sugar
1 tablespoon Dijon mustard
3 tablespoons finely minced fresh dill
3 tablespoons finely minced scallions
5 tablespoons olive oil
Salt and freshly ground black pepper
4 to 5 medium beets (about 1 pound), cooked (see page 17), peeled, and cut into ½-inch dice
1 pound small Kirby cucumbers, peeled and cut into ½-inch dice
⅓ cup diced Gruyère or Swiss cheese

THE BATTER

I cup cake flour or all-purpose
   flour
I cup water
I tablespoon peanut oil
I teaspoon baking powder
½ teaspoon salt

THE DIPPING SAUCE

3 tablespoons soy sauce
2 tablespoons water
Juice of 2 limes
I large garlic clove, peeled and
   mashed
½-inch piece fresh ginger,
   peeled and mashed through
   a garlic press
I teaspoon finely minced
   jalapeño pepper or ¼
   teaspoon crushed red
   pepper flakes
2 teaspoons sugar
2 tablespoons finely minced
   scallions
2 teaspoons Chinese sesame oil

THE VEGETABLES

4 cups peanut oil for deep-
   frying
2 medium beets (about ¾
   pound), cooked, peeled, and
   cut into ⅛-inch slices
I medium-size red onion,
   peeled, cut into ¼-inch
   slices, and separated into
   rings
Coarse salt

Tempura of Beets and Red Onions in Sweet and Spicy Lime Sauce

Fried beets of all things are a popular vegetable preparation in Austrian cooking, and my mother prepared them perfectly. Now I like the idea of teaming the crispy sweet beets with an Oriental dipping sauce similar to that served with traditional Japanese tempura. The beets make an unusual appetizer or a light main course. If you have any leftover batter use it to dip and fry some scallions, a perfect accompaniment to the beets.

1. Combine all the batter ingredients in a large mixing bowl and whisk until well blended. Let the batter rest for 1 hour.

2. Combine all the ingredients for the dipping sauce in a small bowl and whisk until well blended. Set aside.

3. Heat the peanut oil in a large saucepan to 375°F. on a candy thermometer. Dip the beet slices and rings of onion into the batter, letting the excess drip back into the bowl. Add to the hot oil a few at a time and cook until golden brown on one side. Turn and continue cooking until crisp and golden brown. Transfer to a double layer of paper towels to drain.

4. Continue frying the remaining beets and onions in the same manner. Sprinkle with a little coarse salt and serve at once, with the dipping sauce on the side.

SERVES 4 TO 6

Red Beet, Lemon, and Mint Soup with Crème Fraîche

Even non-beet eaters change their minds once they sample this lovely tangy soup. Here the sweetness of the beets is teamed with the clean, refreshing, tart flavor of lemon and some crème fraîche. Add a sprinkling of your favorite herb and serve with a side dish of black bread for a perfect spring or summer starter.

1. In a medium-size casserole, bring salted water to a boil. Add the beets and simmer, partially covered, for 45 minutes, or until tender when pierced with the tip of a sharp knife. Drain and, when cool enough to handle, peel the beets; the skins should slip right off. Trim and cut into ¼-inch dice.

2. Reserve 1 cup of the diced beets, and place the remainder in a food processor. Add 1 cup of the broth and puree until smooth. Set aside.

3. Melt the butter in a heavy 4-quart casserole over medium heat. Add the flour and cook, stirring constantly, for 1 to 2 minutes without browning. Add the remaining broth all at once and whisk until smooth. Bring to a boil, whisk in the beet puree, and season with salt and pepper. Reduce the heat and simmer, partially covered, for 20 minutes.

4. Add the reserved diced beets together with the crème fraîche and lemon juice. Correct the seasoning and simmer for 5 minutes without boiling. Add the mint and serve hot, garnished with a few leaves of mint and dollop of additional crème fraîche, if desired.

SERVES 6

NOTE: You may substitute fresh dill for the mint.

Salt
4 to 5 medium beets, trimmed of all but 2 inches of greens, with roots attached
6 cups chicken broth, preferably homemade (page 360)
4 tablespoons (½ stick) unsalted butter
2 tablespoons all-purpose flour
Freshly ground white pepper
½ cup Crème Fraîche (page 358)
Juice of 1 large lemon
2 to 3 tablespoons finely minced fresh mint

GARNISH
Tiny leaves of fresh mint
Optional: Crème Fraîche

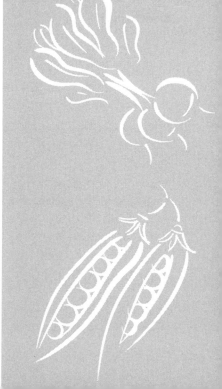

Tuscan Tuna Salad with Parsley Caper Vinaigrette

4 medium beets (about 1 pound), cooked (see page 17), peeled, and cut into ½-inch dice

3 cups cooked white beans (page 364)

1 can (7½ ounces) chunk light tuna, drained

3 tablespoons finely diced red onion

2 tablespoons tiny capers, drained

½ cup fresh parsley leaves

1 large garlic clove, peeled and mashed

2 to 3 tablespoons sherry vinegar

6 tablespoons extra-virgin olive oil

Coarse salt and freshly ground black pepper

I love this gutsy Mediterranean salad, which can be served either as a light main course for a warm-weather lunch or as a side dish to grilled seafood. As a variation you can substitute one half pound of small cooked shrimp for the tuna.

1. In a large serving bowl, combine the beets, white beans, tuna, onion, and capers.

2. Combine the parsley and garlic in a food processor and process until finely minced. Add 2 tablespoons of vinegar and the oil, season with salt and pepper, and process until smooth. Pour the vinaigrette over the beet salad and toss gently. Cover and chill for 4 to 6 hours before serving.

3. Bring the salad back to room temperature about 20 minutes before serving. Correct the seasoning, adding a large grinding of pepper and more vinegar if necessary. Serve with thinly sliced and buttered black bread.

SERVES 4 TO 6

Sweet-and-Sour Roasted Beets with Swiss Chard

Here is one of my favorite spring vegetable dishes, in which the natural beetlike taste of chard is combined with diced roasted beets and simmered with a touch of cream in a delicious sweet-and-sour sauce. I often serve this dish as a starter, but it is also an interesting accompaniment to poultry and veal recipes.

3 cups Swiss chard ribs, cut into 1½ by ½-inch pieces
Salt
3 to 4 teaspoons red wine vinegar
¾ cup heavy cream
3 tablespoons unsalted butter
1¼ pounds small beets, roasted (page 21), peeled, and cut into matchsticks, about 1½ by ½ inches
2 to 3 teaspoons sugar
Freshly ground black pepper

1. Drop the Swiss chard ribs into salted boiling water and cook for 3 minutes. Drain well and run under cold water to stop further cooking. Reserve.

2. In a small bowl, combine 3 teaspoons of the vinegar with the cream and set aside.

3. Melt the butter in a large skillet over medium heat. Add the beets and cook for 2 minutes, tossing lightly in the butter. Sprinkle with 2 teaspoons of the sugar and cook for 1 minute longer or until nicely glazed. Season with salt and pepper.

4. Add the vinegar and cream mixture to the skillet and cook until the mixture is syrupy and heavily coats the beets. Reduce the heat to low, add the Swiss chard ribs, and cook for 1 minute longer, or until just heated through. Taste and correct the seasoning, adding the remaining vinegar and/or sugar if necessary and a large grinding of pepper. Serve hot.

S E R V E S 4 T O 6

Pan-Seared Scallops in a Ruby-Red Vinaigrette

THE VINAIGRETTE
¾ cup diced cooked beets
    (see page 17)
8 tablespoons olive oil
2 tablespoons sherry vinegar
4 tablespoons chicken broth,
    preferably homemade
    (page 360)
Salt and freshly ground black
    pepper

THE SCALLOPS
1½ pounds small sea scallops
4 tablespoons finely minced
    fresh parsley
1½ tablespoons unsalted
    butter
1½ tablespoons olive oil

Vinaigrettes and salad dressings are one type of preparation that has benefited immensely from the creative influences of Nouvelle cuisine; tomato, herb, and spice vinaigrettes add vivid color and flavor to many dishes. Here is one that I find both lovely to look at and delicious. The beet vinaigrette can be teamed with a variety of vegetables, such as asparagus, as well as with seafood. You can be quite creative with the presentations of the dish, topping it, for example, with a sprinkling of diced marinated cucumber or beets, or both. Herbs such as dill, chervil, cilantro, and chives are all good choices. Serve the scallops as a starter or as a main course accompanied by tiny boiled new potatoes.

1. Start by making the vinaigrette: Combine the beets, oil, vinegar, and broth in a blender, a mini chopper, or the beaker of a hand-held immersion blender and process until very smooth and emulsified. Season with salt and pepper and set aside.

2. Dry the scallops thoroughly on paper towels. Place the minced parsley in a small shallow bowl and reserve.

3. Melt the butter together with the oil in a large nonstick skillet until almost smoking. Add the scallops without crowding the skillet and cook for 1 to 2 minutes on each side or until nicely browned. Season with salt and pepper and dip into the minced parsley to coat.

4. To serve, spoon some of the vinaigrette onto each of 4 individual plates to cover the surface completely. Place some of the scallops in the center of each portion and serve at once.

S ERVES 4

NOTE: Large shrimp may be substituted for the sea scallops.

Roasted Beets

Roast a few beets any time you're already using the oven so they will be ready to toss into pastas and salads.

8 medium-size beets (about 2 pounds), whole

1. Keep the beets whole and trim all but 2 inches of their greens. Do not remove the roots.

2. Preheat the oven to 375°F.

3. Place 4 beets on each of 2 sheets of aluminum foil. Tightly crimp the edges of each foil packet to enclose the beets completely and place on a baking sheet. Roast for 1 hour to 1 hour and 15 minutes or until the beets are tender when pierced with the tip of a sharp knife.

4. Remove from the oven and, when cool enough to handle, peel the beets. You will be able to do this with your hands; the skins should slip right off.

SERVES 6

BROCCOLI

BROCCOLI IS CONSIDERED A "NEW" VEGETABLE IN THE UNITED STATES because it has only gained wide popularity in the past twenty years, but in fact it has been around for centuries. Broccoli belongs to the cabbage family and is a close relative of the cauliflower. But while cauliflower, a wonderful "vintage" vegetable, enjoys only moderate popularity, its green relative now is in great demand.

Of all supermarket vegetables, broccoli is by far the best and, moreover, is available fresh and crisp-looking in the winter months when the choices are few and a green vegetable is most needed. The garden-grown vegetable is superior, however, providing florets as well as stalks tender enough for use in the kitchen.

Although everyone seems to agree that broccoli is delicious and easy to prepare, few cooks prepare it with the kind of creativity that this great vegetable deserves. Broccoli is so versatile that it works beautifully as a hot vegetable or chilled; it is a lovely addition to both hot pasta dishes and the cold Marinated Broccoli and Pepper Salad Niçoise on page 31. Pureed broccoli takes on quite a different character; I love its creamy texture in a soup or molded in ramekins. The raw stalk, finely sliced, is a superb addition to the salad bowl or can be served along with other garden vegetables and a tangy dip. And when accompanied by a well-flavored mustard vinaigrette, broccoli can be served just like asparagus, as a starter to a meal or as a separate vegetable course.

Broccoli is wonderful in Oriental preparations. It can be stir-fried and combined with shiitake mushrooms, bean sprouts, and snow peas. A touch of minced garlic and ginger plus a sprinkling of soy sauce completes a quick, spur-of-the-moment dish that I find a most satisfying accompaniment to grilled chicken, broiled fish, or barbecued ribs.

Blanching or steaming broccoli is another matter. The key to success is peeling the stalks with a vegetable peeler or a sharp paring knife. I usually remove all the leaves, trim the stalks, and, if they are hard, cut them lengthwise all the way through the florets into two or three pieces of equal size. To avoid overcooking broccoli, you should trim away all but one and one half inches of the stalks. If the stalks are fresh, crisp, and not woody, they can be scraped, then sliced crosswise into half-inch slices and served cooked or stir-fried. Or use them raw in the recipe on page 25, Country-Style Broccoli and Carrot Pickles. If the stems seem somewhat woody and hollow, I discard all but an inch. Once peeled, the stalks will cook in the same time as the florets.

Although steaming broccoli is a popular method, I prefer cooking it in plenty of salted water for three to four minutes or until the stalks can be pierced with the tip of a sharp knife. (Steaming, I have found, takes somewhat longer, and if the stalks are crowded, the florets tend to lose their bright green color and turn yellow.) Once cooked, broccoli can be braised in a little butter for additional flavoring, or sprinkled with fruity olive oil and some red wine vinegar if it is to be used in a salad.

For cooking in advance, I find that the braising method on page 27 is by far the most successful because you can reheat the vegetable in the skillet in which it has cooked. A broccoli puree is another excellent way to prepare broccoli in advance; you can keep the puree in the top of a double boiler until serving time and enrich it at the last minute with two or three tablespoons of butter.

STORAGE

Broccoli stores well in a plastic bag for up to a week. For longer storage, make a broccoli puree and refrigerate it in a plastic freezer container. You can easily heat the puree right in its container in a water bath or in the microwave.

GARDENING

Adding to broccoli's popularity is the fact that it is remarkably easy to grow and wonderfully productive. Six to twelve plants will suffice for most families. Because maturing florets prefer cool weather, it is best to plant broccoli in very early spring for a late-spring harvest, and again in early to midsummer for harvests during fall. If you live in southern California or the Deep South, you can make a planting in September for winter picking. In the North, if you want to pick broccoli as early in spring as possible, start the seed indoors about six weeks before the last predictable heavy frost.

Some broccoli varieties produce a single magnificent head and ripen all at once. I prefer varieties such as Green Goliath that offer a long harvest season; central heads, after picking, are followed for about a month by lots of harvestable side shoots. Exceptional Bonanza Hybrid boasts side shoots up to five inches across plus a head as broad as the largest single-headed varieties.

As a precaution against diseases that affect the entire cabbage family, do not plant broccoli in spots where any cabbage-family crops grew the previous year.

HARVESTING

When in doubt, err on the side of harvesting early. Ideally, broccoli should be picked before the tight clusters of green buds begin to open and show yellow. Use a sharp knife to cut the stems. To promote continuous production of side shoots, I leave the base of harvested shoots on the plant rather than cutting them back to the main stem. Be sure to remove any spindly side shoots to prevent them from going to seed.

Country-Style Broccoli and Carrot Pickles

Broccoli grown in the home garden has a heavier, longer stem than the supermarket variety, and I like to use the stalks as a separate vegetable, either sautéed or pickled. These garlicky pickles strike just the right note with sandwiches, a grilled flank steak, or a juicy burger.

1. In a medium mixing bowl, combine the broccoli and carrot slices. Add the oil, vinegar, oregano, and salt, season with pepper, and toss well. Bury the garlic cloves among the vegetables, cover, and refrigerate for 24 hours, turning the vegetables often in the marinade.

2. Remove the "pickles" from the refrigerator 20 minutes before serving. Drain well and discard the garlic cloves. Taste and correct the seasoning and serve at room temperature as part of an hors d'oeuvre table.

S ERVES   6

½ pound broccoli stalks, peeled and cut crosswise in ⅛-inch slices
2 medium carrots, trimmed, peeled, and cut crosswise into ⅛-inch slices
6 tablespoons extra-virgin olive oil
2 tablespoons red wine vinegar
¼ teaspoon dried oregano
¾ teaspoon salt
Freshly ground black pepper
2 medium garlic cloves, peeled and crushed

Bright Green Broccoli Florets with a Scallion Sesame Mayonnaise

1 large bunch broccoli (about
1½ pounds), trimmed of
all leaves

Salt

¼ cup peanut oil

¼ cup olive oil

1 tablespoon Chinese
sesame oil

1 extra-large egg

1 extra-large egg yolk

1 tablespoon rice vinegar or
cider vinegar

Freshly ground black pepper

Pinch of cayenne pepper

1 small garlic clove, peeled and
mashed

3 tablespoons finely minced
scallions

1 tablespoon lightly toasted
sesame seeds

Drops of fresh lemon juice to
taste

I *love to serve a cooked vegetable as a first course, a common practice all over Italy and Spain. Nothing fancy, just a nice head of steamed broccoli, string beans, or cauliflower with a drizzle of fruity olive oil and black pepper, a nice vinaigrette, or this zesty, flavorful mayonnaise that also doubles as a dip for raw vegetables.*

1. Trim off all but 1½ inches of the broccoli stems and separate the bunch into spears.

2. Bring salted water to a boil in a vegetable steamer, add the broccoli, and steam, covered, for 2 minutes. Remove and set aside to cool.

3. Combine the peanut, olive, and sesame oils in a liquid measuring cup. In a blender, combine the egg, egg yolk, and vinegar, season with salt, pepper, and cayenne, and blend at high speed for 30 seconds. With the blender still running, add the remaining oil mixture by droplets until the mixture begins to emulsify and thicken. Then add the remaining oil in a slow steady stream until all has been incorporated. The consistency of the mayonnaise should be sauce-like rather than very thick like commercial mayonnaise.

4. Stir in the garlic, scallions, and sesame seeds and correct the seasoning, adding drops of lemon juice to taste. Serve at room temperature with the broccoli spears.

SERVES 6

Pasta with Garlic-Braised Broccoli

I *often make this dish with the broccoli stems only, since the homegrown vegetable usually has longer stems than the store-bought varieties. Either way, be sure to add the steamed florets as a garnish at the end of the preparation. This is a very good-natured dish that can easily be prepared ahead of time and heated in the microwave. The broccoli will lose some of its bright green color but the flavor will not be affected.*

1. Trim the broccoli stalks, removing all leaves. Peel the stalks with a vegetable peeler and cut crosswise in ¼-inch slices. Separate the tops into florets. Reserve.

2. In a heavy 10-inch skillet, heat the oil over medium heat. Add the chili peppers and cook until dark. Discard the chili peppers and add the garlic together with the broccoli stems and cook for 1 to 2 minutes, stirring often. Add the florets and the broth, season with salt and pepper, and simmer, covered, for 10 minutes or until just tender. Add the anchovies and simmer until the anchovies have just "melted." Keep warm.

3. Bring plenty of salted water to a boil in a large casserole, add the penne, and cook until just tender "al dente." Drain well and return the pasta to the casserole. Add the broccoli and anchovy sauce and toss gently over low heat until just heated through. Add the Parmesan and correct the seasoning. Serve hot with crusty peasant bread.

S E R V E S 4 T O 5

VARIATION
Core, seed, and thinly slice a large red bell pepper and sauté in the olive oil together with the broccoli stems and garlic. Continue with the recipe.

1 large bunch broccoli (about 1½ pounds)
3 tablespoons extra-virgin olive oil
2 small dry red chili peppers, broken in half
3 large garlic cloves, peeled and thinly sliced
⅓ cup chicken broth, preferably homemade (page 360)
Salt and freshly ground black pepper
4 to 5 flat anchovy fillets, drained and finely minced
½ pound dried imported penne
⅓ cup freshly grated Parmesan cheese

Saffron Pilaf with Broccoli and Peas

3 cups chicken broth,
    preferably homemade
    (page 360)
1 teaspoon saffron threads
2 cups small broccoli florets
Salt
½ cup shelled peas
4 tablespoons (½ stick)
    unsalted butter
½ cup finely minced scallions
1½ cups long-grain rice
Freshly ground black pepper
3 tablespoons finely minced
    fresh parsley

This is a colorful rice dish that can be made well ahead of time and reheated. It rounds out the plate with almost any roast or sautéed meat, poultry, or fish. I often double the recipe and keep half the rice for a salad, to which I add a well-flavored garlic vinaigrette and finely diced pimientos.

1. Combine the broth and saffron in a small saucepan and simmer, covered, for 20 minutes.

2. While the broth simmers, cook the broccoli in a large pot of boiling salted water until just tender, about 5 to 6 minutes. Remove to a colander with a slotted spoon. Add the peas and cook until tender, 5 to 6 minutes. Drain well.

3. In a heavy 3-quart saucepan, melt the butter over medium low heat. Add the scallions and simmer for 2 to 3 minutes or until soft. Add the rice, season with salt and pepper, and stir well to coat the rice. Add the saffron-infused broth and simmer, covered, for 20 minutes or until the rice is tender.

4. Add the broccoli, peas, and parsley and toss gently. Correct the seasoning and serve hot.

SERVES 4 TO 6

NOTE: If you do not have saffron, you may substitute 1 teaspoon of turmeric. In this case, it is not necessary to steep the turmeric in stock as with saffron. Simply add to the saucepan with rice and stock in Step 3.

Smoky Tuscan Broccoli Soup

I love all soups, but this is one of my favorites. On a cool night, you can easily serve it as a one-dish meal, possibly with some cheese, a salami, some black oil-cured olives, and, of course, crusty bread.

1. Peel the broccoli stalks and cut into thin slices. Separate the tops into small florets and reserve.

2. In a heavy 4-quart casserole, melt the butter together with the oil over medium heat. Add the onions, garlic, carrots, celery, and pork and cook the mixture until the onions are soft but not browned.

3. Add the broth and broccoli stalks, season with salt and pepper, and simmer for 20 minutes or until the stalks are tender. Add the florets and spaghettini and simmer until the pasta is just tender. Taste and correct the seasoning, adding a large grinding of pepper, and serve hot in individual bowls garnished with Parmesan cheese.

S E R V E S 6

VARIATION

For a more substantial soup, I often add 1 cup of cooked white beans and sprinkle each serving with a mild crumbled blue cheese such as Danish blue or Roquefort.

I large bunch broccoli (about 1 ½ pounds), trimmed of all leaves

3 tablespoons unsalted butter

I tablespoon olive oil

2 large onions, peeled and finely diced

2 large garlic cloves, peeled and finely minced

2 medium carrots, peeled and diced

2 celery stalks, finely diced

½ pound smoked pork shoulder butt, cut into ½-inch cubes

6 to 7 cups chicken broth, preferably homemade (page 360)

Salt and freshly ground black pepper

¼ cup imported spaghettini, broken into ¾-inch pieces

GARNISH
Freshly grated Parmesan cheese

Skillet-Braised Chicken with Broccoli and Thyme

1 whole chicken (about 3 pounds), cut into eighths
1 tablespoon unsalted butter
3 tablespoons olive oil
Salt and freshly ground black pepper
1 teaspoon all-purpose flour
⅓ cup dry white wine
3 large garlic cloves, peeled and crushed
3 tablespoons fresh thyme leaves
1 cup chicken broth, preferably homemade (page 360)
3 cups broccoli florets
1 teaspoon arrowroot mixed with a little broth

GARNISH
2 tablespoons finely minced fresh parsley

A *sauté of chicken with crispy broccoli florets simmered in the pan juices makes a flavorful and quick supper dish. A bowl of creamy polenta or a quick couscous are both excellent choices for a side dish.*

1. Dry the chicken pieces thoroughly on paper towels.

2. In a large, deep heavy skillet, melt the butter together with the oil over medium to medium high heat. Add the chicken and sauté, partially covered, until nicely browned on all sides. Season with salt and pepper, sprinkle with the flour, and cook for 2 minutes longer, turning the pieces often, until nicely glazed.

3. Add the wine to the skillet and reduce to 2 tablespoons. Add the garlic, thyme, and ½ cup broth, reduce the heat, and simmer, covered, for 20 minutes. Add the broccoli florets and remaining broth and simmer for 15 minutes longer or until the florets are tender. Transfer the chicken and broccoli to a warm serving dish and reserve.

4. Whisk a little of the arrowroot mixture into the pan juices, bring to a simmer, and cook until the sauce lightly coats a spoon. Correct the seasoning and spoon the sauce over the chicken and broccoli. Sprinkle with the minced parsley and serve hot.

S E R V E S   4

Marinated Broccoli and Pepper Salad Niçoise

With commercial broccoli as plentiful as it is, many gardeners have forgotten the true season for this terrific vegetable. But for those who like to grow it, the rewards of the "real" thing are some delectable spring morsels. Here is a lively salad that can easily serve as a light supper on those first warm days of spring when you are likely to be spending most of your time outdoors getting the garden and the flower borders back into shape. A rather sharp sheep's milk cheese or a slightly aged goat cheese and a bowl of young garden radishes would compliment the salad nicely. Once marinated, the broccoli florets tend to lose some of their bright green color, but this does not affect their taste.

1. In a steamer or large saucepan, add the broccoli and steam, covered, over simmering water until just tender, 5 to 7 minutes.

2. Combine the broccoli, bell pepper, and red onion in a serving bowl and set aside.

3. In a food processor, combine 2 tablespoons of the vinegar with the garlic, parsley, and oil and process until smooth. Season with salt and pepper and pour over the vegetables. Toss gently and let the salad marinate at room temperature for 1 to 2 hours.

4. Add the tuna and the cherry tomatoes, if using, and correct the seasoning, adding the remaining vinegar as needed and a large grinding of black pepper. Garnish with the olives, salami, and hard-boiled eggs and serve lightly chilled.

SERVES 4 TO 6

1½ pounds broccoli florets
1 large red bell pepper, seeded, cored, and thinly sliced
½ cup thinly sliced red onion
2 to 3 tablespoons sherry vinegar
1 large garlic clove, peeled and mashed
1 tablespoon finely minced fresh parsley
6 tablespoons olive oil
Salt and freshly ground black pepper
1 can (7½ ounces) chunk light tuna, drained and flaked
Optional: 8 ripe cherry tomatoes, cut in half

GARNISH
12 small black oil-cured olives
6 slices hard salami, cut into thin strips
2 hard-boiled eggs, peeled and quartered

GARDEN ACCENTS: RADISHES AND SCALLIONS

ALONG WITH TENDER SALAD GREENS, RADISHES ARE AMONG THE FIRST spring crops. Scallions, like chives, are green members of the onion family. In the ways they can be used by the cook, they fall somewhere between an herb and a vegetable. Otherwise unrelated, radishes and scallions have in common their great ability to add flair and flavor to other ingredients. Although rarely served as a dish on their own, they are distinctive additions to others and have become some of the garden's best-loved accent vegetables.

Radishes

As a child, my father grew elongated red and white bicolor radishes that were crisp and slightly pungent yet sweet. We would eat them, picked fresh from the garden with all but two inches of their tops removed, with a side dish of black oil-cured olives, crusty bread, and fresh sweet butter. To this day, I find this a delightful snack.

Radishes are popular everywhere. In the Near East and the Balkan countries you will find radishes served at breakfast along with cool yogurt and fresh farm cheese. And in Austria and throughout northern Europe, finely sliced black radishes are served with buttered black bread at tastings of young wines. The two-toned radish of my youth (appropriately called the French Breakfast radish in the United States) is treated with special reverence in France, where farmers bring these tiny jewels to outdoor markets with a prideful reminder that this is their first crop of spring.

In the United States radishes are often taken for granted and are always available, even if only in cellophane packages. Thanks to modern transportation and the ever-increasing demand for high-quality produce, you now find truly fresh radishes all over the country.

In spite of the recent efforts of some creative cooks to use radishes in cooked dishes, the radish is much more interesting raw. The crisp pungent taste of radishes, whether simply sliced, julienned, or cubed, is so good in so many salads that without this little vegetable the spring and fall garden would not be the same.

STORAGE

In the market, look for uniform, firm radishes, preferably with their greens attached. The tops should be crisp and bright green. Avoid radishes that are soft or have yellowish, wilted leaves.

To store radishes, remove their greens and place in a plastic bag in the vegetable bin of the refrigerator; they will easily keep for up to two weeks.

GARDENING

Radishes mature so early—sometimes in only three weeks—that there is hardly an opportunity for anything to go wrong. The most commonly grown types are the round, red roots, such as mild-tasting Cherry Belle, and the all-white roots, such as the elongated White Icicle. All these varieties, known as spring radishes, require the cool of spring or autumn. For continuous fresh harvests during these seasons, it is best to sow small plantings (one row just a few feet long is enough for most families) about every ten days. I also like to sow radishes between larger, slower-growing crops like cabbage or cauliflower. The tasty roots are ready to pull long before the neighboring crops need the space.

For a heat-resistant radish, try Summer Cross Hybrid, one of the giant white Oriental types known as Daikon. It keeps well and can be stir-fried. Seeds can be sown in mid-spring for an early summer harvest, or in late summer for a fall harvest. So-called winter radishes, such as Round Black Spanish, require cool weather at the end of their relatively long (fifty-five-day) growing season. Plant in summer for a fall harvest.

HARVESTING

Although genetic differences among radish varieties are important in determining pungency, the younger the radishes are when picked, the milder they will taste. Roots allowed to remain in the ground too long may become harsh tasting and pithy.

Scallions

The cultivation of scallions has been perfected to such an extent in the United States that you can now find crisp and uniform bunches with silver-white stalks in most good grocery stores. They also are easy to grow and quick to mature. Some gardeners claim that scallions, besides being a wonderful vegetable, also keep certain pests from nibbling on neighboring crops.

At one time the use of scallions in Western cuisines was essentially confined to the salad bowl. I find their mild taste, lovely green color, and crisp texture a must in an egg, tuna, chicken, or rice salad, as well as in many dressings. They are also delicious poached, grilled, or deep fried and served as either a garnish or a vegetable.

In both Japanese and Chinese cooking, scallions are used more than any other member of the onion family except garlic. Oriental cooks use both the white and green parts of the scallion, either chopped, slant-cut, or shredded, in many stir-fries, soups, and noodle dishes. Because of their color, texture, and natural affinity for garlic and ginger, scallions are the perfect garnish to many Oriental dishes. I also use scallions extensively as a base for soups and in several rice dishes.

When preparing this tender young onion, it is best to remove two or three inches of the greens and peel off their outer layer. Once diced, to prevent them from burning they should be braised in some butter and a touch of broth or water rather than sautéed.

I am frequently asked whether scallions can be used as a substitute for shallots or leeks. They cannot. Although all three belong to the onion family, both leeks and shallots have completely different cooking characteristics and flavors.

GARDENING

Any standard onion variety can be grown as a scallion if harvested early, before the bulbs begin to develop. A convenient space-saving approach is to plant onion sets (small bulbs) or seeds about two inches apart in their rows. When plants reach six inches or more in height, pluck out every other one for use as scallions. The remaining plants are left in the ground, where they will develop into bulbs.

You can also plant the Evergreen Long White Bunching onion, which produces excellent stalks but no bulbs. A ten-foot row yields about ten bunches over a month. Seeds can be sown at any time during the season. The plants are hardy enough to winter over in the garden in most climates, although a protective mulch is advisable in the North. When the ground thaws in early spring, simply pull up scallions as your first harvest of the year.

HARVESTING

Because scallions do not keep very well, it is best to pick them in small quantities as needed.

Middle Eastern Radish and Beet Salad in Scallion Vinaigrette

3 tablespoons olive oil

2 tablespoons red wine vinegar

4 tablespoons finely minced scallions

1½ cups plain yogurt

Salt and freshly ground black pepper

1½ pounds cooked beets (see page 17), peeled and cut into ¾-inch cubes

2½ cups thinly sliced radishes

To many people, radishes are simply snack food, something you nibble on when you are watching your calorie intake. But radishes lend character to many delicious recipes. Combined with beets in a zesty scallion or chive vinaigrette, they move to the top of my list as soon as the weather turns warm. Be sure to serve the salad with good crusty bread and very fresh sweet butter, which tends to intensify the taste of radishes.

1. In a large serving bowl, combine the oil, vinegar, scallions, and yogurt. Season with salt and pepper and whisk until well blended. Add the beets and radishes and fold gently. Cover and refrigerate overnight.

2. The next day, bring the salad back to room temperature. Correct the seasoning and serve as an accompaniment to grilled salmon or chicken, or sautéed veal.

S E R V E S 6

Butter-Braised Scallions

4 tablespoons (½ stick) unsalted butter

6 to 8 medium scallions, trimmed to 6 inches

Salt and freshly ground black pepper

1½ cups chicken broth, preferably homemade (page 360), or water

I often use one or two of these scallions as a finishing touch to pan-seared fish or chops; they're a nice alternative to parsley.

1. Melt the butter in a 10-inch cast-iron skillet over low heat. Add the scallions, season with salt and pepper, and cook, shaking the pan, until lightly glazed.

2. Add the broth or water, partially cover the pan, and simmer for 3 to 4 minutes or until the scallions are well glazed and tender.

Spring Garden Salad with Sweet Mustard Dressing

On a warm spring day when I plan to spend much of my time in the garden, I often opt for this one-dish meal. If you put the vinaigrette in the bottom of the bowl and top it with the greens without tossing, the salad can be refrigerated for many hours without wilting. Simply toss just before serving, correct the seasoning, and pass along a warm crusty baguette.

1. In a large shallow serving bowl, combine the mustard, vinegar, and sugar. Season with salt and pepper and whisk until well blended. Slowly add the oil, whisking constantly, until smooth. Fold in the scallions and top with the mushrooms, but do not mix in. Marinate for 30 minutes.

2. Top the vinaigrette with the radishes, asparagus, endives, and lettuce leaves but do not toss. Cover and refrigerate until serving, up to 6 hours in advance.

3. Remove the salad from the refrigerator about 20 minutes before serving. Toss gently, correct the seasoning, and serve on individual salad plates.

SERVES 4

1½ teaspoons Dijon mustard
2½ tablespoons sherry vinegar
1 teaspoon sugar
Salt and freshly ground black pepper
7 tablespoons olive oil
4 tablespoons finely minced scallions
¼ pound all-purpose mushrooms, wiped, trimmed, and thinly sliced
2 cups thinly sliced radishes
12 asparagus spears, trimmed, peeled, cooked (see page 11), and cut into 1-inch pieces
2 medium-size Belgian endives, cored and cut into a julienne
1 small head of Boston lettuce, leaves separated, washed, and dried
1 small head of red leaf lettuce, leaves separated, washed, and dried

Radish and Endive Salad with Creamy Goat Cheese Dressing

1½ tablespoons sherry vinegar

½ cup mild goat cheese, such as Montrachet, crumbled

3 tablespoons heavy cream

½ cup extra-virgin olive oil

1 teaspoon fresh thyme leaves

2 tablespoons finely minced scallions

Salt and freshly ground black pepper

6 to 7 Belgian endives

8 to 10 radishes, trimmed and thinly sliced

This is a lovely and rather assertive salad. It can only be made successfully with greens and vegetables that will hold up to the somewhat heavy dressing. Radishes and Belgian endives are natural choices, but thinly sliced fennel and even a fine julienne of snow peas can be added to the salad. Be sure to to season the salad well with freshly ground black pepper. Serve as a starter or as a luncheon salad accompanied by a crusty baguette and some sweet butter.

1. In a food processor, combine the vinegar, goat cheese, cream, and oil and process until smooth and creamy. Transfer to a serving bowl and fold in the thyme and scallions. Season with salt and a large grinding of black pepper and set aside.

2. Remove the outer leaves of the endives and rinse quickly under cold water; do not let endives soak or they will get bitter. Drain well and with the tip of a sharp knife remove the hard round core. Cut the endives lengthwise in quarters and then into ½-inch julienne strips. Add them to the serving bowl together with the radishes and toss gently with the dressing. Correct the seasoning and serve at room temperature or lightly chilled.

SERVES 5 TO 6

KOHLRABI

I AM ALWAYS FASCINATED BY THE WAY VEGETABLES ARE SUBJECT TO fashion trends, often "out" for long periods only to be rediscovered by some creative chef. From then on they crop up in every food magazine and on restaurant menus. This seems now to be the case with kohlrabi, which may at last be gaining the popularity it deserves. I hope so! The word *kohlrabi* comes from the German "kohl," meaning cabbage, and "rabi," meaning turnip. The name is appropriate since kohlrabi combines characteristics of both these vegetables. The edible bulb is like a turnip in shape and flavor, while the leaves resemble those of cabbage and can be used creatively in cooking.

Kohlrabi is extremely popular in Austria, Germany, and all over central and eastern Europe, where sweet, tender specimens are always available. In the United States, the kohlrabi I find at the market is sometimes past its prime. The bulbs often are large (a sign of stringiness), with limp yellowish greens (a sign of age). As with all vegetables past their prime, old kohlrabi is simply not worth cooking. Since I grew up eating kohlrabi, sometimes two or three times a week, it has always been an important ingredient in my cooking repertoire. So I began growing it as soon as I had my own garden, discovering that it is easy to grow, extremely productive, and very quick to mature.

Young kohlrabi is delicious finely sliced and served as part of a crudité platter along with a tangy dip. It can be steamed, sautéed, braised, pureed, or pickled. In fact, kohlrabi can be substituted in any recipe that calls for turnips. I often add a handful of cubed kohlrabi to the pan juices of a roasting chicken. By the time the chicken is done, so is the vegetable, adding its sweet taste to the sauce and absorbing the flavorful juices of the chicken. Kohlrabi works beautifully in combination with carrots and peas in a spring fricassee or in a creamy soup spiked with fresh leeks (page 45).

To prepare kohlrabi, you may peel it before cooking, removing all the leaves and skin, or cook it and then peel when the vegetable is tender. The very young bulbs can be sliced and braised in a deep skillet with a little butter, broth, and seasoning. Older bulbs are best reserved for purees, possibly in combination with potatoes or carrots.

STORAGE

Remove all the foliage from the bulbs and store them in perforated plastic bags for up to a week. Store the leaves, which will keep for two or three days, in separate plastic bags. They can be steamed or braised and then finished with a touch of butter, cream, or sour cream, and a sprinkling of herbs.

GARDENING

I enjoy kohlrabi so much that I sometimes make several successive plantings in spring and again starting in midsummer. The bulbs, which grow just above ground, are ready for harvest in seven to eight weeks. Very early (forty-five to fifty days) is Grand Duke Hybrid, a light-skinned variety with crisp white flesh. Early Purple Vienna, with purplish skin and very pale green flesh, matures about ten days later. Kohlrabi's soil must be kept constantly moist, so it is best to apply a thick mulch around the plants. The mulch will also smother weeds, which is important because the shallow roots of kohlrabi are easily damaged during weeding.

HARVESTING

The perfect time to harvest kohlrabi is when bulbs are barely two inches across. Any wider than three inches and bulbs quickly become tough. Use a sharp knife to cut stems near ground level, about an inch below the bulbs.

Kohlrabi Pickles in Sweet-and-Sour Syrup

Most Americans have yet to discover the superb flavor of kohlrabi, a vegetable that is popular and consumed in great quantity all over Europe. Since this sweet, crisp, and crunchy root vegetable does particularly well in my garden, I am always on the lookout for new ways to prepare it. Pickling has become one of my favorites, because it allows my family to enjoy it practically throughout the year. Serve the pickles with a juicy burger, grilled sausages, or a hearty sandwich.

1. Place the kohlrabi in a colander, sprinkle with the salt, and drain for 2 hours. Rinse off the salt, place the kohlrabi in a kitchen towel, and gently squeeze out the excess liquid. Transfer to a mixing bowl.

2. Combine the vinegar and sugar in a small saucepan and bring to a boil. Pour the syrup over the kohlrabi and mix. Divide between two 1-pint jars. Let cool and store in the refrigerator for up to 2 weeks, or process in a hot water bath for 10 minutes (see page 168), cool, and store in a cool place for up to 2 years.

MAKES 2 PINTS

1 pound kohlrabi, trimmed, peeled, and cut into ¼-inch-wide strips
¼ cup coarse salt
1 cup white distilled vinegar
½ cup sugar

Kohlrabi Glazed with
Maple Syrup and Brown Sugar

3 tablespoons unsalted butter

6 medium kohlrabi (about 1½ pounds), trimmed, peeled, and thinly sliced

Salt and freshly ground white pepper

⅓ to ½ cup water or chicken broth

2 tablespoons dark brown sugar

2 tablespoons pure maple syrup

*J*ust like turnips, kohlrabi is delicious when gently braised with a touch of brown sugar and some flavorful chicken broth. I like to serve the kohlrabi as a side dish to roast or grilled chicken, sautéed calf's liver, or a pork roast.

1. In a 10-inch skillet, melt the butter over medium heat. Add the kohlrabi and toss to coat evenly with the butter. Season with salt and pepper. Add the water or broth and simmer, covered, until tender, about 10 to 12 minutes; add the remaining water or broth if the liquid evaporates before the kohlrabi is done. If any liquid remains, remove the cover and cook until reduced.

2. Add the brown sugar and maple syrup, mix well, and cook for 1 to 2 minutes longer until the kohlrabi is nicely caramelized. Serve hot.

SERVES 4 TO 5

Casserole-Roasted Chicken with Thyme, Kohlrabi, and Root Vegetables

Here is a flavor-packed bistro classic that is hard to beat. *Together with carrots, the kohlrabi lends a sweet flavor to the delicious pan juices. Oven-roasted new potatoes or simple buttered orzo would complement the dish nicely.*

1. Preheat the oven to 350°F.

2. In a heavy skillet, melt the butter together with the oil over medium high heat. Add the chicken and brown nicely on all sides. Season with salt and pepper and transfer to a heavy flameproof oval casserole.

3. Add the onions cut side down together with ¾ cup of the broth, the kohlrabi, carrots, garlic, and thyme. Bring to a boil on top of the stove, cover tightly, and braise in the oven for 1 hour to 1 hour and 10 minutes or until the chicken juices run pale yellow; baste every 15 minutes with the pan juices.

4. Carve the chicken into quarters and place on a serving platter together with the vegetables. Cover and keep warm.

5. Degrease the pan juices and return them to the casserole together with the remaining broth. Bring to a simmer and whisk in bits of beurre manié until the sauce lightly coats the spoon. Correct the seasoning and spoon the sauce over the chicken and vegetables. Garnish with sprigs of thyme and serve accompanied by a parslied pilaf of rice.

SERVES 4

2 tablespoons unsalted butter
2 teaspoons corn oil
I whole chicken (about 3½ pounds), dried and trussed
Coarse salt and freshly ground black pepper
3 small onions, peeled and cut in half through the root end
1¼ cups chicken broth, preferably homemade (page 360)
4 small kohlrabi, trimmed, peeled, and quartered
3 medium carrots, trimmed, peeled, and cut crosswise into ½-inch pieces
6 large garlic cloves, peeled and crushed
3 tablespoons fresh thyme leaves
I Beurre Manié (page 361)

GARNISH
Sprigs of fresh thyme

Viennese Braised Kohlrabi with Sour Cream and Green Onions

Salt

6 medium kohlrabi (about 1½ pounds), trimmed, peeled, and cut into ¼-inch-wide matchsticks

¾ cup sour cream

1 teaspoon imported sweet paprika

1 teaspoon all-purpose flour

4 tablespoons (½ stick) unsalted butter

4 tablespoons finely minced scallions

¼ cup chicken broth, preferably homemade (page 360)

Freshly ground white pepper

My very Viennese grandmother and my equally Viennese mother loved to make this dish; as soon as they spotted this spring vegetable at the market, it was on the menu for the duration of the season. Simply braised and combined with sour cream and a touch of good broth, it is an easy dish to love and is good-natured enough to go with just about anything: chicken, seafood, and especially veal chops or veal scaloppine.

1. Bring salted water to a boil in a vegetable steamer. Add the kohlrabi and steam, covered, for 3 to 4 minutes or until just tender. Reserve.

2. Combine the sour cream, paprika, and flour in a small bowl and whisk until well blended. Set aside.

3. Melt the butter in a heavy 10-inch skillet over medium low heat, add the scallions, and cook for 1 minute. Add the kohlrabi and chicken broth and cook until reduced to a glaze.

4. Stir in the sour cream mixture and cook for 2 minutes longer. Season with salt and pepper and serve hot.

SERVES 4 TO 5

Cream of Leek, Potato, and Kohlrabi Soup with Fresh Chives

The rather delicate taste of kohlrabi marries beautifully with that of leeks in this simple yet full-flavored soup. If you can, make it at least a day ahead of time or plan for some leftovers. You can omit the Crème Fraîche if you wish, but a little dollop of yogurt or sour cream in each portion does lend a rich and creamy texture to the soup.

1. In a large casserole, melt the butter over medium low heat. Add the onion and cook until soft but not browned.

2. Add the potatoes, leeks, kohlrabi, and broth, season with salt and pepper, and simmer, partially covered, for 30 to 35 minutes or until the vegetables are tender.

3. Strain the soup and return the broth to the casserole. Puree the vegetables in a food processor until smooth and whisk the puree into the broth. Whisk in the crème fraîche, or yogurt and correct the seasoning. Serve hot, garnished with minced chives.

S E R V E S   5   T O   6

3 tablespoons unsalted butter

I large onion, peeled and finely diced

2 medium all-purpose potatoes, peeled and diced

2 small leeks, trimmed, thinly sliced, and rinsed under warm water

4 medium kohlrabi (about I pound), trimmed, peeled, and diced

6 cups chicken broth, preferably homemade (page 360)

Salt and freshly ground white pepper

½ cup Crème Fraîche (page 358), nonfat plain yogurt, or sour cream

GARNISH

2 tablespoons finely minced fresh chives

LETTUCES AND OTHER GREENS

Over the past few years, growing greens has become an exciting part of the home gardening experience. Aside from the classics, such as
romaine, Boston, and other head lettuce, you will now find a variety of lovely
leaf lettuces, dandelion greens, tiny hearts of Bibb lettuce, and endives. This
is not to mention the new "in" greens, such as radicchio, and the latest fads,
mesclun mixes and corn lettuce, or what the French call *mâche*. For the home
gardener this great variety is truly inspiring.

Essentially, all greens can be categorized as being either buttery (mild
tasting) or acidic (having stronger, more assertive flavors). Today's cooks
should familiarize themselves with the character of the various greens,
including those that double as cooked vegetables, such as collard, dandelion,
sorrel, and mustard greens.

The new American cuisine is rediscovering and refining the salad and
doing so with style, innovation, and great creativity. Indeed, salads have taken
center stage, and while some of the theatrical touches may be overplayed and
somewhat contrived, one thing has become quite clear: Cooks, restaurant
chefs, and gardeners care very much about their salad greens. In addition to
experimenting with a variety of lettuces, they are creating exciting dressings
using unusual oils and vinegars, mustards, and herbs to achieve the kind of
harmony that can set a salad apart and make it a focal point of a meal.

It is fun to add an unusual leaf or two to your salad bowl, but a good
green salad really depends on three basic ingredients only: the freshest
greens, the best oil, and the best vinegar. It is absolutely essential to know
both the proportion of oil to vinegar for a well-balanced vinaigrette and the
amount of dressing to use with regard to the quantity of greens.

Iceberg (Head) Lettuce

Needless to say, iceberg fresh from the garden is better and crisper than that
uninspiring ball you find wrapped in cellophane in most supermarkets. It is

certainly excellent in sandwiches and in combination with tomatoes, cucumbers, and radishes in a Greek salad. But because iceberg tends not to blend well with other salad greens it lacks the kind of flexibility one looks for in a leafy green.

Romaine Lettuce

Romaine is considered an all-purpose lettuce in Mediterranean Europe, where it is often the only choice at the market. In America, good romaine is available year-round in supermarkets and grocery stores, but when it is garden-fresh, it is a different lettuce. Milder and more tender, the fresh leaves have an affinity to just about every other green, cooked or uncooked. In Spain, where romaine is king, the tender leaves are usually served as an appetizer together with a finely sliced spicy hard sausage, some oil-cured black olives, a few radishes, and crusty bread. Cruets of olive oil and vinegar are always on hand and everyone seasons his own salad to taste.

Boston Lettuce

Boston is to central and northern Europe what romaine is to the south: It is the everyday lettuce that most cooks pick up at the market, and it is served in every restaurant. In France, hearts of Boston are classically cooked together with young fresh peas and some tiny spring onions. Whoever first thought of this marriage did, indeed, create one made in heaven.

Boston lettuce likes the company of very few greens, mainly young spinach and arugula. Because of its soft texture, it should be tossed gently in the dressing of your choice at the very last minute.

Bibb Lettuce

Bibb lettuce is considered the most refined of the buttery lettuces. It has a texture similar to Boston, but the smaller, tighter heads and crisper leaves are more flavorful and hold up better in a dressing. Since store-bought Bibb is the most expensive of all lettuces, it is worthwhile to grow a good amount of this lovely salad green in the garden. Bibb is a wonderful addition to a mesclun, the French term for a mixed salad of three to four greens, since it holds its shape so gracefully and lends its buttery yet assertive taste to the other greens without overwhelming them.

Loose-Leaf Lettuce (Red and Green Leaf)

Loose-leaf lettuce is extremely easy to grow, accounting for its popularity in the spring garden. The plants do well even in poor soil. They mature quickly, producing attractive large leaves that are both tender and mild. Of all lettuces, loose-leaf has become the star of the new American salad phenomenon, mainly because it makes an excellent bed for composed salads but also because its mild texture leaves room for many innovative touches. I like to use a tossed salad of loose-leaf lettuce as a backdrop to a julienne of grilled chicken breasts or as an accompaniment to a creamy corn custard. Tossed with the proper amount of cool mustardy vinaigrette, loose-leaf is simply delicious by itself. With the addition of a few dandelion greens, the heart of a tiny Bibb lettuce, and possibly a few bright red radicchio leaves, you have the makings of a memorable salad.

GARDENING

Cool-loving lettuces need full sun when sown in early spring or autumn, while summer crops flourish only if shaded during midday. Adequate shade can be provided by interplanting lettuce among taller plants such as broccoli, or by sowing rows of lettuce next to rows of corn or trellis-grown beans. It is essential that soil remain moist and relatively cool, especially when heads are just beginning to develop. This is most easily accomplished by surrounding the seedlings with a two- to four-inch-thick mulch of salt hay or grass clippings.

Whenever possible, wait until plants reach the "baby" stage before thinning, at which point lettuce makes wonderful eating. For a long harvest season in a small space, thin plants gradually, pulling and using every other plant each time you need some for a salad. When you're down to the suggested spacing (four to twelve inches apart), pick just the outer leaves from each plant and leave the inner ones to mature. Finally, near the end of the season, pull the entire plant.

If this sounds too complicated, and if you have a bit more garden space, plant lettuce seeds every ten to fourteen days until mid-spring, allowing enough time for the last sowing to mature before hot weather starts.

Wash and refrigerate fresh-picked lettuce immediately to prevent leaves from wilting.

Dandelions

When I was child, picking dandelion greens in spring was an unbroken tradition. In mid to late March my father and I would set out to the fields on Saturday mornings looking for the young tender dandelions, and we would pop each handful into a basket. By lunchtime we would return and present my mother with these tangy young wild greens, which soon became the centerpiece part of the meal, usually accompanied by the local garlic-studded sausage, cooked on the grill, and a loaf of farmer's bread.

Dandelions that are really young and tender are still a rare find at the market. Growing your own is very rewarding since you can pick the leaves at the right stage, leaving the more mature ones for a quick stir-fry to be added to a pasta dish. In France, where dandelion is called *pissenlit*, it is serve in a classic preparation that is fast becoming stylish in this country as well. Diced smoky bacon is cooked in a skillet and the fat is tossed with the greens. A splash of vinegar and seasoning is all that is needed to complete this flavorful salad. If you are more adventurous you can also make the salad with duck cracklings, using some rendered duck fat. One of the simplest and most satisfying ways to serve a dandelion salad is with the sweet and sour Pennsylvania Dutch dressing on page 58.

Mature dandelions can be used for a simple stir-fry with two to three sliced cloves of garlic and some minced jalapeño pepper. Tossed with some freshly cooked pasta and seasoned with freshly ground black pepper, this makes a delicious and quick-to-prepare appetizer.

STORAGE

When buying dandelions, look for small crisp leaves that have the mildest flavor. To store, place bunches in plastic bags in the vegetable bin of the refrigerator. Do not wash until just before using. If dandelions are picked with their roots still attached, wrap the roots in damp paper towels and then place in plastic bags.

GARDENING

Dandelion seeds available to vegetable gardeners produce plants as resilient as those that pop up across lawns each spring. But cultivated dandelion boasts leaves that are larger, thicker, and tastier than those from the wild plant. Blanching will help keep the leaves tender enough to eat raw. Simply tie the foliage together so that the outer leaves prevent light from penetrating to the inner leaves.

Be sure to dig out and discard any remaining dandelion plants before they flower and go to seed; otherwise, dandelion will be your primary crop next year.

Arugula

It's called *roquette* in France, rocket or rocket salad in England, and *rucola* in Italy. American horticulturists recognize it as rugula, but somehow most American cooks have settled on arugula, which I've seen spelled a dozen ways. The botanical name is *Eruca vesicaria.*

Many gardeners and cooks consider arugula to be an Italian salad green. Although it is grown in France and Greece, it is by far more popular in Italy than in any other European country. This interesting peppery green is often combined with tiny radicchio leaves, a milder leafy lettuce, or finely julienned Belgian endives and then lightly tossed in extra-virgin olive oil and a touch of red wine vinegar.

To those of us who live in areas that cater to Italian cooks, arugula is a familiar sight at most local vegetable stores. Arugula salads are commonly offered at Italian restaurants, usually in combination with other milder greens that offset the rather sharp taste of this distinctive green.

Unfortunately, store-bought arugula is often too mature and lacking in freshness, which renders it overly strong and pungent. Growing your own arugula is one of the great joys of vegetable gardening, providing a spring-time treasure. Since it is a fast-growing green, you can pick arugula at the peak of flavor, when leaves are about two to three inches high.

STORAGE

Arugula keeps well for as long as a week in a plastic bag in the vegetable drawer of the refrigerator.

GARDENING

As with so many greens, the first arugula crop should be sown very early in spring so it can benefit to the fullest from the season's cool and moist conditions. Plants are ready to harvest in about five weeks. Grow successive crops during spring and begin sowing again in late summer for harvests during fall. Like dandelion, arugula is a rampant weed if it goes to seed, so pull plants before the hot weather causes them to bolt.

Other Greens

In the last few years some of the most traditional greens have emerged as the leafy stars of the French nouvelle cuisine and the new American cuisine.

Sorrel, a hardy perennial that had been relegated to a corner of the vegetable garden, was suddenly rediscovered and is now used with great creativity in many dishes. Other greens, mustard and collard in particular, which never seemed to shine beyond their regional boundaries, are finding their way into many vegetable gardens, supermarkets, and specialty stores and are being picked up by both gardeners and cooks with great enthusiasm.

Although these greens have been around for years, they well deserve their new stardom. Not only are they easy to grow, but they are often interchangeable in many preparations and add flavor, texture, and color to many soups, stews, and salads.

Collards

For years collards were considered a Southern green, associated primarily with soul food. But in recent years, with the new vogue of regional cooking sweeping the country, cooks and restaurant chefs have discovered collards, using them with creativity and imagination.

Closely related to kale, collards have large and somewhat coarse pale green leaves that, when cooked, have an interesting flavor. Most Southern states raise large quantities of both collard and mustard greens, and the regional way of cooking these greens has been a rather lengthy braising with some smoked pork butt or a ham bone. Although collards take well to the smokiness of bacon, I see no reason to overcook this amiable green. Rather, I find that young collards can be quickly stir-fried in good olive oil with some sliced garlic, make a fine addition to spring and summer soups, and are delicious baked in a well-flavored custard (see page 62).

STORAGE

Although they can be stored in the coldest part of the refrigerator for a day or two, collards wilt quickly and should be cooked as soon as possible.

GARDENING

It may come as a surprise that this Southern favorite tolerates cold in the garden better than does cabbage, another collard relative. Unlike many other members of the cabbage family, collards also tolerate heat. Because a single plant can be harvested throughout the season, successive plantings are unnecessary. For summer and autumn picking, I sow seeds in very early spring, as soon as the soil can be worked easily. If you garden in the South, make a second sowing in late summer for harvests during fall and winter. To avoid diseases, do not plant collards in the same spots where cole crops (cabbage, broccoli, kohlrabi, and so on) grew the previous year, and give the plants plenty of room. Collards, which are also known as tree cabbage due to their size and shape, may eventually become three feet high and wide. For smaller, more compact plants, try a variety called Vates.

HARVESTING

Pick the outermost leaves before they become tough. The central rosette of young foliage also makes good eating, but plucking it out puts an end to the plant's productivity. Leaves harvested after a light autumn frost tend to be particularly flavorful.

Mustard Greens

Mustard greens are extremely popular in the South, where they are cooked in a similar fashion to collard greens, usually with a piece of ham bone or salt pork. But with the growing demand around the country for interesting regional greens, you can now find mustard greens featured on the menus of some of the most innovative restaurants.

Today's gardener has a choice of several fast-growing varieties, any of which makes a wonderful addition to the spring garden. None is better than Fordhook Fancy, whose pretty foliage offers delightfully mild flavor.

STORAGE

Store unwashed leaves in a plastic bag. The fresh greens will keep up to five days. Garden-picked mustard greens have to be rinsed in several changes of warm water before drying in a salad spinner or a kitchen towel.

GARDENING

Although modern mustard green varieties are relatively slow to bolt, the plants require cool temperatures for best results. Start sowing seeds as soon as the soil can be worked in spring, and be sure to fertilize before planting. Only in fertile soil kept evenly moist will mustard plants grow rapidly enough to be ready before the weather warms in mid to late spring. For fall harvests, I like to make a second sowing in late summer.

HARVESTING

Like all greens, mustard is at its best when picked at a young, tender stage—about a month after planting.

Sorrel

Ten years ago sorrel was practically unknown in this country. Even in France and England, where it is grown as a perennial in many gardens, it was considered a "vintage" green, used only occasionally in soup. But when the Troisgros brothers, two extraordinarily gifted chefs from the Lyons area of France, created a sublime dish of sautéed salmon fillet in a creamy sorrel sauce, this forgotten green became a star overnight. Now there is scarcely a fine restaurant in Europe or the United States that does not use sorrel.

Sorrel, which grows wild in Russia and Scandinavia, is used primarily for two classic soups. Schave, the Russian version, uses potatoes, while the French *potage à l'oseille* is a velvety soup enriched with egg yolks, cream, and a touch of lemon.

The puckery taste of sorrel has led to its being named "sourgrass," and it is its somewhat sour flavor that makes this green so interesting. Although very young sorrel leaves can be used sparingly in salads, the green is at its best when melted down like spinach—with only the water that clings to the leaves—and then pureed. In combination with cream, it is *the* best accompaniment to salmon fillets, scallops, or fillets of sole. A fine julienne of three to four tablespoons of raw sorrel leaves is often all that is needed to perk up a cream sauce or soup.

Since sorrel is a perennial that comes up year after year with little care, every gardener can enjoy this superb "vintage" green; every gardening cook will wonder how he or she got along without it.

STORAGE

Store sorrel leaves in a plastic bag in the refrigerator and use within a day or two of buying or picking. Sorrel should be washed in several changes of lukewarm water and cooked with just the water that clings to its leaves.

GARDENING

Unlike free-spreading wild sorrel, clump-forming cultivated sorrel is reasonably easy to keep under control. Choose a permanent spot for the plants where the soil is rich and moderately acid and sunlight is direct for at least a few hours daily. Established plants should be fertilized each year and watered generously throughout the growing season. In midseason, I take the time to cut off any developing seed stalks; otherwise, sorrel would propagate itself like a weed. I also pick off old or yellow leaves to encourage plants to continue producing desirable fresh foliage. Every few years, tired clumps should be rejuvenated. Simply dig up the plants, divide them, and then replant the healthiest divisions.

HARVESTING

Always pick the outer leaves first, leaving a rosette of foliage within to ensure additional harvests later on. It is a good idea to cut some foliage regularly even if it is not needed for the kitchen. Otherwise, plants may lose their vigor and outer leaves their tenderness.

Spring Greens in Garlic Vinaigrette with Mozzarella Crostini

1 recipe Provençal Vinaigrette
(page 359)

8 cups mixed salad greens,
such as radicchio, arugula,
and red leaf, corn, and
Boston lettuces, leaves
separated, washed and dried

6 slices French bread, cut ½
inch thick

1 large garlic clove, peeled and
cut in half

3 tablespoons extra-virgin
olive oil

2 teaspoons anchovy paste
or 4 flat anchovy fillets,
finely minced

6 slices whole-milk mozzarella
(about ¼ pound), cut ¼
inch thick

GARNISH

2 teaspoons tiny capers,
drained

*C*risp fresh salad greens are a welcome addition to any meal, but when made with the first young greens of one's own garden or neighboring farm stand, the result is doubly delicious. Besides a well-balanced vinaigrette that must not overpower the delicate greens, I like this simple topping of sliced sautéed or grilled bread with some lightly melted mozzarella to complete this perfect spring starter. For a seasonal addition, shower each portion of salad with a mincing of young basil leaves.

1. Place the vinaigrette in a large mixing bowl and top with the greens, but do not toss. Cover and refrigerate until ready to serve.

2. Preheat the broiler.

3. Rub each side of the bread slices with the cut garlic clove. Heat the oil in a heavy skillet over medium heat. Add the bread and sauté until nicely browned on both sides. Transfer to paper towels to drain.

4. Spread one side of each slice of bread with a little of the anchovy paste, top each with a slice of mozzarella, and run under the broiler until the cheese is just heated through. Reserve.

5. Toss the salad and divide among 6 individual dinner plates. Place one crostini in the center of each portion and sprinkle with capers. Serve at once.

SERVES 6

Crisp-Fried Chicken Wings with Baby Lettuces in a Sesame Vinaigrette

Achange of vinaigrette can add a whole new dimension to a salad, and this one has a decided Asian bent. When I feel like turning the salad into a light meal, I often opt for crisp-fried chicken wings as a topping. For a flavorful variation, add a dash of cayenne to the coating flour or use shrimp instead of chicken wings. Either way a touch of heat such as minced jalapeño pepper works nicely in this salad.

1. Cut each wing in half at the joint and place in a resealable plastic bag. Sprinkle with the cayenne, thyme, cumin, salt, and pepper and toss well. Seal the bag and let marinate at room temperature for 1 hour.

2. While the chicken is marinating, prepare the salad: In a large bowl, combine the soy sauce, vinegar, sugar, mustard, and garlic and whisk until well blended. Add the peanut oil in a slow stream, whisking constantly, until emulsified. Whisk in the sesame oil and scallions and season with pepper. Top with the snow peas, bean sprouts, cucumbers, and lettuces in that order. Do not toss. Cover and chill.

3. Dredge the wings lightly in flour, shaking off the excess. Heat the peanut oil in a large heavy skillet to the depth of ½ inch over medium high heat. When hot, add the wings and fry for 10 to 12 minutes or until crisp and nicely browned. Transfer to a double layer of paper towels to drain.

4. To serve, toss the salad and divide among 4 dinner plates. Top each portion with 4 chicken pieces and serve at once.

SERVES 4

THE MARINADE
- 8 chicken wings, tips removed
- ⅛ teaspoon cayenne pepper
- 1 teaspoon dried thyme
- 1 teaspoon cumin seeds, toasted and crushed (see page 82)
- 1 teaspoon coarse salt
- Freshly ground black pepper
- All-purpose flour for dredging
- Peanut oil for frying

THE SALAD
- 1 tablespoon thin soy sauce
- 1 tablespoon red wine vinegar
- 2 teaspoons sugar
- ½ teaspoon dry mustard
- 1 large garlic clove, peeled and mashed
- 6 tablespoons peanut oil
- 1 tablespoon sesame oil
- 2 medium scallions, finely minced
- Freshly ground black pepper
- 12 snow peas, strings removed, steamed and julienned
- 1 cup mung bean sprouts
- 2 pickling cucumbers, peeled, seeded, and cut into thin matchsticks
- 4 cups mixed baby lettuces, leaves separated, washed, and dried

Young Dandelions with Warm Pennsylvania Dutch Dressing

½ pound young dandelion
    greens (about 8 cups),
    stemmed, washed, and dried
1 tablespoon unsalted butter
5 ounces slab bacon, blanched
    and diced, about 1 cup
4 extra-large egg yolks
6 tablespoons white wine
    vinegar
1 tablespoon sugar
Pinch of dry mustard
3 tablespoons finely minced
    fresh chives
Salt and freshly ground black
    pepper

*I once made the mistake of planting dandelion greens in my veg-
etable garden and spent the next two years yanking out this invasive plant.
Now I follow in the footsteps of my grandmother, who picked the very young
wild greens in the fields and pastures around our house. Tossed in a warm
sweet-and-sour dressing, they were always one of the highlights of early
spring. Be aware that this salad must be consumed the minute it is tossed or
else the greens will wilt. Other greens, especially arugula and New Zealand
spinach, can be substituted for the dandelions. The salad is best served as an
appetizer with some freshly ground black pepper and a crusty baguette.*

1. Place the dandelion greens in a large mixing bowl and set
aside.

2. Melt the butter in a small skillet over medium heat, add
the bacon, and cook until almost crisp. Reserving the drippings in the pan, transfer to a double layer of paper towels to
drain. Crumble and set aside.

3. Combine the reserved drippings with the yolks, vinegar,
sugar, and mustard in a small heavy saucepan, preferably cop-
per, and whisk until well blended. Place over low heat and
whisk constantly until the mixture becomes thick and
smooth. Be careful not to overcook or the yolks will curdle.
Immediately transfer to a bowl, add the chives, and season
with salt and pepper.

4. Pour the warm dressing over the dandelions, toss gently,
and divide the salad among 4 to 6 serving plates. Garnish
with a sprinkling of bacon and serve at once.

SERVES 4 TO 6

Swiss Green Salad with Gruyère Chive Beignets

Salads have become the year-round starters of choice for many cooks. I like to vary them, adding interesting toppings such as these classic cheese beignets. The beignet batter can be made well in advance, but the puffs are best when fried at the last moment. A mixture of cheese such as Parmesan or the more assertive Pecorino Romano can be used. You can also vary the vinaigrette according to your personal taste. Be sure, however, to keep a balance between the taste of the greens and that of the puffs.

1. Place the vinaigrette in a large bowl and top with the greens, but do not toss. Cover and chill.

2. Combine the water, butter, and ¼ teaspoon salt in a heavy medium-size saucepan. Bring to a boil and remove from the heat. Immediately add the flour all at once and beat vigorously with a wooden spoon until the flour is thoroughly incorporated.

3. Return the saucepan to low heat and beat for 1 to 1½ minutes to dry the mixture slightly. Transfer the dough to a food processor and, with the machine running, add the eggs, one at a time, until thoroughly combined. Add the cheese and chives and pulse to combine; the dough will be quite sticky. Transfer to a mixing bowl and let cool to room temperature.

4. In a large saucepan, heat the oil until it registers 350°F. on a deep-fry thermometer. Drop the dough by heaping teaspoonfuls into the hot oil, 4 to 6 at a time, and fry for 5 to 6 minutes, or until the beignets have stopped expanding and are nicely browned on all sides. Transfer with a slotted spoon to a double layer of paper towels. Sprinkle with coarse salt.

5. To serve, toss the salad and divide among 8 serving plates. Top each portion with 3 or 4 beignets and serve at once.

SERVES 8

1 recipe Provençal Vinaigrette (page 359)
8 cups mixed salad greens
½ cup water
3 tablespoons unsalted butter, softened
Coarse salt
½ cup all-purpose flour
2 extra-large eggs
1 cup grated imported Gruyère or other Swiss cheese
2 tablespoons finely minced fresh chives
4 cups corn oil for deep-frying

Nantucket-Style Linguine with Mustard Greens and Littleneck Clams

5 tablespoons extra-virgin olive oil

4 large garlic cloves, peeled and thinly sliced

1 pound mustard greens, stemmed, washed, and dried

Salt and freshly ground black pepper

1 or 2 small dry red chili peppers, broken in half

½ cup fresh parsley leaves

¼ cup dry white wine

24 littleneck clams, scrubbed well

¾ pound imported dried linguine

When properly prepared, linguine in a garlicky, slightly spicy clam sauce is a dish that is hard to improve on. But I like to add a seasonal touch, such as mustard greens or blanched kale. Their slightly bitter taste adds an interesting bite to this year-round favorite.

1. Heat 3 tablespoons of the olive oil in a large skillet over medium heat. Add 2 of the garlic cloves and the mustard greens and cook, tossing constantly, until just wilted. Season with salt and pepper and keep warm.

2. In a large casserole, heat the remaining oil over medium heat. Add the chili pepper, cook until the pepper is dark, and discard it. Add the remaining garlic and the parsley, wine, and clams to the chili oil and cook, covered, until the clams have opened; discard any that do not. Set the clams aside in their cooking liquid. If the liquid is sandy, strain it through a double layer of cheesecloth.

3. Bring plenty of salted water to a boil in a large pot, add the linguine, and cook until just tender "al dente." Drain well and transfer the pasta to a large serving bowl. Add the clams, clam cooking liquid, and warm greens and toss gently. Correct the seasoning and serve hot with plenty of crusty peasant bread.

S E R V E S   4

Skillet-Braised Mustard Greens with Pine Nuts, Crisp Bacon, and Tomato Salsa

This recipe is a takeoff on the popular Catalan stir-fry of spinach with pine nuts and raisins. Because mustard greens have a more assertive flavor than spinach does, they are actually even better suited to this preparation. The addition of a refreshing, slightly spicy salsa is unexpected but inspired; it results in a vaguely Southwestern dish that works beautifully either as an appetizer or as a side dish to grilled fish steaks, grilled lamb chops, or sautéed pork tenderloin medallions.

1. In a large heavy skillet, heat the oil over medium heat. Add the pine nuts and cook, stirring constantly, until lightly browned. Transfer to a side dish and reserve.

2. Add the bacon to the skillet and cook until almost crisp. With a slotted spoon, transfer the bacon to the dish with the pine nuts and set aside.

3. Add the garlic and mustard greens to the skillet and cook, tossing constantly, until just wilted. Add the vinegar and the reserved pine nuts and bacon, season with salt and pepper, and just heat through.

4. Divide the greens among 4 serving plates, top each portion with a dollop of tomato salsa, and serve warm.

SERVES 4

2 tablespoons olive oil
¼ cup pine nuts
2½ ounces slab bacon, blanched and diced, about ½ cup
2 large garlic cloves, peeled and thinly sliced
1½ pounds mustard greens, stemmed, washed, and dried
2 tablespoons sherry vinegar
Salt and freshly ground black pepper
1 recipe Tomato and Avocado Salsa (page 166)

Old-Fashioned Gratin of Collard Greens with Two Cheeses

2 tablespoons unsalted butter

¼ cup plain breadcrumbs

Salt

1½ pounds collard greens, stemmed and washed

3 tablespoons olive oil

2 large shallots, peeled and finely minced

3 large garlic cloves, peeled and finely minced

Freshly ground white pepper

4 extra-large eggs

1½ cups light cream or a mixture of heavy cream and milk

½ cup coarsely grated imported Gruyère or other Swiss cheese

Pinch of nutmeg

3 tablespoons freshly grated Parmesan cheese

Because of their mild flavor, collards are usually teamed with garlic or bacon or both. This rather mellow "gratin" can be further enhanced by adding 8 to 10 double-poached garlic cloves to the custard mixture. Serve the gratin with roast pork, veal, or lamb. Leftovers can be reheated in the microwave with excellent results.

1. Generously butter an oval or rectangular 3-quart baking dish. Sprinkle with the breadcrumbs and set aside.

2. Bring plenty of salted water to a boil in a large saucepan. Add the collards and cook for 10 minutes or until tender. Drain well and when cool enough to handle, gently squeeze to remove all excess liquid. Finely chop and reserve.

3. Preheat the oven to 350°F.

4. Heat the oil in a large skillet over medium heat. Add the shallots and garlic and cook until soft but not browned. Add the collards, season with salt and pepper, and cook for 2 minutes. Set aside.

5. Combine the eggs, cream, and cheese in a large bowl and whisk until well blended. Add the collard greens and season with salt, pepper, and a pinch of nutmeg. Pour the mixture into the prepared baking dish and sprinkle with the Parmesan cheese.

6. Place the baking dish in a large shallow pan and fill the pan with boiling water to come halfway up the sides of the dish. Bake for 25 minutes or until the custard is set and the top is lightly browned; a knife when inserted should come out clean. Remove from the oven and let sit for 10 minutes. Serve hot or at room temperature as an accompaniment to grilled meats.

SERVES 6 TO 8

Catalan Sauté of Collard Greens with Garlic, Anchovies, and Capers

I grew up with this Catalan preparation and have always loved it. The sauce, which is usually served with braised artichoke hearts, works equally well with blanched collards, spinach, and kale. Serve the greens as a light starter or as a side dish to pan-seared fennel sausage, grilled shrimp, or grilled fish steaks.

4 pounds collard greens
Salt
6 tablespoons (¾ stick) unsalted butter
3 large garlic cloves, peeled and finely minced
6 flat anchovy fillets, drained and finely minced
2 tablespoons tiny capers, drained
Freshly ground black pepper

1. With a sharp knife, cut out the entire stem from each collard leaf and discard. Cut the leaves into ¾-inch pieces and rinse 2 to 3 times in warm water to remove all sand.

2. Bring plenty of salted water to a boil in a large casserole. Add the collards and cook for 10 minutes or until just tender. Drain well and, when cool enough to handle, gently squeeze out the excess moisture.

3. Melt the butter in a large skillet over medium low heat. Add the garlic, anchovies, and capers, and cook for 1 minute or until the anchovies have "melted." Add the collards and toss until just heated through. Taste and correct the seasoning, adding a large grinding of black pepper. Serve hot.

SERVES 6

Pan-Seared Salmon with French Sorrel and Lemon Mayonnaise

THE SORREL AND LEMON MAYONNAISE

2 cups tightly packed sorrel
leaves, stemmed

2 extra-large eggs

2 teaspoons white wine vinegar

¾ cup peanut or corn oil

2 tablespoons finely minced
scallions

2 tablespoons finely minced
fresh parsley

Salt and freshly ground black
pepper

Lemon juice to taste

THE SALMON

4 salmon fillets, about 6 to 7
ounces each, with skin on
and preferably center cut

4 tablespoons peanut oil

Coarse salt and freshly ground
black pepper

GARNISH

Tiny leaves of fresh parsley

For decades sorrel was the forgotten vegetable, springing up in innumerable French kitchen gardens year after year but rarely making it beyond the soup pot. All this changed in the 1970s when the brothers Troisgros created their signature dish: salmon braised in a sorrel sauce. I don't think there has been a more copied dish in the past twenty years, and I can't resist offering my own adaptation, in which sorrel is teamed with a light mayonnaise. Served with simply steamed new potatoes, it's still one of the best dishes of the spring season.

1. Wash the sorrel leaves thoroughly under warm water and transfer to a medium saucepan with the water that clings to the leaves. Place over low heat and cook until all the leaves have wilted. Transfer to a strainer and let cool.

2. Combine the eggs and vinegar in a blender or food processor and, with the machine running, add the oil by droplets until the mixture is thick and all the oil has been added. Add the sorrel, scallions, and parsley, season with salt and pepper, and process until smooth. Add drops of lemon juice to taste and set aside.

3. Dry the salmon fillets thoroughly on paper towels.

4. Heat the oil in two 10-inch, nonstick skillets over high heat. Place two salmon fillets in each skillet, skin side down, and cover loosely with foil. Cook for 2 minutes, slightly lower the heat, and cook, without turning, for an additional 3 to 5 minutes, or until the fillets are just done; do not overcook. You may turn the fillets over at the ending of cooking for about 30 seconds if you want the tops to be browned. Season the fillets with coarse salt and pepper.

5. To serve, place 1 fillet on each of 4 dinner plates and spoon a little of the sorrel mayonnaise around each portion. Garnish with parsley leaves and serve hot.

SERVES 4

Farm-Style Sorrel Soup

Spring soups are a lovely introduction to the season. Here is one soup that captures the essence of nature's gifts. Because of the delicate taste of sorrel, it does require a full-bodied homemade chicken stock or at least a well-doctored canned broth. If at all possible, let the soup stand for several hours to allow it to develop its full flavor. Remember that a basket of crusty bread and some sweet butter always make the perfect partners for a good soup.

3 tablespoons unsalted butter
1 large onion, peeled and finely minced
3 medium all-purpose potatoes, peeled and cubed
3 cups tightly packed sorrel leaves, stemmed
6 to 8 cups chicken broth, preferably homemade (page 360)
½ cup sour cream
Salt and freshly ground white pepper
Lemon juice to taste

1. In a heavy 3½-quart casserole, melt the butter over medium heat. Add the onion and cook until soft but not browned.

2. Add the potatoes, sorrel, and 6 cups of the broth. Bring to a boil, reduce the heat, and simmer, covered, for 10 to 15 minutes or until the vegetables are very soft.

3. Strain the soup and return the broth to the casserole. Puree the vegetables in a food processor until smooth, and whisk the puree into the broth. If the soup is too thick, add some of the remaining broth.

4. Whisk in the sour cream and just heat through; do not let the soup come to a boil. Taste and correct the seasoning, adding salt and a large grinding of pepper and lemon juice to taste. Serve hot.

SERVES 6

NOTE: This soup can also be served lightly chilled with an additional dollop of sour cream. Sprinkle with a little zest of either lemon or lime on each portion.

PEAS

When I was a child, shelling peas was a chore I performed almost daily—one that I did not mind too much since I would munch on almost as many as ended up in the bowl. Possibly because of my physical investment in the end product, I loved peas more than any other vegetable. A plateful of freshly cooked sweet peas, sometimes sautéed with bits of smoked ham or air-cured prosciutto, was a favorite first course at our house. Indeed, when in season, cooked peas found their way into many preparations in which their bright green color, unique texture, and delicate sweet taste provided a bit of spring. My mother's version of the Viennese *risi bisi,* a simple but flavorful pilaf of rice that is laced with peas and parsley, is still one of my favorite accompaniments to meats and poultry, as is the classic *salade Russe,* in which fresh-cooked peas, carrots, beans, and potatoes are bound together in a flavorful mayonnaise. In fact, I find that peas are good in just about everything. They are delicious in pasta dishes, in a ragout of veal with mushrooms (page 70), in cold dishes such as a chicken salad, and braised with small white onions or hearts of Boston lettuce.

The reason the peas one buys from a greengrocer so seldom taste fresh is that the sugar they contain turns to starch within hours of picking. In order to enjoy this vegetable at its best, you have almost no choice *but* to grow your own. Since peas demand little care in the garden, they are well worth the effort.

Another lovely garden pea is the snow pea, which has a crunchy and delicious flat pod and is harvested before the little peas develop. Although primarily used in Chinese and other Oriental stir-fries, snow peas are now used creatively in many Western dishes and salads. Simply steamed, they are a wonderful accompaniment to a variety of meats, poultry, and fish. They can be combined with other spring vegetables in a colorful stir-fry, or served by themselves, either sautéed or blanched and buttered. Although snow peas are available in many markets throughout the year, they are quite expensive and often lack that crunchy freshness that makes the garden vegetable so unique.

In recent years the new snap peas have become increasingly popular, and it is easy to see why. They can be eaten pod and all, or the pods can be shelled for the full-size peas within. Unlike snow peas, the snap pea pods are thick and fleshy; they are excellent raw along with a dip, on a relish tray, or eaten alone as a snack. The first variety to be introduced was Sugar Snap, which produces juicy three-inch-long pods, but several varieties have recently become available.

STORAGE

Fresh peas, snow peas, and snap peas can be stored successfully for three to four days in the refrigerator in a plastic bag. Shell the peas just before cooking. Shelled garden peas can be frozen, although they do not retain their crisp texture.

GARDENING

There is no shortage of varieties to choose from. Among the best peas is Maestro; early and highly productive, it is resistant to powdery mildew and other diseases that affect peas. The true soup pea is Alaska, which lends itself to drying and winter use. Oregon Sugar Pod II is a delicious and particularly disease-resistant variety of snow pea.

I usually make a few separate plantings at two- to three-week intervals starting in very early spring. Peas cannot tolerate heat, so plan for the last spring sowing to mature before daytime temperatures average above 75°F. Additional plantings can be made in midsummer for harvest during fall, even after light frosts. Friends in southern California tell me that their pea crops do best in winter.

Before sowing, fertilize the soil and add a granular inoculant of nitrogen-fixing bacteria, which enables roots of peas and other legumes to convert nitrogen from the air into a useful plant nutrient. Chicken-wire cages or garden netting provide excellent support for tall-growing varieties.

HARVESTING

For the sweetest peas, pick pods just before time for cooking. The safest way to harvest is to hold the pod stem in one hand and the pod itself in the other. Then break. Merely yanking or twisting with one hand may uproot the plant.

Sauté of Calf's Liver with Caramelized Onions and Sweet Peas

It is unfortunate that calf's liver has fallen out of favor in this country. Simply pan-seared and served with a side dish of fresh peas and some sweetly caramelized onions it is one of the great springtime meals. You may substitute chicken livers for calf's liver and serve a soft, creamy polenta as a side dish.

1. Cut the liver crosswise into ¼-inch strips. Dry well on paper towels and set aside.

2. In a large heavy skillet, melt 3 tablespoons of the butter together with 1 teaspoon of the oil over medium high heat. Add the onions, sprinkle with 1 teaspoon of the sugar, and season with salt and pepper. Cook for 5 minutes, stirring constantly, until the onions begin to brown. Reduce the heat and cook for an additional 30 minutes or until they are soft and caramelized.

3. While the onions are cooking, prepare the peas: Place the peas in a small saucepan with water to cover. Add the remaining teaspoon of sugar, season with salt and pepper, and simmer for 5 minutes or until just tender. Drain well and set aside.

4. When the onions are done, transfer to a side dish and reserve. Season the liver with pepper only and dredge lightly in flour, shaking off the excess.

5. Add the remaining butter and oil to the skillet over medium high heat. Add the calf's liver and cook quickly until it just loses its pink color, about 1 minute; do not overcook. Immediately remove the pan from the heat, add the onions together with the peas, and season with salt and pepper. Return the skillet to low heat and toss gently to just heat through. Serve hot, garnished with minced parsley.

SERVES 4 TO 5

1 pound calf's liver, thinly sliced
6 tablespoons (¾ stick) unsalted butter
2 teaspoons peanut oil
2 very large onions, peeled, quartered, and thinly sliced
2 teaspoons sugar
Salt and freshly ground white pepper
1½ pounds fresh peas in the shell (about 1½ cups shelled)
All-purpose flour for dredging

GARNISH
2 tablespoons finely minced fresh parsley

Spring Ragout of
Veal Shanks à la Française

6 pounds veal shanks, cut crosswise into 2-inch pieces

4 tablespoons (½ stick) unsalted butter

3 tablespoons olive oil

Salt and freshly ground white pepper

3 cups beef broth, preferably homemade

2 large sprigs of fresh thyme

10 ounces cremini mushrooms, wiped, stemmed, and quartered

1 to 2 teaspoons arrowroot mixed with 1 tablespoon beef broth

1½ pounds fresh peas in the shell (1½ cups shelled), cooked (see page 69)

2 tablespoons finely minced fresh tarragon

GARNISH

2 tablespoons finely minced fresh parsley

*H*ere *is an adaptation of a bistro springtime classic. In France, this earthy stew is usually made with spring lamb, but unfortunately this cut is rarely available in this country. However, I like it just as much made with tender, meaty shanks of veal. Serve the ragout with buttery noodles, mashed potatoes, or quick couscous. Use two skillets so that the shanks can be braised in a single layer.*

1. Dry the veal thoroughly on paper towels and set aside.

2. In each of two large cast-iron skillets, melt 2 tablespoons of the butter together with ½ tablespoon of the oil over medium high heat. Add the shanks in one layer without crowding and brown nicely on all sides. Season with salt and pepper.

3. Add 1½ cups of the broth and 1 sprig of the thyme to each skillet. Cover tightly with foil, then with the lids, and braise over the lowest heat possible for 1 hour and 30 minutes or until the veal is fork-tender but not falling off the bone.

4. While the shanks are braising, heat the remaining 2 tablespoons of oil in a heavy skillet over medium high heat. Add the mushrooms and sauté quickly until nicely browned. Season with salt and pepper and reserve.

5. When the veal is done, discard the thyme and transfer the shanks with a slotted spoon to a shallow serving platter. Keep warm. Degrease the pan juices from both skillets and return them to one of the skillets.

6. Place the skillet over high heat and reduce the juices slightly. Whisk in a little of the arrowroot mixture until the sauce lightly coats a spoon. Add the mushrooms, peas, and tarragon and just heat through. Correct the seasoning and pour the mixture over the shanks. Serve the ragout hot, garnished with minced parsley and accompanied by a pilaf of rice.

SERVES 6

Sugar Snap Pea Salad with Sweet Lemon and Mustard Dressing

Snap peas are becoming increasingly available, but they are still at their very best when picked fresh from the garden or at the farm stand. Steamed snap peas make a lovely simple salad when tossed in tangy lemon dressing and served as a cool side dish to grilled, poached, or pan-seared salmon.

1. Bring salted water to a boil in a vegetable steamer. Add the peas and steam, covered, for 5 minutes or until crisp-tender. Run under cold water to stop further cooking and drain on paper towels. Place in a serving bowl and set aside.

2. In a small jar, combine the lemon juice, oil, mustard, and sugar. Cover tightly and shake until the mixture is smooth and well blended. Add the scallions, season with salt and pepper, and pour the dressing over the peas. Cover and chill for at least 2 hours before serving.

SERVES 6

VARIATION

You may turn this salad into a luncheon dish by simply adding ¼ cup finely diced Gruyère cheese and ¼ cup finely diced smoked ham. Serve lightly chilled on leaves of mixed garden greens accompanied by a crusty loaf of French bread.

Salt
1½ pounds sugar snap peas, strings removed
Juice of 1 large lemon
6 tablespoons olive oil
1 tablespoon Dijon mustard
2 teaspoons granulated sugar
4 tablespoons finely minced scallions
Freshly ground white pepper

Ziti with Peas, Smoked Ham, and Pink Tomato Sauce

2 tablespoons extra-virgin
    olive oil
1 medium zucchini, cut into a
    thin julienne, avoiding as
    much of the seedy center as
    possible
1 large red bell pepper, cored,
    seeded, quartered, and
    thinly sliced
½ cup finely diced smoked
    ham
1 cup shelled fresh peas,
    cooked (see page 69)
1¼ cups Classic Plum Tomato
    Sauce (page 159)
½ cup heavy cream
Salt and freshly ground black
    pepper
½ pound imported dried ziti
⅓ cup julienned fresh basil
    leaves
4 tablespoons freshly grated
    Parmesan cheese

A *pink tomato sauce is one to which a touch of heavy cream or crème fraîche has been added. The sauce is usually reserved for homemade fettuccine, which takes well to creamy sauces rather than the more heavy southern Italian tomato-based ones. But I like a pink tomato sauce so much that I do not restrict myself to the conventional uses; I like to pair it with tubular pasta as well as fettuccine. The addition of fresh peas and a julienne of smoked ham makes it a perfect springtime main course. For a variation, you may add some sautéed asparagus or a stir-fry of bitter greens, such as mustard or beet greens, and top the pasta dish with diced smoked mozzarella or a creamy blue cheese—and, of course, some freshly grated Parmesan.*

1. In a large heavy skillet, heat the olive oil over medium low heat. Add the zucchini and red pepper and cook for 4 to 5 minutes or until just tender. Add the ham and cook for 1 minute longer. Add the peas, tomato sauce, and cream, season with salt and pepper, and just heat through. Keep warm.

2. Bring plenty of salted water to a boil in a large casserole, add the pasta, and cook until just tender "al dente." Drain well and add to the skillet of tomato sauce together with the basil. Toss well to just heat through and correct the seasoning, adding a large grinding of black pepper. Sprinkle with Parmesan cheese and serve directly from the skillet with crusty Tuscan bread.

S E R V E S   4

Mint-Infused Sweet Pea Soup with Crème Fraîche

The thought of pureeing a whole batch of fresh peas may sound rather extravagant to those who have little access to this springtime jewel, but now that shelled peas are available in many markets, this classic English preparation is well worth making. Peas and mint have a particular affinity to one another, but other herbs, especially chervil, dill, and tarragon, will also enhance the soup beautifully. For a real extra treat, I often top each serving with tiny croutons sautéed in clarified butter. Add a dollop of crème fraîche and you have one of the season's very best starters.

1. In a large casserole, melt the butter over medium heat. Add the onion and cook until soft but not browned, 8 to 10 minutes. Add the flour and cook for 2 minutes, stirring constantly, until lightly browned. Add the chicken broth all at once, whisk until well blended, and bring to a boil.

2. Add 3 cups of the peas, reduce the heat, and simmer, partially covered, for 25 minutes or until the peas are very tender. While the soup simmers, cook the remaining shelled peas in salted water to cover for 5 minutes, or until barely tender. Drain.

3. Strain the soup and return the broth to the casserole. Puree the vegetables in a food processor until smooth and whisk the puree into the broth.

4. Whisk in the crème fraîche or yogurt and just heat through. Correct the seasoning. Just before serving, add the separately cooked peas and minced mint and serve hot, garnished with tiny leaves of fresh mint.

S E R V E S 6

3 tablespoons unsalted butter
1 medium onion, peeled and finely minced
2½ tablespoons all-purpose flour
6 cups chicken broth, preferably homemade (page 360)
4 pounds fresh peas unshelled (about 4 cups shelled)
½ cup Crème Fraîche (page 358) or plain yogurt
Salt and freshly ground white pepper
2 to 3 tablespoons finely minced fresh mint

GARNISH
Tiny leaves of fresh mint

Fricassee of Snow Peas with Pan-Seared Scallops and Cilantro

1½ pounds small sea scallops
Salt and freshly ground black pepper
All-purpose flour for dredging
2 tablespoons unsalted butter
2 tablespoons peanut oil
2 large garlic cloves, peeled and crushed
40 snow peas, strings removed
1 teaspoon sugar
2 tablespoons dry sherry
2 tablespoons water
2 to 3 tablespoons fresh cilantro leaves

Snow peas have been closely associated with Asian cooking, to which they add their lovely color and crunchy taste, but now have moved into the everyday American kitchen. Teaming them with a quick sauté of scallops is just one of the many simple and flavorful ways to use this unique spring vegetable. If cilantro is not one of your favorite herbs, dill, flat-leaf parsley, or chives are excellent substitutes. For an accompaniment I usually opt for steamed and buttered new potatoes or a simple loaf of good bread, but it's also lovely with buttered fettuccine.

1. Dry the scallops thoroughly on paper towels. Season with salt and pepper and dredge lightly in flour, shaking off the excess.

2. Melt the butter together with 1 tablespoon of the oil in a large skillet over medium high heat. Add the garlic and cook until browned; remove and discard. Add the scallops, without crowding the pan, and sauté until nicely browned on both sides. Transfer to a side dish and reserve.

3. Reduce the heat and add the remaining oil to the skillet. Add the snow peas, sprinkle with the sugar, and cook for 1 minute to glaze. Add the sherry and water and simmer until the snow peas are just tender and the liquid is reduced and syrupy.

4. Return the scallops to the skillet and toss gently to just heat through. Correct the seasoning, sprinkle with cilantro, and serve hot as an appetizer or as a main course.

SERVES 4 TO 5

Butter-Braised Baby Peas with Scallions and Herbs

In countries such as Spain, Italy, and France, where fresh peas are both expensive and time-consuming to prepare, they are usually served as an appetizer, much like a plateful of freshly cooked asparagus would be. My mother treated these spring treasures with the respect reserved for more important starters. She often added a few small leaves of Boston lettuce to the skillet at the last moment and always enriched the peas with a touch of butter and a sprinkling of sugar, which brought out their natural sweet taste. For an interesting addition of texture, steam a cup of snow peas, first cut lengthwise into a fine julienne, and add them to the skillet just before removing it from the heat. This dish is an unexpected but always well-received first course.

3 pounds fresh peas, about 3 cups shelled
Salt
5 tablespoons unsalted butter
1½ teaspoons sugar
3 tablespoons finely minced scallions
Optional: 4 ounces prosciutto, smoked ham, or smoked turkey, cut into ¼-inch dice
Freshly ground black pepper

GARNISH
2 tablespoons finely minced fresh dill, mint, or chervil

1. Place the peas in a large saucepan with salted water to cover. Add 2 tablespoons of the butter and 1 teaspoon of the sugar, and simmer for 2 to 3 minutes or until barely tender. Drain and reserve.

2. Melt the remaining butter in a large skillet over medium low heat, add the scallions and cook until just wilted, 3 to 4 minutes. Add the prosciutto, ham, or turkey, if using, and the peas. Sprinkle with the remaining sugar, season with salt and pepper, and toss until the peas are tender and nicely glazed. Garnish with the herbs and serve hot.

SERVES 6

VARIATIONS
1. Braise 2 Belgian endives cut crosswise into ¾-inch slices, in 2 to 3 tablespoons of butter together with ⅓ cup chicken broth and a little lemon juice, until just tender. Drain and add to the glazed peas.

2. Sauté ½ pound cubed mushrooms in 2 tablespoons butter together with 1 teaspoon oil and 1 tablespoon finely minced shallots, until nicely browned. Season with salt and pepper and add to the glazed peas.

Sautéed Snow Peas in Mint and Shallot Butter

3 tablespoons unsalted butter, softened

1½ tablespoons finely minced shallots

½ cup loosely packed fresh mint leaves, finely minced

2 tablespoons extra-virgin olive oil

1 pound snow peas, ends trimmed

2 large garlic cloves, peeled and sliced

2 tablespoons dry sherry

¼ cup chicken broth, preferably homemade (page 360)

Salt and freshly ground white pepper

Herb butters are great to have on hand at all times. Just a teaspoon or two allows you to turn sautéed or grilled foods into something more unusual and flavorful. Mint, parsley, shallots, garlic, ginger, and chives are some of my favorite flavorings for compound butters. This mint and shallot combination greatly enhances a simple stir-fry of snow peas, turning it into a lively side dish to grilled meats, chicken breasts, and pan-seared fish fillets.

1. In a small bowl, combine the butter, shallots, and mint and blend well with a fork into a smooth and even paste. Cover and chill.

2. Heat the oil in a large nonstick skillet over medium high heat. Add the snow peas and cook, stirring often, until they start to brown, about 6 minutes. Add the garlic cloves and sherry and continue to sauté until the peas are nicely browned, about 2 minutes longer.

3. Reduce the heat, add the broth, season with salt and pepper, and simmer, covered, for 3 minutes longer or until just tender. Do not overcook.

4. Remove the pan from the heat and fold in the mint and shallot butter. Toss well until the butter just melts into the peas. Correct the seasoning, transfer to a serving bowl, and serve hot.

SERVES 4 TO 5

SPINACH

SPINACH IS POSSIBLY THE MOST VERSATILE OF ALL GREENS. ITS WONDER-ful bright green color, subtle but assertive flavor, and toothsome texture have inspired many classic preparations. Dishes called *alla Fiorentina* (or Florentine) always include spinach, either as a bed for sautéed meats or in stuffings. The all-American spinach and bacon salad makes a most enjoyable year-round starter, as does a well-flavored spinach soup. Spinach pasta and crêpes owe their attractive color to spinach's verdant leaves; Emerald Mayonnaise (see page 9) would be incomplete without it. And there is no other green that blends as well into stuffings, or is as compatible in custards and many other egg dishes.

When I was growing up, spinach was most often braised and served *alla Catalane* with diced sautéed bacon, sautéed pine nuts, and sultana raisins. That always was, and still is, one of my favorite ways to prepare this vegetable. The claim that children do not like spinach surprises me, since there are few greens that taste as wonderful when simply prepared, either buttered or pureed and then enriched with fresh butter and a touch of cream.

While fresh spinach is available practically the entire year in supermarkets and greengrocers, it is a far cry from the tender leafy green of the kitchen garden. In supermarkets, spinach is often sold in cellophane bags, in which you find mostly stems and broken leaves that lend themselves only to cooked preparations. In recent years, more and more truly fresh spinach has become available at good greengrocers, allowing cooks to use it raw in a variety of interesting salads as well as in cooked dishes.

Much of the summer spinach found in West Coast supermarkets is New Zealand spinach, which has elongated thin leaves and is not related to true spinach. Friends of mine in southern California, where temperatures are too warm for standard spinach, have excellent luck with the New Zealand variety because it is heat-resistant. I like it raw in salads (young leaves are best) and find it useful in preparations such as spinach pasta and crêpes.

For many gardeners the excitement that marks the beginning of a new growing season starts with the planting of spinach. Young leaves will be ready for the late-spring salad bowl within six to seven weeks of the first sowing.

Spinach is extremely gritty and takes several soakings in lukewarm water before it is ready to be cooked. Once thoroughly washed, the spinach should be stemmed unless it is very young, in which case the tiny stems add a nice texture to the cooked greens. I like to cook spinach in either a saucepan or a skillet with a very small amount of water, preferably only the water that clings to the leaves after washing. I steam spinach only when it is to be used for a stuffing or as a coloring agent for a mayonnaise or pasta. Spinach can absorb an extraordinary amount of butter, which is the reason why simply buttered spinach is so sinfully delicious.

STORAGE

Spinach will keep for two to three days refrigerated in a plastic bag. If it is to be used in a salad, it should be spun dry in a salad spinner and served as soon as possible.

GARDENING

Timing is of the essence with this otherwise undemanding green. When daytime temperatures rise much above 75°F., spinach plants bolt—that is, they rush into flower and then quickly go to seed, ending their production of harvestable leaves.

I find that the key to success is to start sowing seeds directly in the garden as soon as the soil is workable in early spring. Even if plants are struck by late frost, the hardy foliage will not be damaged significantly. Sow successive crops every couple of weeks, stopping five or six weeks before the first hot weather is expected to arrive. Resume sowing in late summer for additional picking in fall. In regions where winters are warm, it is best to begin sowing in autumn for productive crops in winter and spring. Be sure to use fresh spinach seeds each year.

Water frequently enough to keep soil evenly moist at all times, and fertilize when young plants become about three inches tall. Spinach is ready for harvest when the largest leaves reach six to eight inches in length. Use a sharp knife to cut away the entire plant near ground level or just pick leaves from several plants and let the others continue to grow.

Spinach with crinkled leaves, known as savoy spinach, has a thicker, more appealing texture and also a richer green color than smooth-leaved types. One of my favorite varieties is Bloomsdale Longstanding, which is slow to bolt and sports beautifully savoyed leaves. Also excellent is Avon Hybrid, a fast-growing spinach with semi-crinkled foliage that is large and succulent.

New Zealand spinach is sensitive to cold, so wait until all danger of frost has passed before sowing seeds in the garden. Germination will be hastened if seeds are soaked in water overnight just prior to planting. To encourage thick growth, pinch back the main runners as soon as they begin to spread. Water whenever the top inch of soil becomes dry, and fertilize periodically throughout the season.

HARVESTING

Picking can begin about two months after sowing. For continuous harvests during summer, snip leaves as needed (but at least once a week), allowing new growth to replace whatever is cut.

Soup of Leaf Spinach and Spring Greens

5 tablespoons unsalted butter

2 medium leeks, trimmed of all but 2 inches of greens, thinly sliced and well rinsed

6 cups chicken broth, preferably homemade (page 360)

½ pound fresh asparagus, trimmed, peeled, and cut into 1-inch pieces

1 pound fresh spinach, stemmed and washed

2½ tablespoons all-purpose flour

1 pound fresh peas unshelled (about 1 cup shelled)

½ cup heavy cream

1 small head of Bibb lettuce, leaves separated, washed, and dried

Salt and freshly ground white pepper

GARNISH

2 to 3 tablespoons finely minced fresh chives or ¼ cup watercress leaves

*S*pring soups are a lovely introduction to the season. In a single bowl one can capture the essence of nature's gifts. Do bear in mind that spring greens require a full-bodied homemade stock or at least a well-doctored bouillon to enhance their taste. If at all possible, let the soup stand for several hours before serving to allow it to develop its full flavor. Remember that a basket of crusty bread and some sweet butter always make the perfect partners to a good soup.

1. In a heavy 3-quart saucepan, heat 2 tablespoons of the butter over low heat. Add the leeks and ¼ cup of the broth and simmer, covered, until tender, about 10 minutes. Add the remaining broth together with the asparagus and 2 cups of the spinach leaves and simmer until the asparagus is very tender, about 15 minutes longer.

2. Strain the soup and transfer the broth to a large bowl. Puree the vegetables in a food processor and process until smooth. Whisk the puree into the broth and set aside.

3. Melt the remaining butter in the casserole over medium heat. Whisk in the flour and cook for 1 minute without browning. Whisk in the pureed soup and bring to a boil. Reduce the heat, add the peas, and cook until barely tender, about 5 minutes.

4. Add the heavy cream together with the Bibb lettuce and remaining spinach and simmer until the leaves are just wilted. Season with salt and pepper and serve hot, garnished with minced chives or leaves of watercress.

SERVES 6

Classic Spinach alla Catalane

To me there is simply no better way to prepare spinach than in the traditional Catalan style. If you can use Muscat raisins, they do make a big difference, and Spanish pine nuts also contribute to the lovely taste of this dish. Serve the spinach as a starter or, for a light spring luncheon or simple supper dish, top it with a fried egg cooked in olive oil.

1. Bring plenty of salted water to a boil in a large casserole. Add the spinach and cook for 3 to 5 minutes or until just wilted. Drain well and, when cool enough to handle, squeeze gently to remove all excess liquid. Set aside.

2. Heat 1 tablespoon of the oil in a large heavy skillet over medium low heat. Add the pine nuts and sauté, stirring constantly, until lightly browned. Transfer to a side dish and reserve. Add the remaining oil to the skillet, then add the French bread and sauté quickly on both sides until golden. Reserve.

3. Add the butter to the skillet together with the garlic and cook for 1 minute without browning. Stir in the ham, spinach, and raisins, season with salt and pepper, and cook until all the moisture has evaporated. Add the pine nuts and serve hot, accompanied by the sautéed French bread.

SERVES 6

Salt
3 pounds fresh spinach, stemmed and washed well
4 tablespoons extra-virgin olive oil
2 tablespoons pine nuts
6 slices French bread
4 tablespoons (½ stick) unsalted butter
2 large garlic cloves, peeled and thinly sliced
½ cup finely diced smoked ham
3 tablespoons dark raisins, plumped
Freshly ground black pepper

Moroccan Braised Spinach with Red Potatoes and Yogurt

2 medium-size red potatoes
  (about 12 ounces), unpeeled
Salt
2 tablespoons unsalted butter
6 tablespoons plus 2 teaspoons
  olive oil
Freshly ground black pepper
3 large garlic cloves, peeled
  and thinly sliced
2 pounds fresh spinach,
  stemmed, washed, and dried
1 teaspoon cumin seeds,
  toasted and crushed (see
  Note), or 1 teaspoon ground
  cumin
1/2 teaspoon coriander seeds,
  toasted and crushed, or 1/2
  teaspoon ground coriander
1 cup yogurt
2 tablespoons finely minced
  fresh mint

Quick, *easy, and satisfying are all good words to describe this spinach side dish. It is the perfect accompaniment to marinated, grilled Cornish hens, chicken breasts, and shish kebabs of lamb.*

1. Place the potatoes in a small saucepan with salted water to cover and simmer for 20 to 25 minutes or until tender. Let cool completely in the cooking liquid. Peel and cut into 3/4-inch cubes.

2. Melt the butter together with the 2 teaspoons of olive oil in a heavy skillet over medium heat. Add the potatoes and cook for 5 to 7 minutes, stirring often, until nicely browned on all sides. Season with salt and pepper and reserve.

3. Braise the spinach in three batches: For each batch, heat 2 tablespoons of the oil in a large skillet over medium heat. Add 1 sliced garlic clove and one third of the spinach leaves. Toss until just wilted. Transfer to a colander and press lightly to remove excess liquid. Repeat with the remaining spinach.

4. Return all the braised spinach to the skillet, season with salt, pepper, cumin, and coriander, and cook for 2 minutes; drain off any excess liquid.

5. Add the potatoes and yogurt and cook for an additional 2 to 3 minutes or until the yogurt has been absorbed by the spinach. Add the mint and correct the seasoning. Serve hot.

SERVES 4 TO 6

NOTE: To toast cumin seeds, place them in a small, dry cast-iron or nonstick skillet over medium heat and shake the skillet back and forth until the seeds are fragrant and golden brown. Transfer the seeds to a mortar and pestle or a spice grinder and crush them into a fine powder. This can be done in quantity and the powder stored in a tightly covered jar for 1 to 2 weeks.

Provençal Spinach, Goat Cheese, and Herb Tart

Savory tarts are still the mainstay of provincial France, where a myriad of vegetables are used in their preparation. I first encountered this tart at an outdoor market one early Sunday morning in Avignon. It was in early spring; the air was crisp and the day clear and sunny. Vendors were just starting to unpack their cheeses, fruits, and vegetables from the back of their vans. The tart was still warm and the aroma of goat cheese mingled with that of the still warm buttery dough. I asked the vendor to slice the tart into six pieces and took it with me to the café across the square, where I ordered a large café au lait and gobbled up the entire tart. It was a terrific way to start the day.

1. Preheat the oven to 375°F.

2. Combine the goat cheese, crème fraîche, eggs, Parmesan, thyme, and rosemary in a food processor, season with salt and pepper, and process until smooth.

3. Heat the oil in a heavy skillet over medium heat. Add the garlic and spinach and cook, stirring constantly, until just wilted. Transfer to a colander and press lightly to remove the excess liquid. Season with salt and pepper and spread the spinach over the bottom of the prebaked tart shell. Pour the goat cheese mixture over the spinach and bake for 30 to 35 minutes or until a knife when inserted comes out clean.

4. Remove the tart from the oven and place on a wire rack to cool for 5 minutes or until the custard settles back.

5. Serve as is, either warm or at room temperature. Alternatively, to serve with the optional garnish, preheat the broiler. Cover the top of the tart with the sliced tomatoes, sprinkle with the herbs, and drizzle with the oil. Place a ring of aluminum foil over the rim of the tart and place under the broiler until the tomatoes are just heated through. Garnish with the black olives and serve warm cut into wedges.

SERVES 8

6 ounces mild goat cheese

1¼ cups Crème Fraîche (page 358) or sour cream

4 extra-large eggs

4 tablespoons freshly grated Parmesan cheese

1 tablespoon finely minced fresh thyme leaves

1 teaspoon finely minced fresh rosemary leaves

Salt and freshly ground black pepper

3 tablespoons extra-virgin olive oil

2 medium garlic cloves, peeled and thinly sliced

8 ounces fresh spinach, stemmed, washed, and dried

One partially baked tart shell (page 363), in a 10-inch porcelain quiche dish

OPTIONAL GARNISH

6 ripe plum tomatoes, cut crosswise into ¼-inch slices

1 teaspoon fresh thyme leaves

½ teaspoon fresh rosemary leaves

1½ tablespoons extra-virgin olive oil

16 small black oil-cured olives

Spinach Roulade with Mushroom Dill Filling

THE FILLING

2 tablespoons unsalted butter

½ pound cremini mushrooms, trimmed, wiped, and finely minced

3 tablespoons finely minced scallions

Salt and freshly ground white pepper

1 8-ounce package cream cheese, softened

Optional: ¼ cup sour cream

2 tablespoons freshly grated Parmesan cheese

2 to 3 tablespoons finely minced dill

THE ROULADE

½ cup homemade bread crumbs

Optional: 2 tablespoons freshly grated Parmesan cheese

2 pounds fresh spinach, stemmed, washed, and dried

6 tablespoons unsalted butter, softened

4 extra-large eggs, separated

Salt and freshly ground white pepper

GARNISH

10 to 12 ripe cherry tomatoes, lightly sautéed in 2 tablespoons unsalted butter

2 tablespoons finely minced fresh dill

Try this elegant and unusual hors d'oeuvre for an important evening. The roulade can be made well in advance; reheat, wrap the roulade in foil, place on a baking sheet, and set over a pan of warm water.

1. In a large skillet, melt the butter over medium high heat. Add the mushrooms and sauté quickly until lightly browned and all the liquid has evaporated. Remove the skillet from the heat, add the scallions and toss until just wilted. Season with salt and pepper and allow to cool completely.

2. In a large mixing bowl combine the cream cheese and sour cream, if using, and mash together with the back of a fork. Add the mushroom mixture, Parmesan, and dill. Taste and correct the seasoning, then cover and chill until firm.

3. Preheat the oven to 350°F.

4. Line a jelly-roll pan (15½ × 10½ × 1″) with parchment paper. Butter the paper and sprinkle with the bread crumbs and Parmesan, if using. Set aside.

5. In a large casserole cook the spinach in the water that clings to its leaves over medium low heat, just until wilted. Transfer to a colander, and let cool. Place the spinach in a kitchen towel and squeeze out all of the excess moisture. Finely chop the spinach and set aside.

6. In a large stainless steel mixing bowl, combine the chopped spinach and softened butter, set the bowl over a pan of warm water, and stir until the butter is thoroughly incorporated. Add the egg yolks and mix until well blended. Season with salt and pepper and reserve.

7. In another large mixing bowl, combine the egg whites and a pinch of salt and beat until the whites form soft peaks. Fold gently but thoroughly into the spinach mixture.

8. Spoon the spinach mixture into the prepared pan, using your hands to spread it evenly into a thin layer. Bake for 12 to

15 minutes or until just set (a knife when inserted will come out clean). Remove the pan from the oven and immediately invert the spinach roulade onto a dry kitchen towel. Carefully peel off the parchment paper and trim off a piece, about half an inch wide, from each short side. Leave flat or roll up gently in the kitchen towel. Set aside to cool completely.

9. Spoon a thick layer of the mushroom filling over the entire spinach surface and roll the roulade from a long edge into a tight roll, jelly-roll fashion, using the towel as a support. Transfer carefully to a serving platter and surround with the sautéed cherry tomatoes. Sprinkle the tomatoes with the minced dill, cut the roulade crosswise into $1/2$-inch slices, and serve at room temperature.

SERVES 10 TO 12

Spinach-Mushroom Salad with Creamy Sesame Garlic Dressing

This earthy, full-flavored dressing can be made ahead of time. Refrigerate in a tightly covered jar for up to a week. Bring the dressing back to room temperature before using and whisk until creamy and well blended.

1. In a large serving bowl, combine the egg yolk, vinegar, sugar, and garlic and whisk until well blended. Add the oil by droplets, whisking constantly, until the mixture begins to thicken. Continue to add the oil, in a slow steady stream, until all has been added. Season with salt and pepper.

2. Top the dressing with the red onion, mushrooms, and spinach in that order. Do not toss. Cover and chill until serving.

3. Remove the salad from the refrigerator 15 minutes before serving. Toss gently, correct the seasoning, and serve lightly chilled.

SERVES 5 TO 6

I teaspoon egg yolk

2 tablespoons sherry vinegar

I teaspoon sugar

I medium garlic clove, peeled and mashed

$1/2$ cup peanut oil mixed with 2 tablespoons Chinese sesame oil

Salt and freshly ground black pepper

3 tablespoons thinly sliced red onion

6 medium all-purpose mushrooms, trimmed, wiped, and thinly sliced

8 ounces young spinach leaves (about 8 cups), stemmed, washed, and dried

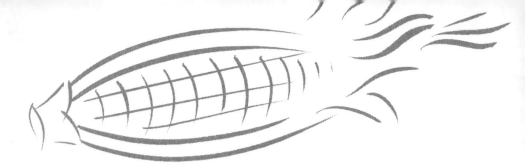

*There's nothing like listening to a shower and thinking
how it is soaking in and around your lettuce and green beans.*

HENRY VAN DYKE

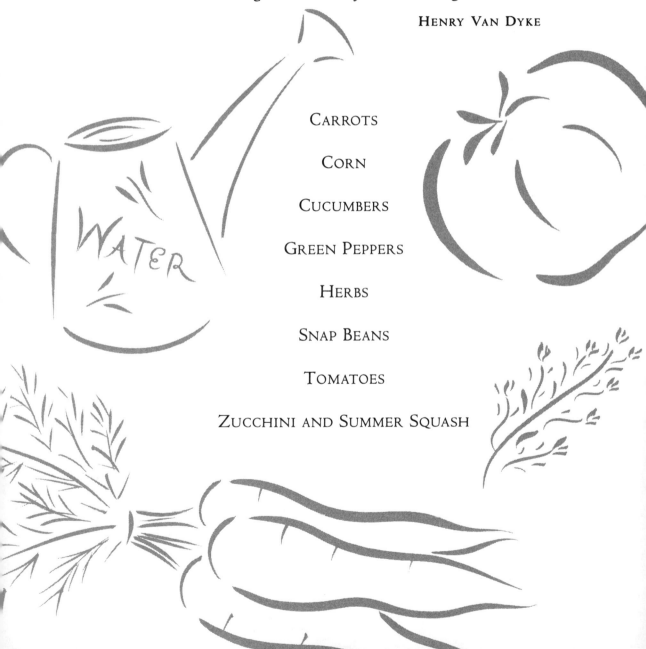

CARROTS

CORN

CUCUMBERS

GREEN PEPPERS

HERBS

SNAP BEANS

TOMATOES

ZUCCHINI AND SUMMER SQUASH

The Main Event:
THE SUMMER GARDEN

If I had my way, I would just close the kitchen and tend to my garden the entire summer. A true glory of the season is the opulence of vegetables that can result from even a small backyard garden patch. For those fortunate enough to have the space and time to devote to a kitchen garden, the effort put in from tilling to tasting returns tenfold in the bounty that bursts on the scene.

These are the moments that memories are made of. Bending over large, sprawling zucchini plants filled with the glorious pale yellow flowers, I spy three—no four—brilliant green squash tucked underneath the giant fuzzy leaves. In a row nearby I gently move the vines aside to reveal enough beans for a nice side dish for four. A tiny, ripe tomato, with its juicy universe of acid and sweet, hides between a bunch of still-green jewels. As I pop it into my mouth together with a basil leaf, it almost feels like lunch—all that is missing is a touch of olive oil and a few grains of salt. I snip a few flowers and some herbs, reminding myself to set aside some time for weeding. But all in all the garden is flourishing, the season is under way, and all is well.

Of course the secret of summer vegetables is that they are essentially undemanding when truly fresh. How do I improve on a plateful of juicy ripe tomatoes interlaced with delicious mozzarella and drizzled with a basil vinaigrette? How do I make corn-on-the-cob taste any better than when it's simply steamed, brushed with melted butter, and lightly salted? And why would I feel the need to adorn the delicate string bean that seems to invite me to eat it raw?

To me, the key to summer cooking and its success lies in dishes that bring the lush charms of the garden, the fields, and the sea into the kitchen and the dining room. There's the urge to eat lighter, cooler foods, and on a particularly hot day, to reinvent the salad.

As if dictated by nature, summer vegetables seem to like one another's company and can be harmoniously combined in many appealing salads as well as in rice, pasta, and seafood dishes. Summer soups, stews, light sauces, vinaigrettes, and marinades all pay homage to the season. There is nothing more satisfying than the pristine taste of a fresh tomato soup, a spicy corn chowder, or a sauté of mixed vegetables served with a nicely grilled piece of fish or chicken. Sometimes I assemble several vegetables from my garden into foil packets and "braise" them on the grill alongside my main course. These wonderful cornucopias of summer need not be relegated to side-course status and can easily be served as light main courses.

Although summer invites simplicity and informality in cooking, I find that a certain sameness seems to set in, which threatens to minimize the extraordinary creative possibilities of this thrilling season. Personally, I make an effort not to resort to the grill at every meal or rely too heavily on the same types of salads and pasta dishes. Instead I try to work with the abundance of nature by incorporating it into novel dishes in a manner that retains their fresh taste and allows the essential flavors to be appreciated.

Many of our garden classics—tomatoes, corn, peppers, beans, and eggplant—have inspired countless cooks all over the world and have become some of our classics. Consider the vegetable paellas of Spain, the Italian minestrone, the French ratatouille, and Southwestern salsas, for example. American cooks and gardeners are equally imaginative when creating classic American cuisine that takes advantage of the world of freshness around us.

Be spontaneous, willing to experiment and take chances, using the season's bounty in innovative ways. I view my repertoire as a building block, always adding a few new ideas to my file of the season's favorites, new small treasures that await the next season of plenty.

CARROTS

HELPING MY FATHER PLANT VEGETABLES REMAINS AMONG MY DEAREST childhood memories. I always waited with great anticipation for the first signs of seedlings, and for carrots, in particular, with their distinctive feathery tops. I could never resist pulling up just one to nibble the tiny beginnings of a sweet, orange root. While tending my garden today, it is no less a pleasure to munch on freshly plucked baby carrots no bigger than a finger.

Carrots are among the most good-natured of vegetables. They are nearly effortless to grow, can be picked when quite young or fully mature, and are adaptable to an endless variety of preparations. Raw, this vegetable is far more versatile than it usually is given credit for, especially for quick summer snacks. One of my longtime favorites is raw grated carrots sprinkled with some sugar and lemon juice. Our refrigerator is always stocked with a dish of this zesty slaw, sometimes enhanced with grated apples, raisins, and diced walnuts. Raw, finely sliced carrots add a welcome crunch to a pasta salad, and can be marinated with cauliflower florets and finely sliced broccoli stalks in a mustard dressing. Despite their differences, when combined the flavors of carrots and broccoli blend to produce a refreshing complement to roast meats, grilled fish, and sautéed or barbecued chicken.

Carrots are essential in stocks and most vegetable soups as well as in many stews and sauces. Steamed or cooked whole, carrots work beautifully as an accompaniment to all meat, fish, and poultry dishes. This is especially so if the roots are young; that is, picked prior to maturity. I usually cook them in a covered, ten-inch skillet with salted water, plus a large dollop of butter. When the carrots are tender, I drain off all but ¼ cup of water, add a generous sprinkling of sugar, and then let the carrots sit and absorb the pan juices. Buttery and sweetly glazed, the results glitter.

Braising is another excellent way to cook this vegetable, and one which I prefer when in need of a dish that can be prepared well in advance and reheated. The French method of braising carrots is by far the most successful:

Cut them into one-inch matchsticks and then braise in a touch of butter with diced bacon, a few garlic cloves, and chicken broth to cover. When done, the carrots have a wonderful mellow flavor quite unlike any other preparation. The finished dish can be varied by adding a touch of cream, a few tiny white onions, or cooked peas during reheating.

Whether they are to be eaten raw or cooked, young garden carrots must first be peeled lightly with a swivel-blade peeler or scraped with a small sharp knife. After a good rinsing, they can be sliced, cubed, diced, or cut into fine julienne strips. Baby carrots need only to be scrubbed with a stiff brush before they are briefly cooked or steamed, and nothing more. With these little jewels of summer, I find the simpler the preparation the better.

STORAGE

When buying carrots, look for bright orange bunches with crisp, green, feathery tops. The carrots should be firm and well shaped. Avoid shriveled carrots with wilted tops.

To store, always remove the green tops and refrigerate the unwashed carrots in a plastic bag. They will keep for two to three weeks. Even after this time, carrots can still be used for stocks and in stews.

A surplus of garden-fresh carrots can be frozen successfully, although, as with many vegetables, freezing changes their texture. I usually keep the baby carrots whole but scrape and then cut the large carrots into $\frac{1}{4}$-inch slices. Once they have been blanched for two to three minutes, I run them under cold water to cool, dry them thoroughly, and then pack them in plastic bags. Frozen carrots will keep for six to eight months.

GARDENING

Your soil will help determine the best type of carrots to grow. All carrots flourish in light, sandy, stoneless loam that can be worked to a depth of ten inches or more. No other soil will do for the long and elegantly tapered varieties such as Gold Pak. I am limited to growing shorter, stubbier varieties because my garden soil is heavy. Among the best baby carrots are Little Finger and Short 'n Sweet. These varieties manage in almost any soil, including planters and pots. Clay soils will certainly be improved by digging in organic matter before planting. But be careful about using manures. Unless they are well rotted, they will cause carrots to become tough or malformed. For a continuous supply of carrots throughout summer, sow successive crops at three-week intervals starting in early spring. It's a good idea to cover newly sown rows with a thin layer of dried grass clippings to prevent the soil from forming a crust; otherwise, tiny carrot sprouts may have trouble pushing through to daylight. The seeds germinate slowly, and soil should be kept quite moist until sprouts appear.

HARVESTING

Harvesting can begin before the full sixty-five to eighty-five days it takes for most carrots to reach full size. Be sure to pick those plants with the biggest tops first. Some people do the reverse, hoping that all remaining carrots will grow as large as possible. With carrots, as with most vegetables, bigger is not better. On the contrary, the smaller the sweeter.

Skillet-Glazed Carrots with Brown Sugar and Mint

Skillet braising is a wonderful way to prepare this terrific year-round vegetable. The addition of garden-grown mint is particularly nice in the summer, but dill, tarragon, and chives are equally good choices. Serve the carrots as a side dish to an "oven-grilled" turkey cooked on a covered kettle grill, lemon and herb–marinated grilled veal chops, or grilled swordfish steaks.

1. Melt the butter in a large skillet over medium heat. Add the carrots and season with salt, pepper, and sugar. Toss the carrots in the butter to glaze, about 3 to 4 minutes. Reduce the heat, add the broth or water, and simmer, covered, for about 10 to 12 minutes or until tender. Remove the cover, raise the heat, and cook until all the liquid has evaporated.

2. Add the brown sugar to the skillet and when melted, add the cream. Simmer until the cream is reduced and the carrots are glazed. Correct the seasoning, adding a pinch of nutmeg. Sprinkle with the mint leaves and serve hot.

SERVES 6

4 tablespoons (½ stick)
   unsalted butter
2 pounds medium carrots
   (about 12 to 14), trimmed,
   peeled, and cut into ½ by ½
   by 1½-inch pieces
Salt and freshly ground white
   pepper
1 teaspoon sugar
½ cup chicken broth,
   preferably homemade
   (page 360), or water
2 tablespoons dark brown sugar
½ cup heavy cream
Pinch of freshly grated nutmeg
2 tablespoons tiny fresh mint
   leaves

Curried Carrot and Potato Soup with Cilantro–Lime Topping

THE TOPPING

1 cup yogurt or sour cream

Juice of ½ lime

3 tablespoons tiny fresh
   cilantro leaves

THE SOUP

3 tablespoons unsalted butter

1 large onion, peeled and finely
   minced

1 tablespoon dark brown sugar

½ teaspoon ground coriander

1 tablespoon imported Madras
   curry powder

¼ teaspoon ground cardamom

Large pinch of freshly grated
   nutmeg

1½ pounds carrots, trimmed,
   peeled, and cubed

2 medium-size all-purpose
   potatoes, peeled and cubed

6 to 7 cups chicken broth,
   preferably homemade
   (page 360)

Salt and freshly ground black
   pepper

*C*arrots have a great affinity to curry powder and other Indian spices, a combination of flavors that works well in this lively soup. Try to make the soup ahead of time to allow the flavors to intensify and add additional character. A dollop of *Crème Fraîche (page 358)*, a mincing of fresh cilantro, and a sprinkling of fresh jalapeño pepper are nice additional garnishes.

1. Start by making the topping: In a small bowl, combine the yogurt or sour cream, lime juice, and cilantro and mix well. Reserve.

2. Melt the butter over medium low heat in a large heavy casserole. Add the onion and cook until soft but not browned. Add the brown sugar, coriander, curry powder, cardamom, and nutmeg and cook for 1 minute longer, stirring constantly.

3. Add the carrots, potatoes, and 6 cups of the broth and season with salt and pepper. Bring to a boil, reduce the heat, and simmer, partially covered, for 30 minutes or until the vegetables are very tender.

4. Strain the soup and return the broth to the casserole. Transfer the vegetables to a food processor and process until smooth. Whisk the puree into the broth and simmer over low heat for 10 minutes. Correct the seasoning and serve the soup hot in individual bowls with a dollop of the cilantro–lime topping.

SERVES 6

NOTE: If you prefer a soup with a bit of texture, finely dice and steam an additional large carrot and add it to the soup just before serving. For a slightly different texture, add the heart of a Boston lettuce, separated into leaves, to the finished soup and simmer until just wilted.

Carrot and Orange Clafoutis

For those who like their carrots sweet, here is a delicious preparation that makes for a nicely sweet—but not too sweet—ending to a meal. It can also be served as a side dish to a well-seasoned chicken curry or roast duck. Leftover clafoutis can be reheated in a low oven or in the microwave without drying out.

1. Preheat the oven to 350° F. Cut the carrots in half lengthwise and then crosswise into ¼-inch slices.

2. In a 10-inch skillet, heat 3 tablespoons of the butter over medium low heat. Add the carrots, sprinkle with 1 tablespoon of the brown sugar, and cook for 3 minutes or until nicely glazed. Season with salt and pepper, add the water, and simmer, covered, for 10 to 12 minutes or until the carrots are tender and all the liquid has evaporated. Reserve.

3. Combine the eggs, flour, milk, and remaining 2 tablespoons of butter in a food processor and puree until smooth. Season with salt, pepper, nutmeg, and orange zest.

4. Place the carrots in a buttered 10-inch porcelain quiche pan or gratin dish and pour the egg mixture over them. Set the clafoutis in a large shallow baking pan and fill the pan with boiling water to come halfway up the sides of the clafoutis dish. Bake for 25 to 30 minutes or until the custard is set and a knife when inserted comes out clean.

5. Remove from the oven and preheat the broiler. Sprinkle the top of the clafoutis with the remaining 2 tablespoons brown sugar and run under the broiler until the sugar becomes crisp (the sugar does not really melt). Serve warm, cut into wedges.

S E R V E S   6

5 medium carrots, trimmed
  and peeled
5 tablespoons unsalted butter,
  melted
3 tablespoons dark brown sugar
Salt and freshly ground white
  pepper
3 tablespoons water
4 extra-large eggs
¼ cup all-purpose flour
I cup whole milk
Large grinding of nutmeg
I tablespoon finely grated
  orange zest

Puree of Carrots with Crème Fraîche and Clover Honey

Salt
2 pounds medium carrots
(about 12 to 14), trimmed,
peeled, and cubed
1 medium sweet potato, peeled
and cubed
2 tablespoons creamed clover
honey
¼ cup Crème Fraîche
(page 358)
3 tablespoons unsalted butter
Freshly ground white pepper

I *like serving this smooth and mellow puree as a side dish to a ragout, pork roast, or turkey, and usually team it with a green vegetable such as pan-seared snow peas, buttered green beans, or braised thyme-flavored zucchini.*

1. Bring salted water to a boil in a large casserole. Add the carrots and sweet potato and cook for 20 minutes or until very tender. Drain well, transfer to a food processor together with the honey, crème fraîche, and butter, and puree until smooth.

2. Season with salt and pepper and serve hot.

SERVES 5 TO 6

NOTE: The carrot puree can be made ahead of time and kept warm in a double boiler or reheated successfully in the microwave.

Creamy Slaw of Carrots, Bell Peppers, and Cabbage

This flavor-packed slaw gets better and better as it sits. Serve it at room temperature as a side dish to a nicely grilled burger, some lamb or fish kebabs, or a plateful of crispy fried chicken wingettes.

1. Place each cabbage in a strainer, sprinkle with a little coarse salt, and let drain for 1 hour. Squeeze out as much moisture as possible from the cabbage and reserve.

2. In a large bowl, combine the mayonnaise, sour cream, 2 tablespoons of the vinegar, the sugar, and the dill, season with salt and pepper, and whisk until well blended. Add the cabbage, carrots, onion, green pepper, and apple and toss gently. Cover and refrigerate overnight.

3. Bring the slaw back to room temperature and correct the seasoning, adding the remaining vinegar if necessary. Serve lightly chilled.

SERVES 6

¾ pound red cabbage, cored and very thinly sliced
¾ pound green cabbage, cored and very thinly sliced
Coarse salt
¾ cup mayonnaise, preferably homemade (page 362)
½ cup sour cream
2 to 3 tablespoons cider vinegar
2 tablespoons sugar
2 tablespoons finely minced fresh dill
Freshly ground black pepper
4 large carrots, peeled and finely shredded
I small red onion, peeled and thinly sliced
I large green bell pepper, cored, seeded, and finely diced
I large Golden Delicious apple, peeled, cored, and finely diced

Carrot and Pineapple Muffins

2 cups all-purpose flour
2 teaspoons baking powder
1½ teaspoons baking soda
Pinch of salt
1 teaspoon ground cinnamon
Pinch of ground nutmeg
Pinch of allspice
Pinch of ground ginger
2 cups sugar
½ cup corn oil
½ cup sour cream or plain
   yogurt
4 extra-large eggs
2 cups grated carrots
1 can (8½ ounces) crushed
   pineapple, drained

I don't know of a better muffin than this one. You can easily get hooked on them, so I suggest you make an extra batch to freeze; the muffins reheat beautifully in a low oven or the microwave.

1. Preheat the oven to 375°F. Lightly butter 3 standard-size muffin pans. Sprinkle each tin with a little sugar, shake out the excess, and set aside.

2. In a large bowl, sift together the flour, baking powder, baking soda, salt, and spices and set aside.

3. Combine the sugar, oil, sour cream or yogurt, and eggs in a food processor and process until smooth. Add the carrots and pineapple and pulse twice. Add to the flour mixture and fold gently but thoroughly. Do not overmix.

4. Spoon the batter into the prepared pans, filling each muffin tin about three-quarters full. Bake for 20 minutes or until a toothpick when inserted comes out clean. Remove from the oven and let cool for 10 minutes. Tip out the muffins onto wire cake racks and cool. Serve warm or at room temperature.

MAKES 18 MUFFINS

Baby Carrots with Spicy Ginger and Mirin Glaze

Here is a lively side dish that is quick, easy, and delicious, the three key "buzz words" for the summer outdoor cook. The natural sweetness of the carrots is much enhanced by the sweet cooking wine, and the ginger adds an interesting and pungent kick of flavor. Several summer herbs such as cilantro, dill, and tarragon can be added to the carrots, depending on what you will be serving them with. I usually team them with sautéed or grilled scallops, grilled salmon, or oven-braised striped bass, but it would go well with any type of poultry or veal dish.

1. In a 10-inch nonstick skillet, melt the butter over medium heat. Add the carrots and broth or water, season with salt and pepper, and simmer, covered, for 12 to 15 minutes or until just tender.

2. Remove the cover, add the mirin, garlic, ginger, and jalapeño pepper, and simmer, stirring often, until the pan juices have reduced and the carrots are nicely glazed.

S E R V E S 4

2 tablespoons unsalted butter

20 medium-size baby carrots, peeled and trimmed of all but 1 inch of greens

4 tablespoons chicken broth, preferably homemade (page 360), or water

Salt and freshly ground white pepper

2 tablespoons mirin (syrupy Japanese rice wine)

1 large garlic clove, peeled and finely minced

2 teaspoons finely minced ginger

1 teaspoon finely minced jalapeño pepper

CORN

I TASTED CORN FOR THE FIRST TIME IN THE MIDDLE EAST, WHERE street vendors sell ears straight from boiling vats as a kind of local fast food. Although the experience was interesting, I never quite understood what made corn so special until I moved to the United States. My first summer, I was introduced to the delicious "eight-row" corn grown in Pennsylvania. I was an instant convert, and fresh corn has been a summer staple in my kitchen ever since.

Initially I bought corn in peak season at the supermarket. But I soon learned that corn, more than any other vegetable, ships poorly and is much better when purchased from roadside farm stands; summer after summer I searched country roads in pursuit of the freshest and juiciest specimens. I gave that up once I began growing corn in my own garden. There simply is no equal to homegrown corn picked just before dinner, boiled briefly, and then served on the cob with no more enhancement than a dab of butter and a sprinkling of salt. Corn "off the cob" is nearly as delightful. Removing the kernels is easily accomplished with a corn cutter and creamer. The versatility of corn is far from exhausted by the recipes that follow, and leftovers can be used to add color and texture to soups or salads.

These days corn is used more creatively than ever in new and spectacular dishes. Aside from such tempting all-American classics as corn spoon bread, corn pudding, and corn fritters, I think you will enjoy experimenting with corn in a sauté of shrimp or in a contemporary roasted pepper and corn dressing.

STORAGE

Ears picked early in the day or bought at a farm stand should be refrigerated immediately, preferably in plastic bags, without removing the husks. Corn that can't be cooked the same day should be saved for soups and chowders. I always try to cook corn the day I get it even if I don't intend to use it right away. I find it best to remove the corn from its cooking water and store it in the refrigerator. The kernels may become a bit soggy, but they still taste wonderful in a mixed pasta salad or as an addition to a flavorful minestrone or other summer soup. To freeze any garden surplus, it is best to blanch the corn, on the cob, for about two minutes. When completely cool, cut the kernels off the cob and pack in small freezer bags.

GARDENING

Freshly picked corn is such a joy that even in a relatively small garden, it's worth finding some space for it. Plants must get full sun all day and should be planted along the garden's northern edge so they won't shade shorter crops. Since corn depends on wind for pollination, it's better to plant at least four short rows side by side than to plant one long row. This way, ears are more likely to produce full sets of kernels.

Corn seeds germinate best when soil becomes warm (65°F.) in mid to late spring. Sometimes I just can't wait to set the seed into the ground, but if it's a little earlier or cooler than usual, I coat the seeds with a fungicide such as Captan. I follow my initial sowing of early, mid, and late season varieties with another sowing of a late variety in about three weeks. By midsummer the first ears are ready for picking. Harvests continue into September, when cool nights seem to make maturing sweet corn even sweeter.

Extra-Sweet, Sugar Extender, Everlasting Heritage (or E.H.), and Illini are designations for many modern corn varieties, all considerably higher in sugar content than the more typical hybrid corn—up to three times as sweet when picked. Moreover, they hold their sweetness much longer than typical hybrids. Whereas most corn converts its sugar to starch within a few days in storage, new varieties such as How Sweet It Is stay sweet and tender in the refrigerator (but not on the stalk) for up to two weeks. Everlasting Heritage types, on the other hand, keep very well on the stalk for an extended harvest. Extra-Sweet and Illini types need to be isolated from other varieties so the pollen doesn't cross, but Everlasting Heritage and Sugar Extender types can be planted without regard to what's in your neighbor's yard—a big advantage for home gardeners.

It seems to me, though, that these new kinds offer more to the farmer who ships corn to market than to the home gardener, who can usually eat what he or she picks within a day or two of harvesting. So I recommend that you do as I do: Grow the varieties that taste best to you. Not everyone likes the candy sweetness of some of the new varieties or the crunchy texture that has replaced the creaminess of the older kinds.

So many new varieties are introduced each year that few of us have a chance to decide on a favorite before another comes along. In my region, and through much of the East, Silver Queen, a white corn introduced in the early 1960s is considered the paragon of corn, so popular that roadside stands and produce markets call all their white corn Silver Queen, although it may in fact be something else.

HARVESTING

Probably the trickiest thing about growing corn is knowing when to pick it. Some people judge corn ripe when the tassels turn brown. I find the hand more reliable than the eye. If the tip end inside the husk is more or less rounded, the ear is ready. A pointed tip means the end kernels haven't matured yet. To pick, simply pull down the ear and twist.

Smoky Corn, Tomato, and Pepper Chowder

Once a New England classic, corn chowders have moved into the mainstream of the new American cooking. Since I love chowders myself, I always look for new and interesting touches to complement the chowder's unique earthiness. Here is one that has become my summer favorite. Laced with smoky bacon and a zesty touch of diced jalapeño pepper, the soup can be served as a substantial starter or as a one-dish meal, followed by an assortment of cheeses, a plate of sliced ripe summer tomatoes, crusty bread, and a bowl of crisp radishes.

1. Bring plenty of lightly salted water to a boil in a large pot, add the ears of corn, and simmer for 5 minutes. Drain well and cut or scrape the kernels from the cobs. You should have about 3 cups. Reserve.

2. Blanch the bacon in boiling water for 30 seconds, then drain, cool slightly, and cut into small dice.

3. In a 4-quart casserole, melt the butter over low heat. Add the bacon and sauté until lightly browned. Remove with a slotted spoon to a side dish and reserve.

4. Discard all but 3 tablespoons of fat from the casserole. Add the onion, jalapeño pepper, and bell peppers and cook for 3 to 4 minutes or until just tender. Add the flour and blend thoroughly. Add the tomatoes and simmer for another 3 minutes.

5. Add the broth, Old Bay Seasoning, cream, zucchini, and reserved corn and bacon to the casserole, season with salt and pepper, and simmer, partially covered, for 15 minutes. Correct the seasoning, garnish with the cilantro, and serve hot accompanied by crusty French bread.

S E R V E S   6

Salt

5 ears fresh corn, husks removed

4 ounces lean slab bacon

1 tablespoon unsalted butter

1 large onion, peeled and finely minced

2 teaspoons finely minced jalapeño pepper

1 small green bell pepper, cored, seeded, and finely diced

1 small red bell pepper, cored, seeded, and finely diced

2 tablespoons all-purpose flour

3 large ripe tomatoes, peeled, seeded, and finely chopped

3½ cups chicken broth, preferably homemade (page 360)

½ teaspoon Old Bay Seasoning

½ cup heavy cream

1 small zucchini, trimmed and diced

Freshly ground black pepper

GARNISH

½ cup tiny leaves of fresh cilantro

Corn and Zucchini Fritters

1 cup cooked fresh corn
   kernels, lightly minced
   (about 2 ears; see page 103)
5 tablespoons all-purpose flour
4 extra-large eggs
½ cup heavy cream
2 teaspoons grated onion
4 tablespoons finely grated
   zucchini skin
Coarse salt and freshly ground
   white pepper
Corn oil for sautéing

Asummer fritter is a welcome preparation at every meal. Serve them at breakfast with a rasher of crisp bacon, as a lunch dish with a bowl of garlic- and herb-flavored yogurt, or as a side dish to grilled or sautéed meats, fish, and chicken. Since these fritters are not intended to be crispy, they can be made ahead and kept warm in a low oven, and any leftover fritters can be reheated successfully the next day, in either a low oven or the microwave.

1. Combine cooked corn, flour, eggs, cream, onion, and zucchini in a mixing bowl, season with salt and pepper, and whisk until well blended. Let the batter rest for 30 minutes.

2. Cook the fritters in batches of about 4 to 6 fritters per batch. For each batch heat 1 tablespoon of corn oil in a 10-inch nonstick skillet over medium heat. Drop the batter by the tablespoonful into the hot oil, without crowding the skillet, and cook for about 1 minute per side or until nicely browned.

3. Sprinkle with a little coarse salt and serve hot.

MAKES ABOUT 2 DOZEN FRITTERS

NOTE: Since the flesh of zucchini is quite watery, it is best to use the skin and only one quarter to one half of the pulp in most zucchini preparations.

Corn-Studded Polenta with Parmesan

A bowl of buttery, soft, mellow-tasting polenta is true soul food. What's more, much like mashed potatoes, it allows for some nice additions such as softened scallions, many of the blue cheeses, or cooked corn. My favorite side dish to this corn-studded polenta is sautéed chicken livers with caramelized onions, but other simple foods are good with it as well, particularly a roast veal or a fricassee of chicken with mushrooms. Leftover polenta reheats beautifully and can also be chilled in a rectangular pan, then cut into squares and either grilled or sautéed in a mixture of butter and oil until crisp and hot.

5 tablespoons unsalted butter
2 cups fresh corn kernels (about 3 ears)
2 tablespoons water
Salt
Pinch of sugar
3¼ cups skim milk or 1½ cups whole milk and 1¾ cups water
¾ cup yellow cornmeal
⅓ cup freshly grated Parmesan cheese
Freshly ground black pepper

1. In a 10-inch skillet, melt 2 tablespoons of the butter over medium heat. Add the corn and water, season with salt and a pinch of sugar, and simmer, covered, for 5 to 7 minutes or until tender. Remove the cover and cook until all the water has evaporated. Reserve.

2. In a heavy 3½-quart saucepan, combine the skim milk and 1 teaspoon of salt and bring to a slow boil. Sprinkle in the cornmeal very slowly to avoid lumping, whisking constantly, until all has been added. Reduce the heat to very low and simmer, covered, for 20 minutes, stirring often. A skin will form on the bottom of the pot; do not be alarmed.

3. Remove from the heat, add the remaining 3 tablespoons of butter, the reserved corn, and the Parmesan, and stir until well blended. Taste and correct the seasoning, adding a large grinding of black pepper, and serve at once.

SERVES 4 TO 6

NOTE: A trick for making polenta without lumps is to place the cornmeal in a grated cheese shaker and shake slowly into the hot milk.

VARIATION
Add 4 ounces of crumbled goat cheese and 2 tablespoons fresh thyme leaves to the finished polenta and just heat through.

Skillet-Baked Corn, Cheddar, and Jalapeño Pepper Bread

2 ears fresh corn, husks removed

1 tablespoon corn oil

1¼ cups yellow cornmeal

¾ cup all-purpose flour

¼ cup sugar

1 teaspoon salt

1 tablespoon baking powder

3 extra-large eggs

1¼ cups whole milk

6 tablespoons (¾ stick) unsalted butter, melted

1 cup finely grated cheddar cheese

1½ teaspoons finely minced jalapeño pepper

A piece of good buttery corn bread served with juicy barbecued ribs is one of the great food marriages, both humble yet satisfying. But corn bread is delicious as an accompaniment to other foods as well, especially marinated oven-roasted pork or barbecued chicken, or as part of a summer picnic table.

1. Cook the corn and remove from cob.

2. Place the oil in a 10-inch cast-iron skillet. Set the skillet in the oven and preheat with the oven to 400° F.

3. While the skillet and oven are preheating, make the corn bread batter: Sift together the cornmeal, flour, sugar, salt, and baking powder into a large mixing bowl.

4. In another bowl combine the eggs, milk, and butter and whisk until smooth. Fold in the corn, cheese, and jalapeño pepper. Pour the mixture into the sifted dry ingredients and fold gently but thoroughly. Do not overmix.

5. Pour the batter into the hot skillet and return to the oven. Bake for 20 to 25 minutes or until a toothpick when inserted comes out clean. Serve warm or at room temperature, cut into wedges.

SERVES 8 TO 10

Spicy Corn, Shrimp, and Red Pepper Salad

Fresh corn is a terrific seasonal addition to a seafood salad. Be sure to let the salad marinate for at least four to six hours before serving and bring it back almost to room temperature. Serve for lunch or a light supper with crusty Tuscan bread, some oil-cured olives, and possibly a side dish of grilled or pan-seared peppers.

1. In a small saucepan, combine the water and Old Bay Seasoning. Simmer for 1 minute, add the shrimp and poach until they just turn pink, about 1 to 2 minutes. Do not overcook. Drain well. Peel and cube the shrimp and set aside.

2. In a small bowl, combine 2 tablespoons of the olive oil, 1 tablespoon of the vinegar, and 1 mashed garlic clove and whisk until well blended. Add the shrimp and season with salt and pepper. Marinate at room temperature for 30 minutes.

3. Combine the remaining oil, vinegar, and garlic together with the lime juice, red onion, and jalapeño pepper and whisk until well blended. Add the shrimp, red pepper, corn, and cilantro, season with salt and pepper and a pinch of cayenne, and toss well. Cover and chill for 2 hours.

4. To serve, bring the salad back to room temperature. Correct the seasoning and garnish with sprigs of cilantro and cherry tomatoes.

SERVES 6

4 cups water
1 teaspoon Old Bay Seasoning
½ pound medium shrimp
5 tablespoons extra-virgin olive oil
2 tablespoons sherry vinegar
2 large garlic cloves, peeled and mashed
Salt and freshly ground black pepper
Juice of 1 lime
1 small red onion, peeled and finely minced
1 to 2 teaspoons finely minced jalapeño pepper
1 large red bell pepper, cored, seeded, and finely diced
4 cups cooked fresh corn kernels (see page 103)
3 tablespoons fresh cilantro leaves
Pinch of cayenne pepper

GARNISH
Sprigs of fresh cilantro
Ripe cherry tomatoes, cut in half

THE VINAIGRETTE

1 large red bell pepper, roasted
and peeled (page 365) and
diced

2 tablespoons sherry vinegar

1 medium garlic clove, peeled
and mashed

6 tablespoons olive oil

½ cup Crème Fraîche (page
358) or sour cream

Coarse salt and freshly ground
black pepper

Pinch of cayenne pepper

1 cup cooked fresh corn
kernels (about 2 ears; see
page 103)

2 tablespoons finely julienned
fresh basil leaves

2 tablespoons tiny fresh
cilantro leaves

THE SWORDFISH

1½ pounds swordfish, cut into
1-inch cubes

All-purpose flour for dredging

3 tablespoons olive oil

GARNISH

Tiny leaves of fresh cilantro

Summer Corn and Roasted Pepper Vinaigrette with Crisp-Sautéed Swordfish

This vinaigrette makes a lovely topping for a ripe avocado or steamed asparagus, or as a sauce for grilled shrimp or shish kebabs of mako. It will keep for up to ten days in a covered jar in the refrigerator, but be sure not to add the garlic to the vinaigrette until an hour or so before serving.

1. Start by making the vinaigrette: Combine the red pepper, vinegar, garlic, and oil in a food processor and process until smooth. Add the crème fraîche or sour cream, season with salt, pepper, and cayenne, and process until well blended.

2. Transfer to a bowl and fold in the corn, basil, and cilantro. Correct the seasoning and reserve. If you plan to make the vinaigrette ahead of time, at this point cover and refrigerate the vinaigrette but bring it back to room temperature before serving.

3. Dry the swordfish well on paper towels and dredge lightly in flour, shaking off the excess.

4. Sauté the swordfish in two batches: For each batch, heat 1½ tablespoons oil in a large nonstick skillet over medium high heat. Add half the swordfish and sauté until crisp and nicely browned on all sides. Season with coarse salt and pepper.

5. To serve, spoon some of the vinaigrette onto individual serving plates and top each portion with some of the sautéed swordfish. Garnish with cilantro and serve hot.

SERVES 4 TO 5

Sauté of Shrimp and Corn Indienne

A quick, spur-of-the-moment dish, this low-fat recipe is both satisfying and delicious. Serve the sauté with a parslied pilaf of rice or quick couscous seasoned with a mincing of fresh basil, cilantro, mint, or a combination of two of your favorite herbs.

1. Combine the garlic, ginger, tomato paste, water, and turmeric in a food processor and puree until smooth. Season with salt and pepper and set aside.

2. Dry the shrimp on paper towels. Heat the oil in a large skillet over high heat, add the chili peppers, and when dark, remove and discard. Add the shrimp to the hot chili oil and cook quickly, shaking the pan back and forth, until the shrimp turn bright pink, about 4 or 5 minutes; do not overcook. Transfer the shrimp to a side dish with a slotted spoon and reserve.

3. Reduce the heat, add the green pepper, corn, and zucchini, and cook for 2 minutes. Add the tomato paste mixture and lemon juice and cook, stirring constantly, for 2 minutes longer. The vegetables should be crisp-tender.

4. Return the shrimp to the skillet together with the yogurt and the cilantro or parsley and just heat through. Correct the seasoning and serve hot directly from the skillet.

SERVES 4 TO 5

5 large garlic cloves, peeled and finely minced
1-inch piece of fresh ginger, peeled and finely minced
3 tablespoons tomato paste
1 tablespoon water
¼ teaspoon turmeric
Salt and freshly ground black pepper
1 pound medium shrimp, peeled
3 tablespoons extra-virgin olive oil
2 small dry red chili peppers, broken in half
1 small green bell pepper, cored, seeded, and diced
1 cup cooked fresh corn kernels (about 2 ears; see page 103)
1 medium zucchini, trimmed and julienned (¼ by ¼ by 2 inches), avoiding most of the seedy center
1 tablespoon fresh lemon juice
⅓ cup plain yogurt
¼ cup tiny fresh cilantro or parsley leaves

Sweet and Hot Corn Relish

4 tablespoons olive oil

2 teaspoons finely minced fresh
ginger

1 to 2 teaspoons finely minced
jalapeño pepper

1 medium red bell pepper,
cored, seeded, and finely
diced

1 medium green bell pepper,
cored, seeded, and finely
diced

4 cups cooked fresh corn
kernels (see page 103)

1 cup mirin (syrupy Japanese
rice wine)

Coarse salt and freshly ground
black pepper

I *was first introduced to a corn and pepper relish by my mother-in-law, who got the recipe from a Pennsylvania Dutch cook. I have since adapted this all-American concoction, giving it an Eastern twist. Serve it with crispy fried chicken wings, a nicely charred tuna steak, a juicy burger, or grilled sausages.*

1. In a 10-inch skillet, heat the olive oil over medium heat. Add the ginger, jalapeño pepper, and bell peppers and cook for 30 seconds, stirring constantly. Add the corn and mirin and simmer until the liquid has reduced to a glaze, about 10 to 15 minutes. Season with salt and pepper.

2. Store the relish in a tightly covered jar in the refrigerator and bring back to room temperature before serving, or ladle into sterilized jars and process in a hot water bath for 10 minutes (see page 168 for canning instructions).

SERVES 6

CUCUMBERS

NOTHING IS QUITE AS SATISFYING AND REFRESHING ON A HOT SUMMER day as the taste of cucumber. Easy to grow, wonderful to have on hand throughout summer and early fall, cucumbers lend their crisp juicy presence to many of the season's best soups and salads.

I often marvel at the tremendous appeal the cucumber has throughout the world. No Scandinavian smorgasbord would be complete without a cucumber salad, nor would the artfully decorated Danish open sandwich. The Viennese serve a sweet cucumber salad much as we do coleslaw; it is considered a "national" salad. The Greeks use cucumbers in combination with yogurt, feta cheese, and mint, while the Indian cucumber salad called Raita acts as a cooling counterpoint to fiery curries and spices.

Several years ago, while on a trip in Russia, I found myself on a bus in Moscow on a hot July day. I was amazed to see several people, including children, snacking on small, unpeeled cucumbers. They reminded me of Americans with granola bars. What a great idea! Later on that same trip, I found that while restaurant menus listed a variety of vegetables, only one was ever available: cucumbers. It was on this Russian journey that I was introduced to a wonderful soup in which diced cucumber is combined with sour cream, buttermilk, lots of minced dill, and diced shrimp. It has since become one of my favorite summer appetizers.

With the recent rise in popularity of burpless (or "gourmet") varieties, cucumber now is being used quite creatively in many warm preparations as well. Some of the finest restaurants in France cut the long and slender flesh, skin intact, into olive-like shapes, which are then braised in a little water, butter, and a pinch of sugar. Sweet yet mellow, the results are a perfect accompaniment to fish—salmon, snapper, and scallops in particular. And more and more cooks are discovering that hot cucumbers combine amazingly well with almost any herb, allowing the cook to experiment with various flavors in the summer kitchen.

Most cucumbers found in American supermarkets throughout the year lack crispness, are extremely seedy, and, because they are usually waxed, have skin that is inedible. When you grow your own cucumbers, peeling and seeding are not required but are merely a matter of personal taste. If garden cukes are regularly picked on the young side, they will have small edible seeds and crunchy, flavorful skins. I peel most homegrown cucumbers but seed only the larger ones and those to be combined with leafy greens in salads or in hot preparations.

In most cases, raw cucumbers release a tremendous amount of liquid and, when added to tossed salads, will dilute the dressing. This can be avoided by salting sliced cucumbers, and draining them for an hour in a colander.

Since cucumber vines tend to produce more fruit than you might care to pick, I find the average kitchen garden needs only a few plants of regular or burpless slicing varieties, a few plants of a pickling variety, plus one of the small gherkin. I especially like West India Gherkin pickled either in a sweet brine or in a sharp vinegar brine much like French cornichons, which are delicious with boiled meats, baked ham, or country pâté. In France, cornichons are served as commonly as our dills; you can make them out of tiny fruits of any pickling variety.

I have been making more and more use of the pickling varieties, such as Kirbys. They are firmer and drier than salad-type cucumbers when eaten fresh, though they are somewhat more bitter. My overall favorite, however, is the burpless cucumber. Here is a perfect vegetable. It is excellent for sautéing and braising; finely sliced, it makes a wonderful garnish; and it adds delicious flavor and crisp texture to salads without watering down. And, of course, burpless varieties are easier to digest than conventional ones.

STORAGE

Because of their moisture content, cucumbers must be refrigerated and kept from drying out. It is best to place the fruit in perforated plastic bags in the vegetable bin, or in brown paper bags near the bottom of the refrigerator. This way, cucumbers will keep for four to six days and often longer.

Cucumber vines are extremely sensitive to the cold, so spring planting should be delayed until the soil warms up to about 60 to 70°F. You will still reap a good harvest of fruit because cucumbers take as little as fifty-five days to mature. Since my growing season is short, I get an early start by germinating seeds indoors in peat pots about a month before planting time. I plant three seeds per pot and later snip away the two weakest seedlings. Peat pots are ideal for cucumbers because the seedlings can be transplanted to the garden, pot and all, without disturbing their particularly sensitive roots.

Untended, the vines will eventually sprawl six feet or more along the ground. In a small garden a practical approach is to train the plants on fences, trellises, or garden netting. The upright plants not only will save space but will produce fruits that are straighter and more attractive than those from trailing plants. Another good idea is to grow some "bush" cucumbers, relatively new varieties whose short, compact vines require about one-third the space of conventional cucumbers.

The traditional way to plant cucumbers is in two-foot-wide mounds, called "hills," which are built to about a foot high with the addition of well-rooted manure or compost. I find, however, that trellised vines and bush varieties do quite well in ordinary rows. Rich, well-drained soil is essential for good productivity, so add compost liberally and apply fertilizer at planting time. Before planting, I roll plastic mulch over the rows where the vines will be allowed to sprawl. The plastic sheeting traps warmth in the soil, conserves moisture, smothers weeds, and protects fruit from soil-borne diseases and insects. You might want to shield seeds and young plants against chilly spring nights with translucent Hotkaps; so protected, seeds germinate and grow quite quickly.

There is no cause for alarm if, at first, flowers appear but do not set fruit. Most cucumber varieties have both male and female flowers on the same vine. Frequently, the first blossoms to unfurl are males. Before long the vines will start producing females, and fruit will be seen soon thereafter. Some of the newer and highest yielding varieties are "gynoecious," that is, they have female flowers only. Male flowers are needed to pollinate the females, so seed packets always include a few seeds of a conventional variety. Gynoecious varieties yield amazingly large crops, and many are also early-bearing and disease-resistant. Among the best and most popular is Burpee Hybrid II, a new gynoecious version of America's first hybrid cucumber, introduced in 1945.

Since cucumbers are pollinated by bees, any necessary pesticides should be used late in the day after the bees have returned to the safety of their hives.

HARVESTING

Cucumbers, like beans, should be picked young and often. If fruits are left on the vine to mature, the plant's productivity will quickly taper off and cease. Most slicing cucumbers can be picked as small as six inches, and must be picked before the skin starts to yellow and the seeds begin to harden. Pickling types can be picked at any stage, depending on whether you want sweet midget pickles or large dills. Use a sharp knife or pruning shears to harvest cucumbers.

Old-Fashioned Cucumber, Garlic, and Dill Dip

Here is one of my favorite dips, which I like to serve with croutons of thinly sliced French bread, rubbed with garlic, brushed with extra-virgin olive oil, and quickly broiled until nicely browned.

1. Combine all the ingredients in a small bowl, season with salt and pepper, and whisk until well blended. Cover and let sit at room temperature for 1 to 2 hours to develop flavor.

2. Serve lightly chilled with croutons of French bread and an assortment of steamed vegetables.

SERVES 4 TO 6

4 pickling cucumbers, peeled and finely diced
2 small dill gherkins, finely diced
¼ cup finely minced scallions
2 tablespoons finely minced fresh dill
1 large garlic clove, peeled and mashed
1 tablespoon red wine vinegar
½ cup sour cream or plain yogurt
¼ cup mayonnaise
Salt and freshly ground black pepper

Ever-So-Sweet Viennese Cucumber and Scallion Salad

I grew up on cucumber salads that were prepared in the typical Austrian way, sweet and watery, and I have always liked them that way. You may, of course, drain some of the cucumber water depending on how authentic you want to be.

1. Place the cucumbers in a colander, sprinkle with coarse salt, and let drain for 1 hour.

2. Combine the vinegar, peanut or corn oil, sugar, and scallions in a bowl and whisk until the sugar is dissolved. Add the cucumbers, season with pepper, and toss well. Serve well chilled with a last-minute grinding of fresh white pepper.

SERVES 6

NOTE: If the cucumbers are large and seedy, cut in half lengthwise and with a grapefruit spoon, scoop out the seeds. In this case, the cucumbers do not need to be salted.

2 pounds medium cucumbers, peeled and thinly sliced
Coarse salt
3 tablespoons white wine vinegar
6 tablespoons peanut or corn oil
1½ tablespoons sugar
3 medium scallions, trimmed and finely sliced
Freshly ground white pepper

Middle Eastern Cucumber, Yogurt, and Mint Salad

4 large cucumbers, peeled, seeded, and cut crosswise into 1/4-inch slices

2 tablespoons white wine vinegar

Coarse salt

1 cup plain yogurt

2 tablespoons olive oil

3 tablespoons finely minced scallions

4 tablespoons finely minced fresh mint

1/2 teaspoon ground cumin

1/4 teaspoon turmeric

1 large garlic clove, peeled and mashed

Freshly ground black pepper

GARNISH
Sprigs of fresh mint

This refreshing Middle Eastern cucumber salad has become a popular preparation, earning a permanent place in many cooks' summer repertoire. I particularly like it with the addition of freshly picked spearmint. The salad is at its best when left to marinate for several hours before serving. It is especially welcome at a meal of lamb, such as a curry or a butterflied grilled leg.

1. Place the cucumber slices in a colander, sprinkle with 1 tablespoon of the vinegar and some coarse salt, and let drain for 1 hour.

2. While the cucumbers are draining, combine the yogurt, oil, remaining vinegar, scallions, mint, cumin, turmeric, and garlic in a serving bowl, season with salt and pepper, and whisk until well blended. Reserve.

3. Dry the cucumber slices thoroughly on paper towels, transfer to the serving bowl, and toss gently. Chill for 2 to 4 hours. Garnish with sprigs of mint and serve lightly chilled.

SERVES 4 TO 6

Fricassee of Cucumbers and Carrots with Tarragon Crème Fraîche

Although they are not traditionally served this way, cucumbers make a lovely hot vegetable. I team them with young tender carrots and lace the braised vegetables with a tarragon-flavored cream. Be sure to use only the "gourmet" or seedless cucumbers in this preparation to ensure that the vegetables are of even crispness when cooked. Serve the fricassee with pan-seared or oven-braised sea bass, pan-seared monkfish medallions, or poached fillets of salmon.

1. Place the cucumbers in a colander, sprinkle with coarse salt, and let drain for 30 minutes. Dry thoroughly on paper towels and set aside.

2. In a large skillet, melt 2 tablespoons of the butter over medium heat. Add the carrots, season with a pinch of sugar, and cook for 2 minutes, tossing in the butter. Add 2 tablespoons of the water, reduce the heat, and simmer, covered, for 5 to 6 minutes or until tender. Remove with a slotted spoon to a side dish and reserve.

3. Melt the remaining 2 tablespoons of butter in the skillet over medium low heat, add the cucumbers, and season with pepper. Add the remaining water and simmer, covered, for 3 minutes or until tender. Remove the cover, raise the heat, and simmer until all the liquid has evaporated.

4. Return the carrots to the skillet, add the crème fraîche, and simmer until slightly reduced and the sauce lightly coats the spoon. Add the tarragon and correct the seasoning. Serve hot.

S E R V E S   4

NOTE: This fricassee is equally delicious with finely minced fresh dill or mint in place of the tarragon.

2 medium cucumbers (seeded if necessary) or 1 large seedless cucumber, unpeeled, cut into ½ by ½ by 1-inch matchsticks
Coarse salt
4 tablespoons (½ stick) unsalted butter
3 medium carrots, trimmed, peeled, and cut into ½ by ½ by 1-inch matchsticks
1 teaspoon of sugar
¼ cup water
Freshly ground black pepper
½ cup Crème Fraîche (page 358)
2 to 3 tablespoons finely minced fresh tarragon

Pan-Sautéed Chicken Breasts with Cucumbers in Lemon Dill Cream

5 pickling cucumbers, peeled, seeded, and cut crosswise into ¼-inch slices

Coarse salt

4 tablespoons (½ stick) unsalted butter

3 whole skinless and boneless chicken breasts, cut in half

Freshly ground white pepper

All-purpose flour for dredging

2 teaspoons peanut oil

¾ cup chicken broth, preferably homemade (page 360)

¼ cup heavy cream

Juice of ½ lemon

1 Beurre Manié (page 361)

GARNISH

2 tablespoons finely minced fresh dill

Now that seedless cucumbers are available year-round, you can make this quick, delicious, and spontaneous dish in a matter of minutes. The chicken breasts take only six to eight minutes to cook. The entire dish can also be reheated successfully in the microwave or in a low oven. Serve the chicken breasts with tiny boiled red-skinned potatoes or a parsley and chive–flavored rice pilaf.

1. Place the cucumbers in a colander, sprinkle with coarse salt, and let drain for 30 minutes. Dry thoroughly on paper towels and set aside.

2. Melt 2 tablespoons of the butter in a large skillet over medium heat. Add the cucumbers and sauté for 3 to 4 minutes or until lightly browned. Transfer to a side dish and reserve.

3. Season the chicken with salt and pepper and dredge lightly in flour, shaking off the excess.

4. Melt the remaining 2 tablespoons of butter together with the oil in the skillet over medium high heat. Add the chicken without crowding the skillet and sauté until nicely browned on both sides. Reduce the heat, add ¼ cup of the chicken broth, and simmer, covered, for 4 to 6 minutes or until the chicken is done and the juices run pale yellow. Transfer the chicken to a side dish and keep warm.

5. Add the remaining ½ cup of broth to the skillet together with the cream and lemon juice. Bring to a simmer and whisk in bits of beurre manié until the sauce lightly coats a spoon. Return the cucumbers and chicken breasts to the skillet and just heat through. Correct the seasoning and transfer to a serving platter. Spoon the sauce over the chicken and cucumbers, garnish with minced dill, and serve hot.

SERVES 4 TO 6

Cool Cucumber, Dill, and Scallion Soup

When *I think of a cool summer vegetable, the first one that comes to mind is the cucumber. What makes this soup so perfect for a warm-weather supper is that it demands no cooking. The taste of cucumbers remains intense, which is not the case when the vegetable is cooked. Many herbs are good with cucumbers, but I usually opt for dill, chives, cilantro, or mint.*

1. Cook the shrimp in a large pot of boiling water just until cooked through, 1 to 2 minutes. Drain, peel, and cut into small pieces.

2. Combine the shrimp with the remaining ingredients in a large bowl. Correct the seasoning and refrigerate 4 hours or overnight.

3. Serve the soup lightly chilled in individual shallow soup bowls, garnished with sprigs of fresh dill.

SERVES 6

NOTE: For the sauerkraut juice, drain and squeeze the contents of one small can of sauerkraut to extract ½ cup of its juice.

½ pound medium shrimp

2 medium cucumbers, peeled, seeded, and diced

2 cups sour cream

5 cups buttermilk

½ cup sauerkraut juice (see Note)

2 medium garlic cloves, peeled and mashed

Salt and freshly ground white pepper

4 tablespoons finely minced fresh dill

½ cup finely minced scallions

GARNISH

Sprigs of fresh dill

GREEN PEPPERS

CHRISTOPHER COLUMBUS DISCOVERED PEPPERS IN THE GARDENS OF Cariban Indians, and within years they were being grown throughout Europe. Today, you can venture into an open-air market almost anywhere in the world and be dazzled by heaps of glistening peppers in shades of green, red, purple, and yellow. In Hungary and the Balkan countries, peppers are staples that have inspired such magnificent regional dishes as chicken paprikash, marinated lamb and pepper kebabs, and spicy stuffed pepper soups. Mexican cuisine as we know it today simply would not exist without the fiery peppers collectively known as chilies. Myriad varieties are cultivated, each with its own special qualities and uses. And in India, where incendiary fare is a way of life, plantings of both hot and sweet peppers became so widespread that early botanists incorrectly believed the plants to be indigenous.

Summer is the time for green peppers. Although all peppers are planted in spring, green peppers are in their glory in the heat of summer, while red and yellow varieties require a longer ripening time and are not ready to harvest until fall (see pages 242–43). In the past few years many more varieties of peppers have become available to the home cook. In addition to purple-skinned bell peppers you can now find red, yellow, and green frying peppers in many summer markets along with various types of hot chili peppers both green and red. The innovative cuisines of chefs in California and the Southwest demonstrate just how exciting and versatile those vegetables can be.

I always add one half cup of finely diced green peppers to tuna, egg, rice, and potato salads; I also love them in a Greek salad, combined with tomatoes, cucumbers, radishes, and onions. I rarely use green peppers in tossed salads, as they tend to dominate the subtle flavors typical of salad greens, but red peppers, which are fully ripened green peppers, are less assertive and will add their welcome color to tossed salads without overwhelming other ingredients. Their delicate sweetness also makes red peppers delicious when quartered raw and served with a zesty dip, stewed in olive oil and butter, or stuffed with rice or a savory meat filling.

When roasted, green peppers acquire a mellow, smoky taste that imparts a new dimension to many dishes. One of my favorite ways to serve roasted peppers is simply quartered and seeded, with the charred skins left on. I place them in a decorative pattern on a round serving platter, dribble them with olive oil, and add freshly snipped thyme leaves and crumbled young goat cheese. A generous grinding of black pepper and a few oil-cured black olives complete this effortless summer appetizer. Late in summer, when both green and red peppers grace the garden, I like to use them together to create unique taste combinations in pastas and ragouts, and with other roasted vegetables such as eggplant and tomatoes.

STORAGE

Whole green peppers can be kept refrigerated in plastic or brown paper bags in the vegetable bin where they will keep up to two weeks. Red peppers have a much shorter storage life than the green because they are already completely ripened and therefore more delicate. However, even peppers that have started to shrivel or show damp spots can still be used successfully in stews and soups. Once sliced, peppers will not keep for more than a day or two. Roasted, peeled, and seeded peppers store well in a jar, covered with about one quarter inch of olive oil and refrigerated.

Freezing peppers changes their texture and renders them limp, but they do retain their flavor and can be used in stews and soups. Core and seed the peppers, cube or slice them, and freeze in freezer bags or containers.

To dry hot peppers, wait until they turn red and then string them together loosely by pushing heavy thread through their stems. Hang in a cool, airy spot out of the sun.

GARDENING

Peppers are quite effortless to grow, but seeds must be started indoors about two months before the last danger of spring frost. In short-season areas, choose fast-maturing varieties so your plants will have enough time to ripen the fruits before fall frosts arrive.

Consider your favorite ways of using peppers and select the varieties best suited for those purposes. Use sweet bell peppers mostly for roasting on the grill or for slicing and dicing in salads, and for stuffing. If you entertain often and enjoy setting a colorful table, grow a few plants of a purple variety along with those that mature to red or yellow. The long narrow varieties like Sweet Banana or the incredibly productive Gypsy Hybrid are best for frying and sautées. Hot peppers are available in degrees of pungency ranging from very mild (Zippy Hybrid) to hot (jalapeño and serrano) to fiery (cayenne).

I plant at least two varieties of sweet bell pepper, a long, sweet Italian-style pepper (usually Sweet Banana) and two hot peppers, which I dry at the end of the season. I also try to include some cherry peppers because the small, round fruit is my favorite for pickling. The plants are so ornamental that, if I run out of room in the vegetable garden, I tuck a couple in a flower bed.

Do not be tempted to set pepper plants out too early in spring. At best, plants will merely be inactive when night temperatures fall below 55°F.; more likely, they will turn yellow and become stunted. Overfertilizing of peppers results in lush foliage but little fruit. Dry soil may cause blossom drop, as may excessively high temperatures or low humidity, but flowering generally will resume as weather conditions become more favorable.

Roasted Pepper Pizza with Red Onion Jam and Smoked Mozzarella

Ahomemade pizza can be both rustic and elegant. What is so nice about making this American favorite at home is that you can have a great time inventing and mixing up a variety of toppings. Here is one that allows plenty of room for additions such as a mild crumbled goat cheese, Gaeta olives, or a sprinkling of your favorite summer herbs.

1. In a large heavy skillet, heat 4 tablespoons of oil over medium high heat. Add the onions and cook for 5 minutes, stirring constantly. Reduce the heat, add the garlic and thyme, and season with salt and pepper. Cook, covered, for 30 to 35 minutes or until soft and lightly browned. Add the anchovies and stir until just melted. Reserve.

2. Preheat the oven to 425°F. Brush a black 12-inch pizza pan with the remaining oil and sprinkle lightly with cornmeal.

3. Roll out the pizza dough on a lightly floured surface into a 9-inch circle. Transfer the dough to the prepared pizza pan and stretch gently from the center outward to the edge of the pan. If the dough becomes too elastic, let rest for 5 minutes and begin again.

4. Spread the red onion jam evenly over the surface of the dough, leaving a ½-inch border. Top with the peppers and a good grinding of black pepper. Bake for 10 minutes. Sprinkle with the mozzarella and bake for an additional 2 to 5 minutes or until the crust is nicely browned and the cheese has melted. Garnish with the olives, cut into wedges, and serve hot.

SERVES 4

NOTE: To grate mozzarella, place it in the freezer until firm, about 20 to 30 minutes. You could also substitute a mild goat cheese, crumbled, for the mozzarella. In this case, drizzle the cheese with a little fruity oil after sprinkling on the pizza.

4 tablespoons plus 1 teaspoon extra-virgin olive oil
4 medium red onions, peeled, quartered, and thinly sliced
2 large garlic cloves, peeled and finely minced
1½ tablespoons fresh thyme leaves
Salt and freshly ground black pepper
4 flat anchovy fillets, finely minced
Coarse yellow cornmeal for sprinkling on pizza pan
½ recipe Quick Pizza Dough (page 359)
2 large green bell peppers, roasted and peeled (page 365) and thinly sliced
6 ounces smoked mozzarella, grated (see Note)

GARNISH
12 small black oil-cured olives

Grilled Pepper Salad with Garlic and Sherry Vinegar Dressing

1 small red onion, peeled,
   quartered, and thinly sliced
2 large green bell peppers,
   roasted, peeled (page 365),
   and thinly sliced
2 large red bell peppers,
   roasted, peeled (page 365),
   and thinly sliced
2 large yellow bell peppers,
   roasted, peeled (page 365),
   and thinly sliced
1 to 2 tablespoons sherry
   vinegar
1 large garlic clove, peeled and
   mashed
Salt and freshly ground black
   pepper
6 tablespoons olive oil,
   preferably extra-virgin

GARNISH
2 tablespoons finely minced
   fresh parsley
12 small black oil-cured olives
Optional: ⅔ cup feta cheese,
   crumbled

Think of this flavor-packed salad the next time you plan to use the grill. Let the peppers marinate for 30 minutes to an hour before serving but not any longer, or the tomatoes with lose too much of their juice and their "crispness" and the salad will become too soupy. For those who use the Weber kettle grill, it is best to put the peppers directly on the hot coals and turn them frequently until they are evenly charred. Of course, a gas grill or a gas flame works just as well, but the salad will lack some of that delicious smoky flavor.

1. Combine the onion and peppers in a shallow serving dish and set aside.

2. In a small bowl, combine the vinegar and garlic, season with salt and pepper, and whisk in the oil in a slow stream. Pour the vinaigrette over the onions and peppers and toss gently. Correct the seasoning and garnish with minced parsley, black olives, and the feta, if using. Serve at room temperature.

SERVES 6

Oven-Roasted Paella-Filled Peppers

When I was young I always looked forward to "leftover day," when my mother used her ingenuity and imagination to make something out of the many leftovers we always seemed to have on hand. Since I prefer the leftover paella rice to freshly cooked, I loved this dish, and to this day I make it whenever I can get crisp, garden-fresh green peppers. If good peppers are not available, try packing the mixture into blanched cabbage leaves and baking them in a little olive oil with a touch of water for 45 minutes to an hour, or until the cabbage is soft and lightly browned. I often add a can of well-drained tuna packed in olive oil to the mixture for additional interest and flavor.

1. Preheat the oven to 375°F.

2. In a large bowl, combine the paella with the cilantro and cumin, correct the seasoning, and mix until well blended.

3. Cut the tops off the peppers and remove the white membranes and seeds. Fill loosely with the paella and stand the peppers in a shallow baking pan. Drizzle with the olive oil and add ½ cup water to the pan. Bake for 1 hour and 15 minutes to 1 hour and 30 minutes, or until the peppers are very tender, basting often with the pan juices. Add the remaining water if the juices begin to dry.

4. When the peppers are done, remove them from the oven and cool. Slice the peppers in half vertically and arrange them on a serving platter. Drizzle with the extra-virgin oil and vinegar, sprinkle with the parsley, and serve warm or at room temperature.

SERVES 10 TO 12

NOTE: The peppers are even better when prepared a day in advance. Refrigerate overnight and then bring back to room temperature before serving.

1 recipe Late-Summer Vegetable
   Paella (page 164)
3 to 4 tablespoons fresh
   cilantro leaves
½ teaspoon ground cumin
Salt and freshly ground black
   pepper
10 to 12 medium-size green bell
   peppers, or a mixture of
   green and red
4 tablespoons olive oil
½ to ¾ cup water

GARNISH
1 tablespoon extra-virgin
   olive oil
1 tablespoon sherry vinegar
3 tablespoons finely minced
   fresh parsley

Mary's Pickled Hot Peppers

Ingredients (sidebar)

2 pounds hot cherry peppers, both red and green

5 cups white vinegar

2 tablespoons fresh oregano leaves

4 large garlic cloves, peeled and thinly sliced

Salt to taste

4 to 5 cups oil (preferably a combination of ½ olive oil and ½ corn oil)

These quickly prepared hot peppers provide a piquant counterpoint to barbecued meats, chicken, or a simple grilled hamburger. I often dice one or two and add them to a summer potato or tuna salad.

1. Remove the stems from the peppers but do not seed. Slice crosswise ¼ inch thick. Place the pepper slices in a large bowl and set aside.

2. Bring the vinegar to a simmer in a medium saucepan and pour over the peppers. Let stand for 25 minutes. Drain well and discard the vinegar.

3. Add the oregano, garlic, salt, and 4 cups of the oil to the peppers and toss well. Transfer the peppers with a slotted spoon to 4 sterilized pint jars, leaving a ¾-inch headspace. Pack down firmly and pour the oil and herb mixture over the peppers, leaving a ¼-inch headspace. Let the jars stand at room temperature, uncovered, overnight.

4. The next day, if the oil has settled so that the peppers are exposed, fill the jars with a little more of the remaining oil to cover the peppers completely. Seal tightly and store in a cool place for 3 to 4 months before opening.

MAKES 4 PINTS

NOTE: There is no need to process the jars in a water bath since the peppers are completely immersed in oil.

Spicy Sauté of Peppers with Fennel Sausage and Basil

Africassee of sautéed peppers and sausages is a favorite Mediterranean preparation, especially common on Spanish and Italian tables. Much depends on the quality of the tomatoes, the peppers, and, of course, the sausage, but when all are good, this is a great peasant dish that deserves to be part of every cook's summer and fall repertoire. Serve with chive or garlic mashed potatoes or a simple well-seasoned salad.

1. In a large heavy skillet, heat the oil over medium high heat. Add the sausage and cook until nicely browned on all sides. Transfer the sausage to a cutting board and cut cross-wise into ½-inch slices. Reserve.

2. Discard all but 3 tablespoons of fat from the skillet. Reduce the heat, add the chili pepper, and when dark, remove and discard. Add the onion and garlic to the hot chili oil and cook until soft and lightly browned, about 5 to 6 minutes.

3. Add the tomatoes, green peppers, oregano, basil, and sun-dried tomatoes, if using, season with salt and pepper, and simmer, covered, for 20 to 25 minutes, stirring often, until the tomato liquid has reduced and the sauce has thickened.

4. Add the sliced sausage and the sautéed eggplant, if using, to the skillet and just heat through. Correct the seasoning and serve hot, directly from the skillet, sprinkled with Parmesan and garnished with basil leaves.

SERVES 4 TO 5

VARIATION
Serve the sauté with Corn-Studded Polenta with Parmesan (page 105). Spoon the polenta into individual serving bowls, top each portion with some of the peppers and sausage, and sprinkle with additional Parmesan.

2 tablespoons extra-virgin olive oil
I pound sweet Italian fennel sausage
I small dry red chili pepper, broken in half
I large onion, peeled and finely minced
2 large garlic cloves, peeled and finely minced
4 large ripe tomatoes, peeled, seeded, and chopped
6 to 8 medium green frying peppers, cored, seeded, and thinly sliced
I tablespoon fresh oregano leaves
½ cup julienned fresh basil leaves
Optional: 8 sun-dried tomatoes, finely diced
Salt and freshly ground black pepper
Optional: 2 cups cubed eggplant sautéed in 3 tablespoons olive oil

GARNISH
½ cup freshly grated Parmesan cheese
Tiny leaves of fresh basil

Viennese Gulasch Soup

3 tablespoons unsalted butter

2 teaspoons peanut oil

2 cups finely minced onions

1 teaspoon finely minced garlic

2 small dry red chili peppers, broken in half

2 pounds beef chuck, cut into ¾-inch cubes

Salt and freshly ground black pepper

2 large green peppers, cored, seeded, and thinly sliced

1 tablespoon imported sweet paprika

1 tablespoon caraway seeds

4 large ripe tomatoes, peeled, seeded, and chopped

8 cups beef broth

1 teaspoon Old Bay Seasoning

1 pound new potatoes, peeled and diced

GARNISH
Sour cream

I am one of those cooks who still like an occasional hearty dish in summer or during those first crisp days of fall, and there is something terrific about food that can be cooked unattended while you work in the garden or enjoy a leisurely drink. What's more, this dish tastes better and better as it sits, which is my idea of the perfect food. Teamed with buttery green beans or some gently braised zucchini, you have the makings of a memorable main course.

1. Melt the butter together with the oil in a large heavy casserole over medium heat. Add the onions, garlic, and chili peppers and cook until soft but not browned. Add the beef and cook, stirring often, until lightly browned. Season with salt and pepper. Add the green peppers, paprika, and caraway seeds and cook for 5 minutes longer.

2. Add the tomatoes, broth, and Old Bay Seasoning and simmer, tightly covered, for 2 hours or until the beef is just tender. Add the potatoes and continue cooking until the potatoes are tender. Correct the seasoning and serve in deep soup bowls garnished with a dollop of sour cream, and serve black bread on the side.

SERVES 6

Curried Pepper, Corn, and Cabbage Jam

I have to warn you, this side dish is truly addictive: once you start nibbling these deliciously spiced corn kernels you just can't stop. Serve this gem, which is a cross between a pickle and a chutney, as an accompaniment to a basketful of crisp fried chicken or lamb shish kebabs.

1. Bring plenty of salted water to a boil. Add the corn kernels and cook for 5 to 7 minutes, or until tender. Drain well.

2. In a stockpot, combine the corn and remaining ingredients. Bring to a boil, reduce heat, and simmer, uncovered, for 25 minutes. Bring back to a boil, then pack in hot sterilized pint jars, leaving a ¼-inch headspace. Adjust the caps and process for 10 minutes in a boiling water bath. Remove and let cool completely. Store for 2 to 3 months before opening.

MAKES 5 TO 6 PINTS

Salt
8 cups fresh corn kernels, about 10 to 12 ears
2 medium-size red onions, peeled and finely diced
½ pound green cabbage, cored and thinly sliced
4 large green bell peppers, cored, seeded, and diced
2 small dry red chili peppers, broken in half
2 tablespoons dry mustard
1 teaspoon ground ginger
2 teaspoons turmeric
2 teaspoons imported curry powder, preferably Madras
12 whole black peppercorns
1 tablespoon coriander seeds
1 tablespoon cumin seeds
1 tablespoon salt
1½ cups sugar
4 cups cider vinegar
1 cup water

HERBS

Each plant is a personality, each kind of herb a fragrant memory
for any visitor to the garden.

ROSETTA E. CLARKSON

THE WORLD OF HERB GARDENING IS MAGICALLY DIVERSE. IT OFFERS AN extraordinary variety of fragrances and tastes, a visual tapestry of blending and contrasting colors, textures, and shapes, and a remarkable sense of connection to different cuisines and cultures. What is so marvelous about herbs is that even non-gardeners can try their hand at growing them, be it on a terrace, on a window sill, or in backyard containers. There is something enchanting about picking up your kitchen shears and cutting a few sprigs of fresh basil, thyme, or mint for that added dash of zest that instantly alters the character and texture of a dish.

Botanically, an herb is defined as a plant that does not develop persistent woody stems. Herb gardeners, though, do not take this definition literally, since many favorite cooking herbs, such as sage, rosemary, and thyme, do not fit this description. A more encompassing and widely accepted definition of an herb is a plant whose roots, stems, leaves, or flowers are valued for their savory, aromatic, and often medicinal qualities.

For me, as for most cooks around the world, few recipes are complete without fresh or dried herbs; they add such dimension, character, and flavor to food that no kitchen garden would be complete without them. Cooking with herbs is deeply rooted in many cuisines, especially those bordering the Mediterranean and those of Mexico, but what has always fascinated me is that an herb such as cilantro, which plays such a major role in Portuguese cooking, is all but unknown in neighboring Spain, while basil, a favorite in Italian cooking, is practically unheard of and hardly ever used in its neighboring Austria, or in Central Europe, for that matter. In the American kitchen herbs are used with abandon in traditional as well as new and innovative preparations. Today chefs and home cooks are experimenting with myriad herbs, using them both fresh and dried to create marinades, rubs, pasta dishes, soups, and rice recipes.

While the great majority of the recipes in this book feature herbal flavorings, the recipes here veritably *revel* in herbs: herbs are integral ingredients, not mere enhancements. Fresh herbs allow the imaginative cook to add distinctive flavor to a dish, or to change its nature entirely by simply substituting one herb for another.

This does not mean that all the new creative interpretations are desirable. For instance, a classic pesto should be made with basil, not cilantro, and a béarnaise is about tarragon, not mint or lemon thyme. But mostly there are no musts in the use of herbs. The key to cooking with these remarkable plants is to infuse foods with just a hint of herbal flavor, to add complexity without dominating the other flavors. Such improvisation is part of the delight of growing both vegetables and herbs.

Over the years I have experimented with a great variety of herbs in the hope that they would do well in my soil. Through trial and error I have now limited my selection to the ones that seem to do well either in my vegetable garden or in a rock garden. Several herbs, particularly rosemary, do well year-round when grown in pots, while others, especially the delicate "accent" herbs such as chervil and dill, love the cool spring weather and a sandy soil (which, in some parts of the country, makes them short season favorites). But by and large, summer is the time for great, fragrant bunches of herbs to be used generously and creatively.

No discussion of herbs would be complete without giving thought to herbal vinegars and oils. Flavored herb oils can be used in as many ways as your imagination allows. They provide infinite inspiration when you want to flavor a piece of fish for grilling or pasta and rice dishes. You can use them in place of butter or oil when sautéing, and they're wonderful for seasoning a platter of raw or roasted vegetables. And for those who are concerned about saturated fats, there's always the option of using canola oil, although I prefer the delicate taste of an olive oil.

Herb oils and vinegars are marvelous additions to the summer kitchen. After all, they give us an opportunity to bottle the very essence of summer.

To Flavor Vinegar with Fresh Herbs

Place one lightly packed cupful of rinsed and dried fresh herbs in a sterilized, dry heatproof jar. Heat two cups of the chosen vinegar to simmering and pour it over the herbs, which should be completely immersed (if not, heat more vinegar and add it). Cap the jar and let the herbs steep for at least ten days, shaking the jar occasionally. Decant the vinegar, filter or strain it if desired, and bottle it in a sterilized, completely dry bottle. Store it, capped, in a cool, dark spot.

STORAGE

Garden-grown herbs will keep well for several days. Just place them in a glass or pitcher of cold water, cover loosely with either a plastic bag or damp paper towel, and refrigerate. (While herbs look pretty when placed in a pitcher and left on the kitchen counter, this is not a good way to keep them fresh.)

When buying herbs in the supermarket be sure to pat them dry with paper towels, but do not wash them. Store in plastic bags and perforate the bags with the tip of a sharp knife. If fresh and not too damp, many herbs will keep for as long as a week to ten days.

Drying herbs is the time-honored—though not always best—method of preserving them. There are two schools of thought about the process. One is to dry the herbs slowly in a cool atmosphere by tying small bunches together and letting them hang upside down for several days. Once dry, the herbs are kept on their stems and crushed just before using.

The second method, and the one I prefer, is to spread the herbs on a rack or baking sheet and dry them in the oven on the lowest possible setting with the door open. Turn them once or twice until they are quite dry and can be crumbled between the fingers.

Freezing is ideal for delicate herbs such as basil, dill, and chives that do not dry well anyway. You can freeze these herbs whole, chopped, or in sprigs in small resealable plastic bags. I do not recommend chopping them in a food processor since it removes much of their flavor.

For most dishes herbs should be chopped, but not too finely minced, since the heat of the knife tends to release the fragrant oils of many and reduce their flavor.

GARDENING

As a general rule most herbs are undemanding and do well in poor soil. In their native habitat many Mediterranean herbs grow in almost arid soils, which proves that they are quite capable of coping with similar conditions in your garden.

In fact, ironically, a deep, rich soil tends to produce herbs with plenty of lush foliage growth, but their flavor is generally inferior to those grown in poorer dry conditions. Unfortunately herbs grown in poor soil do not produce attractive plants and often cannot cope with continued harvesting, so I try to achieve a balance between flavor and good growth.

The key to an herb garden no matter where it is planted geographically is drainage, since herbs will quickly rot in damp conditions. In my garden in the Northeast, where the soil is rather rich and the spring season tends to be long and wet, it is best to grow herbs in raised beds, which allows you to control the soil conditions and provide better drainage. In temperate regions, such as Arizona, California, and Florida, it is important to add some compost material to the herb garden to act as a sponge and hold some moisture in reserve. In coastal areas where the soil is usually very light and sandy, adding some organic matter will greatly aid water retention to keep the roots from drying out.

Heavy applications of fertilizer are totally unnecessary when it comes to herbs, but I usually like to add some bone meal to the young seedlings, which gives them a steady supply of food without causing lush growth or compromising flavor.

Herbs can be grown successfully in containers, pots, and even window-boxes provided that they get enough sun. For those who do not have access to a garden this is a good choice, although the plants are never quite as happy as they are in the ground. Still, with some skill and care you can keep them growing well.

When I first started to grow herbs in the seventies the selection in garden centers and nurseries was quite limited and I used to start almost all my herbs from seed. Now however, with plenty to choose from, I much prefer to buy healthy looking seedlings or small plants, which gives me a head start and eliminates the need to thin the plants.

Be sure to dig holes that will accommodate the roots freely, and do not bury the crown. Firm the soil around the plants and water thoroughly. Annual herbs such as basil, cilantro, and dill can be planted closely together, while such perennials as oregano, marjoram, sage, and thyme need more room since they will spread and form large clumps that should be divided after a few years.

HARVESTING

You can start harvesting your herbs as soon as the plants are well established. In fact, pinching off the tips encourages them to become compact and bushy. However, do not chop off half the plant, even if you need a large amount for a recipe, as this can kill it.

Warm Red Potatoes in Cilantro Avocado Dressing

I recently traveled to the Canary Islands, where I was quite taken with the cuisine, which I found to be full of interesting flavors and textures. This cilantro avocado dressing is an island staple that can be sampled in many variations all over the Canaries. I particularly like it teamed with warm new potatoes, but it is also good served as a dip with grilled squid, shrimp, or scallops. The dressing will keep well for two or three days but may lose some of its brilliant green color. For a more intense cilantro flavor, add half a cup of small whole leaves to the salad.

1. In a food processor combine the avocado and 2 table-spoons of the vinegar and process until smooth. With the machine running, slowly add enough of the oil to make a creamy dressing.

2. Transfer the mixture to a bowl and fold in the minced and the mashed garlic, 1 teaspoon of the jalapeño pepper, the parsley, and the cilantro. Season with salt and black pepper and set aside at room temperature for 30 minutes. Taste and correct the seasoning, adding the remaining vinegar and jalapeño pepper if desired.

3. Meanwhile, place the potatoes in a saucepan with plenty of salted water to cover and simmer until just tender. Drain well, transfer to a serving dish, and, while still warm, toss the potatoes with the dressing. Correct the seasoning and serve warm.

SERVES 4 TO 6

½ ripe avocado, peeled and diced
2 to 3 tablespoons sherry vinegar
½ to ¾ cup olive oil
2 large garlic cloves, peeled and finely minced
1 large garlic clove, peeled and mashed through a garlic press
1 to 2 teaspoons finely minced jalapeño pepper
½ cup loosely packed fresh parsley, finely minced
½ cup loosely packed fresh cilantro leaves, finely minced
Salt and freshly ground black pepper
2 pounds small red potatoes, about 1 to 1½ inches in diameter, unpeeled and cut in half

Thyme-Scented Gratin of Bluefish and New Potatoes

5 tablespoons extra-virgin
   olive oil
2 large red onions, peeled,
   quartered, and thinly sliced
2 large garlic cloves, peeled
   and thinly sliced
½ cup loosely packed fresh
   thyme leaves, finely minced
1 pound small red new
   potatoes, unpeeled, cut into
   ¼-inch slices
Salt and freshly ground black
   pepper
½ to ¾ cup fish bouillon or
   chicken broth, preferably
   homemade (page 360),
   mixed with ¼ teaspoon Old
   Bay Seasoning
3 medium-size ripe tomatoes,
   sliced
1 fresh bluefish fillet, about
   1½ to 1¾ pounds
⅓ cup dry white wine
GARNISH
1½ cups loosely packed fresh
   parsley leaves, finely minced
1 large garlic clove, peeled and
   finely minced
3 to 4 tablespoons fresh
   breadcrumbs
Extra-virgin olive oil
½ cup black oil-cured olives,
   pitted and cut in half

*H*ere is a take off on a typical Catalan dish that has a permanent spot in my summer repertoire. Since bluefish is an oily fish that is only good when superfresh, it is not always available; red snapper and seabass are other good choices for this type of preparation.

1. Preheat the oven to 350°F.

2. Heat 3 tablespoons of oil over medium heat in a large heavy skillet. Add the onions, garlic, and 2 tablespoons of the thyme and cook for 3 to 4 minutes, or until the onions begin to soften. Add the potatoes and season with salt and pepper.

3. Spoon the potato mixture into a rectangular or oval baking dish, add ½ cup of the bouillon and top with overlapping slices of tomatoes. Sprinkle with the remaining thyme and drizzle with the remaining oil. Bake for 15 to 20 minutes or until the potatoes are almost tender; you may need to add the remaining bouillon, depending on the juiciness of the tomatoes. Place the bluefish on top, season with salt and pepper, and add the white wine. Bake until just done, about 30 minutes. Remove the fish from the oven and turn the setting to broil.

4. While the fish is baking, prepare the garnish: Combine the parsley, garlic, and breadcrumbs in a small bowl and add enough oil to moisten. Reserve.

5. Sprinkle the bluefish with the breadcrumb mixture and the olives and run under the broiler for about 2 minutes or until crusty and lightly browned. Serve at once directly from the baking dish.

SERVES 4 TO 5

Parsley Salad

We tend to think of parsley as a basic herb that has little if any personality. To many people it is simply decorative, to be used as a (disposable) garnish. But parsley—and especially flat-leaf parsley—is loaded with taste, and in this adaptation of the popular tabbouleh salad it well proves its case. The addition of mint makes the salad particularly refreshing; you can use a variety of interesting mints depending on what you are growing in your garden. Serve the salad with poached salmon or grilled shrimp, or as part of a picnic.

1. Place the bulgur in a large bowl with warm water to cover and soak until tender and doubled in volume, about 1 to 2 hours. Drain well and return to the bowl. Add the parsley, mint, cucumber, radishes, and onion, mix thoroughly, and set aside.

2. In a small bowl, combine the lemon juice and olive oil and whisk until emulsified. Season with salt and pepper and pour over the salad. Toss gently and marinate for at least 2 to 4 hours at room temperature before serving.

3. Just before serving, taste and correct the seasoning. You may need a touch more lemon juice or oil or both.

S E R V E S   6

1 cup medium-grain bulgur
2 large bunches of flat-leaf parsley, washed, stems discarded, and coarsely chopped
1 heaping cup peppermint, cut into a fine julienne
2 cups peeled, seeded, and diced cucumber, preferably gourmet
1 cup diced radishes
4 tablespoons finely diced red onion
Juice of 2 large lemons
8 tablespoons extra-virgin olive oil
Coarse salt and freshly ground black pepper

Middle Eastern Char-Grilled Skirt Steaks in a Cumin and Cilantro Marinade

¾ cup cumin seeds, lightly
    toasted (see page 82)
4 large garlic cloves, peeled
2 jalapeño peppers, cut in half
2 tablespoons cracked black
    pepper
2 canned chipotle peppers in
    adobo sauce
1 teaspoon Old Bay Seasoning
6 bunches fresh cilantro,
    washed thoroughly and
    dried
1 to 1½ cups olive oil
Coarse salt
3 pounds skirt steak, trimmed
    of all excess fat
½ cup fresh lime juice

GARNISH
Sprigs of fresh cilantro

For years I favored flank steaks as one of summer's best main courses but since discovering the less attractive-looking but juicier skirt steak, I opt for this cut whenever I see it in the market. The intensely flavored and aromatic cilantro marinade further enhances this unassuming cut of beef. Serve with a pan-fried polenta and a spicy corn relish.

1. In a blender, process the cumin seeds until finely crushed. Add the garlic, jalapeño peppers, black pepper, chipotle peppers, Old Bay Seasoning, cilantro, and olive oil, season highly with salt, and process until smooth.

2. Cut the skirt steak into 6 pieces (about ½ pound each) and place them in a large resealable plastic bag. Pour the marinade over them and seal the bag. Set the bag in a shallow dish and refrigerate for 24 hours, turning the steaks in the marinade several times. Four hours before grilling, add the lime juice to the bag.

3. Prepare the charcoal grill. Remove the steaks from the bag and wipe off the excess marinade.

4. When the coals are red-hot, sprinkle each side of the skirt steaks with a little coarse salt. Brush the grill with vegetable oil and place the steaks over the hot coals. Grill 2 to 3 minutes per side until nicely browned for medium rare, about 130 to 135°F. internal temperature on a meat thermometer.

5. Transfer the steaks to a cutting board and let sit for 2 to 3 minutes before slicing. Cut the meat across the grain into thin slices. Garnish with sprigs of cilantro.

SERVES 6

Dill-Cured Carpaccio of Salmon

Quickly marinated raw salmon is a dish that has become popular on both sides of the Atlantic, but speed is not really the name of the game when it comes to proper marinating. It takes 36 to 48 hours for the fish to acquire the right texture and to absorb the flavor of dill and spices. Once marinated, the fish will easily keep for a week.

1. Combine the mustards, sugar, vinegar, and ¼ cup oil or broth in a small bowl and whisk until well blended. If the sauce seems too thick, whisk in the remaining oil or broth. Season with salt and pepper, cover, and refrigerate until needed.

2. Combine the dill, coarse salt, sugar, and white pepper in a small bowl and toss well.

3. In a rectangular porcelain dish, place one salmon fillet skin side down. Spread the fillet with one half of the dill marinade to cover completely. Top with the remaining fillet skin side up. Spread the second fillet with the remaining dill marinade. Cover the dish tightly with foil and place a cutting board that fits inside the dish on top of the fillets. Place 3 or 4 cans or other heavy items on top of the board and refrigerate for 48 hours, turning the whole salmon "sandwich" over every 12 hours and basting with the marinade in the bottom of the dish (the dill marinade will liquefy).

4. After 48 hours, separate the fillets and rinse well under cold water to remove all of the marinade. Pat dry on paper towels. Wrap the fillets loosely in foil and refrigerate until serving. The "gravlax" will keep for up to 8 days.

5. Remove the mustard sauce from the refrigerator about 20 minutes before serving. Cut the salmon crosswise on the bias into thin slices. Place the slices in an even layer on individual serving plates to cover the plates completely. Drizzle each portion with some of the mustard sauce and garnish with sprigs of dill and lemon wedges.

SERVES 12

THE MUSTARD SAUCE
1 cup Dijon mustard, preferably Maille
1 teaspoon dry mustard, preferably Colman's, reconstituted in 1 tablespoon water
3 tablespoons sugar
2 tablespoons white wine vinegar, preferably champagne
¼ to ⅓ cup olive oil or chicken broth
Salt and freshly ground black pepper

THE SALMON
3 medium bunches of fresh dill, with stems, finely chopped
¼ cup coarse kosher salt
¼ cup sugar
2 tablespoons whole white peppercorns, crushed in a mortar and pestle
2 salmon fillets, center cut only, with skin on, about 4½ to 5 pounds total (both fillets must be the same size)

GARNISH
Sprigs of fresh dill
Lemon wedges

Old-Fashioned Baked Mushrooms with Tarragon and Goat Cheese Filling

12 large all-purpose mushrooms, about 2 inches in diameter

6 ounces mild goat cheese, crumbled

1 tablespoon freshly grated Parmesan cheese

1/3 cup fresh tarragon leaves, finely minced

3 tablespoons very finely diced red bell pepper

2 tablespoons very finely diced red onion

Salt and freshly ground black pepper

3 tablespoons extra-virgin olive oil

1 large garlic clove, peeled and thinly sliced

1 large sprig of fresh tarragon

I *still remember a time when the food served at most cocktail parties seemed to come out of a single kitchen. There was always some kind of dip, stuffed cherry tomatoes, and baked cream cheese–filled mushrooms. Well, some foods do come full circle, and the baked stuffed mushroom is one of them. Rather than with cocktails, however, I like to serve these flavorful roasted mushrooms as a starter, perhaps drizzled with an anchovy, caper, and parsley butter or as a garnish for roast veal, chicken, or Cornish hens.*

1. Preheat the oven to 400°F.

2. Carefully remove and discard the stems from the mushrooms. Wipe the caps with a damp paper towel to remove all sand and set aside.

3. In a medium bowl, combine the goat cheese, Parmesan, tarragon, red pepper, and red onion. Season with salt and pepper and mix thoroughly. Fill each mushroom cap with some of the goat cheese mixture.

4. Place a flameproof baking dish over low heat. Add 2 tablespoons of the oil, the garlic, and the tarragon sprig and just heat through. Add the mushrooms to the baking dish and drizzle with the remaining oil.

5. Bake the mushrooms for 20 minutes. Serve hot with a little of the pan juices spooned over each portion.

SERVES 4

Spaghettini with Pan-Seared Eggplant, Olives, and Herbs

The meaty texture of eggplant makes it a perfect addition to pasta dishes. Eggplant is happy in the company of many herbs, especially basil, thyme, oregano, and of course parsley and garlic, so use any of these, alone or in some combination, whenever you make this dish.

1. Place the eggplant cubes in a large bowl, cover with ice water, and add 1 teaspoon of coarse salt. Let soak for 2 hours. Drain the eggplant thoroughly and dry well on paper towels.

2. Sauté the eggplant in 2 batches. For each batch, heat 3 tablespoons of the oil in a large skillet over medium high heat, add half of the eggplant cubes, and sauté quickly until nicely browned on all sides. Remove with a slotted spoon to a side dish and reserve.

3. Add another tablespoon of oil to the skillet. Reduce the heat, add the bacon, and sauté until almost crisp. Remove with a slotted spoon to a side dish and reserve.

4. Discard all but 2 tablespoons of the fat from the skillet and add the remaining 3 tablespoons olive oil. Add the shallots, garlic, and parsley and cook for 1 minute without browning. Add the tomatoes, cover, and simmer for 30 minutes, stirring often to avoid scorching. Season with salt and pepper and if the sauce seems too thick, add a little of the reserved tomato juice. Add the olives and the reserved bacon and eggplant, and just heat through. Cover and keep warm.

5. Bring plenty of salted water to a boil in a large pot, add the spaghettini, and cook until just tender "al dente." Immediately add 2 cups cold water to the pot to stop further cooking. Drain the pasta well and return to the pot. Add the eggplant sauce and correct the seasoning. Transfer to a serving dish and serve hot, sprinkled with minced parsley, accompanied by a bowl of Parmesan cheese.

S E R V E S   4

---

1 medium to large eggplant, unpeeled, cut into ¾-inch cubes

Coarse salt

10 tablespoons extra-virgin olive oil

4 ounces slab bacon, about 1 cup, blanched for 1 minute, drained, and cut into ½-inch dice

2 medium shallots, peeled and finely minced

2 large garlic cloves, peeled and finely minced

3 tablespoons finely minced fresh parsley

1 can (35 ounces) Italian plum tomatoes, drained and coarsely chopped; juice reserved separately

Freshly ground black pepper

1 cup small black oil-cured olives, pitted

¾ pound imported dried spaghettini

GARNISH

3 to 4 tablespoons finely minced fresh parsley

Freshly grated Parmesan cheese

Goat Cheese and Thyme Fondue

½ cup dry white wine

2 tablespoons finely minced shallots

1 large garlic clove, peeled and mashed

12 ounces mild goat cheese, such as Montrachet

3½ ounces grated Gruyère cheese

2 teaspoons Dijon mustard

⅓ cup fresh thyme leaves, finely minced

2 tablespoons unsalted butter

Salt and freshly ground black pepper

6 slices of peasant bread, grilled

*C*heese fondues have always been a popular Swiss specialty and during my student days in Geneva we used to make them often using a variety of local mountain cheeses. Here is a variation of the classic fondue that I like to serve with grilled Tuscan bread, a bowl of oil-cured black olives, and crisp radishes with drinks before dinner. The fondue is also good served as a "melt" for a weekend lunch.

1. In a heavy 1½-quart saucepan, combine the wine, shallots, and garlic, bring to a simmer, and reduce by one half.

2. Add the goat cheese and Gruyère and simmer, stirring often, until the cheeses have melted. Fold the mustard, thyme, and butter, season lightly with salt and a large grinding of pepper, and serve warm with grilled bread for dipping.

SERVES 6

Basil and Spinach Coulis

Herb coulis makes for a most attractive finishing touch for many dishes. A few drops can set off a pan-seared tuna, swordfish, or other fish steaks. Other herbs, especially chives, sorrel, mint, dill, and parsley, make terrific coulis. Even though you can mix two to three herbs such as parsley, chives, and dill, be sure to use one predominant taste and season rather assertively with salt. Herb coulis will keep well for several days in the refrigerator.

1. In a heavy 2-quart saucepan, melt the butter together with the oil over medium heat. Add the shallots, garlic, and mushrooms and cook for 2 minutes, without browning, stirring often.

2. Add the wine, bring to a boil, and reduce to 2 tablespoons. Add the broth and the tomato and reduce by one third, about 5 minutes.

3. Transfer the mixture to a blender together with the spinach and basil and blend until very smooth. Pour the coulis into a bowl and let cool completely.

4. Fold in the sherry vinegar and the olive oil, if using; season with salt and pepper and serve at room temperature.

SERVES 4 TO 6

VARIATION

You may also serve the sauce warm: Place it in a double boiler over warm water and whisk in 3 to 4 tablespoons of unsalted butter for a smooth, velvety sauce.

2 tablepoons unsalted butter
1 teaspoon olive oil
2 tablespoons finely minced shallots
1 large garlic clove, peeled and finely minced
1 cup finely minced all-purpose mushrooms (about 5 or 6 medium mushrooms)
1/2 cup dry white wine
1 cup chicken broth, preferably homemade (page 360)
1 large ripe tomato, peeled, seeded, and chopped
2 cups stemmed fresh spinach leaves
1 1/2 cups loosely packed, stemmed fresh basil leaves
2 teaspoons sherry vinegar
Optional: 2 tablespoons extra-virgin olive oil
Salt and freshly ground black pepper

SNAP BEANS

ALTHOUGH SNAP BEANS ARE AVAILABLE ALMOST YEAR-ROUND, WHAT'S missing from the grocer's vegetable is the audible "snap" of the pods that indicates good crunchy eating. For that, you must rely on beans fresh from the garden. If you pick your beans when they are young, they will be close in texture and appearance to the true French string bean, *haricot vert*, a type increasingly available in the United States.

What endears snap beans to a cook is versatility: they are perfect with every kind of meat, poultry, and fish, and they also make a terrific salad ingredient. One of my favorite bean salads is the classic *salade Niçoise*, from the south of France, which combines cooked beans marinated in a mustard vinaigrette and tossed with slices of tiny new potatoes, flaked tuna, olives, and a handful of basil leaves. For an elegant first course to a summer dinner, try a salad of snap beans and diced shrimp dressed with walnut oil and sherry vinegar. Or revitalize leftover beans with a sprinkling of olive oil and lemon juice and then combine them with some fresh mixed salad greens.

Probably the simplest and most popular way to serve snap beans is steamed and buttered. However, I prefer a different basic preparation, which offers greater possibilities. I cook snap beans in plenty of lightly salted boiling water for three to five minutes, depending on the size and maturity of the pods. (Ideally, cooked beans should soften yet retain some crunchiness— taste one to judge readiness.) As soon as they are done, drain and run under cold water. This stops any further cooking and helps the beans hold their bright green color. To bring out the very best flavor, I melt three tablespoons of butter in a large nonstick skillet and then gently toss the beans for only a minute or two. Do not sauté beans; this causes them to lose both color and flavor. Once the beans are buttered, you can add a variety of fresh herbs, such as dill or chives, or, if you're feeling extravagant, a touch of heavy cream plus two to three spoonfuls of sour cream and a sprinkling of grated Parmesan.

Snap beans should always be cooked whole. Even for a recipe that calls for cut beans, it is best to cut them *after* the pods have been blanched.

STORAGE

Beans keep well refrigerated in a paper bag up to a week. Snap beans freeze well; their texture will be different, but the flavor will be very satisfactory. To freeze, blanch the beans in boiling water for two minutes, then run under cold water to stop further cooking. Cool completely, dry thoroughly, and freeze in freezer bags.

GARDENING

Some snap bean plants are bushy, while others form vigorous vines that attach themselves to poles or other supports. "Bush" beans, which are usually planted in rows, rarely grow taller that two feet. Because they mature in less than sixty days, you can have several harvests throughout summer by making successive plantings from mid-spring to early summer. "Pole" beans take longer to mature than bush varieties but are far more prolific, producing pods for six to eight weeks. For a small garden, I find pole varieties the better choice. Whether trained onto rough-hewn poles (six to eight feet high), wooden tripods, ready-made "bean towers," fences, or garden netting, plants take up air space rather than valuable ground space.

Bean seedlings do not transplant well, so it is best to sow seeds directly in place. But wait until the soil has warmed and frost is no longer a danger. Otherwise, the seeds may fail to germinate. Wherever beans are grown for the first time, it is a good idea to add nitrogen-fixing bacteria to the soil. These microbes enable beans and other legumes to absorb needed nitrogen from the atmosphere. Bigger and better harvests generally result.

Whatever supports you choose for your pole beans should be set in place before seeds are sown. Ten-foot poles should be sunk at least two feet into the earth at two- to three-foot intervals. Trellises should be anchored to the ground to prevent toppling in high wind. At planting time I like to apply some fertilizer to get vines off to a quick start. It may be necessary to guide young vines to their supports. I usually wind the plants counterclockwise—the direction they grow naturally—around the bases of the poles.

Dry soil in mid-season may cause developing pods to shrivel, and yanking nearby weeds can easily damage a bean plant's shallow root system. Applying a four-inch layer of mulch is the best solution to both problems.

There is an embarrassment of snap bean riches to choose from. Among the bush beans, I prefer a variety known as Greensleeves, a disease-resistant plant that sports exceptionally dark green pods. This variety and Tenderpod are extra-tender, require less time in cooking or blanching, and are the varieties of choice for serving raw on relish trays. As a contrast I sometimes grow Brittle Wax, with lemon-yellow pods and a milder, sweeter taste than green varieties. An outstanding pole variety is Kentucky Wonder, with green pods up to nine inches long. For purees, in stews, in a gutsy tomato sauce for braising, I like Romano, whose flat pods have a wonderfully meaty texture. Another interesting and relatively new bean is Royal Burgundy. The pods have a beautiful dark purple color that turns green when cooked.

HARVESTING

Pick bush beans after they are firm enough to snap when bent but before the seeds inside become visibly enlarged. Bean plants are brittle, so harvest with a gentle touch. I hold a pod's stem in one hand while plucking off the pod with the other. It is essential to remove any older or undesirable pods if individual plants are to remain productive for a full two to three weeks.

Green Bean, Radish, and Smoked Turkey Salad

For a lighter version you can substitute well-drained unflavored yogurt for the sour cream.

1. Bring plenty of salted water to a boil in a large saucepan, add the beans, and cook until just tender, about 6 to 7 minutes. Drain and immediately run under cold water to stop further cooking. Dry the beans well on paper towels and set aside.

2. In a large serving bowl, combine the vinegar, oil, sour cream, and scallions. Season with salt and pepper and whisk until well blended. Add the beans and radishes and toss gently. Let the salad marinate at room temperature for 1 hour.

3. Fold in the smoked turkey and correct the seasoning. Serve the salad lightly chilled with a crusty French bread.

S E R V E S   6

Salt
1 pound green beans, trimmed
2 tablespoons sherry vinegar
6 tablespoons olive oil
4 tablespoons sour cream
½ cup finely minced scallions
Freshly ground black pepper
2 cups thinly sliced radishes
  (preferably a combination of
  both red and white)
1¼ cups julienne of smoked
  turkey (about 6 ounces)

Warm Green Bean and Shiitake Mushroom Salad

4 ounces slab bacon

4 tablespoons extra-virgin olive oil

12 large fresh shiitake mushrooms, stemmed and thinly sliced

2 large garlic cloves, peeled and thinly sliced

1½ pounds green beans, trimmed and cooked (see page 149)

Salt and freshly ground black pepper

2 to 3 tablespoons sherry vinegar

GARNISH

2 tablespoons finely minced fresh parsley

I often serve this terrific starter as a main course on weekends, sometimes topped with a crisp potato galette (page 332). Two cups of shredded radicchio leaves added to the shiitake and bacon mixture makes for an interesting variation. Serve with a mild Italian Taleggio or creamy Gorgonzola on the side.

1. Blanch the bacon in boiling water for 1 minute. Drain, cool slightly, and cut into small dice.

2. In a large skillet, heat 1 tablespoon of the oil over medium heat. Add the bacon and cook until almost crisp. Transfer to a side dish and reserve.

3. Discard all but 2 tablespoons of fat from the skillet and add the remaining oil. When hot, add the shiitake mushrooms and garlic and sauté quickly until lightly browned. Add the green beans and reserved bacon, season with salt and pepper, and just heat through. Remove the skillet from the heat, add the vinegar, and correct the seasoning. Sprinkle with the minced parsley and serve warm on individual serving plates.

SERVES 6

Sauté of Two Beans with Tomatoes, Onions, and Tuna

As soon as my garden yields enough beans, I make this mixed bean sauté, which is a fast and attractive seasonal starter. It is also delicious served at room temperature as part of a light luncheon. Add a julienne of red and yellow peppers, drizzle with two to three tablespoons of extra-virgin olive oil, and sprinkle with tiny capers.

1. In a large pot of boiling salted water, blanch the green and yellow beans until just tender, 5 to 7 minutes. Immediately drain and run under cold water. Pat dry with paper towels and cut into 1½-inch pieces.

2. In a large heavy skillet, heat the oil over medium-low heat. Add the onion and garlic and cook until soft but not browned, about 10 minutes. Add the tomatoes, season with salt and pepper, and cook until the tomato juices have evaporated, stirring often. The tomatoes should still retain their shape.

3. Add the green beans, wax beans, and tuna and just heat through. Fold in the basil and correct the seasoning. Garnish with the black olives and serve hot, directly from the skillet.

SERVES 4 TO 6

Salt
½ pound green beans, trimmed
½ pound yellow wax beans, trimmed
3 tablespoons extra-virgin olive oil
1 large onion, peeled, quartered, and thinly sliced
2 large garlic cloves, peeled and finely minced
6 ripe plum tomatoes, quartered
Freshly ground black pepper
1 can (6½ ounces) light tuna, packed in oil, drained and flaked
⅓ cup julienne of fresh basil

GARNISH
16 small black oil-cured olives

Salt
1½ pounds green beans
2 tablespoons extra-virgin
   olive oil
1 small dry red chili pepper,
   broken in half
1 large red onion, peeled and
   finely minced
2 large garlic cloves, peeled
   and finely minced
1½ teaspoons imported sweet
   paprika
6 large ripe tomatoes, peeled,
   seeded, and chopped
Freshly ground black pepper
½ cup sour cream

GARNISH
2 tablespoons finely minced
   fresh parsley

Viennese Fricassee of Green Beans in Piquant Tomato Fondue

Here is a classic Viennese side dish. One of its charms is that the beans are usually somewhat overcooked; while they may lose their bright green color, the wonderful blend of flavors more than makes up for the beans' pallid appearance. The entire dish can be made well ahead of time and reheated. I often use a mixture of both yellow wax and green beans and add a small diced green bell pepper to the onion mixture for a delicious flavor. Serve with pan-braised veal scaloppine or a crispy fried or roast chicken.

1. In a large pot of boiling salted water, cook the beans until tender, 5 or 6 minutes. Immediately drain and run under cold water. Pat dry and cut into 1½-inch pieces.

2. In a large heavy skillet, heat the oil over medium low heat. Add the chili pepper, cook until dark, and discard. Add the onion and garlic and cook until soft but not browned. Add the paprika and cook for 1 minute, stirring constantly to avoid burning.

3. Add the tomatoes, season with salt and pepper, and simmer, uncovered, until most of the tomato water has evaporated, about 10 minutes. Add the green beans to the skillet and simmer for 10 minutes longer.

4. Reduce the heat to low, fold in the sour cream, and just heat through. Correct the seasoning, garnish with minced parsley, and serve hot, as an accompaniment to chicken, veal, or pork dishes.

SERVES 4 TO 6

Puree of Green Beans with Parmesan and Dill

Here is a dish that is especially suitable for the large fleshy Romano beans. In this instance it's fine to break the beans before cooking, since they will be pureed. Seasoned with freshly grated Parmesan, some dill, and a nice lump of butter, this is a classic Mediterranean accompaniment to simply grilled or pan-seared seafood. Other summer herbs, particularly basil and mint, can be substituted for the dill. Leftover puree can easily be reheated in the microwave.

1. Bring plenty of salted water to a boil in a large saucepan, add the beans, and cook until very tender, about 12 minutes. Drain well and transfer to a food processor together with the butter, sour cream or yogurt, and dill. Season with salt and pepper and process until smooth. Reserve.

2. Heat the oil in a large heavy skillet over medium heat. Add the flour and cook, stirring constantly, until the mixture turns a hazelnut brown. Immediately whisk in the puree and just heat through. Add the Parmesan and correct the seasoning. Serve hot.

S E R V E S   6   T O   8

Salt
1½ pounds green beans, trimmed and cut into 1-inch pieces
3 tablespoons unsalted butter
¼ cup sour cream or plain yogurt
3 to 4 tablespoons finely minced fresh dill
Freshly ground black pepper
3 tablespoons corn oil
2 tablespoons all-purpose flour
3 tablespoons freshly grated Parmesan cheese

Snap Bean, Basil, and Pastina Soup alla Milanese

Ingredients

2 cups tightly packed fresh basil leaves

5 to 6 tablespoons extra-virgin olive oil

I medium onion, peeled and finely minced

1½ cups diced green beans

1½ cups diced yellow wax beans

6 cups chicken broth, preferably homemade (page 360)

Salt and freshly ground black pepper

½ cup tiny pasta such as pastina, tubettini, or orzo

GARNISH

I cup freshly grated Parmesan cheese

I *love this simple soup. The secret to its success is the fragrant garlicky basil paste and a garnish of excellent freshly grated Parmesan. The soup is equally good served at room temperature or slightly chilled.*

1. Place the basil in a food processor and process until finely minced. With the machine running, add 3 to 4 tablespoons of the oil until a smooth paste is formed. Reserve.

2. Heat the remaining oil in a heavy casserole over medium heat. Add the onion and cook for 5 minutes, stirring often, until soft but not browned.

3. Add the green beans, wax beans, and broth and season with salt and pepper. Bring to a boil, reduce the heat, and simmer for 20 minutes. Add the pasta and cook for 6 to 7 minutes longer or until the pasta is just tender.

4. Whisk in the basil paste and simmer for 2 minutes longer. Correct the seasoning and serve hot in individual soup bowls with a side dish of grated Parmesan.

SERVES 4 TO 6

VARIATION
To turn this soup into a one-dish meal, add 1½ cups shredded cooked chicken or turkey when adding the basil paste.

Green Beans in Pine Nut and Dill Pesto

Asimple string bean salad dressed with excellent olive oil, a drizzle of lemon juice, and a large grinding of black pepper is hard to improve on, but I always feel that beans can take a more assertive dressing as well. Here is one that has become a warm-weather favorite. Serve the salad as part of a picnic lunch, or as a side dish to grilled chicken, salmon, or veal chops. Basil may be substituted for the dill, but it tends to overwhelm the delicate taste of young beans. The salad is best when made a day ahead of time to allow the pesto to penetrate into the beans.

1. Snap off both ends of the green beans. Place the beans in a large casserole with salted water to cover, bring to a boil, and simmer for 5 to 7 minutes or until just tender. Drain well and immediately plunge the beans into a bowl of ice water. When completely cool, again drain and pat dry on paper towels. Transfer the beans to a serving bowl and set aside.

2. Combine the scallions, parsley, dill, and pine nuts in a food processor and process until very finely minced. Add the vinegar, oil, and broth and process until smooth. Season highly with salt and pepper and pour the pesto over the beans, toss gently, and chill for at least 2 hours before serving. Remove the salad from the refrigerator about 20 minutes before serving, toss, and correct the seasoning.

S E R V E S   6   T O   8

1½ pounds green beans
Salt
½ cup finely minced scallions
3 tablespoons finely minced
    fresh parsley
3 tablespoons finely minced
    fresh dill
¼ cup pine nuts
3 tablespoons cider vinegar
5 tablespoons olive oil
3 tablespoons chicken broth,
    preferably homemade
    (page 360)
Freshly ground black pepper

Sautéed Green Beans with Basil and Tomato Concassée

1½ pounds green beans, trimmed

Salt

2 tablespoons unsalted butter

2 tablespoons extra-virgin olive oil

1 large shallot, peeled and finely minced

Freshly ground black pepper

¾ cup Crème Fraîche (page 358)

3 tablespoons chicken broth, preferably homemade (page 360)

2 large ripe tomatoes, unpeeled and cubed

1 cup loosely packed fresh basil leaves, stemmed and cut into a fine julienne

*H*ere is an adaptation of a Tuscan bean dish which I am very fond of. What sets it apart from similar preparations is that the tomatoes retain their shape and remain refreshingly uncooked. When serving the beans as a starter, you may add a shaving of fresh Parmesan or some crumbled goat cheese to each portion. Other herbs such as thyme and tarragon can be substituted for the basil.

1. Drop the beans into plenty of salted boiling water and cook until just tender, about 6 to 7 minutes. Drain well and run under cold water to stop further cooking. Drain again and dry on paper towels.

2. In a large nonstick skillet, melt the butter together with the oil over medium low heat. Add the shallot and cook until soft but not browned, about 1 minute. Add the beans and sauté until nicely glazed. Season with salt and pepper.

3. Add the crème fraîche and broth and simmer for 2 to 3 minutes or until all the liquid has been absorbed by the beans and the beans are nicely coated.

4. Fold in the tomatoes and basil and just heat through. Do not cook further. Correct the seasoning and serve hot or at room temperature.

SERVES 4 TO 5

TOMATOES

OF ALL HOMEGROWN VEGETABLES, TOMATOES ARE THE GARDENER'S supreme delight. Even before I first made a commitment to have a vegetable garden, I grew tomatoes in large pots on a sunny deck. The unmistakable fragrance of a vine-ripened tomato is so dear to anyone who loves this beautiful vegetable that even non-gardeners often find a way to grow two or three tomato plants.

Tomatoes are extremely easygoing garden specimens. The plants require plenty of sunlight and moisture but are otherwise undemanding. Although there is a vast number of tomato varieties to choose from, the average garden needs only about three or four plants of an early and a main-crop variety, and two more plants if you like cherry tomatoes, to ensure a bountiful supply of fruit. If you plan to pack tomatoes and freeze some of your own tomato sauce for winter use, you should also add four or more plants of the Italian plum type.

Even the most adventuresome chef knows it's hard to improve on a platter of sliced ripe tomatoes seasoned with salt, pepper, and perhaps a fruity oil or sprinkling of fresh basil. But tomatoes are the ultimate in versatility, whether cooked or raw. Many recipes call for peeled and seeded tomatoes. I find the best method of peeling is to cut four or five fine incisions lengthwise into each tomato and then to drop the fruit into boiling water. In thirty seconds, the peels will have separated from the flesh. Next core the fruit. Then to seed, cut the tomatoes in half crosswise, taking care not to squash them. You will see the seeds in their neat compartments. Scoop out the seeds with a teaspoon and season the flesh with coarse salt. Place the pulp in a colander to drain for thirty minutes to an hour before cooking.

Tomatoes, whether whole, quartered, or crushed, are among the easiest vegetables to can, and canning is a wonderful way to store a bountiful harvest. When pressed for time, I freeze tomatoes by placing them, whole and unpeeled, in plastic bags; once defrosted, I pass them through a tomato press. Italian plum tomatoes are best for this, and the best overall for sauce since they are more pulpy and less watery.

At the very end of the season you may find yourself with some green tomatoes, both round and plum types. Aside from pickling, green tomatoes are delicious sautéed in butter and enriched with a little cream and Parmesan. They can be dipped into a batter and deep-fried, or stewed together with eggplant with a touch of sliced garlic and a sprinkling of parsley.

More and more gardeners and chefs are experimenting not only with the popular red cherry tomatoes but with small yellow and orange varieties, which have a somewhat meatier texture and are often sweeter. Aside from lending their sweet juicy taste and lovely shape to many salads, these small tomatoes make an excellent hot vegetable. I often sauté cherry tomatoes in olive oil with a touch of garlic plus a sprinkling of fresh basil and parsley. They can also be tossed into a mixed vegetable fricassee and are delicious served as an hors d'oeuvre filled with tuna salad. Red, yellow, or orange varieties all work equally well in a traditional shish kebab.

STORAGE

Keep not-quite ripe tomatoes at room temperature. If fully mature, refrigerate them in a bowl or the vegetable bin, not a plastic bag. Ripe tomatoes will keep refrigerated for up to ten days. For best flavor, always bring tomatoes back to room temperature before serving. When I have a surplus, I stew them with some olive oil and minced shallots or make the Classic Plum Tomato Sauce (page 159), which keeps for a week and freezes well.

GARDENING

Starting tomato seeds early indoors is standard gardening practice everywhere in the country, since the plants need lots of time to produce a good crop before fall frost. At outdoor planting time, the ideal transplant is no more than eight inches tall and bright green in color, and has a firm and stocky stem as well as a dense root system. If in the past your tomato seedlings turned out weak, spindly, and pale, you either did not provide sufficient light or started the seeds too early. Wait until about six weeks prior to the last expected frost before sowing tomato seeds indoors and follow the spacing requirements specified on seed packets.

There are two main types of garden tomatoes: determinate and indeterminate. Determinate varieties stop growing when fruit sets on the terminal bud. The plants are generally fairly compact and bush-like, and so they're favored by some gardeners with limited space. Since they tend to ripen fruit over a shorter period, they are also chosen by many gardeners in short-season areas and those who grow tomatoes primarily for canning. Determinate varieties are best grown in cages and left unpruned, so they're also a bit easier to grow.

The most popular varieties by far, including Early Girl, Big Girl, and Big Boy, are indeterminate. Indeterminate varieties produce vigorous vines that continue to grow and bear fruit until they are killed by fall frost. The plants often grow to seven or eight feet and, although they can be allowed to sprawl on the ground (or preferably on a mulch), most people prefer to grow them trained on strong stakes or wire cages.

I've had many discussions with gardening friends about whether or not tomato plants should be pruned. According to horticulturists, indeterminate varieties grown in cages may be left unpruned, while plants supported by stakes are best pruned to one or two main stems. This means you need to remove all side stems (called suckers) growing from the leaf nodes. There are advantages to either method. I find that the full, dense foliage of my caged plants shields the fruit from scalding midday sun, but the staking-and-pruning method often yields larger fruits.

When you choose tomato varieties, consider also the relative earliness. Varieties range from Burpee's Pixie Hybrid, which yields ripe tomatoes starting only fifty-two days from transplanting time, to the large beefsteak varieties, for which you'll have to wait eighty days. If you live where the growing season is short, go for the early tomatoes.

Another hotly debated consideration is hybrid versus open-pollinated varieties. Although there are some wonderful open-pollinated varieties such as Delicious and the cherry-size Gardener's Delight, the hybrids, by and large, are more vigorous, more disease-resistant, and better adapted to a wide range of growing conditions, and they yield larger crops.

In the end, I make my choice based on two criteria: how I'll use them and how they taste. Personally, I enjoy growing and serving salad tomatoes such as Early Girl Hybrid, which bears delicious, firm, average-size fruit. For sauces and stir-fries, I prefer a plum tomato such as Roma VF, which offers a meaty texture and few seeds. And in late summer, I love to pick and slice a huge, juicy, vine-ripened Supersteak fruit, a luscious meal in itself.

HARVESTING

The very best-tasting tomato is one that is vine-ripened, picked when the entire fruit is in full blush. (Tomatoes ripen from the bottom upward.) Gently lift by hand until the fruit stem snaps. Toward the end of the season, I sometimes pick tomatoes partially ripe and then let them finish ripening indoors as a precaution against early frost. Contrary to common belief, tomatoes must never be placed to ripen in the sun. They do best in a dark, dry, cool (60 to 70°F.) space. Covering them with a light layer of newspaper encourages tomatoes to ripen more quickly.

Classic Plum Tomato Sauce

For six months out of the year I tell myself that the tomato sauce I make with canned tomatoes is almost as good as what I make with fresh. But as soon as I get enough ripe tomatoes to make fresh sauce, I realize there is no substitute for the real thing. Remember that the sauce is equally good tossed into a quick risotto or as a "bed" for eggs fried in olive oil or goat-cheese crostini.

1. In a large heavy casserole, heat the olive oil over medium low heat. Add the onions and garlic and cook until soft and lightly browned, about 5 minutes.

2. Add the tomatoes, sugar, thyme, and oregano, season with salt and pepper, and simmer, stirring often, for 30 to 35 minutes, or until the sauce becomes thick.

3. Transfer to the workbowl of a food processor in batches if necessary and puree until smooth. Taste and correct the seasoning. Cool completely, cover, and chill. The sauce will keep 6 to 7 days in the refrigerator or up to 2 weeks in the freezer.

MAKES ABOUT 4 CUPS

NOTE: If you use a food mill to puree the sauce instead of a food processor, you can eliminate the step of peeling and seeding the tomatoes. This is especially convenient when making sauce in quantity.

VARIATION
In the fall and winter, for the fresh plum tomatoes, substitute 2 cans (2 pounds 3 ounces each) Italian plum tomatoes, drained and chopped. Always reserve some of the canned tomato liquid to add to the sauce if it becomes too thick too quickly.

---

3 tablespoons extra-virgin olive oil

2 medium onions, peeled and finely minced

2 large garlic cloves, peeled and finely minced

4 pounds ripe plum tomatoes, peeled, seeded, and chopped (see Note)

1 teaspoon sugar

2 tablespoons fresh thyme leaves

2 tablespoons fresh oregano leaves

Salt and freshly ground black pepper

Tomato and Shallot Sauce

4 pounds ripe plum tomatoes,
   peeled, seeded, and
   quartered
Coarse salt
¼ cup extra-virgin olive oil
½ cup finely minced shallots
3 large garlic cloves, peeled
   and finely minced
1 tablespoon fresh thyme
   leaves
2 tablespoons fresh marjoram
   leaves
Freshly ground black pepper

Just as some people cannot be without ice cream in their freezer, I *am* almost never without a jar of this delicious tomato and shallot sauce. *What* do I use it for? Everything. A couple of tablespoons add succulent *flavor* to the pan juices of a roast leg of lamb, and a spoonful atop a tuna *or* lamb burger adds zest. It is also wonderful when added to a sauté of *roasted* summer vegetables. You can extend the shelf life of the tomato *essence* by topping it with one-half inch of fruity olive oil and placing the *jar* in the coldest part of the refrigerator for up to two weeks. Freezing it *makes* it watery, but it can be cooked down again without any serious loss *of* taste. Canning is yet another alternative.

1. Place the tomatoes in a large colander, sprinkle with coarse salt, and let drain for 4 hours. Coarsely chop the tomatoes and set aside.

2. In a large heavy saucepan, heat the oil over medium heat. Add the shallots and garlic and cook for 1 to 2 minutes without browning. Add the tomatoes, thyme, and marjoram, season with salt and pepper, and cook for 15 minutes, stirring often.

3. Reduce the heat and simmer, partially covered, for 40 to 45 minutes or until very thick, stirring often. Taste and correct the seasoning.

4. Place in a tightly sealed jar, top with ½ inch of olive oil, and refrigerate for a week or two, or ladle hot into pint jars and process in a hot water bath for 10 minutes and store immediately.

MAKES ABOUT 4 CUPS

Vine-Ripened Tomato and Rice Soup with Herbed Crème Fraîche

Although most people associate fresh tomato soups with the cooking of the Mediterranean, it is this Central European recipe that I like the most. Personally I prefer garnishing the soup with dill rather than the more predictable basil or cilantro, which gives the soup a more Mexican flavor; but all three herbs are good with it. The keys to success are very ripe, sweet fresh tomatoes and making sure to cook the soup until it is reduced to the right consistency. Leftover tomato soup freezes well, but it does become somewhat watery and will have to be cooked down and have the seasoning adjusted.

1. In a large casserole, melt the butter over medium heat. Add the onions and garlic and cook until soft but not brown, about 5 minutes. Add the thyme, marjoram, parsley, tomatoes, and broth, season with salt and pepper, and simmer, covered, for 40 to 45 minutes.

2. Transfer the soup to a food processor and puree in batches until smooth. Return the puree to the casserole, add the rice, and simmer for 5 minutes.

3. Just before serving, whisk in the crème fraîche or sour cream and the dill and just heat through. Correct the seasoning and serve hot.

SERVES 6

NOTE: This soup is equally delicious served slightly chilled. In this case, substitute yogurt for the crème fraîche or sour cream called for in the recipe.

3 tablespoons unsalted butter
2 medium onions, peeled, quartered, and thinly sliced
1 large garlic clove, peeled and finely minced
1 tablespoon fresh thyme leaves
1 tablespoon fresh marjoram leaves
1 large sprig of fresh parsley
4 large ripe tomatoes, peeled, seeded, and chopped
4 cups chicken broth, preferably homemade (page 360)
Salt and freshly ground black pepper
1/3 cup cooked rice
1/2 cup Crème Fraîche (page 358) or sour cream
1/4 cup finely minced fresh dill

Char-Grilled Lamb Chops with Garlic–Herb Rub and Tomato Essence

2 large garlic cloves, peeled
  and mashed
1 tablespoon fresh marjoram
  leaves, finely minced, or 2
  teaspoons dried
1 tablespoon fresh thyme
  leaves, finely minced, or 2
  teaspoons dried
1 tablespoon fresh rosemary
  leaves, finely minced, or 2
  teaspoons dried
2 teaspoons imported sweet
  paprika
2 tablespoons Dijon mustard
8 loin lamb chops, about 1 inch
  thick
1¼ cups Tomato and Shallot
  Sauce (page 160)
¼ cup julienne of fresh basil
  leaves
Coarse salt and freshly ground
  black pepper

GARNISH
Tiny leaves of fresh basil

I love these flavor-packed chops and can't seem to serve them too often. I always look for "baby" rib chops about half an inch thick and cut off most of the fat along the bone. Once grilled or pan-seared the chops can then be easily picked up by hand, which somehow makes them even more delectable. Serve with a mixed summer salad alongside and perhaps a plateful of grilled vegetables.

1. Combine the garlic, herbs, paprika, and mustard in a small bowl, mix well, and rub the paste on both sides of the lamb chops. Set aside to marinate at room temperature for 30 minutes.

2. While the chops are marinating, prepare the charcoal grill and heat the tomato sauce in a small saucepan over low heat. Add the basil and correct the seasoning. Keep warm.

3. When the coals are white-hot, sprinkle the chops with coarse salt and black pepper and place them on the grill directly above the coals. Grill for 3 to 5 minutes per side or until nicely browned and medium rare.

4. Spoon a little of the tomato sauce on each of 4 individual serving plates, top each portion with 2 grilled lamb chops, and serve hot, garnished with tiny basil leaves.

SERVES 4

Spicy Catalan Gazpacho

Every region of Spain has its own version of this popular summer soup. This flavorful and somewhat spicy gazpacho is my all-time favorite. You may add the traditional garnishes of minced onions, peppers, and cucumbers or serve it with a side bowl of garlic-flavored yogurt and a sprinkling of fresh cilantro.

1. Combine the oil and vinegar in a mixing bowl, add the bread, and toss lightly until the bread has absorbed the dressing. Set aside.

2. Puree the soup in two batches: For each batch, combine half of the cucumbers, tomatoes, jalapeño pepper, onion, garlic, and soaked bread in a food processor or blender and process until smooth. Add half of the tomato juice and half of the chicken broth, if using, and process until well blended.

3. Combine the two batches and whisk until well blended. Season with salt and pepper and chill for at least 6 hours before serving. Serve the soup in individual bowls, sprinkled with a little minced parsley, and pass the vegetable garnishes separately.

SERVES 6 TO 8

¼ cup extra-virgin olive oil
¼ cup sherry vinegar
4 thin slices day-old French bread, cubed and lightly toasted
2 pickling cucumbers, peeled, seeded, and diced
8 large ripe tomatoes (about 3½ to 4 pounds), peeled, seeded, and coarsely chopped
2 teaspoons finely minced jalapeño pepper
½ cup finely minced red onion
2 large garlic cloves, peeled and mashed
2 cups fresh tomato juice
Optional: 1 cup chicken broth, preferably homemade (page 360)
Salt and freshly ground black pepper

GARNISH
4 tablespoons finely minced fresh parsley
1 cup finely minced red onion
1 cup finely diced green bell pepper
1 cup finely diced cucumber

Late-Summer Vegetable Paella

2 tablespoons extra-virgin
    olive oil
I small dry red chili pepper,
    broken
I large onion, peeled,
    quartered, and thinly sliced
2 large garlic cloves, peeled
    and finely minced
1½ teaspoons imported sweet
    paprika
I tablespoon fresh thyme
    leaves
I medium zucchini, trimmed
    and diced
I large red bell pepper, cored,
    seeded, and thinly sliced
I large green bell pepper,
    cored, seeded, and thinly
    sliced
4 large ripe tomatoes, peeled,
    seeded, and chopped
Salt and freshly ground black
    pepper
1¼ cups Italian rice, preferably
    Arborio
3 cups chicken broth,
    preferably homemade
    (page 360)
GARNISH
Finely minced fresh parsley
Lemon wedges

Most people associate paella with chicken, seafood, and sausages, but this Basque-inspired dish allows the vegetables to shine. The paella is good served hot right out of the skillet, but it is even better when the flavors are left to develop for several hours. The dish can be reheated slowly either in a low oven or the microwave. Leftovers can be used as a stuffing for cabbage leaves or small green bell peppers. You can also turn the paella into a rice salad by adding to it a sherry vinegar and olive oil vinaigrette and letting the flavors develop at room temperature for an hour or two.

1. In a large, deep cast-iron skillet, heat the olive oil over medium heat. Add the chili pepper, onion, and garlic and cook, stirring often, until the onion is soft but not browned.

2. Add the paprika, thyme, zucchini, peppers, and tomatoes, season with salt and pepper, and simmer, covered, for 15 minutes.

3. Add the rice and stir to coat well with the tomato mixture. Add the chicken broth and simmer over low heat, covered, for 25 to 30 minutes or until the rice is tender. Taste and correct the seasoning. Garnish with minced parsley and lemon wedges and serve hot, directly from the skillet, accompanied by a well-seasoned green salad.

SERVES 4 TO 6

Smoked Mozzarella, Prosciutto, and Beefsteak Tomato Melts

Open-faced melts are a great and simple solution for summer lunches. Of course, the quality of the ingredients does make a big difference. Dense peasant bread, good smoked mozzarella, and meaty sweet tomatoes are the key ingredients. You can vary the melts by using smoked ham or turkey rather than prosciutto and by drizzling them with a little basil vinaigrette (see page 174).

1. Cut each tomato crosswise into ¼-inch slices, about 12 slices per tomato; do not include end slices. Set aside. Cut each slice of mozzarella in half and reserve.

2. Preheat the broiler.

3. On each of 4 individual ovenproof serving plates or gratin dishes, alternate 6 slices of tomato with 6 slices of mozzarella, in an overlapping pattern, to form a circle. Drizzle each portion with 1 teaspoon olive oil, sprinkle with a little coarse salt, pepper, and ½ teaspoon thyme, and broil until the cheese is just heated through but not melting.

4. Remove from the broiler and drizzle each with the remaining oil. Drape 2 slices of prosciutto over each portion, garnish with 3 basil leaves, and serve at once with a crusty peasant bread.

S E R V E S   4

2 large ripe beefsteak tomatoes
8 ounces smoked mozzarella,
   cut crosswise into 12 slices
   about ¼ inch thick
8 teaspoons extra-virgin
   olive oil
Coarse salt and freshly ground
   black pepper
2 teaspoons fresh thyme leaves
8 thin slices prosciutto

GARNISH
12 fresh basil leaves

Ripe Tomato Vinaigrette

3 large ripe tomatoes, peeled,
  seeded, and chopped
1½ tablespoons finely minced
  red onion
2 tablespoons sherry vinegar
½ cup extra-virgin olive oil
Salt and freshly ground black
  pepper

Since tomatoes are so delicious simply dressed with oil and vinegar, using them as the basis for a zesty vinaigrette is a natural progression. Use the dressing as a sauce for grilled fish and shellfish or vegetables, for sliced mozzarella, or for an open-faced melt. The tomato vinaigrette is also delicious when made somewhat spicy with a touch of minced jalapeño pepper or a few drops of Tabasco sauce.

1. In a blender combine the tomatoes, onion, and vinegar and blend until smooth. With the machine running, slowly add the oil until emulsified.

2. Strain the vinaigrette through a fine sieve into a bowl, season with salt and pepper, and serve at room temperature.

MAKES 2 CUPS

Tomato and Avocado Salsa

2 large ripe tomatoes,
  unpeeled, seeded and diced
2 tablespoons finely minced red
  onion
1 medium garlic clove, peeled
  and mashed
1 to 2 teaspoons finely minced
  jalapeño pepper
Juice of 1 lime
4 to 5 tablespoons extra-virgin
  olive oil
3 tablespoons tiny fresh
  cilantro leaves
1 small avocado, peeled, pitted,
  and diced
Salt and freshly ground black
  pepper

In the last couple of years the word salsa has found its way into every aspect of menu writing. Now even fruit salsas of every description are common. However I still think that a true salsa should be reminiscent of the original, in which tomato plays a key role. I very much like this version including avocados. Be sure to season the salsa assertively and serve it as soon as possible, since avocados do not take well to advance preparations and will turn an unattractive dark color in a short time.

Combine all ingredients in a mixing bowl, season with salt and pepper, and toss gently. Set aside at room temperature for 30 minutes. Correct the seasoning and use in desired recipe or as a garnish to omelettes or grilled fish and poultry.

SERVES 4

Baked Tomatoes with Brown Sugar and Ginger Topping

Until I sampled these delicious sweet baked tomatoes, I had only an intellectual awareness that, as a fruit, they would take well to a sweet preparation. In fact, they are superb, especially when teamed with brown sugar and butter. I like to serve the tomatoes as a side dish to a grilled leg of lamb or grilled chicken, or for lunch with a soft scrambled herb omelette laced with some slightly aged goat cheese. The tomatoes can be prepared ahead of time, but they are at their best when served fresh out of the oven.

1. Preheat the oven to 400°F. Place the tomatoes, cut side up, in a shallow baking dish.

2. In a small bowl, combine the brown sugar and ginger and toss well. Sprinkle each tomato half with 1 teaspoon of the breadcrumbs. Divide the brown sugar mixture evenly and sprinkle on top of the breadcrumbs.

3. Place one piece of butter on each tomato half and season with salt and pepper. Bake for 10 minutes or until hot and bubbly. Serve hot or at room temperature.

SERVES 6

6 medium-size ripe tomatoes, cut in half crosswise
4 tablespoons dark brown sugar
1 teaspoon ground ginger
4 tablespoons unflavored breadcrumbs
6 tablespoons (¾ stick) unsalted butter, cut into 12 pieces
Coarse salt and freshly ground black pepper

10–12 pounds ripe tomatoes
Salt
Sprigs of fresh basil

Canned Tomatoes

Canning is the ideal way to preserve tomatoes for use through-out the colder months; use the canned tomatoes in sauces, soups, and other cooked dishes just as you would store-bought.

"Putting up" produce from the garden is a homey tradition that is well worth reviving, and it is not complicated to do. Just keep these few simple rules in mind when canning food. Sterilize jars, lids, and rings in boiling water each time before using. Don't overfill jars; always allow at least $1/4$-inch headspace. Wipe the jar rims carefully, then screw lids on fairly loosely. Place filled jars on a rack in a large kettle of boiling water that covers the jars by at least 2 inches, and don't overcrowd the kettle. Process the jars as directed once the water returns to a full boil. When processed, allow the jars to cool, then check the lids to make sure they have sealed and tighten.

Due to their high acid content, canned tomatoes must be processed for a relatively long period, but many of the pickles and relishes in this book can be canned successfully in a much shorter time (see the individual recipes for precise processing times).

1. Peel and core the tomatoes and combine in a large bowl.

2. Fill hot sterilized 1-quart canning jars each with $2\frac{1}{2}$ to 3 pounds tomatoes, pressing lightly to yield juice and fill in the empty spaces. Leave a $1/4$-inch headspace. Run a spatula down the sides of the jars to free trapped air bubbles.

3. Add 1 teaspoon salt and a large sprig of basil to each jar. Seal. Process in a boiling water bath for 45 minutes. The jar seals need to pop. Remove from the bath, check the seals, and let cool completely. Store in a cool place. They will keep for up to 1 year.

MAKES 3 TO 4 QUARTS

ZUCCHINI AND SUMMER SQUASH

THE PROLIFIC WAYS OF THE ZUCCHINI PLANT ARE LEGENDARY. IN FACT, IF gardeners cite any problem with this irrepressible vegetable, it is finding enough takers for the inevitable surplus.

Personally, I never tire of zucchini and the other types of summer squash. With their light, unassertive flavors, they are among the most versatile of vegetables. Sautéed, fried, steamed, pureed, stuffed, served cold in salads or even raw, they lend themselves to endless preparations, one of which is my all-time favorite vegetable dish: a plateful of zucchini slivers fried to crisp perfection. Yellow crookneck and straightneck types, and scalloped, round pattypans, offer delightful variations of shapes and colors for the summer kitchen.

Summer squash is so productive that it is best to limit yourself to just a few plants of each of your two or three favorite types. Much like cucumbers, summer squash does not allow even a single day of laziness in picking; one day the fruit is just short of perfect size, and the next thing you know, a giant squash lies heavily on the ground. Some gardeners feel a certain pride at being able to grow giant specimens of summer squash, not realizing that as the fruit gains in size so will it begin to lose its flavor. Now, with the new emphasis on smaller and younger vegetables, many gardening cooks are discovering that great tastes come in small packages.

My favorite time to pick summer squash is at the "baby" stage. Harvested at this prime moment, zucchini and yellow squash offer crisp, distinctive flavors rather than the watery, bland tastes associated with the mature fruit. For sautéing, braising, or for use in salads, I pick the zucchini at no more than four inches in length, at which point they are still wonderfully sweet.

Baby squashes can be picked so young that their yellow flowers are still attached. But be careful; bees love to nestle inside the blooms, so be sure to pick them in the morning when the flowers are open. Italians have a wonderful way of stuffing the flowers with diced mozzarella, minced herbs, and some anchovies or prosciutto. The flowers are then dipped in a light batter and deep-fried. This makes for one of the most tantalizing appetizers of the summer season.

Due to their high water content, summer squashes should be salted and allowed to drain for certain preparations. I always salt grated zucchini, letting it dry over a colander for an hour or two. Sliced zucchini need salting only if they are large or are to be incorporated into a custard or egg batter, where excess moisture may change the texture of the dish. For salads and stuffed squash, it is best to blanch the zucchini first to remove some of the raw crunchiness while retaining the crispness without overcooking. Both yellow and green squashes make delectable pickles.

STORAGE

Refrigerate summer squash in plastic bags. It will keep well for three to five days.

GARDENING

Unlike many winter squashes which grow along sprawling ten-foot-long vines, most summer squashes grow on bush-like plants suitable even for small gardens. Like the closely related cucumber, squash plants are extremely sensitive to cold and should not be set out until the soil warms up and all danger of frost has passed. Squash have finicky root systems and do not transplant very well. Therefore, sow seeds directly in the garden rather than indoors first. If you must use transplants, protect them with Hotkaps immediately after planting.

Some people say it is easier to keep squash seedlings properly moist when grown in "hills," or mounds, but I have had good luck planting them in rows. Either way, it is imperative to condition the soil with a generous amount of well-rotted manure or compost.

Summer squashes are among the crops ideally suited for growing on plastic mulch. The plastic keeps soil moisture in and weeds out and protects the fruit against insects and rotting. I usually apply mulch in between the rows soon after thinning my seedlings. Even with mulch, the plants are subject to destructive borers as well as to mildew and "wilt" diseases. Where space permits, sow a second crop by midsummer to help guarantee harvests until frost. Do not plant squash in the same spots where previous plantings have been affected by wilt.

For excellent flavor, it is difficult to surpass Burpee Hybrid Zucchini. The bush-like plants yield an abundance of medium-green fruit starting just fifty days after planting. Pic-N-Pic Hybrid, a golden yellow crookneck squash, also takes fifty days and, as the name suggests, it is extremely prolific. Be sure to pick crooknecks while they are young and small, before the "handles" get hard. Another fine addition to the garden is Butterstick Hybrid, a new yellow straightneck type. It has a somewhat nuttier taste than zucchini and a firmer, drier texture.

HARVESTING

Always use pruning shears or a sharp knife rather than twisting squash fruit off by hand. Continuous picking promotes nonstop production.

Stir-Fry of Green and Yellow Zucchini with Garlic and Basil

3 medium-size green zucchini, trimmed

2 medium-size yellow zucchini, trimmed

3 tablespoons extra-virgin olive oil

Salt and freshly ground black pepper

2 large garlic cloves, peeled and finely minced

6 large fresh basil leaves, cut into a fine julienne

Fresh garden zucchini need little in terms of embellishment—the less done to them, the better. When cooking medium zucchini, I prefer removing most of their seedy core, which I find makes them watery. But you can omit this step when you are using tiny or small squash.

1. Cut both zucchini in half lengthwise and, with a grapefruit spoon, scoop out the seedy center, as if seeding a cucumber. Then cut crosswise into 1/4-inch slices.

2. In a large heavy skillet, heat the oil over medium high heat. Add both zucchini, season with salt and pepper, and sauté quickly, for 2 minutes or until lightly browned.

3. Reduce the heat, add the garlic and basil, and cook for 1 minute longer; the zucchini should still be crisp. Correct the seasoning and serve hot.

SERVES 4 TO 5

Sweet-and-Sour Summer Squash with Pine Nuts and Raisins

I still remember the first time I sampled this dish. It was at *Mamma Gina, a popular Florentine trattoria. The paper-thin zucchini were still somewhat crispy, and the addition of raisins and creamy pine nuts made the dish truly memorable. I have since incorporated it into my summer repertoire, and as a family we never seem to tire of it. The sauté goes nicely with pan-seared fish steaks such as swordfish, salmon, tuna, and mako. But I like it best of all as a side dish to grilled quail or a simply roasted squab. Leftovers are also good served at room temperature as part of a picnic.*

1. Combine the vinegar and sugar in a small bowl and set aside. Dredge the zucchini lightly in flour, shaking off the excess.

2. Sauté the zucchini in two batches. For each batch, heat 2½ tablespoons of the oil in a large nonstick skillet over medium high heat. Add half the zucchini and sauté until nicely browned. Remove with a slotted spoon to a side dish, season with salt and pepper, and reserve.

3. Wipe the skillet clean and add the remaining 1 tablespoon of oil over medium low heat. Add the pine nuts and cook for 1 to 2 minutes or until lightly browned. Add the garlic and cook for 30 seconds longer. Return the zucchini to the skillet together with the vinegar–sugar mixture and raisins and simmer, covered, until just heated through. Sprinkle with the parsley and serve hot directly from the skillet.

SERVES 4

2 tablespoons red wine vinegar
2 teaspoons sugar
4 to 5 medium zucchini, trimmed and cut lengthwise into ¼-inch strips
All-purpose flour for dredging
6 tablespoons olive oil
Salt and freshly ground black pepper
2 tablespoons pine nuts
3 medium garlic cloves, peeled and finely minced
2 tablespoons golden raisins
GARNISH
2 tablespoons finely minced fresh parsley

Zucchini and Plum Tomato Salad in Basil Vinaigrette

⅓ cup extra-virgin olive oil

⅓ cup loosely packed fresh basil leaves

2 tablespoons red wine vinegar

1 large garlic clove, peeled and mashed

Salt and freshly ground black pepper

1 small red onion, peeled and thinly sliced

½ cup finely diced red bell pepper

6 small zucchini

6 ripe plum tomatoes, quartered

GARNISH

2 tablespoons finely minced fresh parsley

Here is a lovely and refreshing marriage between two of summer's superstars. It is unusual in that the zucchini are cooked whole, then sliced for serving. I often substitute plump ripe cherry tomatoes for the plum tomatoes and use both green and yellow zucchini, which adds both color and a firmer texture to the salad.

1. Combine the oil, basil, vinegar, and garlic in a food processor or blender, season with salt and pepper, and process until smooth. Transfer the vinaigrette to a large serving bowl, stir in the onion and red pepper, and set aside.

2. Bring salted water to a boil in a large saucepan, add the whole zucchini, and blanch for 5 minutes or until barely tender; do not overcook. Immediately run under cold water to stop further cooking. Dry well on paper towels and cool completely.

3. Cut the zucchini in half lengthwise and then crosswise into ½-inch slices. Add the zucchini to the vinaigrette, toss well, and let marinate at room temperature for 1 hour. Taste and correct the seasoning, adding a large grinding of pepper. Arrange the plum tomatoes on top of the salad, garnish with parsley, and serve lightly chilled.

SERVES 6

Pilaf of Zucchini with Tomatoes, Shallots, and Parmesan

The mild tang of zucchini greatly enhances this simple rice pilaf. With the additions of garden-ripe tomatoes and excellent Parmesan, you have the makings of a risotto-style dish that is most satisfying. Serve the pilaf as a first course or as a side dish to grilled or baked salmon.

1. In a heavy 3-quart casserole, heat the oil over medium heat. Add the zucchini and sauté quickly until lightly browned. Remove with a slotted spoon to a side dish and reserve.

2. Add the butter to the casserole and when melted, add the shallots and garlic and cook for 1 minute without browning. Add the tomatoes and oregano, season with salt and pepper, and cook, stirring often, until the juices have evaporated.

3. Add the rice and toss well to coat with the tomato mixture. Add 2½ cups of the broth and simmer, covered, over low heat for 25 to 30 minutes; if the rice absorbs all of the broth before becoming tender, add the remaining broth and continue cooking.

4. Fold in the reserved zucchini together with the Parmesan, parsley, and basil. Correct the seasoning and serve hot.

SERVES 4 TO 6

2 tablespoons olive oil

2 small zucchini, trimmed and cut into ½-inch cubes

2½ tablespoons unsalted butter

2 medium shallots, peeled and finely minced

2 large garlic cloves, peeled and finely minced

2 medium-size ripe tomatoes, peeled, seeded, and chopped

1 teaspoon dried oregano or 1 tablespoon minced fresh oregano

Salt and freshly ground black pepper

1¼ cups Italian rice, preferably Arborio

2½ to 3 cups chicken broth, preferably homemade (page 360)

⅓ cup freshly grated Parmesan cheese

¼ cup finely minced fresh parsley

¼ cup finely minced fresh basil

Zucchini and Orzo Soup with Lemon and Mint

Ingredients

⅓ cup heavy cream

2 extra-large egg yolks

Juice of 1 large lemon

4 tablespoons (½ stick) unsalted butter

1 large onion, peeled and finely minced

2 tablespoons all-purpose flour

4 medium zucchini, trimmed and cubed

Salt and freshly ground white pepper

5 to 6 cups chicken broth, preferably homemade (page 360)

¼ cup imported orzo or other tiny pasta

2 tablespoons finely minced fresh mint

GARNISH

1 medium zucchini, skin only, cut into a fine julienne

Here is one of my favorite summer soups. The piquant taste of lemon beautifully complements the subtle flavor of summer squash. For a variation you may flavor the soup with either fresh tarragon or cilantro. Serve it as a starter, followed by a pasta dish or shish kebabs of swordfish accompanied by the Zucchini and Plum Tomato Salad on page 174.

1. In a small bowl combine the cream, yolks, and lemon juice and whisk until well blended. Reserve.

2. Melt the butter over medium low heat in a large casserole. Add the onion and cook, partially covered, until soft but not browned, about 8 minutes. Stir in the flour and cook for 1 to 2 minutes without browning. Add the cubed zucchini, season with salt and pepper, and simmer, covered, for 10 minutes. Add 5 cups of the broth and simmer for 15 minutes longer or until the zucchini is very soft.

3. Strain the soup and return the broth to the casserole. Transfer the vegetables to a food processor and puree until smooth. Whisk the puree into the broth, add the orzo, and cook over low heat until the orzo is quite tender, about 7 to 8 minutes.

4. Whisk in the reserved cream mixture and just heat through. Do not let the soup come to a boil or the yolks will curdle. Add the mint and julienne of zucchini and correct the seasoning. If the soup seems too thick, add some of the remaining broth. Serve hot.

SERVES 6

NOTE: The soup can be made ahead of time to the point of adding the cream mixture, which should be added just before serving.

Fusilli with Shrimp, Zucchini, and Goat Cheese

Whenever I am asked what is my favorite summer dish, I always turn to this pasta dish, in which the best of summer flavors come together in one terrific zesty combination. For a variation, you may substitute diced sautéed chicken breasts or sautéed bay scallops for the shrimp—or simply omit the shrimp for a very satisfying vegetarian variation.

1. Heat 2 tablespoons of the oil in a large heavy skillet over medium high heat. Add the zucchini and sauté quickly until lightly browned. Transfer to a side dish with a slotted spoon and reserve.

2. Add the remaining 2 tablespoons of oil to the skillet and when hot, add the chili peppers and cook until dark. Remove and discard. Add the shrimp to the hot chili oil and sauté quickly until they turn bright pink, just 4 or 5 minutes. Transfer the shrimp to a cutting board, dice, and set aside.

3. Reduce the heat, add the garlic, ginger, and shallots, and cook for 1 minute without browning. Add the tomatoes, oregano, and thyme, season with salt and pepper, and simmer, covered, until most of the tomato juices have evaporated, about 20 to 25 minutes. Stir in the zucchini and shrimp and remove from the heat.

4. Bring plenty of salted water to a boil in a large casserole, add the fusilli, and cook until just tender "al dente." Drain well and return the pasta to the casserole.

5. Add the tomato and zucchini mixture together with the basil and goat cheese and toss lightly with the pasta; the goat cheese should just be warm, not melted. Taste and correct the seasoning. Transfer to a serving bowl, garnish with the minced parsley, and serve at once with a crusty loaf of French bread.

SERVES 4 TO 5

4 tablespoons extra-virgin olive oil

3 small zucchini, quartered lengthwise and then cut crosswise into thin slices

1 to 2 small dry red chili peppers, broken in half

½ pound medium shrimp, peeled

2 large garlic cloves, peeled and finely minced

1½ teaspoons finely minced fresh ginger

2 large shallots, peeled and finely minced

4 large ripe tomatoes, peeled, seeded, and chopped

2 teaspoons fresh oregano leaves

2 teaspoons fresh thyme leaves

Salt and freshly ground black pepper

½ pound imported dried fusilli

¼ cup finely minced fresh basil

1 cup mild goat cheese, crumbled

GARNISH

2 tablespoons finely minced fresh parsley

Charcoal-Grilled Summer Squash with Plum Tomatoes

4 tablespoons olive oil

2 medium zucchini, trimmed and cut on the diagonal into 1/3-inch slices

2 medium-size yellow squash, trimmed and cut on the diagonal into 1/3-inch slices

6 to 8 ripe plum tomatoes, preferably Roma, cored and cut crosswise into 1/3-inch slices

2 large garlic cloves, peeled and thinly sliced

12 tiny fresh basil leaves

Coarse salt and freshly ground black pepper

This grilled gratin is cooked using the indirect method of grilling. It is sensational hot off the grill, but it's equally delicious when served at room temperature as part of a picnic, garnished with small black oil-cured olives, pitted and cut in half. The vegetable mixture is the perfect complement to grilled lamb dishes.

1. Prepare a charcoal fire with the briquettes mounded on one side only.

2. Brush the inside of a 2-quart gratin dish or baking dish with 1 tablespoon of the olive oil. Alternate the zucchini, yellow squash, and tomato slices in the dish in tight overlapping rows. Tuck the slices of garlic and basil leaves among the rows, sprinkle with coarse salt and pepper, and drizzle with the remaining oil. Cover tightly with aluminum foil.

3. When the coals are white hot, place the dish on the side of the cooking grill opposite the coals; the gratin should not be sitting directly above the coals. Cover the grill and cook for 10 to 12 minutes. Uncover the dish and cook for another 10 to 15 minutes, or until the juices have evaporated and the vegetables are tender.

SERVES 6

NOTE: The gratin can be baked rather than grilled. Bake in a 350°F. oven for 35 to 40 minutes or until the vegetables are tender.

Zucchini Rounds in Parsley and Garlic Butter

This simple zucchini dish is an excellent accompaniment to sautéed or grilled fish. For a variation, you can flavor the parsley and garlic butter with 2 minced anchovy fillets or substitute basil or chives for the parsley.

1. Combine the butter together with the parsley and garlic in a small bowl and mash with a fork until well blended. Season with salt and pepper and chill until needed.

2. Heat the oil in a heavy 10-inch skillet over medium to medium high heat. Add the zucchini and cook for 2 to 3 minutes or until lightly browned. Season with salt and pepper, add the broth, and simmer, covered, for 5 to 7 minutes or just until crisp-tender.

3. Remove the pan from the heat and fold in the parsley and garlic butter. Serve hot.

SERVES 4

3 tablespoons unsalted butter, softened

2 tablespoons finely minced fresh parsley

1 large garlic clove, peeled and finely minced

Salt and freshly ground black pepper

1½ tablespoons olive oil

8 small zucchini, trimmed and cut crosswise into ½-inch rounds

¼ cup chicken broth, preferably homemade (page 360)

Season of mists and mellow fruitfulness.

TO AUTUMN, JOHN KEATS

BRUSSELS SPROUTS AND CABBAGE

CAULIFLOWER

EGGPLANT

LEEKS

MUSHROOMS

RED PEPPERS

TURNIPS AND RUTABAGAS

Late Harvest:
THE FALL GARDEN

It always comes as an unexpected

surprise, when walking down the hill toward my local blueberry patch on a hot

Indian summer afternoon, to see the local farmer already setting up his stand.

Sure enough, a few days later U PICK signs crop up all around, announcing the

start of apple-picking season. The apple, one of the many rewards of autumn, is

a sure sign that the seasonal cycle is again under way—and that the first frosts

that signal the onset of winter are not far behind.

It is nature's way of waving good-bye, of telling us that soon, very soon, we will have time to head indoors to the kitchen and some leisurely cooking, or toward grilling in the fireplace. I think of fall as a crossover season. Its arrival invariably causes me to marvel at how quickly the summer has gone. I look at my garden and so much is still in full bloom: the tomatoes plump, red, and hanging heavily all over the vines, with eggplant, peppers, and basil coming forth in abundance. But now my attention is drawn to the newcomers: tiny Brussels sprouts emerging on their stalks, small heads of snowy-white cauliflower bursting forth from brilliant green leaves, and rows of slender leeks peeking out from the fertile ground.

Around me, the first leaves begin their gentle descent from the trees, and there's a slight nip in the air—a definite indication that the best of all seasons, the glorious New England autumn, is once again upon us. Yes, perhaps singing the praises of the New England fall has become a cliché, but in truth it never fails to make one's soul soar. The earthy smell of the changing leaves, the colorful farm stands, displaying showy heads of kale and myriad brilliantly colored winter squash, are nothing if not glorious. The sun-drenched fields are dotted with pumpkins of every size, and trees are chock-full of pears, apples, and quince. It's a time when the first frost is always on a gardener's mind, whipping us into a frenzy of activity. There seems to be an urgency to get the picking and canning out of the way and to savor the last ripe tomato, the last garden cucumber, the final ear of corn.

Although its arrival is bittersweet for the gardener, who must soon be satisfied with browsing through seed catalogs and relishing the bright flavors of summer in the form of preserved delights stored away on the pantry shelves or in the freezer, fall also presents a welcome change. Just as we have had our fill of tomatoes, cucumbers, peppers, and eggplant, we can also get ready for the wonderful earthy tastes of onions and potatoes. And not to be forgotten are the beautiful green broad-leaved leeks, which emerge from mounds of mulched soil. All of these splendid vegetables seem to vie for our attention within a matter of weeks. At the farm market, stall after stall of glistening cauliflowers, heads of purple broccoli, and baskets filled to the brim with potatoes and onions envelop our senses. An array of outrageously shaped winter squashes, heaped on carts, prompts me to ponder the perennial fall question: where do I find room for all this bounty and when will I have the time to cook all these lovely vegetables?

There's no question that the fall and cold-weather kitchen tends to be more serious than that of summer, mainly because there's more indoor time to devote to leisurely cooking and culinary experimentation. And fall and winter are the key seasons for earthy, homey soups, which play a major role in my cool-weather repertoire. After all, there is a very natural marriage between the bounty of fall—the red peppers, leeks, eggplant, Brussels sprouts, and cauliflower—and the urge to return indoors. As the cooler weather coaxes us inside, we aspire to make the best of the tasty garden gems Mother Nature has provided.

And the glorious colors of autumn never cease to delight the eye—orange, rust, purple, pumpkin, the sharp yellow of early winter squash, interlaced with the pretty, pale green of celery and fennel. Even the tools change with the seasons. As the weather turns colder it is time to give a rest to the outdoor grill and to reach for that favorite black iron skillet or pull out the well-seasoned earthenware casserole.

I grew up in a home where fall's arrival heralded countless gastronomic pleasures. My parents eagerly greeted autumn by spending weekends in search of a variety of mushrooms—finding the glorious cèpe was the highlight of the season. Its flavor still haunts me to this day when I go into the woods near my house in the hope of discovering a similar delicacy. As fall winds down, it becomes, for the gardener, a sentimental journey.

BRUSSELS SPROUTS AND CABBAGE

IN MUCH OF THE COUNTRY BUT ESPECIALLY IN THE NORTHWEST AND the Northeast, cabbage and Brussels sprouts are in season at much the same time. Although the two vegetables are very closely related, few cooks think of them as similar vegetables that, in many dishes, are even interchangeable. Cabbage can be eaten raw, shredded into stews and salads. It is delicious pickled, braised, in soups, and wonderful for stuffing. For the cook who depends on supermarket freshness, Brussels sprouts are often a better bet than cabbage. They are usually quite fresh and will keep well refrigerated for up to a week.

Brussels Sprouts

First cultivated in Belgium in the fourteenth century, Brussels sprouts were introduced in Great Britain in the sixteenth century, where they have enjoyed such popularity that they have virtually become the national vegetable. In fact, my initial acquaintance with these miniature cabbages occurred in England and it was not a happy experience. During my college years, I spent a summer in Yorkshire as an au pair taking care of two children. My parents insisted that the experience would broaden me and do wonders for my English. It turned out to be a miserable, interminable three months. Besides passing too many chilly, rainy, foggy days on a cold beach in Blackpool keeping an eye on the children, I was also subjected to overcooked Brussels sprouts and cabbage two to three times a week! By the end of my stay I vowed never to touch either vegetable again for the rest of my life.

Of course, such impetuous pronouncements are not to be taken too seriously. As soon as I had a garden of my own, I couldn't wait to plant this extraordinary-looking vegetable. A thick tall stalk shoots straight up from the ground and sports a large fan of leaves at the top, giving the plant an umbrella-like appearance. Sprouts form starting at the bottom of the stalk and gradually encircle the entire length. Those marble-size sprouts taste so delicious that they are justification enough for planting a garden.

In England, Brussels sprouts are graded by size so that you can buy them small, medium, or large—a practice that I have seen in this country only in the Northwest. At many farmer's markets they are available on the stalk. Although not very economical, it certainly is one way to get really fresh sprouts of the size you want. When buying Brussels sprouts in the market, look for those that are very small, very firm, and compact, and that have good fresh color. Puffy, soft sprouts are of inferior quality and flavor, and yellowing leaves are a sure sign of age.

STORAGE

Brussels sprouts should be transferred from their containers to a plastic bag and stored in the crisper of the refrigerator. They will keep well for a week or more but, for best flavor, try to cook them within a few days.

GARDENING

Novice gardeners are usually surprised to find that Brussels sprout plants are so large. So-called dwarf types, such as Jade Cross Hybrid, may grow eighteen to twenty inches high, while the tall types such as Dolmic, Valiant, and Oliver can reach three feet. Many gardeners prefer the latter because of their superior productivity, flavor, and quality. Brussels sprouts like full sun and a fertile, moisture-retentive soil. Ideally, the soil should be liberally enriched with organic matter and on the heavy side, not light and sandy. To avoid disease problems, do not plant Brussels sprouts where other members of the cabbage family have grown in the previous year. I sow the seed in early summer and thin or transplant the seedlings to stand two feet apart. Although it may seem brutal to discard so many seedlings, generous spacing between plants is absolutely critical for good sprout formation. Eight to ten stalks will provide plenty of Brussels sprouts for the average home gardener. Regular watering and fertilizing until the sprouts begin to form is also essential. Wind is an enemy of Brussels sprouts because it can loosen the plants' footing, so take care to firm the soil well around the plants and use stakes if necessary. Use insecticidal soap to keep aphids at bay.

HARVESTING

In September you should see the first harvestable sprouts forming along the bottom of the stalks, at the base of each leaf. I cut them off as soon as they are three quarters of an inch across. To encourage production up the full length of the stalk, remove all leaves below harvested sprouts. To halt plant growth and encourage nice, fat little sprouts, I usually pinch out the top tuft of leaves. The flavor of sprouts is noticeably sweetened by frost, and I harvest them until the ground freezes.

Cabbage

The main market in Lisbon is a fascinating place, and on a recent winter trip I found it so intriguing that I visited it for three successive days. To get the real flavor of the place, you had to arrive by six A.M. just as the fishermen finished unloading their catch and the vendors were setting up their stands for the day. The variety and abundance of the seafood was overwhelming, but the choice of vegetables marked this as a less bountiful season. Some stands displayed carrots, onions, and potatoes, but at most the sole offering was cabbage. Everywhere I looked there were heaps and heaps of cabbage, some red, some curly, but mostly greenish white heads with their beautiful gray-green leaves. Almost all the vendors were peasant women. Wrapped in black wool shawls, they sat on small stools surrounded by mountains of cabbage.

Cabbage played an important role in the winter menus of my youth. My mother, an expert with the vegetable, made a wonderful Viennese-style stuffed cabbage using a variety of savory fillings that ranged from mild to spicy. And because my father was Alsatian, his fondness for cabbage and all the regional dishes he grew up with influenced me when I started to cook and garden.

Cabbage deserves praise if only because it has survived centuries of improper cooking, as well as a reputation for being unpleasantly strong, hard to digest, and, most unfortunate of all, boring. Of course, nothing could be farther from the truth; few vegetables are as subtly flavored or have such varied uses as fresh cabbage. When thoughtfully prepared and not overcooked, cabbage tastes more like a sweet, robust lettuce, so mild that it often requires the addition of onions, leeks, and bacon to develop its character. From the Russian white borscht to a whole stuffed cabbage pot-au-feu, not to mention the many delicious soups using cabbage, there are many classic preparations to choose from. Although cabbage has traditionally been regarded as a peasant vegetable, many acclaimed chefs have now discovered its charms and prepare it in imaginative ways, teaming it with monkfish, sea scallops, and pasta or filling it with light mixtures such as red pepper couscous (page 194).

In many parts of the country, buying fresh cabbage can be a frustrating endeavor. Although it is an undemanding vegetable that can be grown almost everywhere, the standard green cabbage is all you are apt to find in supermarkets as well as farmer's markets. While perfect for slaws or just steamed and buttered, it lacks the versatility and depth of flavor of the curly, loose-leaved savoy type. Whenever I see the crinkled, jade-green heads in the market, I change my menu to include it. Quintal d'Alsace and Savoy Ace are two superb varieties. For red cabbage, I like Red Acre and Ruby Ball; Danish Ballhead and the delicious Erdeno are my favorites for green cabbage. No matter which variety I use, when preparing cabbage I always discard the tough outer leaves, quarter the head, and then core it by cutting out the hard center portions.

STORAGE

Cabbage can be stored successfully for several weeks. Be sure to keep it in a plastic bag in the lower part of the refrigerator. For longer storage, remove the outer leaves before placing it in the plastic bag. Savoy cabbage is best used within a week or two of purchase.

GARDENING

Considering that the ancestors of our cultivated cabbages grew wild in cool, damp, coastal climates, it is not surprising that those same conditions produce the best cabbages today. Success with any kind of cabbage depends on four important factors: rich soil, regular fertilizing, plenty of water, and cool weather while the heads are maturing. Deviation from these simple rules will result in disappointment. I suggest using some restraint when planting cabbage unless you plan a pretty steady diet of cabbage dishes and have unlimited cool storage space. I wait until midsummer to start my cabbage, sowing the seed ten to twelve weeks before the first expected frost. When the seedlings are large enough to handle, fertilize and thin or transplant them to stand two feet apart. Continue to water regularly and fertilize several times early in the season. Dusting regularly with rotenone will control most pests. Avoid diseases by planting where no member of the cabbage family has grown the previous year.

HARVESTING

It's a blessing that a single planting of cabbage does not mature all at once. The younger the heads are harvested, the more succulent are the leaves. When the heads become solid, I harvest them as needed, cutting the stalk with a sharp knife. The beautiful red varieties, once they are fully mature, can stand in the garden for several weeks before harvesting. A trick I learned to stretch out the harvest and to keep the heads from cracking once they mature, is to give the entire plant a good, sharp twist and then let it resettle. This severs some of the roots and halts development. Most varieties tolerate light frost, but I try to harvest all of them before really cold weather sets in.

Brussels Sprouts Leaves with Bacon and Garlic

This dish is best made with large, rather overgrown sprouts, whose leaves can easily be separated. The crispy bacon and minced garlic add flavor and texture to this lively and very pretty vegetable dish; serve it alongside sliced grilled pork tenderloin or chicken breasts.

1. Bring plenty of salted water to a boil in a large pan. Add the Brussels sprouts and cook for 4 minutes. Immediately run under cold water to stop further cooking and drain well. Separate the Brussels sprouts into leaves and reserve.

2. In a large heavy skillet, melt the butter over medium heat. Add the bacon and cook until almost crisp. Remove with a slotted spoon to a side dish and reserve.

3. Add the garlic and Brussels sprouts leaves to the skillet and toss for 3 minutes. Add the rosemary, if using, together with the reserved bacon and cook for 1 minute longer. Season with salt and pepper and serve hot.

SERVES 6

Salt
2 pints Brussels sprouts, about
    1 ½ pounds
3 tablespoons unsalted butter
3 ounces slab bacon, blanched
    and diced, about ⅔ cup
2 large garlic cloves, peeled and
    thinly sliced
Optional: 2 teaspoons fresh
    rosemary leaves
Freshly ground black pepper

Gratin of Brussels Sprouts with Fontina and Goat Cheese

Salt
1½ pounds small to medium Brussels sprouts, trimmed
6 tablespoons (¾ stick) unsalted butter
1¼ cups heavy cream
Freshly ground white pepper
¼ pound fontina cheese, cut into ½-inch dice
4 tablespoons mild goat cheese, such as Montrachet or fresh California goat cheese, crumbled

Brussels sprouts take well to many mild cheeses, which tend to balance the rather assertive flavor of the sprouts. Serve the gratin with something very simple such as grilled or roast chicken or roast loin of pork seasoned with garlic and herbs.

1. Preheat the oven to 350°F.

2. In a large saucepan, bring salted water to a boil. Add the Brussels sprouts and simmer for 10 to 12 minutes or until tender. Drain well and cut in half through the root end. Set aside.

3. In a heavy 2-quart saucepan, melt 4 tablespoons of the butter over medium heat. Add the cream and simmer until reduced to ¾ cup. Season with salt and pepper and set aside.

4. Place the Brussels sprouts in a well-buttered, oval gratin dish with a 6-cup capacity and season with salt and pepper. Spoon the reduced cream over the sprouts, sprinkle with the fontina and goat cheese, and dot with the remaining 2 tablespoons of butter. Bake for 15 minutes.

5. Raise the oven temperature to 450°F. and bake for an additional 10 minutes or until the cream is absorbed by the sprouts and the top is nicely browned. Serve hot.

SERVES 4 TO 6

Sauté of Brussels Sprouts Siciliana

Ilike to make this lively side dish with young small sprouts, which can be teamed with a variety of flavorful ingredients. While the pine nuts are mild and buttery, the anchovies give this sauté an interesting punch. For a variation, substitute diced sautéed pecans for the pine nuts and serve the dish as a starter followed by a fall pasta dish or risotto. This dish can be prepared several hours ahead of time and reheated.

1. In a 10-inch cast-iron skillet, heat 2 tablespoons of the oil over medium heat. Add the sliced garlic and sauté until lightly browned. Add the sprouts to the skillet together with the broth and simmer, partially covered, for 8 to 10 minutes or until just tender. With a slotted spoon, remove the sprouts from the skillet and set aside.

2. While the Brussels sprouts are braising, heat 1 tablespoon of the oil in a small skillet over medium heat. Add the pine nuts and sauté until lightly browned. Reserve.

3. Remove the sliced garlic from the skillet the sprouts were cooked in and discard. Bring the pan juices to a boil and reduce to 2 tablespoons. Add the remaining tablespoon of oil to the skillet, and add the minced garlic and anchovies. Cook for 1 to 2 minutes, or until the anchovies have melted. Add the pine nuts and raisins together with the reserved sprouts and toss lightly in the anchovy sauce.

4. Season with salt and a large grinding of pepper and transfer to a serving dish. Sprinkle with the minced parsley and serve hot.

SERVES 4 TO 6

NOTE: If anchovies are salty, place in a little milk for 30 minutes. Drain and finely mince.

4 tablespoons extra-virgin olive oil

2 large garlic cloves, peeled and thinly sliced, plus 1 teaspoon finely minced garlic

2 pints small Brussels sprouts, trimmed and cut in half through the root end

¾ cup chicken broth, preferably homemade (page 360)

¼ cup pine nuts

4 to 6 flat anchovy fillets, drained and finely minced (see Note)

⅓ cup dark raisins, preferably Muscat, plumped in 1 cup warm water

Salt and freshly ground black pepper

2 tablespoons finely minced fresh parsley

Pennsylvania Dutch Cabbage

3 cups shredded green cabbage
3 large green bell peppers,
    cored, seeded, and thinly
    sliced
2 teaspoons coarse salt
2 to 3 tablespoons cider
    vinegar
2 tablespoons sugar
½ cup sour cream
Freshly ground black pepper

Pepper and cabbage slaw is to Pennsylvania Dutch cooking what cole slaw is to the rest of the country. A good pepper slaw is indeed addictive. Its sweet crunchy texture and piquant taste make it the perfect choice for a late-summer picnic, or as a refreshing addition to a juicy grilled tuna or beef burger. The slaw is best when made a day or two ahead of time to allow the full flavors to mix and mingle. As a variation, I often add a large mincing of dill and a few finely diced beets.

1. In a large colander set over a large bowl, combine the cabbage and peppers, sprinkle with the salt, and drain for 1 hour. Press down on the cabbage and peppers with a wooden spoon to extract any excess liquid. Set aside.

2. In a large serving bowl, whisk together the vinegar, sugar, and sour cream until well blended. Add the cabbage and peppers and toss with the dressing. Season with a large grinding of black pepper, cover, and chill overnight.

3. The next day, taste and correct the seasoning, toss well, and serve.

SERVES 6

Red Cabbage and Carrot Slaw in Mustard Dill Vinaigrette

A red cabbage slaw is a lovely alternative to the more common white cabbage slaw. It marries beautifully with a variety of intensely flavored vinaigrettes, and several winter fruits and vegetables can be added to further enhance the slaw. I am especially fond of the crunchiness of apples, the juicy taste of pears, or the characteristic taste of both fennel and celery root. My favorite way to serve the red cabbage slaw is as an accompaniment to a baked ham, pan-seared or grilled sausages, or roasted pork tenderloins.

1. Place the cabbage in a colander, sprinkle with 1 teaspoon of salt, and let drain for 2 to 3 hours. Squeeze out the excess moisture from the cabbage with your hands and set aside.

2. In a large serving bowl, combine the mustard, sugar, and red wine vinegar. Add the oil in a slow steady stream and whisk until well blended. Add the scallions and dill and season with salt and pepper. Add the cabbage and carrots and toss gently. Cover and refrigerate overnight.

3. The next day, taste and correct the seasoning, adding a large grinding of black pepper and more vinegar if necessary. Serve lightly chilled.

SERVES 4 TO 6

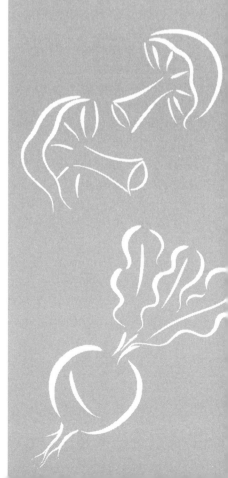

1¼ pounds red cabbage, trimmed and finely shredded, about 5 cups
Salt
3 tablespoons Dijon mustard
3 tablespoons sugar
2 tablespoons red wine vinegar
8 tablespoons olive oil
2 medium scallions, finely minced
3 tablespoons finely minced fresh dill
Freshly ground black pepper
1 cup finely shredded carrots

Mediterranean Cabbage "Bundles" with Spicy Couscous

3 tablespoons unsalted butter

1 teaspoon finely minced jalapeño pepper

1 small red onion, peeled and finely minced

1/3 cup finely diced red bell pepper

1/3 cup finely diced yellow bell pepper

1/3 cup finely diced zucchini

1 cup couscous, preferably imported

3 to 3 1/2 cups chicken broth, preferably homemade (page 360)

Salt and freshly ground black pepper

1 small head of savoy cabbage, about 1 pound

2 teaspoons olive oil

2 garlic cloves, peeled and thinly sliced

GARNISH

Fresh lemon juice

Extra-virgin olive oil

This delicious and light main course makes the most of flavorful curly cabbage. It is also excellent served at room temperature as a starter or as a side dish with a roast or grilled leg of lamb or lamb chops.

1. In a heavy 1½-quart saucepan, melt 2 tablespoons of the butter over low heat. Add the jalapeño pepper and onion and cook for 2 to 3 minutes. Add the peppers and zucchini and continue to sauté until the vegetables are soft but not browned.

2. Add the couscous and 2 cups of the broth to the saucepan, season with salt and pepper, and simmer, covered, for 10 minutes or until all the broth is absorbed and the couscous is fluffy. Taste and correct the seasoning. Set aside.

3. In a large casserole, bring water to a boil. Add the whole cabbage and cook for 3 to 5 minutes. Drain and when cool enough to handle wrap in a large kitchen towel to blot the excess moisture. Remove 12 to 14 leaves and dry well. With a small paring knife, remove an inch of the center rib. Place a heaping tablespoon of the couscous mixture at the bottom of each leaf and roll into a tight package, tucking in the ends to enclose the couscous completely.

4. Preheat the oven to 350°F.

5. In an oval or rectangular ovenproof baking dish, melt the remaining tablespoon of butter together with the oil. Add the sliced garlic and place the cabbage rolls in one layer in the baking dish. Add 1 cup of the broth, cover the dish with foil, and bake for 35 to 40 minutes, adding more broth if needed.

6. When the cabbage rolls are done, they should be lightly browned and the broth almost reduced to a glaze. Serve either hot or at room temperature, sprinkled with a little lemon juice and a drizzle of olive oil.

SERVES 6

South-of-the-Border Cabbage, White Bean, and Root Vegetable Soup

Some vegetables are meant for each other, and when these are combined in the soup pot the result is always harmonious and flavor-packed. While you may use canned beans in this preparation, they are never as good as those that have been soaked in water to cover overnight and cooked separately until tender. Carrots, onions, garlic, and potatoes are also important additions to this homey and ever-so-satisfying autumn soup.

1. In a large casserole, heat the butter and oil over low heat, add the bacon or pork butt, and cook until lightly browned. Add the onion, garlic, and chili pepper and continue cooking until the onion is soft and lightly browned.

2. Add the carrots, potatoes, and broth, season with salt and pepper, and simmer, partially covered, for 25 minutes.

3. Add the cabbage and simmer until tender, about 20 minutes. Add the beans and just heat through. Taste the soup and correct the seasoning. Serve hot, garnishing each portion with a little minced parsley and 1 teaspoon of extra-virgin olive oil.

SERVES 6

VARIATION
You may add 3 or 4 small white turnips, peeled and cubed, to the soup and/or 1 small fennel bulb, quartered and finely sliced, together with 2 to 3 tablespoons finely minced fennel tops.

2 tablespoons unsalted butter
1 tablespoon olive oil
6 ounces slab bacon, cut into 1-inch pieces, or 6 ounces smoked pork shoulder butt cut into 1-inch pieces
1 large Bermuda onion, peeled and finely diced
2 large garlic cloves, peeled and finely minced
1 small dry red chili pepper, crumbled
2 medium carrots, peeled and diced
2 medium red potatoes, peeled and diced
7 cups beef broth
Salt and freshly ground black pepper
1 pound green cabbage, quartered, cored, and thinly sliced
1 cup Cooked White Beans (page 364), preferably Great Northern

GARNISH
2 tablespoons finely minced fresh parsley
6 teaspoons extra-virgin olive oil

Autumn Soup of Curly Cabbage, Beets, and Potatoes

2 large leeks, trimmed of all but 2 inches of greens and finely diced

3 tablespoons unsalted butter

2 large carrots, peeled and finely diced

3 medium red potatoes, peeled and cut into ½-inch cubes

3 medium kohlrabi, peeled and cut into ½-inch cubes

Salt and freshly ground white pepper

5 to 6 medium beets, about 1½ pounds without tops, peeled and finely shredded

8 to 10 cups chicken broth, preferably homemade (page 360)

½ pound green cabbage, cored and finely shredded

1 cup sour cream

2 tablespoons red wine vinegar

2 teaspoons sugar

¼ cup finely minced fresh dill

Being Viennese and growing up in Spain was a strange experience in many ways, but especially so when it came to food. My parents loved and missed everything Austrian. Beets, curly cabbage, and kohlrabi were not available in Barcelona in the 1950s and are still uncommon there. So when we traveled to Austria for our yearly Christmas vacation, we returned home with the car jammed with everything from good Hungarian salami, hazelnuts, and prune jam to black bread and the vegetables needed for this soup. No wonder that for years this one-dish meal seemed so special. Even now, when I can get all the ingredients with ease, I still love this soup; I often serve it as the main component to a lunch or supper with some black bread, good butter, and some cheese—and we all find it most satisfying.

1. Rinse the diced leeks thoroughly under warm water to remove any trace of sand, drain thoroughly, and set aside.

2. In a large casserole, melt the butter over low heat. Add the leeks, carrots, potatoes, and kohlrabi, season with salt and pepper, and cook the vegetables for 3 to 5 minutes. Add the shredded beets and the broth and simmer, partially covered, for 1 hour or until the beets are tender. Add the cabbage and continue cooking for another 20 minutes.

3. Combine the sour cream, vinegar, and sugar in a small bowl and whisk until smooth. Add to the soup and simmer for 10 minutes longer; do not bring to a boil. Taste and correct the seasoning. Just before serving, add the dill to the soup and serve hot.

SERVES 6 TO 8

VARIATION
I also like to serve the soup warm but not hot with an additional dollop of sour cream and sprinkling of fresh dill on each serving. The soup develops more and more flavor and is best made well ahead of time.

Brown Sugar–Braised Red Cabbage with Pears

When I was growing up, red cabbage was often hard to find in the Barcelona markets, so my parents would grow it at our farmhouse in the Pyrenees. Although my mother liked to prepare cabbage the Austrian way, braising it for a long time in red wine with bacon and apples, she also adapted her cooking to Spanish ingredients. Since sherry vinegar was one of her favorites, she often cooked the cabbage in a sweet broth infused with sherry vinegar.

Here is a quick and delicious way to prepare this full-flavored cabbage. Serve it as an accompaniment to grilled pork, lamb, or, best of all, roast duck. You may add one or two Golden Delicious apples to the cabbage or some roasted and peeled chestnuts. If you are using fresh chestnuts, be sure to blanch them until they are almost tender before adding them to the cabbage.

1. Quarter the cabbage and cut into very fine shreds. You can use the fine slicing disc of a food processor or do it by hand with a very sharp knife. You should have about 6 cups total.

2. Place the cabbage in a large bowl, sprinkle lightly with coarse salt, and toss gently, then set aside for two hours. Drain well and taste the cabbage. If it is too salty, rinse quickly under cold water. Squeeze the cabbage with your hands to remove any excess moisture. Reserve.

3. In a 12-inch cast-iron skillet, melt the butter together with the oil over medium heat. Add the shallots and garlic and cook for 1 minute without browning. Add the brown sugar, tomato paste, and vinegar and cook for 30 seconds or until the sugar has melted. Return the cabbage to the skillet and season with salt and pepper. Add the pears and just heat through. Serve at once.

SERVES 4

---

1 small head of red cabbage (about 1½ pounds)
Coarse salt
2 tablespoons unsalted butter
2 teaspoons corn or peanut oil
3 tablespoons finely minced shallots
1 large garlic clove, peeled and finely minced
3 tablespoons dark brown sugar
1 tablespoon tomato paste
2 tablespoons sherry vinegar
Freshly ground black pepper
2 ripe medium-size Bosc pears, peeled, cored, and cut into a very fine julienne

Cabbage and Parmesan Puddings

1¼ cups heavy cream
¾ cup whole milk
4 cups finely shredded savoy cabbage
Salt and freshly ground black pepper
2 large eggs
2 large egg yolks
3 tablespoons freshly grated Parmesan cheese

Here is a super-flavorful little side dish that I like to serve alongside a roast chicken or beef brisket with some of the roast's pan juices spooned over each pudding. The puddings are even more delicious when made a day or two ahead of time and reheated in a slow oven.

1. Preheat the oven to 350°F. Butter the insides of 8 ramekins and set aside.

2. In a heavy 3-quart saucepan, combine the cream and milk and bring to a simmer. Add the cabbage, season with salt and pepper, and simmer for 10 minutes or until very tender.

3. Transfer the cabbage mixture to a food processor and process until smooth. Add the eggs, egg yolks, and Parmesan and season with salt and pepper. Process until thoroughly combined.

4. Divide the cabbage mixture evenly among the prepared ramekins and place them in a very heavy baking dish. Set the dish in the center of the oven and fill the baking dish with boiling water to come halfway up the sides of the ramekins. Bake for 30 to 35 minutes or until the puddings are set; a knife when inserted should come out clean.

5. Remove the puddings from the oven and let cool slightly. Run a knife around the inside of each pudding and unmold onto dinner plates.

SERVES 8

CAULIFLOWER

URING MY COLLEGE YEARS IN GENEVA, MY FRIENDS AND I MET AT A
local café for hot chocolate and buttery croissants every Saturday morning.
Then, shopping baskets in hand, we headed for the market to see what foods
would tempt us that day. We browsed among the stalls, changing our minds
as well as our menus each time we spied a more interesting vegetable, fruit,
sausage, or cheese. My weakness was always the cauliflower—beautiful, pristine heads, the size of large grapefruits, nestled in their lovely blue-green
leaves. I admit that, at that time, my notion of preparing cauliflower was
simply to cook it whole, then douse it with brown "noisette" butter to
which I added a handful of breadcrumbs and some lemon juice. The foamy
brown butter was the only garnish this superb vegetable required. It made a
nice, easy first course, and the leftovers were equally delicious sprinkled with
a little virgin olive oil and some freshly ground black pepper.

At home in Barcelona, cauliflower was one of my mother's favorite fall
vegetables. She loved serving it whole smothered with an exquisite homemade olive-oil–based mayonnaise to which she added minced gherkins,
capers, and a hefty amount of minced parsley and garlic. Accompanied by a
crusty loaf of bread, it was and still is one of my favorite cauliflower preparations. Sometimes I add minced anchovies to the mayonnaise and other
times I flavor it with Middle Eastern spices. Actually, I find the Indian way
with cauliflower the most interesting. The vegetable takes well to assertive
spices like cumin, curry, coriander, and cinnamon, and to various hot peppers when they are subdued a little with yogurt or sour cream.

Some vegetables ship relatively well with little deterioration, but cauliflower is one vegetable that must be harvested and cooked in its prime. Anyone who has either grown this wonderful member of the cabbage family or
bought it fresh from a roadside stand can readily vouch for its delicate flavor
and firm texture, qualities that disappear rapidly when it is subjected to cold
storage. A light cabbagy aroma is fine, but a strong cabbage smell means the

vegetable is well past its peak and will be even stronger tasting when cooked. Unfortunately, most cauliflower arrives in the markets here minus its pretty leaves and sealed in cellophane, safe from discerning noses. Be sure to inspect it closely anyway; brown areas or spots that have been shaved off are a sure sign of age. When buying cauliflower at a roadside stand, look for a dense head with tightly packed curds; a head that has begun to loosen and spread is too old. The leaves, of course, must be crisp and fresh.

To use supermarket cauliflower successfully, add a little milk to the poaching water to keep the curds white and delicate tasting. Very fresh cauliflower is best cooked whole, head down, in plenty of lightly salted water. Test for doneness often so that you do not overcook it. As soon as it is done, I usually transfer it to a bowl of very cold water and cut the head into florets after it has cooled. I prefer to leave cooked cauliflower at room temperature if I am serving it the same day or the next marinated or dressed with a vinaigrette. When using cauliflower in soups I like to let the cauliflower develop flavor for at least a day or two.

STORAGE

To store cauliflower fresh from the garden or a farm stand, cut off the leaves and place it in a perforated plastic bag. It will then keep in good condition for four or five days in the vegetable crisper or the lower part of the refrigerator.

GARDENING

Of all the members of the cabbage family, cauliflower is the most finicky and temperamental. Snow Crown is one of the easier varieties to grow and is of excellent quality. The secret to firm, round heads is rapid, uninterrupted growth with as little stress as possible. That means rich, well-drained soil, monthly fertilizing, regular watering, and cool growing conditions while the heads are forming. The rule of not growing a member of the cabbage family in the same soil for two successive years applies here. Careful soil preparation, with plenty of organic matter worked in for fertility and good drainage, are very important. Sow and seed three months before the first frost and thin seedlings so they are two feet apart. Because cauliflower plants are sensitive about having their roots disturbed, I tackle weeds while the seedlings are small and mulch the row to prevent weeds and conserve moisture. When the heads are about the size of tennis balls, I fold several leaves over them, securing them with string or rubber bands. This blanches the heads, maintaining their snowy whiteness, and protects them from both sun and frost damage later in the fall.

HARVESTING

To avoid a sudden deluge of mature cauliflower, I begin cutting the heads before they attain full size of about six inches across. I've found that when I harvest cauliflower in the morning, still damp with dew, they keep longer.

Cauliflower, Snow Pea, and Grape Salad in Curry Tartar Sauce

1 small head of cauliflower, about 1 pound, trimmed of all leaves

Salt

2 medium carrots, peeled and sliced

¼ pound snow peas, strings removed

¼ cup finely minced red onion

1 cup green seedless grapes, preferably Thompson

2 small sweet gherkins, finely diced

2 extra-large egg yolks

2 teaspoons red wine vinegar

1 teaspoon finely minced jalapeño pepper

1 teaspoon imported curry powder, preferably Madras

Pinch of ground cumin

¾ cup peanut oil or corn oil

Freshly ground white pepper

GARNISH

Tiny leaves of fresh cilantro

On a recent trip to India, I sampled a deliciously fiery chutney made with cauliflower and raisins. The taste stayed with me, and upon my return I tested several recipes in which I combined fruit with one of fall's best vegetables. I came up with this light and tasty salad that is a welcome addition to a seasonal weekend lunch.

1. Break the cauliflower into florets about ¾ inch in diameter, removing most of the stalk. Bring salted water to a boil in a vegetable steamer, add the cauliflower florets, and steam, covered, until just tender, about 5 to 7 minutes. Transfer to a salad bowl and reserve.

2. Steam the carrots and snow peas until tender and add to the cauliflower together with the onion, grapes, and gherkins. Set aside.

3. In a blender, combine the egg yolks, vinegar, jalapeño pepper, curry powder, and cumin and process until smooth. With the machine running, add the oil by droplets, until the mixture begins to thicken. Add the remaining oil in a slow steady stream until a smooth and thick mayonnaise is formed. Season with salt and pepper. Spoon the tartar sauce over the cauliflower mixture, toss gently, and chill 2 to 4 hours before serving.

4. Just before serving, taste the salad and correct the seasoning. Garnish with cilantro leaves.

SERVES 4 TO 6

Mediterranean Cauliflower and Feta Salad in Raita Vinaigrette

You'll find the best cauliflower in the markets from late August to early September, and that's the time to make this delicious preparation. Serve the salad as a side dish to grilled chicken or lamb shish kebabs. You can also add finely minced jalapeño pepper to the yogurt vinaigrette and garnish the salad with tiny cilantro leaves rather than parsley. Be sure to make the salad a day ahead to let the cauliflower fully absorb the vinaigrette.

1. In a large saucepan, bring salted water to a boil. Add the cauliflower florets and cook until just tender, about 3 to 5 minutes. Do not overcook. Immediately drain and run under cold water to stop the cauliflower from cooking further. Transfer the cauliflower to a serving bowl and set aside.

2. In a small bowl combine the yogurt, garlic, oil, and vinegar and whisk until well blended. Season with salt and pepper and pour the vinaigrette over the cauliflower. Add the remaining ingredients to the salad, toss lightly, and chill the salad for 4 to 6 hours before serving.

3. Thirty minutes before serving, bring the salad back to room temperature and correct the seasoning. Garnish with the minced parsley and serve as part of an hors d'oeuvre table.

S E R V E S   5   T O   6

NOTE: To remove the moisture from yogurt, transfer a pint of yogurt to a strainer lined with cheesecloth and set over a bowl. Refrigerate overnight. The result will be a denser, better-tasting yogurt.

Coarse salt
2 pounds cauliflower, trimmed and broken into uniform florets
1 cup well-drained plain yogurt (see Note)
1 large garlic clove, peeled and mashed
3 tablespoons extra-virgin olive oil
1½ tablespoons red wine vinegar
Salt
Freshly ground black pepper
1 cup finely diced red bell pepper
⅓ cup finely diced red onion
1 cup finely cubed feta cheese
15 to 18 pitted Gaeta olives (or other small oil-cured black olives), cut in half
1 medium cucumber, peeled, seeded, and diced

GARNISH
2 to 3 tablespoons finely minced fresh parsley

Curried Cauliflower and Sweet Potato Soup

3 tablespoons unsalted butter
2 medium onions, peeled and
    finely diced
2 tablespoons dark brown
    sugar
¼ teaspoon ground ginger
¼ teaspoon ground cardamom
¼ teaspoon ground coriander
1 medium head of cauliflower,
    about 1½ pounds, trimmed
1 large sweet potoato, peeled
    and diced
7 cups chicken broth,
    preferably homemade
    (page 360)
Salt and freshly ground black
    pepper
Large grinding of nutmeg
¼ cup heavy cream
GARNISH
1½ cups tiny cauliflower
    florets, steamed
1 cup sour cream
3 tablespoons tiny whole
    cilantro leaves

Cauliflower loves the company of assertive herbs and spices, which is probably why it is used so extensively in Middle Eastern and Indian cooking. I recently was about to make curried cauliflower and potato soup, a favorite of my family, when I found myself without potatoes but with a couple of sweet potatoes in the vegetable bin. The result is this soup, which can be made with or without curry.

1. In a large heavy 4-quart casserole, melt the butter over medium heat, add the onions, and cook until soft but not brown. Add the brown sugar and spices and continue to sauté for another 2 to 3 minutes.

2. Add the cauliflower, diced yam, and broth and simmer, partially covered, for 35 minutes or until the vegetables are very soft.

3. Cool slightly and puree the soup in batches in a food processor. Pass through a food mill or a fine sieve and return to the casserole. Season with salt, pepper, and nutmeg, add the cream, and just heat through.

4. Place a few steamed cauliflower florets in each individual soup bowl and ladle some of the soup over each portion. Serve hot with a generous dollop of sour cream and a few cilantro leaves.

S E R V E S   4   T O   5

Tandoori-Style Cauliflower Fricassee

Here is another recipe inspired by a cauliflower preparation I sampled in India. There the dish was extremely spicy and the seasonings seemed to overwhelm the rather delicate vegetable. I have tamed the spices, but if you like it hot by all means stoke up the fire. Serve the cauliflower as a side dish to simply grilled or pan-seared fish steaks such as tuna, mako, or mahimahi, or with lamb kebabs.

1. Place the eggplant in a colander, sprinkle with a little salt, and let drain for 1 hour. Dry the eggplant thoroughly on paper towels.

2. In a heavy 12-inch skillet, heat 3 tablespoons of the oil over medium high heat. Add the eggplant cubes and brown nicely on all sides. Remove with a slotted spoon to a side dish and reserve.

3. Add the remaining 3 tablespoons of oil to the skillet and when hot, add the chili peppers and cook until dark. Remove and discard the peppers. Add the onions, garlic, and ginger, reduce heat, and cook for 5 minutes, stirring often until soft and lightly browned.

4. Add the cumin seeds, paprika, and turmeric and cook for 30 seconds. Add the tomatoes, tomato paste, and cilantro, season with salt and pepper, and cook until all the tomato liquid has evaporated.

5. Add the cauliflower, potato, and broth and stir well to coat the vegetables. Reduce heat to low and cook, covered, for 20 minutes or until the vegetables are tender when pierced with a knife. Add the eggplant and just heat through. Taste and correct the seasoning, sprinkle with the cilantro leaves, and serve directly from the skillet.

S E R V E S   6

1 small eggplant, about $\frac{1}{2}$ pound, cut into 1-inch cubes
Coarse salt
6 tablespoons extra-virgin olive oil
2 small dry red chili peppers, broken in half
2 medium onions, peeled and finely minced
2 large garlic cloves, peeled and finely minced
1-inch piece of fresh ginger, peeled and finely minced
1 tablespoon cumin seeds, toasted and crushed (see page 82)
1 teaspoon imported sweet paprika
$\frac{1}{4}$ teaspoon turmeric
2 large ripe tomatoes, peeled, seeded, and chopped
2 teaspoons tomato paste
$\frac{1}{4}$ cup fresh cilantro leaves
Freshly ground black pepper
$1\frac{1}{4}$ pounds cauliflower florets
1 large all-purpose potato, peeled and cut into 1-inch cubes
$1\frac{1}{2}$ cups chicken broth, preferably homemade (page 360)

GARNISH
Tiny leaves of fresh cilantro

Salt

1 medium head of cauliflower,
about 1½ pounds, trimmed
of all leaves

5 tablespoons unsalted butter

4 tablespoons freshly grated
Parmesan cheese

Freshly ground black pepper

2 tablespoons breadcrumbs,
preferably homemade

1 tablespoon fresh thyme
leaves

1 recipe Tomato and Shallot
Sauce (page 160), warm

Shoulder Season Gratin of Cauliflower

I very much like this preparation in which the cauliflower is
allowed the company of tomatoes and a dash of herbs. It is a nice way to
celebrate a new season while taking advantage of one of the previous season's great stars. Serve as a starter sprinkled with smoked mozzarella or a
flavorful goat cheese, or as a side dish to grilled flank steak.

1. Preheat the oven to 400°F.

2. Bring plenty of salted water to a boil in a large casserole,
add the whole cauliflower, and cook for 10 minutes or until
tender. Drain well and separate into florets. Reserve.

3. Spread 1 tablespoon of the butter on the bottom and
sides of a 1½-quart baking dish. Sprinkle with 2 tablespoons
of the Parmesan and top with cauliflower florets in a single
layer. Season with salt and pepper and sprinkle with the
breadcrumbs, thyme, and remaining Parmesan. Set aside.

4. In a small saucepan, melt the remaining 4 tablespoons of
butter over medium heat and whisk until it turns a light
hazelnut brown, being careful not to burn. Immediately drizzle the butter over the florets and bake for 15 to 20 minutes
or until the breadcrumbs are golden brown and the cauliflower is heated through. If you prefer, run the dish under the
broiler to brown a bit more. Serve hot with the tomato and
shallot sauce on the side.

SERVES 4

Mashed Cauliflower and Onion Fritters

I like vegetable fritters of every kind and try to experiment with new ones as often as I can. Cauliflower lends itself particularly well to this kind of preparation and, with a side dish of yogurt flavored with garlic, parsley, and dill, it makes for a sensational light main course or side dish to seafood, poultry, or lamb.

Coarse salt
1 small head of cauliflower, about 1 pound, trimmed of all leaves
3 extra-large eggs
3 tablespoons all-purpose flour
1 teaspoon baking powder
2 teaspoons grated raw onion
Freshly ground white pepper
Peanut oil for frying

1. Bring plenty of salted water to a boil in a large casserole, add the cauliflower, and cook for 15 minutes or until very tender. Drain well and separate the head into florets. Trim off the stalks and mash the florets lightly with the back of a fork. You should have about 2 cups. Set aside.

2. In a large mixing bowl, combine the eggs, flour, baking powder, and grated onion, season with salt and pepper, and whisk until well blended. Fold in the mashed cauliflower and let the batter rest at room temperature for 1 hour.

3. Heat the oil to a depth of $\frac{1}{3}$ inch in a heavy 10-inch skillet over medium heat. Drop the batter by heaping tablespoons into the hot oil without crowding the pan; fry in 3 batches of about 5 to 6 fritters per batch. Cook for 1 to 2 minutes per side or until nicely brown, adjusting the heat so that the fritters do not brown too quickly.

4. Remove with a slotted spoon to paper towels to drain. Sprinkle with coarse salt and serve hot.

MAKES 16 TO 18 FRITTERS

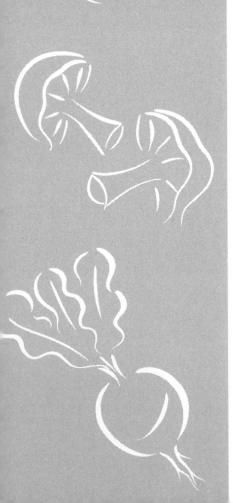

I large head of cauliflower trimmed of all leaves, about 2 pounds, separated into small florets

⅓ cup coarse salt

½ cup sugar

1½ cups white distilled vinegar

2 tablespoons dry mustard

I tablespoon imported curry powder, preferably Madras

2 small dry red chili peppers, broken in half

I teaspoon coriander seeds

2-inch piece of cinnamon stick

Spicy Pickled Cauliflower

When cauliflower is pickled, the buds get a nice crunchy taste similar to that of the raw vegetable. I enjoy making this easy, quick pickle and serving it as a condiment to a spicy chicken curry, brochettes of lamb, or a nicely seared burger.

1. Place the cauliflower florets in a large bowl, sprinkle with the salt, and let stand for 3 hours. Rinse thoroughly under cold water and drain well.

2. In a large saucepan, combine the sugar, vinegar, mustard, curry powder, chili peppers, coriander seeds, and cinnamon stick. Bring to a boil, reduce the heat, and simmer for 5 minutes. Add the cauliflower florets and simmer, partially covered, for 8 minutes longer or until tender.

3. Remove the florets with a slotted spoon and pack into 2 or 3 hot pint jars. Pour the hot liquid over the florets, leaving a ¼-inch headspace. Remove all the visible air bubbles by sliding a thin knife down the sides of the jars, adjust the caps, and process for 10 minutes in a boiling water bath. Remove and let cool completely. Store for 2 to 3 months to develop flavor before opening.

MAKES 2 TO 3 PINTS

EGGPLANT

EGGPLANT, OR AUBERGINE AS IT IS KNOWN IN EUROPE, IS A UNIQUELY beautiful vegetable. The Victorians so admired its distinctive shape and rich violet color that they considered it an ornamental plant. In fact, the lovely plants with their big purple blossoms and glossy purple fruits are decorative enough to grow in containers or even in front of a flower border. Heaped in a basket along with red tomatoes and peppers, the voluptuous fruits make a display that is the essence of late summer and early autumn bounty.

Aside from its good looks, eggplant plays an essential role in many cuisines. In the Orient and Middle East it is often a substitute for meat and it is a feature of many Mediterranean dishes. Classics like Greek moussaka, French ratatouille, and the eggplant parmigiana of Italy are all based on this wonderful vegetable. Traveling through Sicily in early summer, I have noticed that every restaurant serves eggplant in at least six different ways. It is one of the few vegetables that is substantial enough to serve as a main course or even as a one-dish meal.

My only complaint with many eggplant dishes is a tendency to greasiness. Eggplant absorbs a great quantity of oil in cooking, only to release it in the finished preparation. Also, older large specimens can have bitter juices. The trick to solving both difficulties is to allow the eggplant to release its juices before cooking. Slice the eggplant and sprinkle the slices with coarse salt, cover them with a double layer of paper towels, and weight them down with a heavy pan or skillet for an hour. In Spain, cooks use a different but equally effective method: Submerge eggplant slices in a bowl filled with salted ice water. Drain after twenty minutes and dry well.

Besides sautéing and braising, a favorite method of mine for cooking smaller eggplants is to grill them over a charcoal fire, a gas flame, or even the coils of an electric stove. (Do not prick the skin during grilling or the delicious juices will escape.) Once the eggplant is charred on all sides, let it cool, slit it open, and scoop out the pulp onto a cutting board. Chop it fine and it is then ready for delectable eggplant "caviar," custard, or fritters. I think eggplant caviar, surrounded by cherry tomatoes, black olives, and cucumber sticks, is the most delightful of all vegetable dips. Some variations on the theme include the Middle Eastern version mixed with tahini (sesame paste), a little crushed garlic, and lemon juice. Chinese cooks sauté the chopped, smoky pulp in oil with minced garlic and fresh ginger and then combine it with minced scallions, sesame oil, soy sauce, and a drop of hot chili oil. It's a splendid accompaniment to barbecued spareribs. My own favorite dip is chopped eggplant simply mixed with mayonnaise, minced scallions, and a generous amount of freshly ground pepper.

Baby eggplants are very appealing, but if they are very immature they tend to be quite bitter. Braising is the best way to handle them. I usually insert slivers of garlic and fresh herbs into deep incisions made in the flesh, then cover them with a rich tomato sauce and braise them for one to one and a half hours in a low oven so that they do not burst.

A fine eggplant, in its prime, should not weigh more than one and a half pounds. Heavier fruit is usually quite seedy. Oversize eggplants can be used in many dishes, but you must first peel the toughened skin, which means the fruit will not hold its shape during cooking. One the other hand, it is not necessary to peel the tender skin of fresh young eggplants. The skin is attractive and tasty and helps to hold the eggplant together.

STORAGE

Garden and farm-fresh eggplant will keep up to one week when stored loosely in the vegetable bin, while store-bought eggplant should be used within three to four days. Be sure never to store eggplants in a plastic bag. Sautéed, broiled, grilled, or baked eggplant will keep well refrigerated for another three to four days.

GARDENING

Being a tropical plant, eggplant likes nothing better than to bask in the sun of a long hot summer. If summers in your area are short, consider one of the early maturing varieties such as Early Beauty Hybrid, which bears early over a long season, or Millionaire, an extra-early Japanese type with long thin fruits. Another early variety that is a favorite of mine is Dusky Hybrid. A superb heirloom variety is Violette di Firenze, which produces large lavender and white fruits. I also like to grow some of the baby types, such as Little Fingers and Slim Jims, a lavender variety in containers. Because eggplants take nearly four months from seed to maturity, I start my plants indoors eight to ten weeks before the last frost and transplant them to organically enriched soil when days are warm and nights stay above 50°F. I fertilize the plants every three to four weeks and water regularly so that the soil stays evenly moist. (A mulch is helpful.) Taller varieties laden with fruit may need staking.

HARVESTING

Start picking as soon as the fruits are the size you like. Do not let eggplants overripen because they will taste bitter and the plants will stop producing. The stems are tough, so use pruning shears to cut them.

Fricassee of Eggplant, Zucchini, and Two Mushrooms

2 medium eggplants, trimmed, unpeeled, and cut into ¾-inch cubes

Coarse salt

1 ounce dried porcini mushrooms, thoroughly rinsed under warm water to remove all grit

1½ cups chicken broth, preferably homemade (page 360)

9 tablespoons olive oil

¾ pound all-purpose mushrooms, wiped and stems removed

2 small zucchini, trimmed, cut in half lengthwise and then cut crosswise into ½-inch slices

2 large garlic cloves, peeled and finely minced

2 large shallots, peeled and finely minced

Freshly ground black pepper

3 to 4 tablespoons finely minced fresh parsley

*I*n Mediterranean cuisines eggplant is prepared in endless exciting ways, and this Galician fricassee is just such an example. What makes this dish particularly interesting is the fact that it does not contain tomatoes, letting both eggplant and mushrooms shine without their powerful garden partner.

1. Place the eggplant in a large bowl with ice water to cover, add 1 teaspoon salt, and soak for 1 to 2 hours. Drain thoroughly and dry well on paper towels. Reserve.

2. While the eggplant is draining, prepare the porcini: In a saucepan, combine the porcini and broth and simmer, covered, for 25 to 30 minutes or until tender. Remove the porcini from the broth and finely dice; reserve. Strain the broth through a double layer of cheesecloth and reserve separately.

3. In a large 12-inch skillet, heat 2 tablespoons of the olive oil over high heat. When hot, add the all-purpose mushrooms and sauté quickly until nicely browned. Remove with a slotted spoon to a side dish and reserve.

4. Add 1 tablespoon of the oil to the skillet and sauté the zucchini quickly until nicely browned. Remove with a slotted spoon to a side dish. Add 3 more tablespoons of oil to the skillet and when hot add half the eggplant and sauté quickly until nicely browned on all sides. Transfer to a colander with a slotted spoon and repeat with the remaining oil and eggplant.

5. Add 1 garlic clove and the shallots to the skillet and cook for 1 to 2 minutes without browning. Add the porcini and reserved porcini broth, bring to a boil, and reduce to 3 tablespoons. Reduce the heat, add the eggplant, zucchini, and all-purpose mushrooms, and cook for 2 to 3 minutes or until most of the liquid has evaporated. Season with salt and pepper, sprinkle with the remaining garlic and the parsley, and serve directly from the skillet.

SERVES 6

Provençal Ragout of Eggplant, Fall Vegetables, and Sausage

The appeal of this simple fall main course depends entirely on the quality of the sausage and of the eggplant, which must be snow-white inside and not seedy. Serve the ragout with couscous or a buttery polenta.

1. Place the eggplant cubes in a large bowl with ice water to cover. Add 1 tablespoon salt and let soak for 1 hour. Drain well and pat dry on paper towels.

2. Place the quartered tomatoes in a medium mixing bowl. Toss gently with 1 tablespoon of the olive oil and set aside.

3. In a large heavy skillet, heat 3 to 4 tablespoons of the olive oil over medium high heat. When the oil is hot, add the eggplant cubes and sauté quickly until nicely browned on all sides. Transfer to a colander set over over a bowl and set aside.

4. Add 1 to 2 tablespoons of the olive oil to the skillet, add the zucchini, and sauté quickly until nicely browned on all sides. Transfer to the colander with the eggplant.

5. Add 2 more tablespoons of the oil to the skillet. Add 1 chili pepper and cook over medium heat; when dark, remove and discard. Add the sausage and sauté until nicely browned on all sides but still pink in the center. Transfer the sausage to a cutting board, cut crosswise into ½-inch slices, and set aside.

6. Add another 1 to 2 tablespoons of the oil to the skillet. Add the garlic, onions, red and green peppers, and the remaining chili pepper. Season with salt and pepper and cook, partially covered, for 25 to 30 minutes.

7. Add the reserved eggplant, zucchini, and sausage, the oregano, and the thyme and season carefully with salt and pepper. Partially cover and cook for 10 minutes longer. Add the marinated tomatoes and toss gently just to heat through.

8. Transfer to a warm shallow serving platter, garnish with the minced parsley, and serve at once.

SERVES 4 TO 6

1 large eggplant, unpeeled, cut into 1-inch cubes
Coarse salt
8 ripe plum tomatoes, peeled, quartered lengthwise, and seeded
10 to 12 tablespoons extra-virgin olive oil
2 medium zucchini, trimmed and cut into ¾-inch cubes
2 small dry red chili peppers, broken in half
¾ pound sweet Italian sausage, preferably fennel sausage
2 large garlic cloves, peeled and finely minced
2 large red onions, peeled, quartered, and thinly sliced
1 large red bell pepper, cored, seeded, and thinly sliced
1 large green bell pepper, cored, seeded, and thinly sliced
Freshly ground black pepper
1 teaspoon dried oregano
1½ teaspoons dried thyme

GARNISH
2 to 3 tablespoons finely minced fresh parsley

Grilled Eggplant, Onion, and Tomato Gratin

2 small eggplants, unpeeled,
    cut crosswise into ½-inch
    slices
7 tablespoons extra-virgin
    olive oil
4 medium red onions, peeled,
    quartered, and thinly sliced
Coarse salt and freshly ground
    black pepper
3 ripe medium tomatoes, cut
    crosswise into ¼-inch slices
2 teaspoons finely minced fresh
    thyme leaves
2 teaspoons finely minced fresh
    rosemary leaves

GARNISH
12 small black oil-cured olives

Here is an obvious marriage of ingredients. All three are stars of the early fall garden—and, if you think about it, nature truly has a way of producing the most wonderful vegetables at the right time. This simple gratin is satisfying, delicious, and an excellent choice either as a starter or as an accompaniment to lamb, marinated grilled chicken, or, for a change, a nicely roasted shoulder of veal well seasoned with garlic and rosemary.

1. Prepare the charcoal grill.

2. Brush the eggplant slices with a little olive oil, using 2 tablespoons in all. When the coals are very hot, place the eggplant slices on the cooking grill, directly above the hot coals, and grill for about 1 minute on each side or until nicely browned. Do not overcook; the slices should still be firm. Remove and set aside.

3. In a heavy 10-inch skillet, heat 4 tablespoons of the olive oil over medium high heat, add the onions, and cook for 5 minutes or until they begin to brown. Reduce the heat, season with salt and pepper, and cook, partially covered, for 25 to 30 minutes or until soft and nicely browned.

4. Preheat the broiler.

5. Spread the onions evenly in the skillet and top with the eggplant slices in an overlapping pattern, covering the onions completely. Place the tomato slices in an overlapping pattern on top of the eggplant. Drizzle with the remaining tablespoon of olive oil and sprinkle with coarse salt, pepper, thyme, and rosemary. Bring to a simmer on top of the stove and immediately place under the broiler 6 inches from the source of heat. Broil 1 to 2 minutes or until the tomatoes are lightly browned. Garnish with the black olives and serve directly from the skillet.

SERVES 6

Asturian Stuffed Eggplant with Tuna, Capers, and Olives

Everyone remembers a dish or two their mother made particularly well. My mother stuffed eggplants in many ways, sometimes using leftovers such as couscous or even mashed potatoes, mixing them with the baked eggplant pulp and topping them with plenty of grated sheep's milk cheese. But my all-time favorite was this version in which she used canned tuna, lots of fresh tomatoes, herbs, and plenty of good seasoning. The result was always so satisfying that I am not quite sure my efforts will ever duplicate the savoriness of her recipe. Nevertheless my version is delicious in its own right. Be sure to have some leftovers, since the stuffing is even more delicious the next day and the next.

1. Preheat the oven to 350°F.

2. Cut a lengthwise slice off each eggplant. With a melon-ball cutter, scoop out the pulp, leaving a ¼-inch shell, being careful not to damage the skin. Finely mince the pulp and set aside. Reserve the eggplant shells separately.

3. Heat 3 tablespoons of the olive oil in a large skillet over medium heat. Add the minced eggplant pulp and sauté until lightly browned. Add the tomato sauce, breadcrumbs, parsley, basil, garlic, olives, capers, and tuna, season with salt and pepper, and cook for 2 minutes.

4. Fill the eggplant shells loosely with the tomato mixture and top each with a sprig of fresh oregano. Place in a heavy shallow dish, drizzle with the remaining 3 tablespoons of oil, and add 3 tablespoons of water to the dish. Bake for 35 to 40 minutes or until the eggplants are tender, adding a little water to the dish and basting with the pan juices every 15 minutes.

5. When the eggplants are done, remove from the oven, sprinkle with finely minced parsley, and serve warm or at room temperature.

SERVES 6 TO 8

6 to 8 small eggplants, about 4 inches long
6 tablespoons olive oil
1 cup Tomato and Shallot Sauce (page 160)
¾ cup homemade breadcrumbs
2 tablespoons finely minced fresh parsley
2 tablespoons minced fresh basil
2 large garlic cloves, peeled and finely minced
½ cup small black oil-cured olives, pitted and coarsely chopped
2 tablespoons tiny capers, drained
1 can (6½ ounces) tuna, packed in oil and drained
Salt and freshly ground black pepper
6 to 8 tiny sprigs of fresh oregano
⅓ cup water
GARNISH
Finely minced fresh parsley

Grilled Eggplant and Plum Tomato Soup

6 to 8 large ripe plum
   tomatoes
3 tablespoons extra-virgin
   olive oil
1 medium onion, peeled and
   finely minced
2 large garlic cloves, peeled
   and finely minced
1 tablespoon finely minced
   fresh oregano
2 medium eggplants, about 1
   to 1¼ pounds each, roasted
   (page 219) and pulp finely
   diced
3 cups chicken broth,
   preferably homemade
   (page 360)
Salt and freshly ground black
   pepper
Pinch of cayenne pepper

THE BASIL PASTE
2 cups packed fresh basil
   leaves, well washed and
   dried
3 to 5 tablespoons extra-virgin
   olive oil
Optional: 4 ounces mild goat
   cheese, such as Montrachet
1 large garlic clove, peeled and
   mashed

GARNISH
Tiny leaves of fresh basil

I like eggplant nearly every way, but when grilled it takes on a unique smoky taste. Here it is combined with tomatoes that have been roasted on the open gas flame. Although the skin is removed, the tomato also becomes slightly smoky, and the combination of the two vegetables in this simple soup is a perfect marriage of taste and textures.

1. Pierce the tomatoes onto a long fork through the stem end and hold the tomatoes over a medium high gas flame. "Grill" until the skin blisters on all sides. Peel the tomatoes carefully and cut in half crosswise. Remove the seeds from the pockets and roughly chop the tomato pulp.

2. In a heavy 3-quart casserole, heat the oil over medium heat. Add the onion, garlic, and oregano and sauté the mixture until the onion is soft but not browned, about 5 minutes. Add the tomatoes, eggplant, and broth, season with salt, pepper, and cayenne, and simmer, partially covered, for 35 minutes.

3. Let the soup cool slightly, transfer to a food processor, and process until smooth. You may have to puree in batches. Pass the soup through a food mill to catch all the remaining seeds. Return the soup to the casserole, season with salt and pepper, and keep warm.

4. Make the basil paste: Combine the basil leaves in the food processor with enough of the olive oil to make a smooth paste. Add the goat cheese, if using, and process the mixture until smooth. Add the mashed garlic and season with salt and pepper to taste.

5. Spoon the soup into individual soup bowls and top each portion with a dollop of the basil paste. Garnish with tiny whole basil leaves. Serve hot, accompanied by crusty French bread.

SERVES 4 TO 5

Eggplant Sandwiches with
Onion Jam á là Genovese

I first discovered this way of serving eggplant in a restaurant in Umbria. It was part of a lovely antipasti table that was memorable in its simplicity and seasonality: roasted whole onions, a big platter of roasted red peppers, marinated sardines, several bowls of olives, and of course a huge beautiful hunk of prosciutto. Once I tasted the eggplant sandwiches, I could only wonder why I had not thought of preparing them this way before. I usually serve one sandwich per person as an appetizer or for lunch drizzled with either a garlic, roast pepper, or tomato vinaigrette.

1. Slice the eggplants crosswise ½-inch thick, about 16 slices total. Place the eggplant slices in a large bowl with ice water to cover. Add the coarse salt and let soak for 1 hour.

2. While the eggplants are soaking, prepare the onion jam: In a medium skillet, heat 5 tablespoons of the oil over medium high heat. Add the onions and cook for 10 minutes, or until they start to brown. Reduce the heat, add the garlic, and continue to cook, partially covered, until the onions are soft and nicely browned, about 30 to 35 minutes.

3. Add the tomatoes and herbs, season with salt and pepper, and cook, uncovered, until all the tomato liquid has evaporated and the mixture is thick. Set aside to cool completely.

4. Drain the eggplant slices and dry thoroughly with paper towels. Dredge lightly in flour, shaking off the excess.

5. Heat 3 tablespoons of the oil in a large skillet over medium high heat. Sauté the eggplant slices a few at a time, adding oil as needed, until nicely browned on both sides. Transfer to paper towels and set aside.

6. Place 8 slices of eggplant on a serving platter. Top each with a dollop of the onion jam and then the remaining eggplant slices. Garnish with minced parsley, roasted pepper or pimientos, and black olives, and serve at room temperature.

SERVES 8

3 small eggplants, unpeeled, about ¾ to 1 pound each
1 teaspoon coarse salt
½ to ¾ cup olive oil
2 large onions, peeled, quartered, and thinly sliced
2 large garlic cloves, peeled and finely minced
4 to 5 large ripe tomatoes, peeled, seeded, and chopped
2 teaspoons fresh oregano leaves
2 teaspoons fresh thyme leaves
2 tablespoons finely minced fresh basil
Freshly ground black pepper
All-purpose flour for dredging

GARNISH
2 to 3 tablespoons finely minced fresh parsley
Thinly sliced roasted pepper or pimientos
Tiny black oil-cured olives

Baked Tomatoes with Roasted Eggplant and Goat Cheese

1 cup finely minced Roasted
   Eggplant (page 219)
1 extra-large egg
1 tablespoon finely minced
   shallots
2 tablespoons Crème Fraîche
   (page 358)
1 teaspoon finely minced fresh
   thyme leaves
3 tablespoons mild goat
   cheese, crumbled
Salt and freshly ground black
   pepper
6 ripe medium tomatoes
4 tablespoons olive oil

GARNISH
Sprigs of fresh parsley

I have found through my teaching that most cooks stop short when it comes to interesting vegetable preparations. While seasonality and freshness are becoming a matter of course, particularly when it comes to tomatoes, treating them creatively in warm preparations seems to involve too much time. Yet stuffed tomatoes make a wonderful appetizer, and when served as an accompaniment to a grilled veal or lamb chop, a grilled roast leg of lamb, or simple seared fish steak, they elevate a simple main course and round it off beautifully. Grill the eggplant over charcoal to give it the smoky flavor that is key to its preparation. If you do not plan to grill the main course, roast the eggplant on top of a gas stove directly over the high flame or put them directly on medium hot coils of an electric stove.

1. Preheat the oven to 350°F.

2. In a medium bowl, combine the eggplant, egg, shallots, crème fraîche, thyme, and goat cheese and mix well. Season with salt and pepper and set aside.

3. Cut a ¼-inch slice off the bottom (side opposite the stem end) of each tomato and reserve these "caps."

4. Hollow out each tomato leaving a ⅓-inch-thick shell. Fill each cavity with some of the eggplant mixture, mounding slightly, and place cut side up in a heavy baking dish. Top each tomato with one of the reserved "caps" and drizzle with the olive oil. Bake for 25 to 30 minutes or until the tomatoes are tender, basting often with the pan juices. Garnish with parsley and serve hot or at room temperature as a side dish or part of a buffet table.

SERVES 6

Roasted Eggplant

2 medium eggplants, unpeeled

I have to admit that eggplant is probably my favorite vegetable. It has a great affinity with many other vegetables, can stand on its own in many preparations, and can be teamed with almost every meat, poultry, and seafood. Simple roasting is the easiest but also one of the most delicious ways to serve it.

1. Prepare the charcoal grill.

2. When the coals are very hot, place the eggplants directly on the coals. Grill, turning often, until the skin is charred on all sides and the eggplants are quite tender. Be careful not to char beneath the skin.

3. Remove the eggplants carefully from the grill and transfer to a cutting surface. When they are cool enough to handle, scoop out the pulp, being careful not to include any part of the charred skin. Roughly chop the pulp and use as desired.

MAKES ABOUT 2 CUPS

LEEKS

FOR TOO MANY YEARS, AMERICANS HAVE REGARDED LEEKS PRIMARILY AS either a flavoring for soups and stews, or a vegetable to use only in combination with root vegetables or potatoes. The eager cook would go to the market to buy "a leek" only to learn that it was the most expensive item on the grocery list. So much for the French expression "poor man's asparagus"! They are indeed costly here (a good reason to grow your own), and consequently are rarely bought in quantity or served on their own. The subtle flavor of leeks vies with that of shallots as the mildest of the onion family. They also have a more intense flavor and better texture than scallions. I keep leeks on hand at all times as one of the basics in my kitchen, along with carrots, onions, parsley, and celery. This elegant vegetable is also beautiful to look at, with its characteristic long white stalk and fan of flat, deep green leaves.

In France, Belgium, and England, leeks are savored as a vegetable in their own right. Leeks served in a mustard vinaigrette is a classic preparation, a favorite bistro appetizer. In Catalonia, they are regarded as a delicacy, simply grilled in the embers of a wood fire and served whole, accompanied by a spicy mayonnaise. The smoky sweet taste is unforgettable. Top restaurants, both here and abroad, are now preparing leeks imaginatively and giving them gourmet vegetable status. You can sample poached leeks wrapped in prosciutto and served in a pool of green mayonnaise or try braised leeks dressed with Beluga caviar—possibly the most extravagant way of presenting this elegant vegetable. Cooked leeks are memorable wrapped in thin slices of ham and gratinéed or baked in a custard. Some cooks are substituting leeks for onions in many risottos and even tomato sauces. A fine julienne of leeks, braised in cream, is a favorite accompaniment to many elegant seafood dishes and has even been used as a topping for poached oysters.

Braising is the traditional and simplest way of preparing leeks, and many more elaborate recipes call for this preliminary step. When braising them, be sure to use a deep skillet filled with just enough water to cover them. I usually add two to three tablespoons of butter and a pinch of sugar to the water. Test the leeks several times for doneness and remove them from the water as soon as they are tender. A rich homemade chicken bouillon can be used instead of water and will greatly enhance their delicate flavor. After the leeks are tender, I like to enrich the bouillon slightly with butter and some herbs and spoon it over them. Other delicious accompaniments to braised leeks are mayonnaise-based sauces flavored with curry, mustard, or herbs. Serve leeks hot or at room temperature; refrigeration kills their sweet, mild taste.

Leeks are easy to grow, and the fall and winter harvest of this member of the onion family is a delightful addition to one's autumn cooking repertoire. For those who do not garden, leeks are now available by the bunch in most good markets practically year-round. This allows you to make a leek and potato soup on the spur of the moment or to enhance a simple pilaf of rice. When they first come into the markets at the beginning of the season, you can buy them just three quarters of an inch thick, in bunches of uniform size. Whether I get them from my own garden or from the market, I remove all but two inches of the green tops before storing them. However, I do not wash them until I am ready to use them.

When you are ready to cook the leeks, trim off the roots and slit the stalk with a sharp paring knife to within one half inch of the white bulb. Fan out the leaves and run under warm water to flush out the grit. Alternatively, you may soak leeks for an hour or two in a basin of warm water for an even more thorough job. If you are going to dice or mince the leeks, omit cleaning them first and rinse the minced leeks in a colander. My garden specimens are usually far grittier than store-bought leeks.

STORAGE

Placed in a plastic bag, the leeks will keep well for as long as a month. You will want to check them occasionally and, if the leeks are slippery, simply rinse them and remove the outer layer, dry them well with paper towels, and store again in a clean plastic bag.

GARDENING

Leeks would undoubtedly enjoy the popularity they deserve if gardeners and cooks knew that it is nearly impossible *not* to grow a good crop. Besides, many of the fine European varieties are increasingly available. Broad London is a reliable old standby, but I am especially fond of Blue Solaise, the superb Carina, and the long slender King Richard. Leeks like full sun, fertile soil enriched with organic matter, regular watering, and some patience on the part of the gardener. They are slow and will take 14 to 21 days to germinate and 110 to 130 days to mature, so be prepared to wait. Three weeks before the last spring frost, sow the seeds directly in the garden, as thinly as possible. Thin the grass-like seedlings to stand six inches apart and, as they grow, hill the soil up around the stems to blanch them.

HARVESTING

By autumn, you can begin to harvest young slender leeks—or use them even earlier as you would scallions. From then on, right through the winter and into spring, I have what I consider one of the greatest luxuries available only to the home gardener: fresh leeks, anytime I want them. I use a spading fork to carefully lift just as many as I need. Many varieties are perfectly winter-hardy, and a thick mulch of straw can keep the soil workable in all but the coldest climates. If the ground freezes really hard, harvest the remainder in spring.

Leek and Polenta Spoonbread

Leeks and corn overlap in the kitchen garden in early fall, and I always try to find ways of combining them at this time of year. This lovely, light soufflé-like preparation allows both vegetables to shine. Serve the spoonbread as a side dish to a hearty vegetable or meat chili or with the Fricassee of Eggplant, Zucchini, and Two Mushrooms on page 212.

1. Place the leeks in a colander and run under warm water to remove all sand and grit. Drain well and set aside.

2. In a large heavy skillet, melt 3 tablespoons of the butter over medium low heat. Add the corn and leeks and season with salt and pepper. Add the water and braise the vegetables, covered, for 5 to 8 minutes, or until tender. Remove the cover, raise the heat, and cook until all juices have evaporated. Reserve.

3. Preheat the oven to 375°F. Generously butter the bottom and sides of a 3-quart baking dish. Set aside.

4. Bring the milk to a simmer in a 2-quart saucepan and add the cornmeal, sprinkling in a little at a time, while constantly whisking, to avoid lumps. When all the cornmeal has been added, cook, partially covered, for an additional 15 minutes, stirring often, until very thick. Remove from the heat, stir in the remaining 4 tablespoons of butter, and set aside to cool.

5. Season the polenta with salt, pepper, and cayenne pepper. Add the egg yolks and whisk until well blended. Add the corn and leek mixture and fold gently. Cover and keep warm.

6. In a large mixing bowl, beat the egg whites with a pinch of salt until they form stiff peaks. Fold the whites gently but thoroughly into the polenta and pour into the prepared baking dish. Bake for 45 to 50 minutes or until the edges are quite firm, yet the center is still a little soft; the top of the spoonbread should be nicely browned and crusty.

7. Remove from the oven and let rest for 10 minutes. Cut into squares and serve hot.

SERVES 8 TO 10

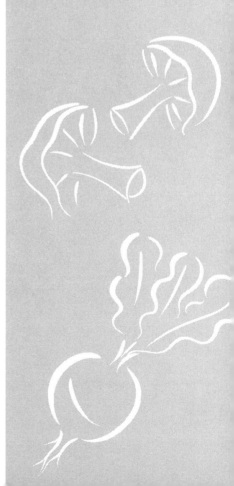

4 medium leeks, trimmed of all but 1 inch of greens, thinly sliced
7 tablespoons unsalted butter
2 cups fresh corn kernels (about 2 to 3 ears)
Salt and freshly ground white pepper
¼ cup water
3 cups whole milk
1 cup white cornmeal
Large pinch of cayenne pepper
3 extra-large egg yolks
4 extra-large egg whites

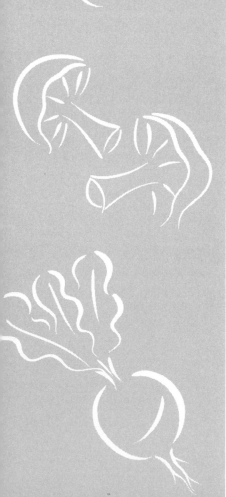

Braised Leeks and Carrots in a Rich Broth

12 small leeks

6 small carrots with their greens

3 cups chicken broth, preferably homemade (page 360)

3 tablespoons unsalted butter

Salt and freshly ground black pepper

GARNISH

Tiny leaves of fresh mint or dill

Select tender, small leeks of uniform size so that they will cook evenly. You can also prepare the vegetables in advance and reheat them in the microwave.

1. Trim the leeks of all but 1½ to 2 inches of greens. Remove and discard the first outer leaves of each leek and with a sharp knife, cut through the green part lengthwise. Place in a shallow dish, cover with warm water, and let soak for 30 minutes to 1 hour.

2. Trim the carrots of all but 1 inch of greens. Peel the carrots and set aside.

3. In a large, low-sided pan that will fit the leeks and carrots comfortably, add the broth, leeks, and carrots and simmer, partially covered, for 10 to 12 minutes or until tender. Remove the vegetables to a side dish with a slotted spoon, cover, and keep warm.

4. Raise the heat to high and reduce the broth to 1 cup. Taste the broth often while reducing and if you feel that at any given point the broth is salty enough, stop reduction immediately and measure only 1 cup. Whisk in the butter and season with salt and pepper to taste.

5. Cut each carrot and leek in half lengthwise and place 4 leek halves and 2 carrot halves on each of 6 individual serving plates in a crisscross pattern. Spoon some of the sauce around the vegetables and serve warm garnished with tiny leaves of mint or dill.

SERVES 6

Roast Cornish Hens with Stewed Leek and Tomato Compote

Cornish hens like the company of many seasonal vegetables, and in the summer–fall shoulder season I like to team them with braised leeks and a few ripe stewed plum tomatoes for a delectable one-dish meal that needs only some crusty bread for dipping into the good pan juices.

1. Preheat the oven to 375°F.

2. Dry the Cornish hens thoroughly and season. Place sprigs of thyme and basil in the cavity of each and truss.

3. In a heavy baking dish, melt 2 tablespoons of the butter with 1 teaspoon oil over medium heat, add the hens, and brown well on all sides. Place the pan in the center of the oven and roast the hens for 45 minutes to 1 hour; add 2 to 3 tablespoons of broth to the pan every 10 minutes and baste. The hens are done when their juices run pale yellow.

4. While the hens are roasting, carefully wash the leeks in a colander in warm water. Drain well.

5. Melt the remaining 2 tablespoons of butter in a large skillet over medium heat, add the leeks and water, and braise until soft, about 5 minutes. Add the tomatoes, season with salt and pepper, and cook the mixture until all the tomato juices have evaporated and the mixture is thick.

6. When the Cornish hens are done, remove and discard the trussing strings and cut the hens into serving pieces. Transfer to a serving platter and keep warm.

7. Thoroughly degrease the pan juices and return to the baking dish with the remaining broth and tomato-leek mixture. Place over medium heat and just heat through. If the sauce is too thin, whisk in bits of beurre manié until it lightly coats the spoon. Correct the seasoning. Spoon the juices around the hens and garnish with sprigs of thyme and basil.

S E R V E S   4

4 Cornish hens, about 1¼ pounds each
Salt and freshly ground black pepper
4 sprigs of fresh thyme
4 sprigs of fresh basil
4 tablespoons (½ stick) unsalted butter
1 teaspoon peanut oil
1½ cups chicken broth, preferably homemade (page 360)
3 large leeks, all but 2 inches of greens removed, thinly sliced
2 tablespoons water
3 large ripe tomatoes, peeled, seeded, and chopped
Optional: 1 Beurre Manié (page 361)

GARNISH
Sprigs of fresh thyme and basil

Leek and Parsnip Chowder

3 tablespoons unsalted butter
3½ tablespoons all-purpose
   flour
6 to 7 cups chicken broth,
   preferably homemade
   (page 360)
4 cups peeled and cubed
   parsnips
2 cups finely diced leeks, well
   rinsed and drained
2 cups peeled and finely diced
   red potatoes
Salt and freshly ground black
   pepper
½ cup heavy cream
GARNISH
2 tablespoons finely minced
   fresh parsley

As with all root vegetable soups, this one is at its best when made at least a day ahead of time. This allows the flavors of the vegetables to mingle and particularly allows the flavor of the rather delicate parsnip to stand out. For a touch of color you may add one cup of diced carrots to the soup as well or, instead of parsley, add two cups of fresh spinach leaves just after adding the cream. Let the soup heat through and serve immediately; do not let the spinach become overcooked or it will spoil the appearance of the soup.

1. In a heavy 3-quart saucepan, melt the butter over low heat, stir in the flour, and cook for 1 minute without browning. Add 6 cups of the broth and whisk constantly until the broth comes to a boil. Reduce the heat, add the parsnips, leeks, and potatoes, and season with salt and pepper. Simmer, partially covered, for 25 minutes or until the vegetables are tender but not falling apart.

2. Add the cream, correct the seasoning, and simmer for another 5 minutes. If the soup is too thick add the remaining broth.

3. Spoon the soup into individual soup bowls, garnish with minced parsley, and serve with crusty French bread.

S E R V E S   4   T O   6

Baked Penne with Leeks, Roquefort, and Thyme

This decidedly French-style pasta dish proves that pasta indeed has become a "cross-cultural" food. I first sampled this robust entrée in a small Italian–French restaurant in Nice, and it has since earned a permanent spot in my winter repertoire. I often substitute other cheeses, especially Stilton or a mild Gorgonzola. Be generous with the thyme in this dish and pass a bowl of freshly grated Parmesan.

1. Start by making the Roquefort and thyme cream: In a heavy 2½-quart saucepan, melt the butter over low heat. Add the shallots and 1 garlic clove and cook for 1 minute, or until soft but not brown. Add the flour, stir well, and cook for 1 minute longer. Add the broth, thyme, and cream, season with salt and pepper, and simmer over very low heat, partially covered, for 30 minutes, stirring often.

2. While the cream is simmering, prepare the leeks: Melt the butter in a 10-inch nonstick skillet over low heat. Add the leeks and season with salt and pepper. Add the broth, cover, and simmer until just tender, about 10 minutes. Add the leeks to the sauce together with the Roquefort, Parmesan, and remaining garlic and fold gently but thoroughly. Taste and correct the seasoning and keep warm.

3. Preheat the oven to 350°F.

4. In a large casserole, bring plenty of salted water to a boil. Add the oil and penne and cook until just tender "al dente." Drain well. Return the pasta to the casserole, pour the sauce over the pasta, and toss gently.

5. Transfer the pasta to a well-buttered, heavy rectangular baking dish or gratin dish, sprinkle with the ⅓ cup Parmesan, and cover with aluminum foil. Bake for 30 minutes or until hot and bubbly. Remove from the oven, let sit for 5 minutes, and serve with a bowl of Parmesan on the side.

SERVES 6

THE ROQUEFORT AND THYME CREAM

4 tablespoons (½ stick) unsalted butter

¼ cup finely minced shallots

2 large garlic cloves, peeled and mashed

⅓ cup all-purpose flour

⅔ cup chicken broth, preferably homemade (page 360)

1 tablespoon fresh thyme leaves

2 cups heavy cream

Salt and freshly ground black pepper

6 ounces Roquefort or other mild blue cheese, crumbled

½ cup freshly grated Parmesan cheese

THE LEEKS

4 tablespoons (½ stick) unsalted butter

2½ cups thinly sliced leeks, well rinsed and drained

Salt and freshly ground black pepper

¼ cup chicken broth, preferably homemade (page 360)

THE PASTA

Salt

1 tablespoon olive oil

¾ pound imported dried penne

⅓ cup freshly grated Parmesan cheese

Skillet-Braised Leeks with Provençal Mayonnaise

THE LEEKS
12 to 18 baby leeks
3 cups chicken broth,
 preferably homemade
 (page 360), or bouillon
Salt and freshly ground black
 pepper

**THE PROVENÇAL
MAYONNAISE**
2 cups tightly packed fresh
 spinach leaves, stemmed
 and washed
3 tablespoons finely minced
 scallions
4 tablespoons finely minced
 fresh parsley
2 large garlic cloves, peeled
 and crushed
4 to 6 flat anchovy fillets,
 drained and finely minced
½ cup sour cream
1 cup mayonnaise, preferably
 homemade (page 362)
Juice of 1 large lemon, or more
 to taste
Salt and freshly ground black
 pepper

GARNISH
1 hard-boiled egg, peeled and
 sieved
Sprigs of fresh parsley

This bright-green Provençal mayonnaise can be made several days in advance, but do not add the garlic until the day of serving. Though a homemade mayonnaise is much better, a good-quality commercial mayonnaise will work as well. Be sure to select leeks of uniform size to ensure even cooking.

1. Start by poaching the leeks: Trim the leeks of all but 1½ to 2 inches of greens. With a sharp knife, cut through the green part lengthwise. Place in a shallow dish, cover with warm water, and let soak for 30 minutes to 1 hour.

2. In a large, low-sided pan that will fit the leeks comfortably, add the broth and bring to a simmer. Add the leeks and season with salt and pepper and simmer, partially covered, for 10 to 12 minutes or until tender. Remove the leeks with a slotted spoon to a double layer of paper towels to drain. Set aside.

3. Make the mayonnaise: Place the spinach with the water that clings to its leaves in a small saucepan, set over medium heat, and cook, covered, until the spinach has just wilted. Drain and when cool enough to handle, gently squeeze the spinach to remove not all but most of the excess liquid. Set aside.

4. In a food processor, combine the spinach, scallions, parsley, garlic, and anchovies together with a little sour cream and process until smooth. Add the mayonnaise, remaining sour cream, and lemon juice, and process until just combined. Season with salt and pepper and chill for 4 to 6 hours before serving.

5. Cut the leeks in half lengthwise and arrange them decoratively on a rectangular platter. Spoon some of the sauce over the leeks and garnish with a sprinkling of sieved hard-boiled egg and sprigs of parsley. Serve as an appetizer or as part of an hors d'oeuvre table.

SERVES 6

Risotto of Leeks, Fennel, and Sea Scallops

Much like pasta, risotto likes the company of many seasonal vegetables. Leeks and rice are especially well suited to one another. When you add some sweet fennel and a few small sea or bay scallops, you have a winner of a recipe. Although the method for cooking the rice is not classic, it works beautifully and is easier on the cook. You must, however, keep a watchful eye on the rice so that it does not dry out or become mushy. If you cannot get scallops, shrimp would do nicely in this dish; or keep the risotto simple with just a large grating of fresh Parmesan and a sprinkling of fennel tops.

1. In a heavy 3-quart saucepan, melt 2 tablespoons of the butter together with the oil over medium high heat. Add the scallops and sauté just until nicely browned. Do not overcook. Remove with a slotted spoon to a side dish and reserve.

2. Add 2 tablespoons of butter to the saucepan. Add the leeks and fennel and sauté until soft and lightly browned. Add the rice, season with salt and pepper, and stir well into the fennel and leek mixture. Add 2 cups of the broth, cover the pan tightly, and simmer over very low heat for 12 minutes.

3. Raise the heat to medium and uncover the saucepan. Add the broth, ¼ cup at a time, stirring the rice constantly until each addition has been absorbed, for the next 10 minutes; you may not need all of the remaining broth. The rice should be tender on the outside but still somewhat chewy on the inside.

4. Add the heavy cream, if using, and the scallops together with their juices and fold gently into the risotto. Fold in the parsley and the Parmesan, if using, correct the seasoning, and serve immediately.

SERVES 5 TO 6

NOTE: A touch of Pernod or ½ teaspoon of fennel seed will increase the fennel flavor in the risotto. Parmesan is usually not used in a seafood risotto, but in this case the Parmesan, if of excellent quality, is a good addition.

---

4 tablespoons (½ stick) unsalted butter

2 teaspoons extra-virgin olive oil

½ pound small sea scallops

1½ cups finely minced leeks, rinsed and drained

1 medium fennel bulb, trimmed and thinly sliced

1½ cups Italian rice, preferably Arborio

Salt and freshly ground black pepper

4 to 5 cups chicken broth, preferably homemade (page 360), or bouillon

Optional: ¼ cup heavy cream

Finely minced fresh parsley

Optional: Freshly grated Parmesan cheese

Quick Couscous with Leeks, Red Peppers, and Zucchini

5 tablespoons unsalted butter

3 tablespoons very finely diced red bell pepper

3 tablespoons very finely diced zucchini, avoiding seedy center

2 small leeks, all but 2 inches of green removed, very finely diced, washed, rinsed, and drained

Salt and freshly ground black pepper

2 cups chicken broth, preferably homemade (page 360)

1 cup quick couscous, preferably imported

2 to 3 tablespoons finely minced fresh parsley

What did we do before quick couscous? This good-natured grain has certainly taken its permanent place on my pantry shelf, and I find that I serve it at least once a week. Combined with braised leeks, red pepper, and a possible addition of cumin, full-flavored saffron, or curry, it makes a satisfying and quick side dish that is good with just about any grilled or pan-braised main course as well as Roast Chicken with Fennel and Garlic (page 289), roast turkey (page 306), or pork tenderloins (page 298).

1. In a small skillet, melt 3 tablespoons of the butter over medium heat. Add the red pepper, zucchini, and leeks and season with salt and pepper. Reduce the heat and simmer, covered, for 5 minutes or until just tender. Set aside.

2. Bring the broth to a boil in a small saucepan. Add the couscous, bring back to a boil, cover, remove from heat, and set aside for 5 minutes. Add the remaining 2 tablespoons of butter while still warm and mix well. Stir in the vegetable mixture together with the parsley, mix well, and correct the seasoning. Serve hot.

SERVES 6

MUSHROOMS

WHEN I WAS GROWING UP, AUTUMN WAS SYNONYMOUS WITH WONderful mushrooms. For me, picking them was an eagerly anticipated annual event. My parents and I would make weekend excursions to the foothills of the Pyrenees during October and early November in search of the great boletus mushrooms that resemble the French cèpes and Italian porcini. Often we would come upon a farmhouse with a small makeshift stand out front where the farmer, his wife, or one of the children could be found grilling these big meaty mushrooms, pierced with slivers of garlic, over a small wood fire. Served on grilled peasant bread and doused with fruity olive oil and coarse salt, they were incomparable. On a lucky weekend, we could find our own to pick and return home bearing four or five pounds of this treasure. My mother always treated them with the respect appropriate to such a delicacy.

Throughout Italy, Spain, France, Germany, and Japan, mushrooms are the culinary highlight of the autumn season. Many wild varieties are brought into the markets during fall, and some are prized as highly as caviar or foie gras.

For decades, recipes calling for mushrooms did not specify any particular kind. It was simply assumed that the cook would purchase the ubiquitous round white variety commonly found in markets everywhere. In France, this variety goes by the rather elegant name of "Champignons de Paris" because it was cultivated in the disused quarries near Paris in the seventeenth century. In appearance, the white mushroom is certainly attractive enough, but compared to wild varieties, it has a bland, inconsequential flavor. Although many classic French dishes make use of this variety, its chief merit is that it adds a pleasant texture to salads and other dishes.

With the growing culinary interest in all things wild and unusual, cooks in the United States are exploring the vast and exciting world of this extraordinary gift of nature. A diversity of mushrooms is at last available in markets of more cosmopolitan areas, while ethnic markets offer many dried varieties.

Delicious and flavorful varieties such as shiitake, portobello, enoki, oyster, and cremini mushrooms are in fact cultivated, but they are well worth adding to your autumn repertoire. The only two truly wild varieties available commercially are the fall chanterelle from the Northwest and the springtime morel picked in Minnesota. They're worth their weight in gold, and are priced accordingly.

When buying mushrooms, freshness is the quality to look for. The common white mushroom can be considered fresh if the cap is creamy white and closed tightly around the stem. Avoid those with wide-open caps and dark gills or any that look spongy and discolored. The more exotic kinds are generally sold loose rather than prepackaged. Purchase them at a market that has a rapid turnover and be sure they look fresh and moist.

STORAGE

Cremini, shiitake, and the common white mushroom will all keep well for several days in a brown paper bag or a plastic bag into which a paper towel has been placed to absorb moisture. More delicate varieties, especially oyster and enoki mushrooms, should be used within a day of purchasing. Never wash mushrooms until just before you are ready to use them, and then a quick rinse in cool water is sufficient.

GARDENING

Mushroom kits are available from seed companies and garden centers. These are filled with planting medium and spawn and will provide several small flushes of mushrooms over a three- to four-month period. Only the common white and brown varieties are available in this form. Spawn for some of the more unusual varieties is also available from a few seed companies specializing in exotic or gourmet vegetables. For those gardeners determined to grow their own mushrooms from scratch, a fair amount of effort is required. It involves preparing the mushroom compost from poultry manure and wheat straw, ripening it to just the right stage, and filling wooden boxes with it. The mushroom spawn is then planted in the compost and covered with a layer of subsoil and peat. The whole business is kept watered and the temperature is monitored carefully. A basement is the place to do this as the mushrooms must be out of direct sunlight to grow. The first flush of mushrooms should appear in three weeks. Some mushroom spawn can be sown outdoors.

A word of caution. Although many varieties of wild mushrooms are to be found in this country, do not attempt collecting your own unless you are thoroughly familiar with the whole world of wild fungi and can absolutely differentiate between edible varieties and those that are poisonous. Some mushrooms are deadly.

Roast Shiitake Salad in Shallot Vinaigrette

THE SALAD

4-ounce piece of Parmesan cheese

20 large shiitake mushrooms, about 10 ounces, stems removed

2 to 3 tablespoons extra-virgin olive oil

Coarse salt and freshly ground black pepper

2 large garlic cloves, peeled and thinly sliced

2 large Belgian endives

1 medium head of radicchio

2 heads of Bibb lettuce

1 bunch of arugula, stems removed

THE VINAIGRETTE

2 tablespoons red wine vinegar

1 tablespoon sherry vinegar

8 tablespoons extra-virgin olive oil

1 large shallot, peeled and finely minced

1/4 teaspoon dry mustard

Coarse salt and freshly ground black pepper

While simple, this salad can nevertheless take its place as the starter of a rather elegant meal. The shiitake mushrooms become extremely flavorful when roasted and add an interesting touch to the cool greens. Be sure to use only the best Parmesan if you are going to serve "shavings" of it, since the cheese will otherwise be quite harsh tasting and dominate the buttery lettuces.

1. With a vegetable peeler, shave the Parmesan into thin shavings. Set aside.

2. Preheat the oven to 400°F.

3. Toss the shiitakes in a little of the oil, season with salt and pepper, and place on a baking sheet together with the sliced garlic. Roast for 10 to 12 minutes or until tender. Remove from the oven and cut into 1/4-inch slices. Return to the baking sheet, cover with foil, and keep warm in the turned-off oven.

4. Cut the endives into fine julienne strips. Break each radicchio leaf in two, removing the tough white part with the tip of a sharp knife. Thoroughly wash the Bibb lettuce and separate into leaves. Rinse the arugula and pat all the lettuces dry. Set the salad greens aside.

5. Make the vinaigrette: Place both of the vinegars in a large bowl and add the oil in a slow steady stream, whisking constantly, until the vinaigrette has emulsified. Add the shallot and dry mustard and season with salt and pepper.

6. Add the salad greens to the bowl and, just before serving, toss the salad thoroughly. Transfer to individual salad plates, top with warm shiitake slices, and sprinkle with Parmesan shavings. Serve immediately.

SERVES 4 TO 5

Frittata with Chanterelles, Scallions, and Goat Cheese

The unique chanterelle mushroom has a particular affinity to eggs and mild herbs, and indeed, when I was growing up, my mother used these lovely delicate wild mushrooms almost exclusively as an addition to scrambled eggs or as a filling for a fluffy omelette. Serve the frittata as a starter or a light main course along with some small roasted potatoes. Do not be tempted to serve a salad on the side, since a tart vinaigrette might overwhelm the delicate chanterelles.

1. Preheat the oven to 375°F.

2. In a heavy 10-inch skillet, melt 3 tablespoons of the butter over medium high heat. Add the chanterelles and cook, tossing often, until the mushrooms are tender and the juices have reduced to a syrupy glaze, about 5 minutes. Season with salt and pepper and transfer the mushrooms with their juices to a bowl. Reserve.

3. Reduce the heat and add the remaining 2 tablespoons of butter to the skillet. Add the scallions and cook until just wilted; add to the bowl containing the chanterelles.

4. Place the eggs in a large bowl, season with salt and pepper, and whisk until well blended. Add the mushroom mixture, goat cheese, and thyme and fold gently but thoroughly.

5. Heat the olive oil in a heavy ovenproof 10-inch skillet, preferably iron, over medium heat. When the oil is hot, add the egg mixture and disperse the mushrooms evenly. Cook for 1 to 2 minutes, or until the bottom is just set. Place the skillet in the oven and bake for 15 to 18 minutes, or until the eggs are just set and the top is lightly browned.

6. Remove from the oven and loosen the sides of the frittata if necessary by running a sharp knife around the sides. Carefully slide the frittata onto a large serving platter or invert onto the platter. Serve warm, cut into wedges.

S E R V E S   6

5 tablespoons unsalted butter
¾ pound fresh chanterelles, trimmed and cut in half or quartered if large
Salt and freshly ground black pepper
3 medium scallions, trimmed and finely minced
10 extra-large eggs
5 to 6 ounces mild goat cheese, crumbled
1 tablespoon fresh thyme leaves
2 tablespoons olive oil

Soup of Fall Mushrooms with Shallots and Garlic

1 ounce dried porcini
  mushrooms
6 cups beef broth
7 tablespoons unsalted butter
$\frac{1}{2}$ pound cremini mushrooms,
  stemmed, rinsed, and finely
  diced
$\frac{1}{2}$ cup finely minced shallots
2 medium garlic cloves, peeled
  and mashed
3 tablespoons all-purpose flour
$\frac{1}{2}$ cup heavy cream
Salt and freshly ground black
  pepper

GARNISH
6 all-purpose mushrooms,
  stemmed, cleaned, and
  thinly sliced
3 to 4 tablespoons finely
  minced fresh parsley

Mushroom soups are probably as popular as tomato soups, and while both are easy enough to make, I rarely come upon a truly tasty version in restaurants. Here is one that is chock-full of flavor. Packed with the unique smoky taste of porcini mushrooms, it is a cool-weather soup that goes well with just about any main course and also freezes beautifully.

1. Rinse the dried mushrooms thoroughly under cold running water to remove all sand and grit. Place in a medium saucepan together with the broth and simmer, covered, for 30 minutes or until tender. Drain the mushrooms and finely mince. Reserve the broth and minced mushrooms separately.

2. In a heavy 3$\frac{1}{2}$- to 4-quart casserole, melt 3 tablespoons of the butter over medium heat. Add the cremini and sauté quickly until nicely browned. Transfer with a slotted spoon to a side dish and reserve.

3. Reduce the heat to low, melt the remaining 4 tablespoons of butter in the casserole, and add the shallots, garlic, and 2 tablespoons of the reserved mushroom broth. Cover and simmer for about 3 minutes or until the shallots are soft.

4. Add the flour and stir until well blended. Add the remaining mushroom broth and whisk until well blended. Add the reserved Chilean and cremini mushrooms and simmer, covered, for 20 minutes.

5. Add the cream and just heat through. Taste and correct the seasoning and serve hot in individual soup bowls, garnished with a few thinly sliced all-purpose mushrooms and a sprinkling of parsley.

SERVES 6

Savory Mushroom and Shallot Timbales

Come fall, I crave all types of mushroom preparations. Although most mushrooms we eat are commercially grown and therefore available year-round, fall is the natural season for this wild delicacy. I often serve the timbales surrounded by cooked green lentils dressed in a garlic and sherry vinegar vinaigrette. The timbales are also a perfect side dish to a roast turkey or a juicy roast chicken. They can be made in advance and reheat well in either the microwave or a 200° F. oven.

2 tablespoons unsalted butter
2 tablespoons finely minced shallots
¾ pound all-purpose mushrooms, wiped, trimmed, and finely minced
Salt and freshly ground white pepper
2 extra-large eggs
1 extra-large egg yolk
¼ cup heavy cream

1. Preheat the oven to 350° F. Butter 6 (4-ounce) porcelain ramekins and set aside.

2. In a heavy 10-inch skillet, melt the butter over medium heat. Add the shallots and cook for 1 minute, or until soft but not browned. Add the mushrooms and cook, stirring often, until all the liquid has evaporated. Season with salt and pepper and reserve.

3. In a large mixing bowl, combine the eggs, egg yolk, and cream and whisk until well blended. Fold in the reserved mushroom mixture and season with salt and pepper.

4. Pour the mixture into the prepared ramekins and place in a large shallow baking dish. Fill the dish with water to come halfway up the sides of the ramekins. Place in the oven and bake for 20 to 25 minutes or until a knife inserted into one of the timbales comes out clean. Unmold and serve hot.

SERVES 6

Roasted Portobello Mushrooms in Garlic, Caper, and Anchovy Cream

THE ANCHOVY CREAM
- ½ cup (1 stick) unsalted butter
- 4 to 6 flat anchovy fillets, drained and finely minced
- 1 large garlic clove, peeled and mashed
- ⅓ cup heavy cream or Crème Fraîche (page 358)
- 1½ tablespoons well-drained capers, preferably nonpareil
- Coarse salt and freshly ground black pepper

THE MUSHROOMS
- 6 slices all-purpose white bread
- 6 tablespoons extra-virgin olive oil
- 6 large portobello mushrooms
- Freshly ground black pepper
- Coarse salt

GARNISH
- Tiny leaves of fresh parsley or basil

You can brush the toast rounds for these elegant canapés with olive oil and either sauté them or broil them in the oven. You can also substitute olive oil for the butter in the sauce, adding a touch of lemon juice or balsamic vinegar for additional taste and texture.

1. Start by making the cream sauce: In a heavy 2-quart saucepan, melt the butter over low heat. Add the anchovies and garlic and cook for 3 to 4 minutes, or until the anchovies have melted. Whisk in the heavy cream or crème fraîche, add the capers, and season the sauce carefully with a touch of pepper. You may not need any additional salt. Set aside.

2. With a large cookie cutter, cut the bread into rounds approximately the same size as the mushrooms.

3. In a large nonstick skillet, heat 2 tablespoons of the oil over medium heat. Add three bread slices and sauté until nicely browned on both sides. Transfer to a side dish and reserve. Add another 2 tablespoons of oil and sauté the remaining bread slices.

4. Preheat the oven to 400°F.

5. Brush the mushrooms on both sides with the remaining olive oil, season with freshly ground pepper, and place on a baking sheet. Roast for 10 to 12 minutes, or until tender and well heated through. Remove from the oven and season with coarse salt.

6. Place a toast round on each of 6 individual appetizer plates. Top each one with a mushroom. Reheat the sauce until it comes to a low simmer; do not let it come to a boil. Spoon some of the sauce over each mushroom and garnish with tiny parsley or basil leaves. Serve immediately.

SERVES 6

Ziti with Parmesan Mushroom Ragout

Every season brings with it a pasta dish that becomes my very favorite for a few weeks. Here is one of fall's top ten: a full-bodied preparation that combines either fresh or dried noodles with a toothsome, flavor-packed mushroom ragout.

1. Rinse the porcini well under warm water to remove any sand; drain thoroughly. Combine the porcini with the broth in a small saucepan and simmer for 20 minutes. Drain the porcini, reserving the broth, and cut them into a fine julienne.

2. In a heavy 10-inch skillet, heat the olive oil over medium heat, add the shiitakes, and sauté quickly until lightly browned. Remove with a slotted spoon to a side dish.

3. Melt the butter in the skillet, add the cremini mushrooms, and sauté quickly until nicely browned. Add the garlic, shallots, and parsley and cook for 1 minute. Add the reserved porcini broth and cook until it is reduced to 2 tablespoons.

4. Return the sautéed shiitakes and the porcini to the skillet and cook for 2 minutes longer. Add the heavy cream, season with salt and a large grinding of black pepper, and just heat through. Whisk in the additional butter, if using, cover, and keep warm.

5. Bring plenty of salted water to a boil in a large pot. Add the ziti and cook until just tender "al dente." Immediately add 2 cups cold water to the pot to stop further cooking and drain the pasta well.

6. Return the ziti to the casserole together with the mushroom ragout, Parmesan, and prosciutto or ham and toss well. Taste and correct the seasoning and transfer to a serving dish. Garnish with the minced parsley and serve hot with a bowl of Parmesan on the side.

SERVES 4

---

1 ounce dried porcini mushrooms

1 cup chicken broth, preferably homemade (page 360)

2 to 3 tablespoons olive oil

4 to 6 large fresh shiitake mushrooms, stemmed and cubed

3 tablespoons unsalted butter

8 to 10 medium cremini mushrooms, stemmed and cut into ½-inch cubes

1 teaspoon finely minced garlic

2 tablespoons finely minced fresh shallots

2 tablespoons finely minced fresh parsley

½ cup heavy cream

Salt and freshly ground black pepper

Optional: 2 to 3 tablespoons unsalted butter for enrichment

½ pound imported dried ziti

⅓ cup freshly grated Parmesan cheese

½ cup finely diced prosciutto or smoked ham

GARNISH

2 to 3 tablespoons finely minced fresh parsley

Bowl of freshly grated Parmesan cheese

Swordfish Scaloppine with Sautéed Mushrooms and Peppers

1 tablespoon peanut oil

10 fresh shiitake mushrooms, sliced

2 very small zucchini, trimmed and cubed

2 medium-size red bell peppers, cored, seeded, and thinly sliced

2 medium-size yellow bell peppers, cored, seeded, and thinly sliced

1 medium garlic clove, peeled and finely minced

1½ tablespoons black or dark soy sauce

4 swordfish steaks, cut about ½ inch thick

Salt and freshly ground black pepper

All-purpose flour for dredging

3 tablespoons olive oil

GARNISH

3 tablespoons finely minced fresh parsley

Here is a popular Catalan way of serving salt cod or monkfish that I found adapts extremely well to thin swordfish steaks. Serve the scaloppine on a bed of the mushroom and red pepper sauté, or top them with it; either way, this quick and flavorful preparation will undoubtedly become a permanent addition to your fall repertoire.

1. In a large heavy skillet, heat the peanut oil over high heat. Add the mushrooms, zucchini, and peppers and cook for 2 minutes, tossing constantly. Add the garlic and soy sauce and cook for 10 seconds longer. Keep warm.

2. Cut each steak in half crosswise to yield 8 scaloppine about ¼ inch thick.

3. Dry the swordfish on paper towels and season with salt and pepper. Dredge lightly in flour and set aside.

4. You will have to sauté the swordfish in two batches. For each batch, heat 1½ tablespoons of the olive oil in a large nonstick skillet over very high heat. When almost smoking, add 4 of the swordfish scaloppine without crowding the skillet and sauté for 1 to 2 minutes per side, or until just done; do not overcook. Transfer to a platter and keep warm while you sauté the remaining scaloppine.

5. Place two scaloppine on each of 4 individual serving plates and top each portion with some of the mushroom and pepper sauté. Garnish with minced parsley and serve at once.

SERVES 4

Sauté of Chicken Breasts with Porcini Mushrooms and Dill

Chicken breasts are probably the most popular part of the bird, yet they are so often overcooked and dry that I seldom order them in restaurants. Here they are teamed with porcini and quickly braised. The dish is done and ready to serve in 8 to 10 minutes. Creamy polenta, mashed potatoes, or the cabbage and parmesan pudding on page 198 make the perfect accompaniments.

1. Place the porcini in a strainer and rinse in warm water.

2. Combine the porcini and broth in a small saucepan and simmer, covered, for 25 to 30 minutes or until the mushrooms are tender. Remove the porcini with a slotted spoon to a cutting board, cut into a fine julienne, and reserve. Strain the stock through a double layer of cheesecloth and set aside.

3. Dry the chicken breasts thoroughly on paper towels. Season both sides with salt and pepper and dredge lightly in flour, shaking off excess.

4. In a large heavy skillet, melt the butter together with the oil over medium high heat. Add the chicken breasts without crowding the skillet and sauté until nicely browned on both sides. Transfer the chicken breasts to a side dish.

5. Add the shallots to the skillet and cook for 1 minute or until soft and lightly browned. Add the reserved porcini broth and return the chicken breasts to the skillet. Reduce the heat and simmer, covered, for 5 minutes. Transfer the chicken breasts to a serving platter, cover, and keep warm.

6. Add the porcini and heavy cream, if using, to the skillet and reduce slightly over medium high heat. Whisk in bits of beurre manié until the sauce lightly coats the spoon. Add the dill and correct the seasoning. Spoon the sauce over the chicken breasts and garnish with sprigs of fresh dill.

S E R V E S   6

1 ounce dried porcini mushrooms
1½ cups chicken broth, preferably homemade (page 360)
3 whole chicken breasts, boned, skinned, and cut in half
Salt and freshly ground black pepper
All-purpose flour for dredging
3 tablespoons unsalted butter
2 teaspoons peanut oil
3 tablespoons finely minced shallots
Optional: ½ cup heavy cream
1 Beurre Manié (page 361)
3 tablespoons finely minced fresh dill

GARNISH
Sprigs of fresh dill

RED PEPPERS

WHEN I FIRST CAME TO THIS COUNTRY IN THE LATE 1960S, I MISSED red peppers more than any other fall vegetable. Come autumn, the Barcelona market stalls were laden with red peppers. Giant bell peppers, small round cherry peppers, long red cayenne peppers, and reddish-green Italian frying peppers abounded. This bounty inspired the creation of richly flavored soups, fiery stews, and brilliant garlicky mayonnaise, similar to the aioli that my mother served with her bouillabaisse.

Not too long ago, the only place you could find fresh red peppers here was in Italian or farmer's markets for a few weeks in the fall. Now supermarkets boast a veritable rainbow of peppers including red, yellow, orange, and purple, all year round. Many are imported from Holland and are shockingly expensive, although that does not seem to affect the demand. Few people realize that there really is a season for red peppers, a time when they are plentiful and inexpensive. And few people know that a richly colored pepper is nothing more than a fully ripened green pepper, bursting with vitamins and sweet flavor. Being fully ripe, red peppers are quite perishable and must be used quickly.

Red peppers can be roasted over hot coals, over a gas flame, or directly on the coils of an electric stove. I do not recommend broiling the peppers in the oven; the result is soft and flabby. Once the skin of the pepper is charred all over, I wrap it in a double layer of damp paper toweling to create steam between the flesh and the skin. When the pepper is cool, I simply rub off the blackened skin. Now the peppers are ready for many exciting yet simple preparations. The least complicated is to core and quarter the peppers and drizzle fruity olive oil over them, along with some sherry or balsamic vinegar and coarse salt. Minced shallots or finely sliced red onion will further enhance this simple Mediterranean first course and classic antipasto ingredient. Diced roasted peppers are also a delicious addition to pastas, along with a creamy tomato sauce. Another of my favorites is an earthy roasted pepper soup in which I combine the peppers with sautéed onion and diced peeled potatoes. I simmer the vegetables in a flavorful chicken broth, puree the whole concoction, and finish it off with a little sour cream and a large grinding of black pepper. Gardeners with a surplus of red peppers at the end of the season can put the roasted peeled peppers in jars and cover them with a good olive oil. Refrigerated, they will keep you in roasted peppers right into the winter. Another alternative is to pickle them, which makes a marvelous Christmas gift. (See pages 121–22 for gardening information.)

STORAGE

Red peppers will store well in the refrigerator crisper for several days as long as they are not in a plastic bag. Hot peppers can be strung together loosely with sturdy thread and hung to dry. Snip them off as needed.

HARVESTING

Peppers can be harvested when they are the size and color you want. The plants will continue to produce until frost. Use a sharp knife or pruning shears to cut the peppers from the plant.

Basque Red Pepper, Tomato, and Zucchini Soup

3 tablespoons olive oil

2 medium onions, peeled, quartered, and thinly sliced

2 teaspoons imported sweet paprika

5 to 6 cups chicken broth, preferably homemade (page 360)

4 large ripe tomatoes, peeled, seeded, and chopped

3 large red bell peppers, cored, seeded, and finely diced

Salt and freshly ground black pepper

2 small zucchini, trimmed and finely diced

Pinch of cayenne pepper

½ to ¾ cup sour cream

GARNISH

2 to 3 tablespoons fresh cilantro leaves

In Basque cooking, tomatoes and peppers are teamed in a seemingly endless variety of dishes, all of which have marvelous flavor. This zesty soup is rather sweet tasting but it can also be made spicy by sautéing a tablespoon of finely minced fresh jalapeño pepper along with the onions. Serve the soup hot or slightly chilled. A garnish of mint leaves is a nice finishing touch.

1. Heat the oil over medium heat in a large casserole. Add the onions and cook, covered, for 8 to 10 minutes or until soft but not browned. Add the paprika and cook for 1 minute, stirring constantly.

2. Add the broth, tomatoes, and peppers, season with salt and pepper, and simmer for 15 minutes. Add the zucchini and simmer for 10 minutes longer or until tender. Correct the seasoning, adding a pinch of cayenne.

3. Just before serving, whisk in the sour cream and just heat through. Do not let the soup come to a boil. Serve hot, garnished with fresh cilantro.

SERVES 4 TO 6

Steamed Maine Mussels
in Spicy Pepper Sauce

Here is a wonderful Basque preparation in which the delicious mussel broth is mixed into a spicy red pepper sauce. Be sure to serve with plenty of peasant bread and a chilled Pinot Grigio or fruity French white wine. If you buy farm-raised mussels (ones that come in two- or three-pound bags), they will need little scrubbing. If the mussels have plenty of beards and feel gritty, be sure to scrub them thoroughly and then place in a large bowl of very cold water mixed with 1 tablespoon of flour. The flour and water mixture will force the mussels to expel their grit.

1. Scrub the mussels well under cold running water and remove beards; discard any open mussels.

2. In a large casserole, heat the oil over medium heat, add the chili pepper, shallots, garlic, and parsley, and cook for 1 minute. Add the wine and the mussels and steam, covered, until the mussels open. Transfer with a slotted spoon to a large bowl. Discard any mussels that do not open. Strain the mussel broth through a double layer of cheesecloth and return to the casserole.

3. Add the bell peppers, tomatoes, and herbs and simmer until the peppers are tender and the broth has reduced by one half to one third, tasting several times. Stop the reduction when the sauce has the right amount of saltiness. Add the crème fraîche and a large grinding of black pepper and whisk in bits of the beurre manié until the sauce lightly coats the spoon.

4. Return the mussels to the sauce and just heat through. Transfer to a deep serving bowl and garnish with fresh parsley and basil. Serve with plenty of napkins and crusty French bread.

S E R V E S   4

5 pounds small Maine mussels
⅓ cup extra-virgin olive oil
1 small dry red chili pepper, broken in half
3 tablespoons finely minced shallots
4 large garlic cloves, peeled and finely minced
½ cup finely minced fresh parsley
½ cup dry white wine
2 large red bell peppers, seeded, cored, and cut into ½-inch dice
3 large ripe tomatoes, peeled, seeded, and chopped
1 teaspoon fresh thyme leaves
1 teaspoon fresh oregano leaves
¾ cup Crème Fraîche (page 358)
Freshly ground black pepper
1 Beurre Manié (page 361)

GARNISH
Finely minced fresh parsley
Julienne of fresh basil leaves

Grilled Kebabs of Lamb and Two Peppers in Chili Marinade

THE MARINADE
1/2 cup extra-virgin olive oil
Juice of 1 lemon
1 teaspoon finely minced
   jalapeño pepper
1 large onion, thinly sliced
1 tablespoon finely minced
   fresh parsley
2 garlic cloves, finely minced
1 tablespoon pure ground chili
   powder
1 tablespoon whole cumin
   seeds, toasted and crushed
   (see page 82)
1 teaspoon turmeric
1 tablespoon finely minced
   fresh ginger
1 teaspoon dried oregano
2 tablespoons soy sauce
2 teaspoons dry sherry

THE KEBABS
1 leg of lamb, about 6 pounds,
   cut into 1 1/2-inch cubes
2 large red bell peppers, cored,
   seeded, and cut into
   1 1/2-inch squares
2 large yellow bell peppers,
   cored, seeded, and cut into
   1 1/2-inch squares
1 large Bermuda onion, cut
   into 1 1/2-inch squares
16 large mushrooms, wiped
   and stems removed
Coarse salt
Vegetable oil

GARNISH
Sprigs of fresh cilantro

*H*ere is a marinade that truly enhances the meat and gives it a unique and delicious flavor. The kebabs are interlaced with chunks of sweet peppers in the traditional style and simply grilled. Serve with the Pennsylvania Dutch Cabbage on page 192 and the Red Bliss Potato Salad on page 324 for a terrific weekend picnic or supper.

1. Start by making the marinade: In a large mixing bowl, combine all the ingredients for the marinade and whisk until well blended.

2. Place the cubes of lamb in a large resealable bag, pour the marinade over the lamb, and seal the bag. Set the bag in a bowl and refrigerate overnight, turning the bag several times.

3. The next day, prepare the charcoal grill.

4. Remove the lamb cubes from the marinade and thread them on 8 metal skewers, alternating with red and yellow peppers and squares of onion. Add a mushroom cap to each end of the kebabs, sprinkle with coarse salt, and set aside.

5. When the coals are white hot, brush the cooking grill with a little vegetable oil. Place the kebabs on the cooking grill over the coals and grill for 4 minutes, or until nicely browned. Turn over and grill for another 2 to 3 minutes, or until medium rare. Remove from the grill and serve hot, garnished with sprigs of cilantro and accompanied by a pilaf of rice or couscous.

SERVES 6 TO 8

Early Fall Risotto with Peppers, Thyme, and Two-Tone Zucchini

There is no question that when it comes to popularity, Italian cuisine has led the pack for years. However, many everyday cooks are still resistant to incorporating risottos into their repertoires, opting for quickly cooked pasta dishes rather than stirring rice for 25 minutes. This dish will be welcome for those who like rice as much as pasta. Here the rice is covered and cooked without stirring for 12 minutes. Once the rice is tender, the rest of the broth is added and the risotto is stirred for 3 to 5 minutes longer. The result is delicious, creamy, and very much like the authentic dish.

1. In a 10-inch skillet, heat 3 tablespoons of the oil over medium low heat. Add the peppers and cook for 5 minutes. Add the zucchini and squash and continue to cook for 2 minutes longer, or until the vegetables are tender. Add the tomatoes, season with salt and pepper, and cook for 4 minutes, or until the juices have reduced slightly. Set the mixture aside.

2. Heat the remaining 3 tablespoons of oil in a heavy 3½-quart casserole over medium heat. Add the onion and cook until soft but not browned. Add the rice, season with salt and pepper, and cook for 1 minute, stirring constantly. Add 2 cups of the chicken broth and the saffron, if using; reduce the heat to very low and simmer, tightly covered, for 12 minutes.

3. Raise the heat to medium and uncover the casserole. Add the remaining broth, ¼ cup at a time, stirring the rice constantly until each addition has been absorbed, for the next 5 to 10 minutes; you may not need all of the remaining broth. The rice should be tender on the outside but with a firm kernel on the inside. Season carefully with salt and pepper.

4. Fold in the vegetable mixture and the butter, if using, and correct the seasoning. Serve in individual bowls, topped with a grating of fresh Parmesan.

SERVES 4 TO 5

6 tablespoons extra-virgin olive oil
1 small yellow bell pepper, cored, seeded, and diced
1 small red bell pepper, cored, seeded, and diced
1 small zucchini, trimmed and diced
1 small yellow squash, trimmed and diced
2 ripe medium tomatoes, peeled, seeded, and diced
Salt and freshly ground black pepper
1 medium onion, peeled and finely minced
1¼ cups Italian rice, preferably Arborio
3 to 3½ cups chicken broth, preferably homemade (page 360)
Optional: ¼ teaspoon powdered saffron
Optional: 2 to 3 tablespoons unsalted butter

GARNISH
Freshly grated Parmesan cheese

Oven-Roasted Bell Pepper, Zucchini, and Eggplant Pizza

3 small Italian eggplants or 2 small eggplants, trimmed

3 tablespoons plus 1 teaspoon extra-virgin olive oil

2 large garlic cloves, peeled and thinly sliced

1 large red bell pepper, cored, seeded, and quartered

1 large yellow bell pepper, cored, seeded, and quartered

2 small zucchini, trimmed and cut into ½-inch slices

Coarse salt and freshly ground black pepper

Coarse yellow cornmeal for sprinkling on pizza pan

½ recipe Quick Pizza Dough (page 359)

1 teaspoon herbes de Provence

⅓ cup freshly grated Parmesan cheese

Early fall is a great time for homemade pizza. With all the "star" vegetables in abundance, it is a good way to use eggplant, tomatoes, red onions, peppers, and more peppers. You can oven-roast the vegetables or use the outdoor grill. The dough takes minutes to prepare and there is really nothing out there that tastes as good as your own pizza, which will be neither trendy nor traditional—just delicious.

1. Preheat the oven to 375°F.

2. Cut the Italian eggplants in half lengthwise, or if using 2 small eggplants, cut them into quarters lengthwise and then in half crosswise. Set aside.

3. In a large, heavy baking dish, heat 3 tablespoons of the olive oil over low heat. Add the sliced garlic and top with the vegetables in a single layer, slightly overlapping. Set the dish in the oven and roast for 45 minutes or until the vegetables are tender and nicely browned, turning the vegetables carefully with a spatula once or twice during roasting. Season with salt and pepper and reserve.

4. Raise the oven temperature to 425°F. Brush a black 12-inch pizza pan with the remaining oil and sprinkle lightly with cornmeal. Set aside.

5. Roll out the pizza dough on a lightly floured surface into a 9-inch circle. Transfer the dough to the prepared pizza pan and stretch gently from the center outward to the edge of the pan. If the dough becomes too elastic, let rest for 5 minutes and begin again.

6. Spread the pepper mixture evenly over the surface of the dough, leaving a ½-inch border. Sprinkle with the herbes de Provence and bake for 12 to 15 minutes, or until the crust is nicely browned. Sprinkle with Parmesan, cut into wedges, and serve hot.

SERVES 4

Cavatelli with Peppers, Tomatoes, and Roasted Shiitake Mushrooms

Cavatelli *is a relatively new pasta shape that may not yet be as widely available as fusilli, penne, or ziti, any one of which could be substituted for the cavatelli with equal success. Dry shiitake mushrooms could also stand in for the fresh ones in this dish; simply reconstitute the dry mushrooms in some chicken broth over low heat and, when tender, drain, slice thin, and add them to the pasta.*

1. Preheat the oven to 375°F.

2. Blanch the bacon in boiling water for 1 minute; drain, then dice. In a large heavy skillet, heat 2 tablespoons of the olive oil over medium heat, add the bacon, and sauté until almost crisp. Add the garlic and peppers and continue to sauté until the peppers are soft and lightly browned. You may need to add 2 to 3 tablespoons of water to the skillet to prevent the peppers from being scorched. Add the tomato sauce, season with salt and pepper, and just heat through. Reserve.

3. Place the shiitake in a shallow baking dish, drizzle with the remaining tablespoon of olive oil, and season lightly with coarse salt. Roast for 10 to 12 minutes or until tender and lightly browned. Cut the mushrooms crosswise into ¼-inch slices and add to the pepper mixture.

4. Bring plenty of salted water to a boil in a large casserole. Add the cavatelli and cook for 10 to 12 minutes or until tender. Drain the pasta, reserving about ½ cup of the water (see Note); transfer to the skillet and fold gently but thoroughly into the sauce. Serve on individual plates sprinkled with Parmesan and a large grinding of black pepper.

SERVES 4 TO 5

NOTE: Always keep some of the pasta cooking water. It has great flavor and is most useful for thinning out the pasta sauce if it is too thick.

2½ ounces slab bacon
3 tablespoons extra-virgin olive oil
2 large garlic cloves, peeled and thinly sliced
2 large red bell peppers, cored, seeded, quartered, and thinly sliced
I large yellow bell pepper, cored, seeded, quartered, and thinly sliced
Optional: 2 to 3 tablespoons water
½ to ¾ cup Classic Plum Tomato Sauce (page 159)
Coarse salt and freshly ground black pepper
12 large fresh shiitake mushrooms
I pound fresh or frozen cavatelli
Freshly grated Parmesan cheese

Roasted Red Pepper Salad in a Pesto Vinaigrette

8 to 10 medium-size red bell peppers, roasted and peeled (page 365)

½ small red onion, peeled, cut in half again, and very thinly sliced

1 large garlic clove, peeled and finely minced

1 cup tightly packed fresh basil leaves

¼ cup coarsely minced fresh parsley

2 to 3 tablespoons sherry vinegar

6 to 8 tablespoons extra-virgin olive oil

Salt and freshly ground black pepper

1 tablespoon tiny capers, drained

1 hard-boiled egg, finely minced

In the summer I never seem to tire of a plateful of sliced ripe tomatoes, and the same goes for a platter of fleshy red peppers in the fall. I like to team them with a variety of interesting vinaigrettes, especially this one that includes basil, capers, and garlic. For a terrific variation, top the peppers with two or three tablespoons of sautéed pine nuts. A crusty Tuscan bread and a semi-ripe goat cheese would complete perfectly this rather classic Italian starter, and it works well with just about any fall main course.

1. Quarter the roasted peppers, remove the seeds and membranes, and arrange decoratively on a serving platter. Sprinkle with the sliced onion and set aside.

2. In the workbowl of a food processor, combine the garlic, basil, parsley, vinegar, and olive oil and process until smooth. Season carefully with salt and add a large grinding of black pepper. Stir in the capers and hard-boiled egg. Spoon some dressing over the peppers and serve at room temperature with the remaining dressing on the side.

SERVES 6

Basque Sweet Pepper Soup
with Cilantro Sour Cream

Green, red, yellow, hot, and mild, peppers are probably the vegetable used most extensively in Basque cooking. Here is an everyday soup that you would find served in homes as well as in some of the best restaurants. On a recent visit to the region, I sampled this soup spooned into shallow individual soup plates to which grilled scallops and a pesto-filled zucchini blossom were added. It was delicious and memorable.

1. In a 3-quart cast-iron casserole, melt 2 tablespoons of the butter together with the oil over medium heat. Add the onions and garlic and sauté until soft but not browned. Add the tomatoes, peppers, and 6 cups of the broth and season with salt and pepper. Simmer the soup, partially covered, for 45 minutes.

2. Cool slightly and puree in batches in a food processor. Pass the soup through a food mill or fine sieve and reserve.

3. Melt the remaining 2 tablespoons of butter in the casserole over low heat. Add the flour and whisk until well blended. Add the pureed soup and again whisk to make sure the mixture is smooth. Add the cream, if using, taste and correct the seasoning, and just heat through. If the soup is too thick, add some of the remaining broth. Serve the soup in individual soup bowls either hot or at room temperature, garnished with a dollop of sour cream and a sprinkling of either cilantro leaves or minced dill.

S E R V E S 6

---

4 tablespoons (½ stick)
   unsalted butter
2 teaspoons olive oil
2 medium onions, peeled
   and finely minced
2 large garlic cloves, peeled
   and sliced
6 large ripe plum tomatoes,
   cubed, or 2 cups canned
   plum tomatoes, drained and
   chopped
8 large red bell peppers, cored,
   seeded, and cubed
6 to 7 cups chicken broth,
   preferably homemade
   (page 360)
Salt and freshly ground black
   pepper
2 tablespoons all-purpose flour
Optional: ⅓ cup heavy cream
GARNISH
Sour cream
Tiny whole fresh cilantro leaves
   or finely minced dill

TURNIPS AND RUTABAGAS

TURNIPS AND RUTABAGAS ARE MEMBERS OF THE SAME VEGETABLE FAMILY, but while turnips have a mild and delicate taste, the rutabaga has a far more assertive flavor. Both have an affinity to roasts, stews, and other hearty cool weather dishes.

Turnips

Baby turnips are one of spring's great garden treasures. I still have fond memories of my mother's Easter lamb stew, which boasted tiny garden peas, the first new potatoes, carrots, baby artichokes, and turnips. It was a homey dish, full of robust flavor, and I have never been able to duplicate it. Often, as a starter to a meal, we would enjoy a plateful of sweet marble-size turnips tossed in brown butter and sprinkled with pepper. A simple enough ritual, but it always heralded the beginning of the growing season in our garden.

Here, turnips are essentially a fall vegetable, especially in the Northeast where the spring growing season is short. Because heat has a detrimental effect on their flavor, they are at their best when grown for a fall crop. By the time young fresh turnips appear, most cooks are more than a little weary of the summer bounty of zucchini, tomatoes, corn, and cucumbers. Coupled with other vegetables of autumn, such as curly cabbage, leeks, and winter squash, turnips nudge your cooking repertoire toward a celebration of the new season.

Tracking down truly fresh young turnips is not easy, and the quality of store-bought turnips varies greatly from one region to another. In some parts of the South, turnips are sold with their bright green leaves still intact, a definite sign of freshness. In the North, their tops are most often trimmed to improve their shelf life. With or without leaves, a really fresh turnip feels solid and very firm and has a vibrant rosy shoulder. The taste of a good turnip falls somewhere between a tart apple and a crisp radish; when turnips are old they become unpleasantly woody and bitter.

Turnips often are described as dull, but nothing could be farther from the truth. Young turnips love the company of carrots, potatoes, and virtually all root vegetables. They add their own distinctive texture and flavor to any kind of vegetable soup and can also be substituted for potatoes in many recipes. Traditionally, they have been combined with duck and pork, but their delicate flavor also works beautifully with veal as well as seafood.

STORAGE

When buying turnips, look for fairly small, firm young roots, two or three inches in diameter. If the turnips are sold with their greens, cut these off and store separately. Place the turnips in a plastic bag and keep in your refrigerator's crisper. Use within ten days.

GARDENING

Easy to grow and quick to mature, turnips are a most rewarding vegetable for even the novice gardener. Because they are most definitely a cool-weather crop, you will have best results by sowing seed from mid to late summer for a fall harvest. Some varieties, such as the Japanese hybrid Tokyo Cross (all white) and the French De Milan, obligingly mature in just thirty-five days. Purple-Top White Globe and Milan Early Red Top are among the most popular. Gilfeather is an heirloom variety from Vermont with an especially sweet flavor. If you are fond of succulent turnip greens, you will want to try Shogoin, another Japanese import, bred for its tops. In frost-free areas, turnips are a fine winter crop. Sow turnip seed one half inch deep in any soil in a sunny location in midsummer, about two months before the first expected frost. Water regularly to encourage rapid growth. I like to sow the seed rather closely so that I can have an abundance of the tender young leaves from the thinnings end up with seedlings spaced at the recommended three to four inches apart. Make a couple of successive sowings two weeks apart.

HARVESTING

To me, the whole point of growing this vegetable is to have the luxury of baby turnips. Pulling the roots when they are golf-ball size is my ideal, although I always leave plenty to mature to three or four inches in diameter. Then the flavor is a little more developed but the texture is still delightfully crisp. A light touch of frost makes them even sweeter. Left in the ground too long, they rapidly become tough and woody.

Rutabagas

I must confess that it was several years before I tried growing rutabagas. Of course I had seen them in the markets in the autumn and winter, but their bulbous shape and dull coloring did not inspire me. Nor was I impressed with their assertive flavor, which seemed to dominate other foods. My feelings about rutabagas have since changed for the better, thanks to a Canadian friend who introduced me to her garden-grown version. I now enthusiastically include them in my garden as well as in my cold-weather menus.

The secret to enjoying this delicious fall vegetable is to harvest it or buy it small, no more than three or four inches in diameter. Local farm stands are a reliable source of small rutabagas if you don't grow your own. Once peeled, the moist, crisp, golden flesh of a rutabaga comes as a surprise. Delicious and versatile, rutabagas can be used in velvety purees and creamy soups, can be butter-braised in a gratin, or can be used as a substitute in many dishes that call for potatoes. The distinctive flavor of this humble vegetable mellows when properly cooked, and I prefer to enhance rather than subdue it. I particularly like rutabagas braised with an onion jam. The taste also marries beautifully with dried fruits such as prunes, apricots, and figs or with robustly flavored meats like roast loin of pork, applewood smoked turkey, or a spicy beef chili.

STORAGE

Look for smallish, well-shaped rutabagas. Unlike turnips, rutabagas from the market can be stored for as long as a month without deteriorating in quality. While I prefer the smaller ones to the large paraffin-coated roofs found in supermarkets, the latter can be quite delicious and will store well for several months. Rich in vitamins, rutabagas retain their food value well in storage.

GARDENING

Like turnips, rutabagas are undemanding to grow but they do need a long growing season, being tolerant of hard frost but not summer drought and heat. Although I am always tempted to start them in the spring along with the bulk of the garden, I have learned to wait until early or mid summer to sow the seed. The idea is to have them mature in late fall, before the ground freezes, so they will be sweet and tender. Purple Top Yellow is the leading variety and matures in about three months. Makes sure they get plenty of water throughout their growing season or their growth will be stunted and they will become pithy. When the seedlings have been up three to four weeks, thin them to stand eight inches apart and fertilize them. By harvest time in the fall, the roots will have filled in the wide spacing.

HARVESTING

Any time after the first hard frost is fine for harvesting your crop. If you're impatient or want to thin them more, go ahead and pull some when they are small and young. Their flavor will be mild and sweet but not as sweet as when fully matured. Because the roots are so hefty, I often break the tops when I try to pull them. I find that carefully sliding a spading fork under the rutabagas and popping them upward is the easiest and most back-saving method. Cut the tops off near the crown.

Gratin of Turnips à la Dauphinoise

3 tablespoons unsalted butter

4 to 5 medium turnips, peeled and very thinly sliced

Salt and freshly ground white pepper

¾ cup heavy cream

2 tablespoons finely shredded Gruyère cheese

*T*ruly fresh turnips with their almost transparent white/purplish skins are one of fall's most glorious vegetables. I really like them best when simply prepared as in this top-of-the-stove gratin, which cooks far more quickly than the conventional oven method. Be sure that the turnips are sliced thinly and evenly and do not let the pan juices run dry or the turnips will burn and turn bitter. For a slightly richer but delicious variation, add two to three tablespoons of crème fraîche and a mincing of tarragon, chives, or dill to the pan juices and cook to coating consistency. Serve with pan-seared sea scallops, scrod, salmon, or chicken breasts.

1. In a 10-inch ovenproof nonstick skillet, melt the butter over low heat. Add the turnips, season with salt and pepper, and add the heavy cream. Simmer, covered, for 20 to 25 minutes or until the turnips are tender and all but 2 tablespoons of the cream have been absorbed.

2. While the turnips are cooking, preheat the broiler.

3. Sprinkle the turnips with the Gruyère and run quickly under the broiler until the cheese has melted and browned nicely. Serve hot, directly from the skillet.

SERVES 4

Cream Cheese, Chive, and Turnip Custards

I *like to serve these delicate custards as a centerpiece to a meal of pan-seared shrimp, topped with a light lemon and garlic sauce. They also make a lovely side dish to a veal piccata or any chicken preparation. The custards can be made a day or two ahead, unmolded, and reheated either in a low oven or in the microwave. Whatever side dish you decide on, be sure that it does not overwhelm the delicate taste of the turnips.*

1. Preheat the oven to 350°F. Butter 6 to 8 (4-ounce) porcelain ramekins and set aside.

2. In a heavy 10-inch skillet, melt the butter over medium heat. Add the turnips and water or broth and season with salt, pepper, and a pinch of sugar. Reduce the heat and braise, partially covered, until the turnips are very soft and all the water has evaporated.

3. Transfer the turnips to a food processor and puree until smooth. Add the cream cheese and eggs and season with salt and pepper and chives, if using. Process until very smooth.

4. Spoon the mixture into the prepared ramekins and place in a large shallow baking dish. Fill the dish with boiling water to come halfway up the sides of the ramekins. Place in the center of the oven and bake for 25 minutes, or until lightly browned and the custard is set. A knife when inserted will come out clean.

5. Unmold the custards onto a serving platter. Garnish with sprigs of parsley and serve hot.

SERVES 6

2 tablespoons unsalted butter
1½ pounds medium turnips, trimmed, peeled, and thinly sliced
¼ to ½ cup water or chicken broth, preferably homemade (page 360)
Salt and freshly ground white pepper
Pinch of sugar
4 ounces cream cheese, softened
5 extra-large eggs
Optional: 2 to 3 tablespoons finely minced fresh chives

GARNISH
Sprigs of fresh parsley

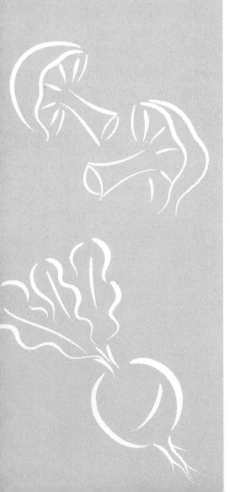

**3 pounds medium turnips,
about 8 to 9, trimmed,
peeled, and cut into ¾-inch
cubes**

Salt

**3 medium russet potatoes,
peeled and cut into ¾-inch
cubes**

**4 tablespoons (½ stick)
unsalted butter**

Freshly ground white pepper

3 tablespoons sour cream

**3 tablespoons finely minced
fresh chives**

Mashed Turnips
with Russet Potatoes

As any aficionado of bistro food knows, turnips and potatoes
have enjoyed a long and tasty friendship; together with carrots they comprise
the "backbone" of many home-style bistro dishes. Here the two root vegetables are teamed in a creamy smooth puree that is perfect with a flavorful
roast or a gutsy ragout of pork.

1. Place the turnips in a large saucepan with lightly salted
water to cover and simmer for 25 minutes, or until almost
tender. Add the potatoes and continue cooking until the
potatoes and turnips are very tender, about 15 minutes
longer.

2. Drain the vegetables and pass through a food mill into a
large bowl. Add the butter and salt and pepper to taste and
mix well. Whisk in the sour cream, and correct the seasoning.

3. Return the puree to the saucepan, place over low heat, and
cook for 2 to 3 minutes, stirring constantly, until the puree
thickens. Fold in the chives and serve hot.

SERVES 4 TO 6

Rutabaga and Sweet Potato Puree with Caramelized Pears

While *I am a great fan of turnips, I never liked the assertive taste of rutabaga until I started to grow my own and was able to pick them on the small side. I suddenly realized that this is truly a superb vegetable that works well with game, pork, and duck and has a lovely affinity to several fall fruits, particularly apples and pears. In the past two years more and more small rutabagas seem to appear in the markets, often unwaxed, which is the best way to buy them. This is delicious with a roast veal, duck or grilled pork tenderloins. The puree can be made a day or two ahead of time and reheated in a low oven or microwave.*

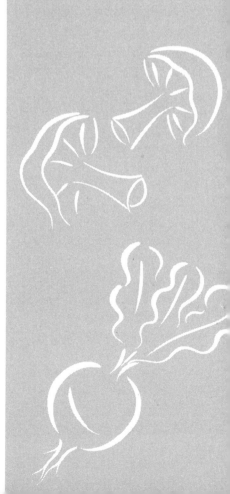

¾ pound rutabagas, about
  2 small bulbs
2 medium sweet potatoes
Coarse salt
2 medium-ripe Bartlett pears,
  peeled and cored
4 tablespoons (½ stick)
  unsalted butter
1½ teaspoons sugar
Large grinding of fresh nutmeg
2 to 3 tablespoons sour cream
Freshly ground black pepper

1. Peel the rutabagas and cut into 1-inch cubes. Peel and cube the sweet potatoes.

2. In a large saucepan, combine the rutabaga with salted water to cover and cook for 5 minutes over medium heat. Add the sweet potatoes and continue to cook until both vegetables are very tender, about 20 minutes longer. Do not drain. Set aside.

3. Cut the pears into ¾-inch cubes. In a 10-inch cast-iron skillet, melt 2 tablespoons of the butter over high heat. Add the pear cubes, sprinkle with the sugar, and sauté until the pears are well browned and caramelized. Add a large grinding of fresh nutmeg and set aside.

4. Drain the vegetables well and puree in a food processor. Add the remaining 2 tablespoons of butter and 2 tablespoons of the sour cream and season the puree carefully with salt and pepper.

5. Return the puree to the saucepan, bring almost to a simmer over medium heat, and stir constantly with a wooden spoon until thick; be careful not to burn it. Fold in the caramelized pears, correct the seasoning, and add the remaining sour cream if desired. Serve the puree hot.

SERVES 4 TO 5

Union Square Cafe's Puree of Rutabaga with Crispy Shallots

Salt

2 medium rutabagas, about 3 pounds, peeled and cut into 2-inch pieces

1 medium all-purpose potato, peeled and cut into 1½-inch pieces

4 tablespoons (½ stick) unsalted butter

2 to 3 tablespoons sour cream

Freshly ground white pepper

1½ tablespoons peanut oil

3 large shallots, peeled and thinly sliced

This side dish has become a staple at Union Square Cafe in Manhattan. It is one of those delicious little dishes that are simply addictive. I order it whenever I get the chance to eat at this wonderful restaurant.

1. Preheat the oven to 250° F.

2. In a large saucepan, bring plenty of salted water to a boil, add the rutabagas and potato, and cook until both vegetables are very tender.

3. Drain well and transfer the vegetables to a food processor together with 3 tablespoons of the butter and 2 tablespoons of the sour cream. Season with salt and pepper and if the mixture is not quite creamy, add the remaining tablespoon of sour cream. Transfer to an ovenproof dish, cover, and set in the center of the oven to keep warm.

4. In a heavy 8-inch skillet, melt the remaining tablespoon of butter together with the oil over medium high heat. Add the shallots and sauté until nicely browned and crisp-tender, about 4 minutes. Fold the shallots into the potato and rutabaga mixture and correct the seasoning. Serve hot.

SERVES 6

Lemon-Glazed Purple Turnips

Crisp young turnips take beautifully to pan braising. The key to the success of this simple dish is that the turnips are sliced very thinly and evenly and simmer over low heat in a heavy pan, preferably an old-fashioned cast-iron skillet. Once the turnips are tender, they are best reheated in a slow oven or in the microwave.

1. Place the turnips in a vegetable steamer, set over simmering salted water, and steam, covered, for 3 to 4 minutes, or until just tender. Remove from the steamer and set aside.

2. Melt the butter in a 10-inch nonstick skillet over medium heat, add the turnips, and cook for 1 minute. Add the broth and lemon juice and cook until reduced to a glaze that coats the turnips. Whisk in the optional beurre manié if you prefer more "sauce." Season with salt and a large grinding of pepper. Serve hot, garnished with a sprinkling of minced chives.

SERVES 4 TO 6

6 medium turnips (about 1½ pounds), trimmed, peeled, and cut into ¼-inch matchsticks
Salt
4 tablespoons (½ stick) unsalted butter
½ cup chicken broth, preferably homemade (page 360)
Juice of 1 large lemon
Optional: ¼ teaspoon Beurre Manié (page 361)
Freshly ground white pepper

GARNISH
2 tablespoons finely minced fresh chives

A Soup of Winter Bounty (with Turnips, Celery, and Potatoes)

2 large leeks, all but 2 inches
of greens removed

4 tablespoons (½ stick)
unsalted butter

5 large celery stalks, trimmed
and finely diced

1 medium all-purpose potato,
peeled and cut into ½-inch
cubes

3 medium turnips, peeled and
cut into ½-inch cubes

7 cups chicken broth,
preferably homemade
(page 360)

Salt and freshly ground white
pepper

¾ cup heavy cream

I am often accused by my family of having a "soup fetish" for I usually choose soup as a starter to most meals, year-round. As soon as the cool weather sets in, I start to crave the taste of root vegetables. All I need to do is reach into the freezer for a homemade chicken stock and thirty minutes later I get the first whiff of the hearty delicious soup that promises to satisfy my cravings. Served with either crusty French or black bread, there are few dishes that can top this as a way to begin a fall meal.

1. Finely dice the leeks, place in a colander, and run under warm water to remove all sand. Drain and reserve.

2. In a large heavy casserole, melt the butter over medium low heat. Add the leeks and celery and cook until soft but not brown, about 5 minutes.

3. Add the potato, turnips, and broth and season with salt and pepper. Simmer, partially covered, for 30 minutes or until the vegetables are very soft.

4. With a slotted spoon remove 1½ cups of the vegetables to a side dish and reserve. Transfer the remaining vegetables and broth to a food processor and process until smooth.

5. Return the soup to the casserole together with the reserved vegetables, add the heavy cream, and just heat through. Taste and correct the seasoning and serve hot or at room temperature.

SERVES 6

Turnip Tempura
with Soy–Chili Sauce

This is also a wonderful way to prepare strips of peppers and lengths of whole scallions.

1. Start by making the sauce: Combine all the ingredients for the sauce in a small mixing bowl and whisk until well blended. Let stand for 30 minutes to 1 hour to develop the flavor.

2. Preheat the oven to 250°F.

3. Next, make the batter: In the workbowl of a food processor or blender, combine the baking powder and flour. Add the peanut oil, sesame oil, and ¾ cup of the water and process until the mixture is smooth. Add the sesame seeds and scallions, season with salt and pepper, and pulse to combine.

4. In a wok or heavy casserole, heat the oil until it registers 375°F. on a thermometer. Test the batter by dipping a turnip slice in it; the batter should drip slowly off the turnip. If too thick, add the remaining water.

5. Dip the turnip slices in the batter, letting the excess drip off, and carefully add them a few at a time to the hot oil. Deep-fry until golden brown on all sides. Remove with a slotted spoon to paper towels and keep warm, uncovered, in the oven while continuing to deep-fry the remaining slices. Serve hot with soy–chili sauce.

SERVES 4 TO 6

THE SOY–CHILI SAUCE
- 5 tablespoons black or dark soy sauce
- 3 tablespoons water
- 2 teaspoons Chinese sesame oil
- 2 teaspoons hot chili oil
- 1 large garlic clove, peeled and mashed
- 1 tablespoon finely minced gingerroot

THE TEMPURA BATTER
- 1 tablespoon baking powder
- 1 cup all-purpose flour or rice flour
- ⅓ cup peanut oil
- 1 teaspoon Chinese sesame oil
- ¾ to 1 cup water
- 2 tablespoons sesame seeds, lightly toasted
- 4 medium scallions, trimmed and finely minced
- Salt and freshly ground black pepper

- 4 cups peanut oil or corn oil for deep-frying
- 3 to 4 medium turnips, peeled and cut into thin slices

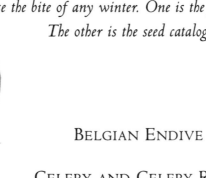

*There are two seasonal diversions that can
ease the bite of any winter. One is the January thaw.
The other is the seed catalogues.*

HAL BORLAND

BELGIAN ENDIVE

CELERY AND CELERY ROOT

FENNEL

ONIONS, GARLIC, AND SHALLOTS

PARSNIPS

POTATOES AND SWEET POTATOES

WINTER GREENS

WINTER SQUASH

Come November the vegetable garden has finally given its all and it is time to head indoors for a bit of armchair gardening and some well-deserved rest. Autumn has quietly tiptoed away and the last of the vegetables—onions, potatoes, Brussels sprouts, leeks—have been picked. A row or two of parsnips remain tucked into the ground where they will await winter's first frost, which will allow them to acquire their distinct sweetness.

With the success and failures of another gardening season behind me, I am ready to return to my cozy kitchen for some down-to-earth, earnest cold-weather cooking. To me, winter is a season of plenty in its own subdued way. With a definite chill in the air, the warmth of the kitchen seems to welcome the opportunity for reflection and for inspiration. Now after months of hectic gardening, picking, and preserving, I finally find the time to experiment with new dishes, to read recipes, and do more in-depth cooking, complete with stews, soups, side dishes, and hearty desserts. Now my thoughts turn invariably to old favorites, such as a savory cabbage tart, a ragout, and some flavorful vegetable fricassees.

I rather like the fact that my New England garden will remain dormant over the next few months, allowing me time to cook for my family and friends in a way that the growing seasons never seem to permit me to do. It is also a time of year in which my attention naturally turns to the supermarket experience. Without the cold cellar of yesteryear in which we used to store potatoes, onions, and apples for the season, the produce area of the supermarket becomes the natural alternative and, with some creativity, it can offer many interesting cold-weather choices to which I turn my full attention. I still sidestep the hothouse tomatoes, the Chilean asparagus, and the seemingly perfect berries that have been flown in from several time zones away. Even though hothouse herbs lack the intensity of those grown in the garden, I still settle for some varieties while bypassing those of which I have had my fill over the summer and fall months.

The winter kitchen may seem somewhat limited in its selection, but it still offers endless interesting possibilities. The selection may not be as picture perfect as those born out of the summer kitchen, but winter vegetables, with their subdued colors and shapes, make up for these slight shortcomings with their incredible versatility and depth of flavor. I often marvel at the innumerable tastes I seem to get out of the humble potato, out of a few pearl onions, out of simple pan-seared winter greens or a fennel fricassee. Amazingly, these slightly imperfect but flavor-packed vegetables have a wonderful way of complementing each other in countless combinations, be it in soups, stews, or side dishes. Personally, I rarely feel the need to use out-of-season produce, and although occasionally I like to roll with the punches and include some brilliant red and yellow peppers in my repertoire, I find plenty to keep my winter menus fresh and seasonal.

And then, before you know it, comes January and, in between testing and tasting, the colorful seed catalogs start arriving and with them the cycle of planning and mapping out next year's garden starts again. Of course, I am keenly aware that while my garden is still going through its seasonal hibernation, gardeners in other regions can take immediate advantage of their seed catalog offerings and in milder climates have already begun their gardening cycle. With a touch of envy, perhaps, I can't help but transport myself mentally to sunny garden plots in Florida or California where gardeners have a head start on true freshness.

But whether I like it or not, nature takes its course and for now I can be content to just sit back and relax as my armchair plans begin to take shape. Being an armchair gardener has its advantages, and I like the fact that I can keep an eye on my roast or a soup simmering on the corner of the stove while I check off my favorite types of tomatoes, cucumbers, and corn.

This is a good time of year for new gardeners to start planning their vegetable plots. Now you have time to ponder and decide what it is that you would like to grow most, what you can rely on the farm stand for, and what kinds of vegetables you consider a must in your garden. Winter may seem like it is here forever but soon the days will become longer and warmer, spring is in the air, and winter is again three seasons away.

BELGIAN ENDIVE

BELGIAN ENDIVE WAS DISCOVERED BY ACCIDENT. BELGIAN FARMERS HAD grown chicory for its roots, which were dried, roasted, and ground as a coffee substitute. When of the chicory a farmer noticed delicate white sprouts, called *chicons,* growing from the roots one winter, a new delicacy was born. Because the production of chicons demands intensive hand labor, they have never been grown on a commercial scale in this country, but they are rewarding to cultivate for home use throughout the fall and into the winter months.

Belgian endive is one of the most common cool-weather vegetables in Switzerland, France, and of course Belgium, where it is called *witloof* (Flemish for white leaf). During the winter months, its availability and affordability made it a staple in my diet when I was a college student in Geneva. My roommates and I were always trying to devise new ways of preparing it. As if I didn't have enough Belgian endive throughout the week, I often faced the prospect of still more on weekends at home. Belgian endives were considered a delicacy in Spain, so at my mother's request I frequently took a supply with me home to Barcelona on the overnight train. This meant a weekend full of mixed salads to which my mother would add one carefully sliced Belgian endive. By the end of my school years, I had had quite enough of this winter root.

When I arrived in this country I was finally ready to include Belgian endives in my winter cooking repertoire once again, only to find that, as in Spain, they were very pricey and hard to get. Times have changed and now this versatile winter vegetable is the darling of both chefs and home cooks. Like fennel, Belgian endive can be used both as a salad green and a cooked vegetable. Used raw, it shines either mixed with other lettuces or served alone. It takes kindly to many vinaigrettes, especially a sweet mustard and lemon dressing or one made with sherry vinegar, shallots, and virgin olive oil.

When braised or baked, Belgian endive assumes a more mellow, delicate taste, losing almost all of its bitterness while keeping a highly distinctive flavor that is complementary to veal, chicken, and roast duck. Whole endives can also be blanched or steamed. (I find that a heel of stale rye bread added to the water removes any bitterness.) When the endives are tender I braise them in a little butter and lemon juice in a heavy skillet either on the top of the stove or in the oven. My favorite preparation is to julienne them lengthwise and then cook them in a heavy cast-iron skillet with butter and a touch of sugar until they are brown and caramelized—a delectable accompaniment to pan-seared or braised salmon, sautéed scallops, chicken breasts, or veal scaloppine.

All the endives we buy are imported from Belgium and apt to be expensive, another good reason to give these unusual plants a go in your garden. When you do buy them, they should still be in the shipping box and wrapped in paper to protect them from light, which causes them to turn green and very bitter. Choose only endives that are creamy yellow with no trace of green, tightly closed, and free of brown spots.

STORAGE

Store Belgian endives in a plastic bag in the refrigerator crisper, where they will keep for several days, but long storage increases bitterness. Wash endives just before using them. If the outer leaves turn brown, simply remove them, dry the root, and return them to the refrigerator. When you are ready to use them, clean the endives by rinsing them quickly in cold running water; never let them soak, as that will also make them bitter. Remove any wilted outer leaves and, with the tip of a sharp knife, cut out the small, round white core.

GARDENING

Growing Belgian endives is a two-step process that is not difficult but is a little involved. Sow the seeds in early summer in rich, well-drained soil and let them grow until late fall. Then pull out the roots and cut off the inedible, romaine-like tops, leaving a two-inch stub. The roots will be about ten inches long; I like to trim them at the bottom so that they are all a uniform length of six to eight inches. I use a bushel basket for the next step, although any large pot or crate is satisfactory. Fill it with four inches of soil, stand the roots upright so that they are just touching, and fill in with more soil or sand to four inches above the stubs. Keep the container in total darkness (I keep it in the cellar) and the soil evenly moist. The shoots or chicons will appear in three to four weeks.

HARVESTING

When the chicons are four to five inches tall, cut them off just above the crown. If you have used good stout roots, you can water the whole business again and get a second crop. Rather than bring all the roots in from the garden at once, I pull several at a time for forcing until the ground freezes. That way I have an ongoing crop of chicons. Alternatively, you can store the roots in sand or sawdust in a cool place until you are ready to force them.

Sweet-and-Sour
Braised Endives

If you have only served endives raw in salad you'll be surprised by how much their natural bitterness is reduced when the vegetable is braised with a touch of vinegar and sugar. Serve the endives with a roast or sautéed chicken, braised pork tenderloins, or pan-seared scallops.

1. In a heavy 12-inch skillet, melt the butter together with the peanut oil over medium high heat. Add the endives and do not stir until the endives begin to brown.

2. Season with salt, pepper, vinegar, and sugar. Toss the endives and continue to sauté until they have become nicely browned and caramelized. Serve at once as an accompaniment to roasted or grilled meats.

S E R V E S 4 T O 6

4 tablespoons (½ stick)
  unsalted butter
2 teaspoons peanut oil
2 pounds Belgian endives, cut
  lengthwise into ½-inch
  julienne and covered
Salt and freshly ground white
  pepper
2 tablespoons sherry vinegar
1½ teaspoons sugar

Belgian Endive and Stilton Cheese Salad in Anchovy and Shallot Vinaigrette

2 flat anchovy fillets, drained and finely minced

2 tablespoons finely minced shallots

1½ tablespoons sherry vinegar

5 tablespoons walnut oil

Salt and freshly ground black pepper

6 large endives, cored and cut lengthwise into a fine julienne

3 ounces Stilton cheese, or other mild blue cheese, crumbled

GARNISH

2 tablespoons finely diced radishes

2 tablespoons finely diced cucumbers

Rather than have them play second fiddle to other greens, I like a salad of nothing but endives simply tossed with some diced full-flavored blue cheese and dressed in a zesty vinaigrette. If you wish to add a green, my suggestion would be arugula, which has great affinity to Belgian endives as well as to blue cheese. This is a lovely lunch salad but can also be served as a starter to a variety of menus.

1. In a medium bowl, combine the anchovies, shallots, vinegar, and oil and whisk until well blended. Season with salt and pepper and top with the endives, but do not toss the salad. Cover and refrigerate until serving.

2. Twenty minutes before serving, toss the salad gently and divide among 4 individual serving plates. Sprinkle each portion of salad with some of the cheese, garnish with the radishes and cucumbers, and serve at once.

SERVES 4

Endive Flans

Vegetable flans are a mainstay of French home cooking; leftover cooked cabbage, leeks, or spinach is folded into a well-seasoned custard mixture and baked in individual ramekins until just set. Here the flans are made with endives, which permeate the custard with their sweet but somewhat bitter flavor. Serve these custards with a nice roast, as an appetizer surrounded by sautéed or grilled sea scallops, or as a "centerpiece" for a bed of cool greens tossed in a shallot and sherry vinegar dressing. The flans can be made hours or even a day ahead of time and then reheated in a 250°F. oven or microwave.

1. Preheat the oven to 350°F. Butter the insides of 6 (4-ounce) ramekins. Place a circle of parchment in the bottom of each ramekin, butter the parchment, and set the ramekins aside.

2. Remove and discard the outer leaves from the endives. Core the endives with the tip of a sharp knife. Cut the endives in half lengthwise and then crosswise into ½-inch pieces.

3. Melt the butter in a large cast-iron skillet over medium high heat. Add the endives and sauté for 2 to 3 minutes, or until they begin to brown. Add the broth and season with salt, pepper, and the sugar. Reduce the heat and simmer, covered, for 6 to 8 minutes, or until very tender. Uncover the skillet and cook until all the liquid has evaporated. Reserve.

4. In a large bowl, combine the eggs, cream, and cheeses and whisk until well blended. Add the endives and season lightly with salt and pepper. Pour the mixture into the prepared ramekins and place them in a large baking dish.

5. Set the baking dish in the oven and fill with boiling water to come halfway up the sides of the ramekins. Bake for 25 minutes, or until the tip of a knife when inserted comes out clean.

6. Remove the flans from the oven and let cool for 5 minutes. Unmold them onto each dinner plate and serve immediately.

SERVES 6

- 1 pound Belgian endives
- 2 tablespoons unsalted butter
- 3 tablespoons chicken broth, preferably homemade (page 360)
- Salt and freshly ground white pepper
- 1 teaspoon sugar
- 3 extra-large eggs
- ¾ cup heavy cream
- 2 tablespoons freshly grated Gruyère cheese
- 2 tablespoons freshly grated Parmesan cheese

Endive and Scallop Salad with Creamy Mustard Vinaigrette

4 large Belgian endives

2 cups chicken broth, preferably homemade (page 360)

½ pound fresh bay scallops

4 tablespoons Crème Fraîche (page 358)

2 teaspoons Dijon mustard

¼ cup olive oil

2 tablespoons red wine vinegar

Salt and freshly ground black pepper

2 tablespoons finely minced fresh chives

Much like salmon and cucumbers, scallops and endives have had a happy long-standing relationship that works in both hot and cold combinations. Be sure to use only Massachusetts bay scallops or small sea scallops and avoid bay scallops from the Carolinas or Florida if possible. Serve this appetizer salad within an hour or two of preparation.

1. Remove the wilted outer leaves from the endives. With the tip of a sharp knife, remove the hard core. Cut the endives crosswise into ¼-inch slices, transfer to a salad bowl, and chill until serving time.

2. In a small heavy saucepan, bring the chicken broth to a simmer. Add the scallops and poach, without letting the broth come to a boil, for 1 minute, or until the scallops just turn opaque. Chill the scallops in their poaching liquid for 30 minutes, or until ready to serve.

3. In a small mixing bowl, combine the crème fraîche, mustard, oil, and vinegar and whisk until smooth. Season with salt and pepper and fold in the chives.

4. To serve, drain the scallops very well and add them to the salad bowl with the endives. Pour the dressing over the salad, toss lightly, and correct the seasoning, adding a large grinding of pepper. Serve at once as an appetizer, accompanied by a crusty French bread.

SERVES 4

Cream of Belgian Endive, Fennel, and Arugula Soup

Idevised this soup during my college days, when Belgian endives were plentiful and inexpensive. Now with the addition of fennel and a julienne of arugula it becomes a far more sophisticated and interesting soup. It has to be made a day or two ahead of time to allow the endives to give up their full flavor. Although it is not a must, a good full-bodied homemade chicken stock does make a difference in this kind of creamy, delicate soup.

1. Trim the endives of any wilted outer leaves and rinse quickly under cold water. Cut in half lengthwise and then crosswise into fine julienne slices.

2. Trim the fennel of all leaves and stalks and remove the outer layer if it is bruised or brown. Quarter the bulb and cut crosswise into thin slices.

3. In a 10-inch cast-iron skillet, melt 2 tablespoons of the butter over high heat, add the endives and fennel, and cook until the vegetables begin to brown. Add the sugar, lower the heat, and continue to sauté the mixture, stirring it well with a wooden spoon, until nicely browned and caramelized. Be very careful not to burn the vegetables. Reserve.

4. In a 3½-quart casserole, melt the remaining 3 table-spoons of butter. Add the flour and stir until well blended. Whisk in 5 cups of broth all at once. Bring to a boil and add the vegetable mixture. Season with salt and pepper and simmer, partially covered, for 35 minutes. Add the cream and correct the seasoning. If the soup is too thick, add the remaining broth.

5. Just before serving reheat the soup, add the arugula or Bibb lettuce, and simmer until the greens have just wilted. Serve the soup hot accompanied by a bowl of grated Parmesan and crusty French bread.

SERVES 4 TO 5

6 large Belgian endives
1 medium-size fennel bulb
5 tablespoons unsalted butter
1 teaspoon sugar
3 tablespoons all-purpose flour
5 to 6 cups chicken broth, preferably homemade (page 360)
Salt and freshly ground white pepper
½ cup heavy cream
1 large bunch of fresh arugula, stems removed, or 1 cup tightly packed small Bibb lettuce leaves, well washed and drained

GARNISH
Coarsely grated Parmesan cheese

Roast Chicken à la Flamande

1 whole chicken, about
   3½ pounds
Coarse salt
Freshly ground white pepper
1½ teaspoons dried thyme
1 large garlic clove, peeled
   and mashed
3 tablespoons unsalted butter
1 tablespoon corn or peanut oil
4 large Belgian endives,
   trimmed and cut in half
   lengthwise
1 to 1½ cups chicken broth,
   preferably homemade
   (page 360)
Optional: 1 teaspoon Beurre
   Manié (page 361)

GARNISH
Finely minced fresh parsley

There is nothing simpler than roasting a chicken with a garniture of seasonal vegetables. Carrots, turnips, small onions, and whole peeled garlic cloves are just a few of the vegetables that come to mind. But my favorite is a Belgian bistro classic that I never tire of. Contrary to most vegetables, which seem to sweeten the pan juices excessively, Belgian endives do not. It's a perfect one-dish meal that can be ready to serve in less than an hour. You may also pair it with Caramelized Oven-Roasted Parsnips (page 315) or Potato Puree Danoise (page 330).

1. Preheat the oven to 400°F. Season the chicken with salt, pepper, and thyme, rub with the mashed garlic, and set aside.

2. In a large cast-iron skillet, melt the butter together with the oil over high heat. Add the chicken and brown on all sides. Add the endives cut side down, season with salt and pepper, and add ⅓ cup of the broth. Place the skillet in the oven and roast for 45 minutes to 1 hour or until the juices run pale yellow, basting every 10 minutes with a little broth. Turn the endives halfway through cooking to be sure they do not burn.

3. When the chicken is done, cut it into quarters and transfer to a serving platter. Garnish with the roasted endives and keep warm.

4. Degrease the pan juices and return them to the skillet. Place the skillet over direct heat, add any remaining broth, and whisk in a little beurre manié to thicken the pan juices, if desired. Spoon over the chicken and garnish with minced parsley.

S E R V E S   3   T O   4

CELERY AND CELERY ROOT

CELERY AND CELERY ROOT ARE OF THE SAME VEGETABLE FAMILY, BUT most Americans are more familiar with Pascal celery. The root vegetable is just starting to gain the popularity it deserves. The vegetables are interchangeable as a flavoring for soups, and both are delicious simply braised or pureed.

Celery

Celery is a year-round staple in many kitchens. Many people wouldn't dream of making tuna salad or cole slaw without it, while others only think of celery as a vegetable to keep on hand for nibbling. Even in Europe, celery is sold primarily as a soup green. Few cooks take celery very seriously as a vegetable in its own right. That's too bad, because this versatile vegetable has a lot of merit.

To me, raw celery is strong and overpowering, but when cooked it has a delicate, subtle flavor. It is an essential ingredient in stocks and soup bases. I enjoy it served alone and like to gently braise it in the oven in a full-flavored stock with a little butter. (Boiling or steaming destroys the natural flavor of celery, leaving it tasting flat.) Prepared this way, it makes an elegant accompaniment to seafood, veal, and poultry dishes. A classic English soup made with celery and Stilton cheese is one of my favorite winter appetizers; a handful of diced celery adds an interesting crunch to a buttery risotto.

Pascal celery is the kind most commonly grown here commercially and sold in bunches in the supermarket. In some supermarkets, we can even choose from varieties like the very delicate White Ice and the toothsome Golden Self-Blanching, which are usually sold in packages of two hearts. While celery will probably never enjoy the newfound popularity of its close cousin, celery root, it is a fine addition to the winter kitchen and deserves to be used creatively.

STORAGE

Celery can be stored successfully for several weeks. I usually trim about two inches from the leaf tops and place them in a separate plastic bag. The stalks will then fit in their own plastic bag to be kept crisp and moist. If after a couple of weeks the celery starts to yellow and the outer stalks show signs of decay, simply remove them and trim the inner stalks and place in a clean plastic bag. The celery leaves are a fine addition to stocks and soups.

GARDENING

Make no mistake about it, celery is a demanding vegetable to grow, but you will feel very proud when you produce your own beautiful stalks. I urge you to try a row in your garden. Basically there are two types of celery; the self-blanching types like Golden Self-Blanching and the more nutritious green-stalked types which include old standbys like Tendercrisp and Summer Pascal, as well as the newer, tall Utah 52-70 R. All can be grown in virtually any part of the country if you can provide acceptable growing conditions. Celery is a greedy plant, requiring a very fertile soil and copious amounts of moisture and high-nitrogen fertilizer. The soil where it is to grow should be enriched with liberal amounts of organic matter. Celery takes at least six months from sowing seed to harvest. Except in frost-free areas, I recommend that you start the seed indoors in spring ten weeks prior to the last frost. Germination will take about three weeks of that time. Seven or eight weeks later, transplant the seedlings to the garden, allowing five inches between the plants. Fertilize at transplanting time and every six weeks thereafter and keep moist at all times. If you like your celery stalks white, pull up the soil around the stalks to the top of the leaves four weeks before harvesting. Blanching does tenderize the stalks but cuts down the nutritional value.

HARVESTING

Begin harvesting as soon as the stalks look large enough to use, usually in September, about four months after transplanting. Initially I pick just the outer stalks, allowing the plant to continue growing. Celery tolerates mild frost and can stand in the garden well into fall if it is mulched with straw. To harvest, slide a spading fork under the entire plant and lift it up.

Celery Root (Celeriac)

Celery root is hardly a vegetable you would pick up at the market for its good looks. But beneath that brown, knobby, coarse exterior lies a tender heart. It enjoys enormous popularity in central Europe and France, and anyone familiar with French cooking will recognize celery root as the delicious main ingredient of the mustardy remoulade salad that is possibly that country's most popular appetizer. Besides grating it raw for salads, use this adaptable, earthy root vegetable for gratinées, or mash, boil, sauté, and even deep-fry it for superb winter dishes. Celery root is especially delicious combined with potatoes in a puree or cream soup, and although it is one of the few vegetables that I wouldn't use with tomatoes or other Mediterranean-type vegetables, celery root is outstanding with dishes containing apples or pears.

In markets throughout Europe, you can find giant celery roots that are fresh, crisp, and juicy, but that is seldom the case in America. Here, even in fall and winter, the roots are apt to be rather tired and flabby, a sure indication that they will be stringy, hollow, and dry. A good fresh celery root will have a distinct celery aroma, a characteristic not present in old roots that have been sitting in the market too long. When using celery root, peel it first and put it immediately into acidulated water to keep it from turning brown. I also add some milk to the cooking water to whiten the root when I poach or boil celeriac.

STORAGE

Store celery root in a perforated plastic bag in the vegetable bin of the refrigerator. It will keep for a week to ten days. If there are any signs of rotting or decay be sure to change the bag.

GARDENING

Alabaster is the time-honored variety of celeriac that is found in most gardens, but the Dutch have recently introduced Zwindra, a superior variety that is very easy to grow and has firm, fine-textured flesh. The growing requirements of celeriac are essentially the same as for celery: a long growing season, soil liberally enriched with organic matter, and plenty of water, especially in dry weather. Like celery, celeriac also takes a long time to mature, at least 120 days. I start mine indoors about ten weeks before the last frost and transplant them to the garden so that they are ten to twelve inches apart. Setting the plants out when nights are still very cold will cause the plants to go to seed. I feed them with a balanced fertilizer at transplanting time and two or three more times before harvest. I've learned that the secret to getting nice, large, firm roots is to mound the soil over the roots during the first eight weeks of growth or apply mulch. Midway through the growing season, around midsummer, I gradually push the soil back, exposing the crown, and remove the older, lower leaves. This produces smoother, larger roots.

Harvesting

Once the roots are three to four inches across, you can begin harvesting them as needed. They are impervious to frost and can be left in the ground through winter, covered with a thick mulch of straw to facilitate pulling.

Skillet-Braised Celery Puree

Celery has never had a strong presence in my cooking repertoire, since I grow it primarily as a pot herb. But in the winter months, I have come to appreciate its wonderful taste and varied uses. Braising it gently in a little butter and enriching it with a touch of cream or crème fraîche brings out its true mellow and unique flavor. Serve it with sautéed chicken breasts or salmon fillets. An addition of minced herbs such as dill or parsley makes for a nice variation.

1. In a large cast-iron skillet, melt the butter over medium low heat. Add the celery and broth, season with salt and pepper, and simmer, partially covered, for 20 minutes or until the celery is very tender. Remove the cover, raise the heat, and cook until all the liquid has evaporated.

2. Transfer the celery to a food processor and process until smooth. Add the crème fraîche, process until just combined, and return the puree to the skillet. Set aside.

3. In a small skillet heat the peanut oil over medium heat. Add the flour and whisk until the mixture turns a hazelnut brown, being careful not to burn.

4. Add the oil mixture to the celery puree, place over medium low heat, and stir until well blended and heated through, about 1 to 2 minutes. Serve hot.

S E R V E S 6

4 tablespoons (½ stick) unsalted butter

2 large bunches celery, about 3½ pounds, trimmed of all leaves and diced

1½ cups chicken broth, preferably homemade (page 360)

Salt and freshly ground white pepper

3 to 4 tablespoons Crème Fraîche (page 358) or sour cream

2 tablespoons peanut oil

2 tablespoons all-purpose flour

Three-Celery Risotto
with Creamy Gorgonzola

3 cups chicken broth,
preferably homemade
(page 360)
1 cup celery leaves
1 teaspoon celery seeds
¾ cup finely diced celery
¾ cup finely diced celery root
2 tablespoons unsalted butter
½ cup finely diced onion
1¼ cups Italian rice, preferably
Arborio
Salt and freshly ground white
pepper
⅓ cup crumbled mild
Gorgonzola, preferably
Gorgonzola dolce
⅓ cup freshly grated Parmesan
cheese
⅓ cup heavy cream

The mild taste of celery and the more assertive flavor of the celery root play off each other beautifully in a quick but lovely risotto. For the best flavor, don't shy away from a couple of tablespoons of butter for enrichment, and if at all possible use a Gorgonzola dolce which is sweet, mild, and not too salty. Otherwise, use a bit less cheese than called for here.

1. In a small saucepan, combine the broth, celery leaves, and celery seeds and simmer, partially covered, for 20 minutes.

2. Strain the broth and discard the leaves and seeds. Return the broth to the saucepan, add the diced celery and celery root, and simmer for 5 minutes, or until tender. Strain the broth once again and reserve the vegetables and broth separately.

3. Melt the butter in a heavy 3- to 3½-quart saucepan over medium low heat. Add the onion and cook until soft but not brown. Add the rice, season with salt and pepper, and stir well to coat with the butter and onion mixture. Add 2 cups of the reserved broth and simmer, covered, over low heat for 12 minutes.

4. Remove the cover and start adding the remaining broth, ¼ cup at a time, stirring well after each addition and making sure all is absorbed before adding the next, until the risotto is done. The grains of rice should be soft on the outside but still quite chewy on the inside.

5. Add the reserved celery and celery root. Fold in the Gorgonzola, Parmesan, and heavy cream and just heat through. Taste and correct the seasoning and serve at once.

SERVES 4 TO 5

Smoky Lentil and
Celery Root Soup

I am particularly fond of lentils, since unlike other dried legumes they do not require presoaking, and I serve them often in the cooler months. The French way of teaming lentils with root vegetables, be it carrots, leeks, parsnips, celery root, or a combination of several, remains my favorite. Here the lentils play host to celery root, which gives the soup a special character. You may substitute a combination of parsnips and diced celery for the celery root.

1. Finely dice the leek, place in a colander, and run under warm water to remove all grit. Drain well.

2. In a large heavy casserole, melt the butter over medium heat. Add the leek, carrot, celery root, and onion and cook for 2 minutes. Add the bacon, lentils, and broth or water, season with salt and pepper, and simmer, partially covered, for 2 hours.

3. Remove 2 cups of the cooked vegetables from the soup, being careful to avoid the bacon, and transfer to a food processor. Process until smooth and return to the casserole. Stir over medium low heat until well blended and just heated through.

4. Taste and correct the seasoning. Ladle the soup into individual bowls and garnish with parsley. Drizzle each portion with oil and serve hot.

SERVES 5 TO 6

VARIATION
Garlic-flavored crème fraîche is a richer and delicious substitute for the olive oil garnish.

1 large leek, trimmed of all
    but 2 inches of greens
3 tablespoons unsalted butter
1 large carrot, peeled and finely
    diced
1 large celery root knob, peeled
    and finely diced
1 large onion, peeled and finely
    minced
6 ounces slab bacon
1½ cups dried lentils
8 cups chicken broth,
    preferably homemade
    (page 360), or water
Salt and freshly ground black
    pepper
GARNISH
Tiny leaves of parsley
Extra-virgin olive oil

FENNEL

JUST AS THE GARDEN IS WINDING DOWN AND ROOT VEGETABLES DOMI-
nate the menu, crisp fennel brings its refreshing taste and light, crisp touch to
winter meals. Fennel occupies a special place in my kitchen, both as an herb and
as a vegetable. I have grown the feathery green herb fronds for years, using them
extensively in fish marinades, fennel butter, rice pilaf, and pasta dishes. The vegetable, Florence fennel (Italian *finocchio*), is a deliciously sweet, anise-flavored bulb
that is cultivated both for the bulb and for its hollow stalks and seeds.

I still remember traveling with my parents through the charming hill
towns of southern France and stopping at the open markets, where farmers
sold giant, fragrant stalks of fennel and large sachets of the pungent seed. In
Provence, the stalks are dried and used as a bed for grilled fish, a memorable
eating experience. Local cooks use the seed to flavor sausages, pâtés, and
especially the full-flavored court bouillon used to poach fish and vegetables.
In the area around Nice, fennel bulb is always included on a platter of cru-
dités (raw vegetables) and served with a garlicky dip.

The Italians love their fennel both cooked and raw. When using it raw,
they usually serve it as a salad that invariably includes arugula and Belgian
endives. Dressed simply with virgin olive oil and a generous cracking of
black pepper, it is one of my favorite light winter appetizers. Italians, especially those in the region around Naples and in Sicily, use fennel most creatively. Braised, blanched, sautéed, and in fricassees, it is a cool-weather
staple that complements seafood, veal, and poultry.

As authentic Italian cooking becomes more popular in this country, good
fresh fennel, which once was found only in Italian markets, is now widely
available in supermarkets. I find that commercially grown fennel does not
have enough pungency, however, and I usually add a few drops of Pernod (an
anise-flavored liqueur) or a dash of roasted fennel seeds to dishes in which I
want a pronounced fennel taste. Fortunately an exceptional Italian variety,
Romy, is available to gardeners. It has fine, crisp flesh and is succulently

sweet and full flavored. Other varieties that produce good bulbs are Neapolitan and Zefa Fino.

STORAGE

Remove the feathery leaves before storing Florence fennel. Trim any bruised parts and store the bulbs in a plastic bag in the vegetable crisper of the refrigerator. Fennel will keep well for several days.

GARDENING

Growing fennel for a late fall crop ensures that the bulbs will develop into a good harvestable size. Planted in the spring, it tends to bolt and go to seed quickly in the heat of summer. I sow the seed eight to ten weeks before the first expected frost. In frost-free areas, sow the seed in late winter or very early spring. Because I like to use the young stalks in many preparations or raw, as I would use celery, I take my time about thinning the plants. Allowing ten inches between them leaves plenty of room for the bulbs to develop. Any good rich garden soil will do, although I recommend fertilizing about four weeks after sowing for really big, fleshy bulbs. If the weather is dry, water promptly to prevent the plants from bolting.

HARVESTING

As the bulb swells, cover it with soil to blanch it. When it reaches tennis-ball size, use a sharp knife to cut it away from the roots, close to the ground. Don't forget that you can use the feathery fronds at any time during the growing period, just as you would use the herb fennel.

Caramelized Fennel and Onion Tart

6 tablespoons (¾ stick)
  unsalted butter
1 teaspoon peanut oil
3 medium onions, peeled,
  quartered, and thinly sliced
1½ pounds fresh fennel, about
  3 large bulbs, trimmed of
  stalks
Salt and freshly ground white
  pepper
½ cup water
1 cup heavy cream
3 extra-large eggs
¾ cup grated Gruyère cheese
One partially baked tart shell
  (page 363), in a 10-inch
  porcelain quiche pan
3 tablespoons freshly grated
  Parmesan cheese

*L*ike its cousin the frittata, a homey vegetable tart is great cool-weather food. Caramelized fennel and onions make a winning combination, and if you add a salad of mixed greens tossed in a mustard and garlic vinaigrette, plus some nice bread, dinner is on the table.

1. In a heavy 10-inch skillet, melt 3 tablespoons of the butter together with the peanut oil over medium low heat. Add the onions and cook, partially covered, until they are soft and nicely browned, about 30 to 35 minutes, stirring often.

2. While the onions are cooking, quarter the fennel bulbs, core, and slice thin.

3. Melt the remaining 3 tablespoons of butter in another heavy 10-inch skillet over medium high heat. Add the sliced fennel, season with salt and pepper, and cook 3 to 4 minutes or until the fennel begins to brown. Add the water, reduce the heat, and simmer, partially covered, until the fennel is very tender and nicely browned, about 15 minutes. Transfer the fennel to a large mixing bowl and when the onions are done, add them to the fennel and set the mixture aside.

4. Preheat the oven to 350°F.

5. In another bowl, combine the cream, eggs, and Gruyère and whisk until well blended. Add the fennel and onion mixture and fold gently but thoroughly. Season the mixture carefully, adding a large grinding of pepper.

6. Pour the custard into the prepared crust and sprinkle with the Parmesan cheese. Place in the oven and bake for 35 to 40 minutes, or until puffed and nicely browned. The tip of a knife when inserted should come out clean.

7. Remove the tart from the oven, let cool slightly, and serve hot, cut into wedges.

SERVES 6 TO 8

Oven-Roasted Fennel

Oven-roasted vegetables, in particular peppers, zucchini, and eggplant, have become the trendy side dish of the nineties to be found at antipasti tables, at take-out gourmet stores, and on many restaurant menus. Fennel has joined the ranks of these vegetables with much success. Be sure to use plenty of olive oil when roasting fennel and turn it several times in the roasting pan to ensure even browning. Once the fennel is done, you can spoon off any excess oil. Roasted fennel can be reheated either in a low oven or in the microwave. It is best served with lamb, pork, or roasted whole fish such as snapper or sea bass.

4 medium fennel bulbs
3 to 4 tablespoons olive oil
Coarse salt and freshly ground
  black pepper

1. Preheat the oven to 350°F.

2. Trim the fennel bulbs of all feathery tops and stalks. Do not core the fennel bulbs. Cut them through the root end into eighths.

3. Bring water to a boil in a medium casserole, add the fennel, and blanch for 3 minutes. Drain well and dry on paper towels.

4. Place the fennel on a well-oiled baking sheet or roasting pan, drizzle with the olive oil, and season with salt and pepper. Roast for 45 minutes to 1 hour or until the fennel is nicely browned and quite tender, turning once or twice during roasting.

5. Serve hot or at room temperature.

S E R V E S 4

NOTE: For a more assertive anise flavor, you may add 1 tablespoon of Pernod to the roasting pan before the fennel is done.

Ragout of Fennel, Cremini Mushrooms, and Pearl Onions

20 pearl onions, unpeeled

3 tablespoons unsalted butter

2 tablespoons plus 2 teaspoons olive oil

12 ounces cremini mushrooms, trimmed, wiped, and quartered

Coarse salt and freshly ground black pepper

2 large fennel bulbs, trimmed of stalks, about 1 pound, cored and cut into ½-inch squares

½ cup chicken broth, preferably homemade (page 360)

3 tablespoons finely minced fresh parsley

1 large garlic clove, peeled and finely minced

Skillet-braised vegetables were the backbone of my mother's cooking. She would come up with the least likely combinations, yet the result would always be a delicious blend of flavors and textures. In this dish, fennel, mushrooms, and pearl onions are simmered together with a touch of broth until tender and well glazed. While the vegetables should not be mushy, they should also not be too crispy or the dish loses its charm.

1. Bring water to a boil in a small saucepan, add the onions, and blanch for 1 minute. Drain and run under cold water to stop further cooking. Peel and set aside.

2. In a 10-inch cast-iron skillet, melt 2 tablespoons of the butter together with 2 teaspoons of the oil over high heat. Add the mushrooms and sauté quickly until nicely browned. Season with salt and pepper and transfer with a slotted spoon to a side dish. Reserve.

3. Add 2 tablespoons of oil to the skillet and reduce the heat to medium. Add the onions and roll back and forth until the onions are nicely browned. (The onions will not brown evenly.) Transfer to a side dish and reserve.

4. Add the remaining tablespoon of butter to the skillet together with the fennel and cook, stirring often, until nicely browned. Return the onions to the skillet and season with salt and pepper. Add ¼ cup of the broth and simmer, covered, over low heat for 20 to 25 minutes or until tender; if the juices run dry before the vegetables are tender, add the remaining broth. If there are any pan juices left in the skillet once the vegetables are tender, remove the cover, raise the heat, and simmer until the juices have evaporated.

5. Return the mushrooms to the skillet together with the parsley and garlic and just heat through. Correct the seasoning, adding a large grinding of black pepper, and serve hot.

SERVES 4

Roast Chicken with Fennel and Garlic

Here is a gutsy one-dish meal, perfectly suited for the busy cook. Once the chicken is seasoned and browned, add the fennel and garlic and roast together with the chicken, being sure to baste every 10 minutes with a little broth. The result will be a delicious blend of flavors and textures. A fluffy pilaf of rice, possibly flavored with some porcini and freshly grated Parmesan, will nicely complete this all-in-the-pot main course.

1. Preheat the oven to 400°F. Dry the chicken thoroughly and season inside and out with the thyme, salt, and pepper.

2. Melt the butter together with the oil in a heavy flameproof baking dish over medium high heat. Add the chicken and brown nicely on all sides. Add the fennel and garlic to the baking dish together with ⅓ cup of the broth and roast for 1 hour or until the juices run pale yellow; a meat thermometer should register an inner temperature of 180°F. During roasting, add a little broth to the pan every 10 minutes and baste with some of the pan juices. Do not let the pan juices run dry.

3. When the chicken is done, remove from the oven and transfer to a carving board. Set aside. Transfer the vegetables to a side dish and reserve.

4. Degrease the pan juices thoroughly, return them to the baking dish together with the Pernod, and reduce slightly. Add the remaining broth and the cream, if using, and whisk in bits of beurre manié until the sauce lightly coats a spoon. Return the vegetables to the baking dish and just heat through. Keep warm.

5. Carve the chicken and quickly run under the broiler if you prefer a crisper skin. Transfer to a serving platter, pour the sauce over the chicken, and surround with the vegetables. Garnish with minced fennel tops and serve at once.

SERVES 4

I whole chicken, about 3½ pounds
1 tablespoon fresh thyme leaves
Coarse salt and freshly ground black pepper
2 tablespoons unsalted butter
1 teaspoon peanut oil
2 medium fennel bulbs, trimmed and each cut into 6 wedges
12 large garlic cloves, peeled
1½ to 2 cups chicken broth, preferably homemade (page 360)
¼ teaspoon Pernod
Optional: ¼ cup heavy cream
1 Beurre Manié (page 361)

GARNISH
2 tablespoons finely minced fennel tops

Sweet Lemon-Braised Fennel

4 medium fennel bulbs

3 tablespoons unsalted butter

1 teaspoon olive oil

½ teaspoon sugar

Juice of ½ lemon or more to taste

Salt and freshly ground white pepper

1 cup chicken broth, preferably homemade (page 360)

Optional: 2 tablespoons unsalted butter

Braised fennel is a wonderful winter or spring vegetable that works well with both meat and seafood. The entire dish can be prepared several hours or a day ahead and reheated in a low oven or in the microwave. The fennel tops can be finely minced and used as a garnish. As elsewhere, for a more intense fennel taste, you may add a few drops of Pernod to the finished pan juices.

1. Remove the feathery leaves and stalks from the fennel bulbs and trim off the outer layer from the bulbs. Quarter the bulbs through the root end or, if larger, cut into eighths; do not core.

2. In a large cast-iron skillet, melt the butter together with the oil over medium heat. Add the fennel and brown nicely on all sides. Reduce the heat to medium low and sprinkle with the sugar and the lemon juice. Season with salt and pepper and continue to sauté until the fennel is glazed and brown.

3. Add ½ cup of the broth and braise, tightly covered, for 10 minutes, adding more broth as needed. When the fennel is tender but not falling apart, transfer with a slotted spoon to a side dish and reserve.

4. Add the remaining broth and additional lemon juice to taste. Whisk in the additional butter, if using, for enrichment and spoon the pan juices over the fennel. Serve hot.

SERVES 4 TO 6

Marinated Mushroom and Fennel Salad in Dill and Parsley Vinaigrette

Fall salads are a nice way to start a meal, and they do not always have to be based on greens. Mushrooms, fennel, and leeks are a welcome change after a long summer of mixed green salads. Be sure to give the mushrooms a chance to absorb the vinaigrette by letting them marinate for 2 to 4 hours. For a light but most satisfying meal, serve the salad slightly chilled with sautéed or grilled Tuscan or French bread.

1. Place the mushrooms in a large bowl and sprinkle with salt, pepper, and 2 tablespoons of the vinegar. Toss gently and marinate for 30 minutes.

2. In a food processor, combine the mustard, egg yolk, sugar, and remaining 2 tablespoons of vinegar and process until smooth. With the machine running, add the oil in a slow, steady stream until all has been incorporated. The vinaigrette should resemble a very loose mayonnaise. Add the parsley and dill and process until finely minced. Transfer the vinaigrette to a large serving bowl; fold in the scallions and season with salt and pepper. Set aside.

3. Quarter the fennel bulbs lengthwise and, with a very sharp knife, remove and discard the core. Slice each quarter thin and add to the bowl containing the vinaigrette.

4. Drain the mushrooms well and also add to the serving bowl. Toss the vegetables gently in the vinaigrette, cover, and refrigerate for 2 hours.

5. Before serving, remove the salad from the refrigerator and correct the seasoning. Serve slightly chilled.

S E R V E S   4   T O   5

I pound all-purpose mushrooms, wiped, trimmed, and thinly sliced
Salt and freshly ground black pepper
4 tablespoons red wine vinegar
2 teaspoons Dijon mustard
½ teaspoon egg yolk
I teaspoon sugar
9 tablespoons olive oil
½ cup fresh parsley leaves, coarsely chopped
½ cup fresh dill, coarsely chopped
3 tablespoons finely minced scallions
I pound trimmed fennel bulbs

ONIONS, GARLIC, AND SHALLOTS

PROBABLY THE MOST IMPORTANT FLAVORINGS IN THE KITCHEN, ONIONS, garlic, and shallots add flavor, interest, and texture to innumerable preparations. There is not a single cuisine that would be complete without them.

Onions

If I had to pick one vegetable that I couldn't do without, it would be the onion. Virtually anything, from a simple tomato sauce to a soup, stew, or pilaf of rice, is enhanced by the addition of onions. Onions are also an important vegetable in their own right; without onions there would be no French onion soup, french-fried onion rings, or sinfully rich Swiss onion tart. Recently onions have enjoyed an unprecedented popularity, as the new sweet varieties have inspired deliciously sweet onion jams, oven-roasted onions enhanced with fresh herbs, and simply grilled onion slices.

We are particularly fortunate to have a broad selection of onion varieties available year-round in the United States. You can find them large or small; sweet or pungent; yellow, white, or red; and flat, round, or cylindrical. The variety and quality of onions is largely a regional affair. For the longest time I thought that Bermuda onions came from Bermuda and Spanish onions were from Spain. Not necessarily so. The names really refer to two types of non-hybrid onions that grow well in most parts of the country. In Texas, Arizona, and California, where onion growing is a big industry, the quality is superior and the choice is wide. Onions from this area are often classed as "new onions": sweet, very mild, and succulent. Because their high sugar content makes them more perishable, they should be purchased in small quantities and refrigerated. Onions that come from the Northeast, Northwest, and Midwest are usually called "old onions"; they store well and are the basic, all-purpose onions we buy throughout the year. They also tend to have a more pungent and robust flavor. Red or creole onions, which until recently were primarily used raw in salads, are now very popular and have an affinity to strong herbs such as thyme and rosemary. I like to braise them gently in olive oil with a dash of sherry vinegar and a little brown sugar or simmer them with honey and red wine. The best red onions are imported from Italy, although one variety, Red Torpedo, is available as seed here. Look for them from midsummer through fall. The large, flat, purplish-red onions from California appear in the markets about the same time. I find the flavor of the latter much too assertive and their shape awkward to work with.

There are also the gourmet varieties such as Vidalia, grown in Georgia; Maui, from the Hawaiian island; and Walla Walla, from the state of Washington. Sweet and juicy with thick, firm flesh, these varieties are known for their exceptional sweetness and can be best enjoyed raw in salads or sandwiches or quickly grilled and served as a topping for fancy pizzas.

Pearl onions, too, play a major role in the fall kitchen. There are red, white, and yellow varieties, but the white is most widely available. Peeled and braised, these little onions can turn a simple roast chicken into a great dish. I love to add them to the pan juices from a roast turkey or a ragout of veal, or I braise them in an iron skillet with diced bacon, brown sugar, and a cupful of dark raisins. Once cooked, the caramelized pearl onions can be refrigerated for weeks in a jar, ready to serve like chutney with country pâté, roast meats, and poultry.

STORAGE

Be sure to buy onions with brittle, dry skins. They should be firm and hard with thin, compact necks. You can also tell a good onion by its smell. Properly stored and dried, onions have no strong smell whatsoever. Store them in a cool, dry place; they will keep for many weeks in a loosely woven mesh bag or loose in the vegetable bin of the refrigerator.

GARDENING

If your experience with growing onions has been limited to using sets, you're in for a treat. Onion sets will only produce strong, storage-type onions used in winter. If you want big, sweet, mild onions for autumn use, you must start them from seed. To make big bulbs, onions need very rich, mellow soil that is full of compost or other organic matter. Although they require copious amounts of water, they also demand good drainage. If your soil is on the acidic side, add some lime. Choose a long-day type if you live anywhere except the South or the coastal areas south of San Francisco. There, short-day varieties are in order. Sow the seed thinly in furrows one-half inch deep after the last hard freeze when the soil begins to dry out. I thin the seedlings to two inches apart initially (I use scissors to snip the shoots off) and then gradually to five inches apart by using the seedlings as scallions. Be diligent about weeding, remembering that onions are shallow rooted and won't make good growth if they have to compete with unwelcomed guests. I like to use a fairly deep mulch of straw. Water generously until the tops start to fold over, a sign that the bulbs are mature and beginning to cure.

HARVESTING

When the tops of the onions collapse and turn yellow, it's time to dig them up. Do this on a dry, sunny day, lifting the bulbs from the soil with a spading fork. I brush the soil off and let them lie on top of the ground to dry off and then spread them out in an airy sheltered spot to further cure for two weeks. Once they are cured, I braid the tops and hang them up. Big sweet onions, like the Walla Walla type, are not good keepers and should be used within two weeks.

Garlic

Tales abound of the miraculous curative powers of garlic. It is credited with reducing high blood pressure and preventing cancer, as well as curing asthma, head colds, and virtually every other ill known to man. Whether or not there is any truth to these attributes, I do believe one thing: garlic is great!

The garlic I grew up with was powerful stuff. One clove was certainly enough to give a dish character, but at home in my mother's kitchen one clove was rarely enough. We started the day with peasant bread, grilled and then rubbed with garlic. A pungent mixture of minced garlic, parsley, and lemon rind (known as a gremolata) was my mother's favorite garnish for just about everything short of dessert. To this day, I find it nearly impossible to be objective about garlic because I love its distinctive taste and aroma so much.

One of my most unforgettable experiences with garlic occurred in the south of France, where I was served a roast leg of spring lamb with a garlic confit. The roast arrived surrounded by at least fifty tender, slightly caramelized garlic cloves and tiny roasted potatoes, redolent of rosemary. The taste of the garlic was haunting. That was in the early 1970s. It would be another ten years before chefs and home cooks in this country discovered the Mediterranean techniques of cooking with garlic. Roasted, poached, double-poached, and glazed, versatile garlic takes on a different character with each preparation.

How you prepare garlic determines how much flavor and aroma it adds to a dish. Slice or mince it with a small stainless-steel knife if you want a mild flavor. For a stronger taste, I prefer the Mediterranean method of sprinkling the clove with coarse salt and then mashing it with a knife over passing it through a garlic press. The press releases the garlic oil and produces a strong, almost bitter flavor. To peel garlic, place a few cloves on a cutting board, hold the flat side of a chef's knife over them, and rap your fist on the blade. Do this firmly enough to crack the skin, which will then peel off easily, but not hard enough to crush the cloves. Garlic cloves can also be poached or roasted in their skins and then peeled when tender.

My favorite garlic is the variety that produces small lavender-pink bulbs. Even in Spain, a country that grows much of the garlic used in this country, this variety is often hard to find. When I am in Barcelona, I always look for the peasant women who bring their home crop to the market daily, selling it in little plastic bags of four or five heads. Although the heads are small, the cloves are plump and loaded with natural oil. Italy and Mexico also produce a pink variety, more aromatic and pungent, that is worth searching for. The varieties closest to it that are available here are Italian Purple and German Red.

White garlic heads, such as the California Silverskin, are readily available and easier to peel and can be stored longer. However, the cloves have less natural oil and therefore tend to burn rather quickly. Burnt garlic imparts a bitter taste and can easily ruin a dish. White garlic is my first choice for a confit or for double poaching. In both cases the cloves should be used whole.

STORAGE

Although garlic cloves store well in a dry, airy place, I find that they last even longer when refrigerated. I keep the heads in a small bowl in the vegetable crisper. Be sure that the bowl is always dry or the garlic will rot.

GARDENING

See Shallots, below.

HARVESTING

See Shallots, below.

Shallots

The shallot is a cross between the onion and garlic. Like garlic, it is divided into cloves; unlike garlic, its flavor is sweet and delicate. If differs from onions in that it does not add pungency but actually sweetens the flavor of a sauce. Shallots have a characteristic of "melting" in the pan juices of a ragout or stew, making it unnecessary to strain or puree the liquid. Shallots enjoy a long tradition as an essential ingredient in such French haute cuisine as escargot butter and buerre blanc sauce. Because their delicate flavor has a great affinity to wine and lemon juice, shallots are essential in the preparation of many fish dishes. In fact, I keep minced or sliced shallots covered with white wine in a jar in the refrigerator at all times. I prefer their subtle taste to that of onions or even scallions in salad dressings, too. Adding shallots definitely improves a quick tomato sauce made from canned tomatoes, giving it more complexity and depth. Whether roasted, stewed, caramelized, or double-poached, shallots are one of a cook's best friends.

Because they are so much in demand now, shallots are widely available in supermarkets. Their price, however, is prohibitive, so growing your own is especially rewarding, allowing you to then use them lavishly. The Dutch Yellow shallot is the variety most often found in the market, but a little searching through catalogs can turn up some fine French heirloom types, such as Brittany shallots, for the gardener.

STORAGE

Store shallots at room temperature in a dry place or, as I prefer to do, in the refrigerator. If they are not kept dry, they will soften and sprout.

GARDENING

Garlic and shallots are very easy to grow, and any cook who uses quantities of either should reserve a place for them in the garden. As with other members of the onion family, they require fertile soil rich in organic matter. Addition of a well-balanced fertilizer is also beneficial. Start them in early spring as you would onion sets, setting the individual cloves about eight inches apart, and cover with two inches of soil. That's all there is to it.

HARVESTING

When the tops begin to wither and brown, about 90 to 110 days after planting, shallots and garlic are ready to be harvested. Pull up the clumps, brush off the soil, and let the bulbs dry in the sun for a day or so. Then spread them out in a dark, dry, airy place to finish curing for a couple of weeks. I always save some of the crop for replanting the following spring.

Pork Tenderloins in Red Onion–Thyme Sauce

THE PORK MARINADE

2 large garlic cloves, peeled
  and sliced

4 tablespoons olive oil

Juice of I large lemon

1½ tablespoons fresh thyme
  leaves

2 teaspoons cracked black
  pepper

2 whole pork tenderloins,
  trimmed, about ¾ to 1
  pound each

**THE RED ONION–THYME
SAUCE**

3 tablespoons olive oil

6 medium-size red onions,
  thinly sliced

I teaspoon sugar

2 tablespoons finely minced
  fresh thyme

Salt and freshly ground black
  pepper

½ cup dry white wine

I cup Crème Fraîche (page
  358), or heavy cream

I teaspoon green peppercorns,
  drained and crushed

Optional: 2 tablespoons
  unsalted butter

2 tablespoons unsalted butter

Coarse salt

½ cup chicken broth,
  preferably homemade
  (page 360)

GARNISH

Sprigs of fresh thyme

Come October, I start buying up as many red onions as will fit into my vegetable bins. By then I have gone through my own fall crop and the imported Italian onions are by far the best in the market. Red onions stewed in olive oil and flavored with fresh thyme make a wonderful vegetable on their own, but they also are one of my favorite toppings for a homemade pizza or as a bed for grilled fish. I especially like the marriage of this rather assertive jam with a well-seasoned pork tenderloin. A bowl of creamy polenta or a risotto would complete this delightful main course.

1. Start by marinating the pork: Combine the garlic, oil, lemon juice, thyme, and cracked pepper in a shallow dish and whisk until well blended. Add the pork tenderloins and let stand, covered, at room temperature for 30 minutes, turning often in the marinade.

2. Preheat the oven to 425°F.

3. While the pork is marinating, prepare the onions: In a large heavy skillet, heat the oil over medium high heat. Add the onions and cook, stirring constantly, until the onions are nicely browned. Add the sugar and thyme and season with salt and pepper. Add the wine, bring to a boil, and reduce to 2 tablespoons. Add the crème fraîche or heavy cream and peppercorns and simmer until reduced to 3 to 4 tablespoons. Cover and keep warm.

4. Remove the pork tenderloins from the marinade and pat dry. In a very heavy baking dish, melt the butter over medium high heat. Add the pork to the skillet and brown nicely on all sides. Season with coarse salt and add ¼ cup of the broth to the skillet. Place in the oven and roast for 16 to 20 minutes, or until the juices run clear or a meat thermometer registers an inner temperature of 155°F. Add a little broth during roasting and baste often with the pan juices. Be careful not to overcook.

5. When the tenderloins are done, remove from the oven and transfer to a carving board. Set aside.

6. Degrease the pan juices thoroughly and add them to the red onion–thyme sauce. Whisk in the butter, if using, and correct the seasoning. Cut the pork crosswise into thin slices. Place some of the red onion–thyme sauce in the center of 6 warm individual serving plates and top each with 4 or 5 slices of pork. Garnish with sprigs of fresh thyme and serve at once.

S E R V E S 6

Chunky Pickled Onions with Ginger and Black Pepper

I love all kinds of pickles, and onions take especially well to this treatment. Paired with ginger and plenty of black pepper, they are nicely crunchy and slightly spicy. I serve the onions as a condiment with a burger, but I also like them as a side dish to a spicy chicken or lamb curry.

1. Layer the onions with the coarse salt in a large bowl. Cover with ice cubes and let stand for 2 hours. Rinse under cold water and drain well.

2. Combine the remaining ingredients in a large casserole. Bring to a boil, add the onions, and bring back to a boil.

3. Immediately remove the onions with a slotted spoon and pack into 4 to 5 hot pint jars. Pour the hot liquid over the onions, leaving a ¼-inch headspace. Remove all the visible air bubbles, adjust the caps, and process for 10 minutes in a boiling water bath (see page 168). Remove and cool completely. Store for 2 to 3 months before opening, to develop flavor.

M A K E S 4 T O 5 P I N T S

4 pounds medium onions, peeled and cut into ⅓-inch slices
¼ cup coarse salt
3 cups cider vinegar
2 cups sugar
1½ tablespoons yellow mustard seeds
2½ teaspoons turmeric
2½ teaspoons celery seeds
1½ teaspoons ground ginger
¾ teaspoon whole black peppercorns

Braised Red Onion, Gruyère, and Herb Tart

2 tablespoons unsalted butter

5 ounces slab bacon, blanched and finely diced, about 1 cup

4 medium-size red onions, peeled, quartered, and thinly sliced

Salt and freshly ground black pepper

1 tablespoon fresh thyme leaves

1 teaspoon fresh rosemary leaves

3 extra-large eggs

1 cup heavy cream

2/3 cup grated Gruyère cheese

One partially baked tart shell (page 363), in a 9-inch tart pan with a removable bottom

2 tablespoons freshly grated Parmesan cheese

Savory tarts are finally regaining their well-deserved popularity, and although there is plenty of room for creativity as far as the fillings are concerned, they are really at their best when made with the simplest of ingredients, such as onions, cabbage, leeks, and herbs. Here is a Swiss version, a favorite of Frédy Girradet. Frédy finds it amusing that people ooh and aah at a tart that is a classic of the region and can be bought well prepared in many of the local pastry shops. At Girradet, the tiny buttery and flaky onion tarts are served as part of the finger-food selection appropriately called "les amuse-bouches," translated as "mouth-amusing" selection.

1. In a large skillet, melt the butter over medium heat. Add the bacon and cook until lightly browned, about 5 minutes. Remove with a slotted spoon to a side dish and reserve.

2. Discard all but 3 tablespoons of fat from the skillet, add the onions, and cook, stirring constantly, for 5 minutes or until they begin to brown. Season with salt, pepper, thyme, and rosemary. Reduce the heat and cook, covered, for 30 minutes or until soft and nicely browned. Set aside.

3. Preheat the oven to 350°F.

4. In a large mixing bowl, combine the eggs and cream, season with salt and pepper, and whisk until well blended. Add the onions together with the bacon and Gruyère and mix well.

5. Pour the custard into the partially baked tart shell, sprinkle with the Parmesan, and bake for 30 to 35 minutes or until the custard is set and the surface is nicely browned. Remove from the oven and let sit for 10 minutes. Serve warm or at room temperature, cut into wedges.

SERVES 6

Caramelized Onion and Garlic Soup

Here is a soup that epitomizes the simplicity of Mediterranean cooking. What could be more flavorful and easy to make than a potful of tender caramelized onions enhanced by the delicious pungency of sweet garlic? When prepared well, this is a memorable soup indeed. Be sure to take your time cooking the onions and use juicy purple garlic when at all possible. For a garnish I love to top each portion of soup with a slice of grilled French bread and a hefty spoonful of coarsely grated Parmesan or a Spanish manchego cheese.

1. In a heavy 3-quart casserole, melt the butter together with the oil over medium heat. Add the onions, sprinkle with the sugar, and season with salt and pepper. Cook for 10 minutes, or until the onions begin to brown.

2. Reduce the heat and continue cooking the onions, partially covered, for 30 to 35 minutes, or until they are soft and nicely browned. Add the garlic and cook for 2 minutes longer.

3. Add the flour and stir well into the onions. Add 6 cups of the broth all at once and stir until the soup comes to a boil. Simmer, covered, for 20 minutes.

4. Let the soup cool slightly. Strain and return the broth to the casserole and set aside. Transfer the onions to a food processor and process until smooth.

5. Whisk the pureed onions into the broth, add the cream, and season with salt and pepper. Add some of the remaining broth if the soup is too thick. Just heat through. Serve the soup hot in individual bowls, garnished with minced parsley.

SERVES 6

2 tablespoons unsalted butter
1 tablespoon peanut oil
6 cups onions, peeled, quartered, and thinly sliced
1 teaspoon sugar
Salt and freshly ground black pepper
2 large garlic cloves, peeled and finely minced
2 tablespoons all-purpose flour
6 to 7 cups beef broth
¼ cup heavy cream

GARNISH
2 tablespoons finely minced fresh parsley

Early Winter Minestrone (with Onions, Garlic, and Tomatoes)

3 tablespoons extra-virgin olive oil

2 Bermuda onions, peeled, quartered, and thinly sliced

1 teaspoon sugar

Salt and freshly ground black pepper

2 teaspoons fresh thyme leaves or 1 teaspoon dried

3 large garlic cloves, peeled and finely minced

1 teaspoon fresh oregano leaves or ½ teaspoon dried

2 tablespoons finely minced fresh parsley

2 tablespoons all-purpose flour

1 teaspoon tomato paste

6 large ripe tomatoes, peeled, seeded, and chopped, or 1 can (35 ounces) Italian plum tomatoes, drained and chopped

6 to 8 cups chicken broth, preferably homemade (page 360)

½ teaspoon Old Bay Seasoning

½ cup imported dried tiny pasta, preferably tubettini

GARNISH

3 tablespoons finely minced parsley

¼ cup freshly grated Parmesan cheese

Certain preparations fall into the all-season category, and this flavor-packed minestrone is one of them. I start with a good brand of canned tomatoes such as the ones imported from San Marzano or the Naples area and drain them well, reserving the juice for when and if I need it. The minestrone is the perfect one-dish meal for the weekday cook since it can be prepared on the weekend when time is less tight, and served throughout the week, either preceded by a salad or as a starter followed by a frittata or cool-weather risotto.

1. In a large heavy casserole, heat the oil over medium high heat. Add the onions, sprinkle with the sugar, and season with salt and pepper. Cook for 10 minutes, stirring often, until the onions begin to brown. Reduce the heat, add the thyme, garlic, oregano, and parsley and cook, partially covered, for 30 to 40 minutes, or until the onions are soft and nicely browned.

2. Add the flour and stir to blend thoroughly into the onions. Add the tomato paste, tomatoes, and 6 cups of the broth and the Old Bay Seasoning and bring to a boil. Reduce the heat and simmer, partially covered, for 35 minutes. Add the pasta and continue to simmer until the pasta is tender. If the soup is too thick, add the remaining broth. Taste and correct the seasoning. Serve the soup in individual bowls, garnished with minced parsley and Parmesan cheese.

SERVES 6

Grilled Onions in Mint Butter

Grilled onions can be quite addictive. They are a terrific addition to an antipasti table or as a side dish to a late summer grill buffet. The mint butter adds a nice mellow flavor that I find most welcome. You may vary the herbs, using cilantro, thyme, or basil or a combination. Leftover grilled onions are lovely served at room temperature with a drizzle of sherry vinegar and a large grinding of black pepper. Be sure to cook the onions over the lowest possible heat, especially if you are using a kettle-type grill.

1. In a small bowl, combine the softened butter and mint, season with salt and pepper, and mix well. Chill until needed.

2. Prepare the charcoal grill, placing the coals only on one side of the grill.

3. Place the onions on a large double layer of heavy-duty aluminum foil. Sprinkle with coarse salt and pepper, add the oil and 2 tablespoons of the water, and enclose the onions completely with the foil.

4. When all the coals are white hot, place the foil packet on the cooking grill on the side opposite the coals (not directly over the coals). Cover the grill and cook for 45 minutes to 1 hour, adding a little water to the packet every 15 minutes and basting with the juices and turning the onions, until they are tender. You will need to add about 8 to 10 more coals to the pile of burning coals to ensure the heat is constant.

5. Open the foil packet, add the mint butter, and grill, covered, for about 5 minutes longer. Serve the onions warm, as an accompaniment to grilled lamb or pork.

SERVES 4 TO 5

VARIATION
You may also bake the onions in a 350°F. oven in the foil packet set on a baking sheet, for about 1 hour or until tender and lightly browned.

4 tablespoons (½ stick) unsalted butter, softened
2 tablespoons finely minced fresh peppermint
Coarse salt and freshly ground black pepper
6 large onions, peeled and sliced
2 tablespoons olive oil
⅓ cup water

Catalan Roasted Onions with Sherry Vinegar

5 tablespoons extra-virgin olive oil

12 small onions, about 1½ to 2 inches in diameter, unpeeled, cut in half crosswise

Coarse salt and freshly ground black pepper

2 tablespoons sherry vinegar

1 large garlic clove, peeled and finely minced

3 tablespoons finely minced fresh parsley

Slow-roasted onions are a classic in Catalan cooking—where the onion reigns supreme. Onion jams find their way into open-faced frittatas and sautéed calamari and they are the basic ingredients of a good paella. My favorite way to serve them is over soft polenta or buttery mashed potatoes. A dollop placed under pan-seared skate or a fillet of sole adds a terrific punch to a simple spur-of-the-moment dish.

1. Preheat the oven to 350°F.

2. Coat the bottom of a large heavy baking dish with 2 tablespoons of the olive oil. Place the unpeeled onions in the dish cut side down, drizzle with 1 tablespoon of the oil, and season with salt and pepper.

3. Roast the onions for 1 hour and 15 minutes to 1 hour and 30 minutes, or until tender and nicely browned, basting several times with the oil in the dish. Turn the onions once during roasting if necessary.

4. Remove the dish from the oven and carefully peel off the skin and discard. Transfer the onions to a shallow serving platter, cut side up. While still warm, drizzle with the remaining 2 tablespoons of olive oil and the sherry vinegar. Sprinkle with the minced garlic and parsley and correct the seasoning.

5. Let the onions sit at room temperature for 1 to 2 hours before serving. Serve as part of a buffet or hors d'oeuvre table.

SERVES 6

Skillet-Braised Chicken Legs with Double-Poached Garlic

For those who still object to the pungent taste of garlic, double-poaching the cloves is the answer. The sweet cloves contribute a texture rather than a distinct garlic bite. I like to add as many as a handful to skillet-braised chicken or to a veal ragout. Be sure to start this dish a day ahead of serving.

1. In a bowl, combine the garlic, pepper, lemon juice, and oil and whisk until well blended. Place the chicken pieces in a large resealable plastic bag and pour the marinade over them. Seal the bag and place in a shallow dish. Refrigerate overnight, turning the bag several times.

2. The next day remove the chicken from the marinade and dry thoroughly with paper towels. Reserve.

3. In a 12-inch cast-iron skillet, melt the butter together with the oil over high heat. Add the chicken pieces and brown nicely on all sides. Remove to a side dish, season with salt and pepper, and reserve.

4. Discard all but 2 tablespoons of fat from the skillet. Add the shallots and cook until soft and lightly browned, about 1 minute. Add the wine, bring to a boil, and reduce to a glaze. Add the thyme sprigs and half of the broth. Return the chicken to the skillet and simmer, tightly covered, for 25 minutes, adding a little broth to the pan every 10 minutes.

5. When the chicken is done, transfer to a side dish and reserve. Thoroughly degrease the pan juices and return them to the skillet. Add the poached garlic and crème fraîche and simmer until the sauce is reduced and lightly coats a spoon. Taste and correct the seasoning. Return the chicken pieces to the skillet and spoon the sauce over them. Simmer for another 2 to 3 minutes or until just heated through. Transfer to a warm serving platter and serve with a parslied rice pilaf or couscous.

S E R V E S   4   T O   6

6 large garlic cloves, peeled and finely minced

2 teaspoons coarse salt

Freshly ground black pepper

Juice of 1 large lemon

1/3 cup extra-virgin olive oil

6 small whole chicken legs (with thighs attached), cut in half at the joint

2 tablespoons unsalted butter

2 teaspoons olive oil

3 tablespoons finely minced shallots

1/3 cup dry white wine

2 large sprigs of fresh thyme

1 cup chicken broth, preferably homemade (page 360)

8 large garlic cloves, double poached (page 308)

1 cup Crème Fraîche (page 358)

Roast Turkey with Caramelized Pearl Onions and Chestnuts

Few people realize the wonderful affinity turkey has to all root vegetables. Here is one of my favorite ways to serve this most popular winter bird. If possible, choose red or yellow pearl onions rather than the white ones. They are usually sweeter and more mellow tasting and also will cook to a nicer, softer consistency. The French vacuum-packed chestnuts are the perfect choice for this dish, but if you can find peeled frozen chestnuts imported from Italy, their taste and texture are even closer to the fresh nuts. Either is a less time-consuming option than roasting and peeling the nuts yourself, but that is, of course, the best!

1. Preheat the oven to 425°F.

2. Dry the turkey thoroughly with cotton kitchen towels. Season with salt, pepper, and thyme and truss. Set aside.

3. In a large heavy baking dish, melt 2 tablespoons of the butter together with the oil over medium high heat. Add the turkey and brown nicely on all sides. Add ¼ cup of the broth to the pan and roast for 1 hour and 30 minutes to 1 hour and 45 minutes, or until the internal temperature on a meat thermometer registers 180°F. and the juices run pale yellow. Turn once during roasting. Add a little broth to the pan every 10 to 15 minutes and baste with the pan juices. If the turkey becomes too dark, tent loosely with foil.

4. While the turkey is roasting, drop the onions into boiling water and blanch for 30 seconds. Drain well and when cool enough to handle, peel and set aside.

5. In a large heavy skillet, melt the remaining 2 tablespoons of butter over medium heat. Add the bacon and cook until almost crisp. Transfer with a slotted spoon to a side dish and reserve.

6. Add the onions and brown nicely, shaking the pan back and forth to brown evenly. Add the brown sugar, vinegar, and tomato paste, season with salt and pepper, and add ½ cup of

Ingredients

- 1 fresh whole turkey, about 8 pounds
- Coarse salt and freshly ground black pepper
- 2 tablespoons fresh thyme leaves
- 4 tablespoons (½ stick) unsalted butter
- 1 teaspoon peanut oil
- 3½ cups chicken broth, preferably homemade (page 360)
- 2 pints pearl onions, unpeeled
- ½ pound slab bacon, blanched and diced, about 1⅔ cups
- 4 tablespoons dark brown sugar
- 2 tablespoons sherry vinegar
- 1½ tablespoons tomato paste
- 2 cups roasted and peeled chestnuts, either fresh or jarred
- 2 teaspoons arrowroot mixed with 1 tablespoon chicken broth

GARNISH
- 2 tablespoons finely minced fresh parsley

the broth. Simmer, partially covered, for 20 minutes. Add the chestnuts and bacon and simmer 10 minutes longer, or until the onions are tender. If the pan juices run dry before the onions are done, add another 2 to 3 tablespoons of broth to the skillet.

7. When the turkey is done, remove it from the oven and transfer to a carving board. Reserve. Degrease the pan juices and return them to the baking dish together with the remaining broth. Bring to a boil and reduce by half. Add the onion mixture and whisk in a little of the arrowroot mixture until the sauce lightly coats a spoon. Taste and correct the seasoning. Keep warm.

8. Carve the turkey and place on a large serving platter. Spoon some of the onion sauce around the turkey and garnish with the minced parsley. Serve hot.

SERVES 6

Double-Poached Garlic

4 heads garlic, separated into cloves and peeled
Olive oil for storing

*C*ertain vegetables benefit tremendously from double poaching, and garlic is one of them. Discarding the first cooking water allows the garlic to become tender without any trace of bitterness. I use double-poached garlic in many ways, especially as a last-minute addition to the pan juices of a roast or to a pasta dish.

1. Bring plenty of water to a boil in a medium saucepan, add the garlic cloves, and bring back to a boil. Cook for exactly 1 minute.

2. Drain and discard the poaching liquid. Return the blanched garlic to the saucepan, cover with more water, and again bring to a boil. Reduce the heat and simmer, uncovered, for 15 to 20 minutes, or until tender when pierced with the tip of a sharp knife. Drain well. The garlic is now ready to be used.

3. To store the garlic, place in a jar, cover with olive oil, seal tightly, and place in the refrigerator. The garlic will keep for up to 3 months. Bring the desired amount back to room temperature before using.

MAKES 4 HEADS

Roasted Garlic

Not all garlic takes to roasting. If the heads are purple, they are usually full of natural oil and will roast well. The white heads are usually less oily and will lose most of the oil during roasting, rendering them rather dry. To prevent this, coat the outside skins with some oil and roast the heads whole wrapped in foil. To serve, cut the heads in half and serve each person half a garlic head with some grilled country bread as a side dish to well-seasoned grilled lamb chops or a winter cabbage soup.

3 heads garlic, unpeeled
1 tablespoon extra-virgin
    olive oil
Coarse salt
Freshly ground black pepper
Large pinch of sugar
Olive oil for storing

1. Preheat the oven to 375°F.

2. Separate the garlic into cloves but do not peel. Place the whole cloves of garlic in the center of a large piece of aluminum foil, drizzle with the olive oil, and sprinkle with coarse salt and black pepper. Bring the ends of foil up over the garlic and crimp to seal the cloves completely.

3. Place the foil packet in the center of the oven and roast for 45 minutes, or until the garlic is soft to the touch. Open the foil packet, sprinkle the garlic with the sugar, and continue to roast, uncovered, for 15 minutes, or until golden brown.

4. Remove the garlic from the oven and when cool enough to handle, peel the cloves carefully so that they remain whole. Place the roasted garlic cloves in a small container, cover completely with olive oil, and cover the container. Store in the refrigerator for up to 3 months. Bring the desired amount back to room temperature before using.

MAKES 3 HEADS

Marsala-Glazed Shallots

2 tablespoons unsalted butter

3 teaspoons olive oil

24 large shallots, unpeeled

Coarse salt and freshly ground
black pepper

2 tablespoons dark brown
sugar

¾ cup sweet Marsala wine

½ to ¾ cup beef bouillon or
chicken broth, preferably
homemade (page 360)

My friend the writer Tom Harris gave me this recipe. I think Tom likes to cook and eat as much as I do, and he does it with great gusto and style. When we get together we always seem to come up with new little dishes that soon become my favorites. Delicious glazed shallots are one such invention, the perfect match for grilled or roasted lamb, duck, turkey, or whole roasted fish.

1. Preheat the oven to 350°F.

2. In a 10-inch cast-iron skillet, melt the butter together with the oil over medium heat. Add the shallots, season with salt and pepper, and sauté for 2 minutes, or until they start to brown. Add the brown sugar, Marsala, and half of the broth and roll the shallots in the mixture until they are well coated.

3. Place the skillet in the oven and braise the shallots for 1 hour and 15 minutes. Add a little more broth every 20 minutes and roll the shallots in the pan juices to ensure that they braise evenly.

4. When the shallots are tender and well glazed, remove them from the oven and transfer to a bowl. If the pan juices are not well reduced, place the skillet over direct heat and simmer until the sauce is thick and syrupy. Return the shallots to the skillet and coat them well. Serve at once.

SERVES 6 TO 8

Caramelized Shallot "Marmalade"

Caramelized shallots can be made in quantity and stored in a jar, and they will keep for weeks. Small pearl onions can be prepared in the same manner, but the subtle, more delicate taste of the shallot produces more interesting results.

1. In a large cast-iron skillet, melt the butter over medium heat. Add the shallots and sugar and cook until the sugar has melted and the shallots begin to brown.

2. Reduce the heat, add the red wine, Cassis, and vinegar, and cook for 25 to 30 minutes, or until all the liquid has evaporated and the shallots are soft and nicely caramelized. Season with salt and pepper and serve.

SERVES 6

VARIATION
You may add ½ cup plumped dark raisins and ¼ cup pine nuts, sautéed in a little olive oil, to the marmalade for a more unusual taste and texture.

6 tablespoons (¾ stick)
   unsalted butter
2 pounds shallots, peeled
   and thinly sliced
¼ cup sugar
3 cups dry red wine
¼ cup Cassis
1½ tablespoons sherry vinegar
Salt and freshly ground black
   pepper

PARSNIPS

THE PARSNIP MAY VERY WELL BE THE MOST OVERLOOKED AND UNDER-rated vegetable around. I think of it as a "vintage" vegetable, as it has been cultivated since the Romans took it to England, where it quickly became a staple. While one sees parsnips stacked in plastic bags in the supermarkets nearly year-round, a freshly dug parsnip is almost a different vegetable. My introduction to fresh parsnips occurred, appropriately, in England just a few years ago. I was visiting a friend in the Cotswolds, and as we strolled through her kitchen garden, she stopped to dig up three enormous roots that resembled the parsley roots I knew in Spain. She peeled the knobby skin to reveal a creamy smooth root which, even raw, tasted as if it had been dipped in sugar. We decided to add them to the pan juices of the pork roast that was in the oven, along with some small onions and cut-up carrots. The result is still a delicious memory.

I determined to grown my own parsnips when I found that really fresh ones were nowhere to be found. I think if more home cooks grew their own they would think of them more kindly, instead of associating them with the woody, pithy variety found in supermarkets. As it is, people either love this slim, pristine root vegetable or loathe it.

In my kitchen, I lavish special attention on parsnips. My favorite way of preparing them is to slice and bake them in a buttery gratin with a little cream and a dash of nutmeg or allspice. I also enjoy a creamy parsnip soup made with a full-bodied chicken stock and enhanced with leeks and carrots. As a cold-weather first course, it's unbeatable. Parsnips can also be substituted in many recipes that call for carrots. Indeed, quick breads, cakes, and puddings are among the best ways to use parsnips.

Unfortunately, if you do not grow parsnips, buying fresh ones can be a frustrating experience; look for smooth, cream-colored roots that are firm and well shaped. Avoid any that are limp or have brown spots.

STORAGE

Parsnips will keep well for many weeks stored in a plastic bag in the crisper of the refrigerator. Rinse and peel them when you are ready to use them.

GARDENING

My first attempt at growing parsnips was a dismal failure. The rocky Connecticut soil produced knobby, distorted roots that bore little resemblance to those I had sampled in England. I now know that proper soil preparation is the only demand of this easily grown vegetable. In spring, I make fifteen-inch-deep cone-shaped holes, fill them with sifted soil and compost, and sow a few seeds a half inch deep on the top of each hole. Seed can also be sown in mounded rows of deeply worked, stone-free soil. Parsnips are slow to germinate and need a good six months to develop. I like to sow quick-germinating radish or lettuce seed along with the parsnip seed to mark the rows and get a little extra mileage from the row. A side dressing of general fertilizer when the sprouts appear is beneficial, but too rich soil will cause forked roots. Hollow Crown is an excellent variety that produces large, tender white roots; Harris Model is long, slim, and delicately flavored; and Cobham Improved, a new English variety, is exceptionally sweet.

HARVESTING

One of the nicest things about parsnips is that you can harvest them as you need them once they have reached a good size. Frost sweetens the roots, and they can be left in the garden over winter even after the ground freezes. A thick mulch will enable you to retrieve them during winter, or you can wait until the ground thaws in earliest spring to harvest them again.

Cream of Parsnip and Carrot Soup with Fragrant Indian Spices

3 tablespoons unsalted butter

1 large onion, peeled and finely minced

1 tablespoon dark brown sugar

½ teaspoon ground coriander

1 tablespoon imported curry powder, preferably Madras

¼ teaspoon ground cardamom

Large pinch of freshly grated nutmeg

¼ teaspoon ground ginger

1 pound carrots, trimmed, peeled, and cubed

3 medium parsnips, trimmed, peeled, and cubed

6 cups chicken broth, preferably homemade (page 360)

Salt and freshly ground black pepper

1 cup heavy cream

GARNISH

2 ripe, medium-size tomatoes, unpeeled, seeded and finely diced

3 tablespoons fresh cilantro leaves

Parsnips and carrots have a lovely friendship that extends way beyond the garden. They both take well to a number of spices, and I especially like the combination in this mellow and comforting soup. If possible, make the soup a day or at least several hours ahead to allow the flavors to mature, and add a dicing of either blanched or roasted cubed parsnip to it for more texture.

1. In a large heavy casserole, melt the butter over low heat. Add the onion and cook until soft and lightly browned, 5 to 6 minutes. Add the brown sugar, coriander, curry powder, cardamom, nutmeg, and ginger and cook the mixture for 1 minute longer.

2. Add the carrots, parsnips, and broth and season with salt and pepper. Reduce the heat and simmer the soup for 30 minutes, or until the vegetables are very tender. Cool the soup slightly and transfer to a food processor or blender and process until smooth.

3. Return the soup to the casserole. Add the cream, blend well, and simmer for another 10 minutes. Taste and correct the seasoning. Serve hot in individual soup bowls and garnish each with 1 tablespoon diced raw tomato and a sprinkling of fresh cilantro.

S E R V E S   6

Caramelized Oven-Roasted Parsnips

Oven roasting brings out the essential sweetness in parsnips. If the vegetable is picked fresh from the garden, especially those that are left in the soil well into the cold season, it can be roasted without blanching or the addition of sugar. Store-bought parsnips do need a little extra help: add a touch of sugar to the water when blanching to bring out their sweetness. Parsnips make a terrific side dish to all roast poultry, baked ham, and roast pork.

1. Preheat the oven to 350°F. Cut the parsnips in half lengthwise and then again crosswise.

2. Melt the butter in a cast-iron skillet over medium heat. Add the parsnips, season with salt, pepper, and sugar, and sauté for two minutes or until parsnips are lightly browned.

3. Add ½ cup of the broth and place the skillet in the oven. Roast for 15 minutes or until tender. If the pan juices become dry, add the remaining broth. Transfer the parsnips to a serving platter, season with a large grinding of pepper, and serve hot.

SERVES 4

NOTE: Parsnips reheat perfectly in the microwave. Cover with plastic wrap and cook on high for 1 minute.

1½ pounds fresh parsnips, peeled
3 tablespoons unsalted butter
Salt and freshly ground black pepper
1 teaspoon sugar
½ to ¾ cup chicken broth, preferably homemade (page 360)

Parsnip, Apple, and Onion Rösti

5 tablespoons unsalted butter

2 teaspoons peanut oil

1 large Bermuda onion, peeled, quartered, and thinly sliced

Salt and freshly ground black pepper

1 pound parsnips, trimmed, peeled, and grated

1 medium Golden Delicious apple, peeled, cored, and grated

1/3 cup plus 1 tablespoon all-purpose flour

3 extra-large eggs

A *good rösti is one of the great potato dishes. An all-parsnip variation is an interesting twist on the classic. Serve the rösti as a side dish to a classic veal piccata, a nicely grilled veal chop, or sautéed swordfish scaloppine.*

1. In a heavy skillet, melt 2 tablespoons of the butter together with 1 teaspoon of the oil over medium high heat. Add the onion and cook for 5 minutes, stirring constantly, until the onion begins to brown. Season with salt and pepper, reduce the heat, and cook, partially covered, until the onion is soft and nicely browned, about 20 minutes.

2. When the onion is done, transfer to a large mixing bowl. Add the parsnips, apple, flour, and eggs. Season with salt and pepper and mix until well blended.

3. In a 10-inch nonstick skillet, melt 2 tablespoons of the butter and the remaining oil over medium high heat. When hot, add the parsnip mixture and press down gently into an even disk, covering the entire skillet. Reduce the heat to medium low and cook, covered, for 10 minutes, or until the bottom is nicely browned.

4. Invert the rösti onto a large dinner plate, browned side up. Melt the remaining tablespoon of butter in the skillet and slide the rösti carefully into the skillet, browned side up. Cook for an additional 10 minutes, or until nicely browned.

5. Transfer to a round serving dish and serve hot, cut into wedges.

SERVES 4 TO 5

Sweet Parsnip and Lemon Quick Bread

To be honest, there is hardly a quick bread I don't like; but one made with parsnips and a touch of lemon is one of my favorite breakfast starters. If the parsnip is not very juicy, add one tablespoon of sour cream to the batter and increase the sugar by one or two tablespoons. The bread is delicious served with a nice cup of tea or an afternoon cappuccino.

1. Preheat the oven to 350°F. Butter the bottom and sides of a standard loaf pan. Sprinkle with 2 tablespoons of the sugar and shake out the excess. Set aside.

2. Sift together the flour, baking soda, baking powder, and salt and reserve.

3. In a large mixing bowl, combine the eggs, remaining sugar, lemon zest, lemon juice, and vanilla extract. Beat with an electric hand beater until fluffy and pale yellow. Add the oil and crème fraîche or sour cream and beat until well blended. Fold in the sifted dry ingredients until they are just blended; do not overmix. Add the parsnips and fold gently but thoroughly. Pour the batter into the prepared loaf pan, place in the center of the oven, and bake for 50 to 55 minutes, or until a toothpick when inserted comes out clean.

4. Remove from the oven and let cool slightly. Carefully remove the bread from the pan and let cool completely on a wire rack. Serve at room temperature, cut into thin slices.

S E R V E S 8

NOTE: The bread is best made a day in advance. It also freezes beautifully.

1¼ cups plus 2 tablespoons sugar

1½ cups all-purpose flour

1 teaspoon baking soda

½ teaspoon baking powder

Pinch of salt

2 extra-large eggs

1 teaspoon finely grated lemon zest

1 tablespoon fresh lemon juice

1 teaspoon vanilla extract

⅓ cup corn oil

2 tablespoons Crème Fraîche (page 358) or sour cream

2 cups grated parsnips

POTATOES AND SWEET POTATOES

Potatoes

The potato is among the most important of all the world's vegetables, a staple in the everyday diet of millions of people. The French are justly famous for their Duchesse potatoes and Pommes Soufflés, but other cuisines have also produced great classic potato dishes that, unfortunately, have not been given the gourmet status they deserve. In Spain the flavorful potato omelet still reigns as the most popular everyday dish, but it is rarely found beyond the local tapas bar and small country restaurant. The Belgians created the best french fries in Europe years ago, but those have been relegated to "street food" mostly sold in small paper bags along with a hefty dollop of spicy mustard. Italy has given us potato gnocchi, a dish as popular as pasta but seldom seen outside the neighborhood trattoria. Only in Ireland, Germany, and Austria have potatoes enjoyed an honored place in the national cuisine. In even the best restaurants in Austria, the famous Wiener schnitzel arrives accompanied by a Viennese-style potato salad, while in Germany, potatoes, simply boiled and parslied, are served with many elegant main courses. And, of course, the potato is to the Irish what pasta is to Italians.

My introduction to American potatoes is still fresh in my mind. I had recently arrived in this country and was invited to spend a weekend in Bridgehampton, on the eastern end of Long Island. My friends' house bordered a potato field, which, I soon found out, produced some of the finest potatoes I've ever tasted. It was early fall and the potatoes had just been harvested. We walked through the barren fields collecting the small, leftover potatoes and, with a basketful, headed for the kitchen, where we scrubbed them and cooked them in their skins. With a bit of melted butter, a sprinkling of fresh thyme, and a dash of salt and pepper, those buttery, marble-size potatoes were unforgettable.

Even if you don't grow your own (or live beside a potato field), you can now find more flavorful and unusual varieties, such as the Yellow Finn potato, in markets during winter months. Potatoes come in assorted sizes, shapes, and colors, and each has distinctive cooking characteristics. Basically there are three varieties to be found in supermarkets practically year-round: large, oval Russet potatoes have a mealy texture and are best used for baking; medium-size, round, all-purpose potatoes such as Kennebec or Katahdin are suitable for boiling and french fries; and small red- or white-skinned potatoes such as Red Norland or Irish Cobbler are often sold as tiny "new potatoes." What aren't available unless you grow them yourself or find them at roadside stands are the fine European and heirloom varieties, such as Green Mountain, Ladyfinger, Ruby Crescent, and Carole, that have such unique flavor and texture. There are several varieties of potatoes that have colored flesh and skins—pink, yellow, lavender, and even blue! They taste superb and add an unusual touch to many dishes.

There's good news on the nutritional front too. In these days of almost obsessive concern with weight loss, the potato has come into its own. For years, it was regarded as a high-calorie food. However, a plain, unadorned potato contains only about 100 calories—the same as an apple. And those calories are in the form of carbohydrates, not fat. Furthermore, a potato is a rich and valuable source of minerals and fiber. As a result, home cooks are now using the vegetable as an important nutritious basic in family meals.

BUYING

It is extremely important to know the cooking characteristics of the different potato varieties so that you can take full advantage of their seasonal availability and flavor. Always buy potatoes at a market that has a rapid turnover. Personally, I prefer to buy potatoes loose rather than bagged, but you may not always have that choice. Most all-purpose, round potatoes are now marketed prepackaged in five- to ten-pound, see-through bags. When purchasing these bags, check to see that the potatoes are firm and free from cuts. Avoid potatoes that are greenish, a sign that they have been exposed to light and are bound to have a short shelf life and unsatisfactory flavor.

STORAGE

If you do not have a cool, dry place with good air circulation in which to store potatoes, buy just enough for a week's supply. Potatoes should not be refrigerated because the cold moist air turns the starch to sugar and produces an unpleasant taste. Store potatoes in paper rather than plastic bags.

GARDENING

As you might expect, given that they are such a basic part of the diet of so many countries, potatoes are easy to grow. Although they take up more space than lettuce, root crops, or beans, I find that the broad range of varieties and the unsurpassed flavor of freshly dug new potatoes earn even a small crop its place in my garden. Depending on the variety, just one fifteen-foot row can yield as many as 120 tubers, with some to use as "new" potatoes and plenty left to mature. Because they are essentially cool-weather plants, start your potatoes about two weeks before the last frost. Potatoes need a location in full sun all day as well as light, well-drained, acidic soil and plenty of water. I start my plants the easy way, using certified seed potato sets, which are readily available from garden centers and mail-order houses. Dig a furrow four to five inches wide and six to eight inches deep, working an all-purpose 5-10-5 fertilizer into the soil. Set the potato sections, with the eyes pointing up, nine to twelve inches apart along the furrow and cover each with four to five inches of soil. When the plants stand about five inches high, hill up soil from the sides of the furrow around the plant to almost cover the leaves. Continue this process every time the plants grow another five inches. As the tubers form near the surface, the mounded soil keeps the plants cool and protects the tubers from light, which causes them to turn green. Be careful when cultivating around the plants not to cut into the young potatoes. Be sure to keep the soil moist throughout the growing season.

HARVESTING

When the first blossoms appear on the plants (usually in midsummer or about fifteen weeks from planting), I run my hands just an inch or two under the soil to seek out those first tiny new potatoes that are so delicious. If you do this carefully, you can pick a few without disturbing the plant, and it will continue to produce more tubers. Potatoes are so accommodating about providing these early treasures while the main crop continues to mature. About two weeks after the leaves have turned yellow and died back is the time to harvest your main crop. I use a garden fork to lift the tubers, most of which will be in the top six inches of soil. Store them immediately in a cool, dark, humid place for two weeks and then move them to a dark, dry location for longer storage.

Sweet Potatoes

When it comes to distinguishing yams from sweet potatoes, confusion reigns. For that matter, they really aren't potatoes at all but belong to the morning glory family. The elongated tubers have skin that ranges in color from yellowish tan to coppery brown and either dry yellow fresh or moist, deep-orange flesh. What we know as yams in this country are really the moist-fleshed type of sweet potato. The sweet potato is one of the most complete foods known, being exceptionally rich in vitamin A, and is a staple in the diet of tropical and subtropical areas. The true yam is a tuber grown only in tropical regions that rarely finds its way to northern markets except for an occasional Hispanic or Asian one. These exotic yams are very large, sometimes growing from one to three feet in length, and are much sweeter than our yams. If you ever come across them, they are well worth trying and can be used in any recipe calling for sweet potatoes. The only sweet potato or "yam" that I use in my kitchen is the kind with sweet and moist, vivid orange flesh.

Sweet potatoes are relatively new to my kitchen. My introduction to them was at my first Thanksgiving dinner in this country twenty years ago. I found them interesting but associated them with traditional holiday food, something to eat with turkey at Thanksgiving and Christmas. My innate curiosity about all vegetables finally led me to explore the creative possibilities of sweet potatoes. Now they're an important basic that I use in many ways. They are delicious made into a hearty soup, in which I combine them with root vegetables, onions, and parsley. Spiced with a dash of cayenne and garnished with fresh cilantro, it is a delicious first course to a winter meal. And of course there is nothing better than a yam baked whole in its skin and served simply with butter and a touch of sour cream. Sweet potatoes can be substituted for white potatoes in many dishes such as creamy gratins and fried or sautéed potatoes. Mashed, they are wonderful in custards and pancakes, or simply served as a puree. I find they have a great affinity to Indian and Mexican spices yet are also suitable for Mediterranean dishes.

Throughout fall and winter you should be able to find top-quality sweet potatoes in the markets. Choose the small to medium tubers, as they are the sweetest. They should be firm, heavy, and well shaped. Avoid any that have a wrinkled, shriveled look or discolored ends.

STORAGE

You can store sweet potatoes for several weeks in the refrigerator or in a cool, dark, dry place.

GARDENING

Those who grow sweet potatoes for the first time are often pleasantly surprised to find that they are decorative plants with lovely dense foliage. In addition to the vining type, sweet potatoes are also available in bush types so that they can be grown even in small gardens. Vardaman and Bush Porto Rico are two superb bush varieties, the latter having a distinctive chestnut flavor. Georgia Jet is a standard variety that is well suited to northern gardens, maturing in just ninety days instead of the usual four months. Sweet potatoes are easy to grow and thrive in poor, sandy soil that is slightly acidic, so don't bother about fertilizing or enriching the soil where they are to grow. Rich soil yields a good crop of leaves but few tubers. Sweet potatoes are started from sprouts or slips in late spring. I plant them in mounded rows to ensure good drainage, covering all but the top leaves, and give them one deep watering to get them started.

HARVESTING

Dig the roots when the leaves begin to wither and before frost kills the vines. Use a fork to gently lift the tubers, taking care not to bruise the tender skin. Place in a warm, dry place for ten days to toughen the skins, and then move them to a cool, dark place.

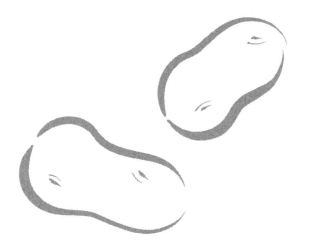

Red Bliss Potato Salad with Capers and Gherkins

THE VINAIGRETTE

I medium garlic clove, peeled
   and crushed

4 flat anchovy fillets, drained
   and finely minced

2 medium scallions, finely
   minced

1/3 cup fresh parsley leaves

5 tablespoons extra-virgin
   olive oil

2 tablespoons sherry vinegar

Salt and freshly ground black
   pepper

THE SALAD

Salt

1 1/4 pounds small red Bliss
   potatoes, unpeeled

I small red bell pepper, cored,
   seeded, and cut into 1/2-inch
   cubes

I small green bell pepper,
   cored, seeded, and cut into
   1/2-inch cubes

I tablespoon capers, drained,
   preferably nonpareil

1/4 pound smoked ham or
   smoked turkey, cut into a
   fine julienne

2 tiny dill gherkins, finely
   minced

*H*ere is a popular Austrian potato salad, one that you will find
at most butcher shops since it is the classic partner for grilled or boiled hot
dogs. You may, of course, vary the salad, adding to it the herbs and spices
of your choice—dill, chives, and flat parsley all work well. Make the salad
at least 6 hours before serving and reseason carefully.

1. Start by making the vinaigrette: In a food processor, combine the garlic, anchovies, scallions, and parsley and process
until finely minced. Add the oil and vinegar, season with salt
and pepper, and process until smooth. Reserve.

2. Bring salted water to a boil in a vegetable steamer, add the
whole potatoes, and steam, covered, for 15 to 20 minutes or
until tender. When the potatoes are done, run them under
cold water to stop further cooking. Peel the potatoes and cut
crosswise into 1/4-inch slices.

3. Transfer the potato slices to a large serving dish and add
the red and green peppers, capers, ham, and minced gherkins.
Pour the vinaigrette over and toss the salad gently but thoroughly. Taste and correct the seasoning, cover, and refrigerate
overnight.

4. The next day, bring the salad back to room temperature.
Taste and correct the seasoning, adding a large grinding of
pepper and more vinegar if necessary.

SERVES 6

Red Potato, Spinach, and Caramelized Onion "Tortilla"

When Spanish cooks think of potatoes they automatically think of a potato tortilla. I take the basic recipe a step farther by folding caramelized onions and some blanched spinach into the egg and potato mixture. I usually serve the tortilla as a main course simply accompanied by a salad, but it is delicious at room temperature cut into thin wedges.

1. In a small skillet, melt the butter together with 1 tablespoon of the oil over high heat. Add the onions and sugar and cook for 3 to 5 minutes, stirring constantly, until the onions begin to brown. Reduce the heat, season with salt and pepper, and cook, covered, for 25 to 30 minutes, or until nicely browned and very soft, stirring often. Set aside.

2. Preheat the oven to 375°F.

3. In a food processor, combine the cooked spinach and parsley and process until finely minced. Add the eggs and a few drops of Tabasco, to taste, and process until smooth. Transfer the egg mixture to a large mixing bowl and fold in the caramelized onions and reserved sliced potatoes, making sure to separate the potato slices so that they will be surrounded on all sides by the egg mixture. Season highly with salt and pepper and reserve.

4. In a heavy 10-inch skillet, heat the remaining 2 tablespoons of olive oil over medium high heat. When the oil is hot but not smoking, add the egg–potato mixture, spreading the potato slices evenly. Cook for 1 to 2 minutes, or until the bottom begins to set and is lightly browned. Sprinkle with the Parmesan cheese and bake for 12 minutes, or until the eggs are just set and lightly browned. Do not overcook.

5. When the tortilla is done, remove it from the oven and let it cool slightly. Slide onto a serving platter and serve hot or at room temperature, cut into wedges.

SERVES 6 TO 8

---

3 tablespoons unsalted butter
3 tablespoons olive oil
2 large onions, peeled, quartered, and thinly sliced
Pinch of sugar
Freshly ground black pepper
2 cups tightly packed, stemmed, fresh spinach leaves, cooked and squeezed
3 tablespoons finely minced fresh parsley
10 extra-large eggs
Drops of Tabasco sauce
2 medium-size red potatoes, boiled and sliced ¼ inch thick
3 tablespoons freshly grated Parmesan cheese

"Melted" Russet Potato Custard Tart

Despite *the overall popularity of potatoes, the rich golden potato tarts of provincial France have never made it into the American cook's repertoire. This is unfortunate, because potatoes are the perfect vegetable for this kind of creamy, custardy, and comforting preparation. When teamed with a fresh crisp green salad and, if the waistline permits, some rashers of crisp bacon or grilled sausages on the side, you have the makings of an outstanding winter meal.*

Salt

2 large russet potatoes, about 1¼ pounds, peeled and sliced very thin

One uncooked tart shell (page 363) in a 10-inch tart pan with a removable bottom

2 tablespoons unsalted butter

Freshly ground black pepper

1 extra-large egg

⅓ cup Crème Fraîche (page 358)

½ cup finely grated Gruyère cheese

1. Preheat the oven to 375°F.

2. In a large saucepan, bring salted water to a boil. Add the potatoes and simmer for 5 minutes. Drain well and pat dry.

3. In the bottom of the tart shell, place one third of the potato slices in an overlapping pattern to cover the bottom completely. Dot with a bit of the butter and season with salt and pepper. Make 2 more layers of potatoes, dotting each with butter and seasoning with salt and pepper.

4. Cover the tart tightly with foil, place in the center of the oven, and bake for 45 to 50 minutes, or until the potatoes are tender when pierced with the tip of a sharp knife.

5. While the tart is baking, combine the egg and crème fraîche in a small bowl and whisk until well blended. Season with salt and pepper and set aside.

6. When the potatoes are done, remove the tart from the oven and remove the foil. Pour the egg mixture over the potatoes and sprinkle the entire surface with the Gruyère. Return to the oven, and bake uncovered for 20 to 25 minutes, or until the custard is set and the top has browned nicely. Let the tart sit for 10 minutes before serving. Cut into wedges and serve warm or at room temperature.

SERVES 8

Curry-Spiced Red Potato and Smoked Chicken Salad

Potatoes and chicken are both extremely receptive to a myriad of spices, especially cumin and curry. Here I give them a chance to mingle in a delicious main-course salad that is good for lunch, supper, or as part of a mixed-salad picnic. If you cannot get smoked chicken, you can use smoked turkey or ham with excellent results.

1. In a small bowl, combine all the ingredients for the curry mayonnaise. Season with salt and pepper and whisk until well blended. Set aside for 30 minutes to develop flavor.

2. Bring salted water to a boil in a medium casserole, add the potatoes, and cook until just tender. Drain and, while they are still warm, peel and quarter the potatoes.

3. Place the warm potatoes in a serving bowl, drizzle with the oil and vinegar, and season with salt and pepper. Toss gently and set aside to cool completely.

4. When the potatoes are cool, add the smoked chicken or turkey, onion, red pepper, and curry mayonnaise. Toss gently but thoroughly, cover, and refrigerate for 2 to 4 hours.

5. Thirty minutes before serving, bring the salad back to room temperature. Taste and correct the seasoning, adding more lemon juice if necessary.

S ERVES   6

THE CURRY MAYONNAISE
½ cup sour cream
½ cup mayonnaise, preferably homemade (page 362)
2 teaspoons imported curry powder, preferably Madras
Large pinch of turmeric
¼ teaspoon ground cumin
Juice of I lemon, or more to taste
I to 2 teaspoons finely minced jalapeño pepper
Salt and freshly ground black pepper

THE SALAD
Salt
2½ pounds small red potatoes
3 tablespoons olive oil
I tablespoon red wine vinegar
Freshly ground black pepper
½ pound smoked chicken or turkey, diced
I small red onion, peeled and finely diced
I large red bell pepper, cored, seeded, and finely diced

Baby Red-Skinned Potatoes in Maple–Nutmeg Butter

1 pound small red potatoes,
  unpeeled
3 tablespoons unsalted butter
¼ cup pure maple syrup
Salt and freshly ground black
  pepper
Pinch of freshly grated nutmeg

Here is a fast and unusual way to prepare new potatoes in the fall. I often sauté ½ cup of diced blanched slab bacon and add it to the skillet for the last 3 to 4 minutes of cooking; the smokiness of the bacon enhances the sweet flavor of the maple syrup. This would be the perfect accompaniment to a roast turkey, loin of pork, or baked ham.

1. Preheat the oven to 375° F.

2. Place the potatoes on a shallow baking sheet and bake for 45 to 50 minutes, or until just tender when pierced with the tip of a sharp knife. Remove the potatoes from the oven and cool slightly. Cut in half and set aside.

3. In a 10-inch cast-iron skillet, melt the butter over medium heat, add the potatoes cut side down, and sauté until lightly browned. Add the maple syrup, season with salt and pepper, and continue to sauté until the potatoes are well glazed and caramelized. Taste and correct the seasoning and add a pinch of freshly grated nutmeg. Serve the potatoes hot.

SERVES 4

Creamy Sweet Potato and Carrot Soup with Allspice

I *find it hard to resist the temptation of teaming sweet potatoes with spices, especially when it comes to soups. But rather than go with the more expected flavorings such as nutmeg, cinnamon, and cloves, I like the more elusive taste of allspice. Still, the flavor options here are wide open: curry, garam masala, a touch of cayenne, ginger, cardamom, and coriander all add interest to the soup when used sparingly. As with most soups, this one benefits from being made ahead of time and can easily be frozen. Be sure to adjust the seasoning carefully if you have made the soup in advance.*

1. In a small saucepan, combine 1 cup of the diced carrots and 1 cup of the broth and simmer, covered, for 12 to 15 minutes, or until the carrots are tender. Drain and reserve the carrots and broth separately. Set aside.

2. Melt the butter in a large heavy casserole over medium heat. Add the onion and cook until soft but not browned. Add the remaining carrots, the sweet potatoes, the reserved carrot broth, and 5 cups of the remaining broth to the casserole. Simmer, partially covered, until the vegetables are very tender, about 30 minutes.

3. Strain the soup and set the vegetables aside. Return the broth to the casserole and reserve. Transfer the vegetables to a food processor and process until very smooth. Add the puree to the broth together with the cream and whisk until well blended. Season with allspice, salt, and pepper and simmer the soup for 10 to 15 minutes, or until the allspice has permeated the soup, whisking often. If the soup is too thick, add the remaining broth.

4. Add the reserved diced carrots and just heat through. Serve hot, garnished with tiny leaves of cilantro.

SERVES 6 TO 8

6 medium carrots, peeled and cut into ¼-inch dice
6 to 6½ cups chicken broth, preferably homemade (page 360)
2 tablespoons unsalted butter
1 large onion, peeled and finely minced
2 large sweet potatoes, peeled and cut into ¼-inch dice
½ cup heavy cream
Large pinch of ground allspice
Salt and freshly ground white pepper

GARNISH
Tiny leaves of fresh cilantro

Salt
4 medium all-purpose potatoes,
about 2 pounds, peeled and
cut into eighths
4 tablespoons (½ stick)
unsalted butter, cut into 4
pieces
¾ cup mascarpone
3 tablespoons red salmon
caviar
3 tablespoons finely minced
fresh dill
2 tablespoons finely minced
fresh chives
Freshly ground black pepper

Potato Puree Danoise

Mashed, riced, and pureed potatoes have regained their status
as an all-American favorite. In fact, they are equally popular in Europe,
where chefs are reinventing and adorning this homey classic. Even those
who shy away from too many calories cannot resist a few spoonfuls of this
best of all potato preparations. Here the puree is enriched with some butter
and mascarpone cheese, which gives it a nice tang. A couple of tablespoons
of minced chives, some sautéed shallots, or a mixture of minced parsley and
garlic are some of my favorite variations.

1. In a large saucepan, bring salted water to a boil. Add the
potatoes and simmer until very tender, about 25 to 30
minutes.

2. Drain the potatoes thoroughly and pass through a food
mill or ricer; do not use a food processor, as the texture will
be too gummy.

3. Return the riced potatoes to the saucepan. Set the pan
over very low heat, add the butter, and stir until it is absorbed
by the potatoes. Fold in the mascarpone, caviar, dill, and
chives and season with salt and pepper. Heat gently just until
warmed through. Transfer to a serving bowl and serve hot.

SERVES 6

Rum-Infused Sweet Potato Crème Brûlées

Few desserts have captured the imagination—and tastebuds—of as many people as has the crème brûlée. Every restaurant and home cook must have a favorite version by now, so coming up with a tasty "yammy" version was just the next step in the natural evolution of this dish. You can substitute Grand Marnier or Cointreau for the rum.

1. Preheat the oven to 350°F.

2. Place the potato on a baking sheet and bake for 50 minutes, or until fork tender, turning once or twice during baking. Remove from the oven and when cool enough, peel and cut into eighths. Set aside. Keep the oven at 350°F.

3. In a food processor, combine the sugar and egg yolks and process until well blended. Add the potato, rum, vanilla, lemon zest, nutmeg, and cream and process until smooth. Transfer to a large mixing bowl and skim off the foam or bubbles from the surface with a large spoon.

4. Pour the custard mixture into 8 to 10 four-ounce porcelain ramekins so that they are three quarters full. Place in a large heavy baking dish and set in the center of the oven. Fill the baking dish with boiling water to come halfway up the sides of the ramekins and bake for 20 minutes, or until the custard has just set. Remove from the water bath and let cool completely. Cover and refrigerate until very cold, about 2 hours.

5. Make the caramel: In a heavy saucepan, combine the sugar and water, bring to a boil over high heat, and stir once to dissolve the sugar. Continue to cook without stirring until the mixture turns a hazelnut brown. Immediately remove the pan from the heat and carefully pour a little of the hot caramel over each cold custard, quickly tilting each ramekin back and forth to cover the surface completely. Chill the custards until serving time.

SERVES 8

THE CUSTARDS
1 medium sweet potato, about 10 ounces, unpeeled
⅓ cup sugar
5 extra-large egg yolks
1 tablespoon dark rum
1 teaspoon vanilla extract
Finely grated zest of 1 large lemon
Large pinch of freshly grated nutmeg
2 cups warm heavy cream

THE CARAMEL
¾ cup sugar
¼ cup water

**6 tablespoons (¾ stick)
  unsalted butter, melted
1 large baking potato (about
  8 ounces)
Freshly ground black pepper
Coarse salt**

Crispy Potato Galettes

Nothing can be simpler or more delicious than this trditional
and unassuming potato dish. Thinly sliced potatoes are placed in a single
layer in an overlapping circle and baked until crisp. If brushed with melted
clarified butter (page 358), they will be even more delicious. I like to serve
the galettes as a bed for grilled quail or some nicely seared sea scallops,
but I also use them to add a welcome crunch to a well-seasoned mixed
green salad.

1. Preheat the oven to 425°F. Brush each of 2 baking sheets,
preferably nonstick, with 1 tablespoon of the melted butter.

2. Peel the potato and slice as thin and even as possible.

3. Dip the potato slices individually into the remaining
melted butter, and arrange 8 to 10 to make a circle on the
prepared baking sheet, overlapping slightly. It should be
about 6 inches in diameter. You can also use flan rings if you
prefer a more uniform appearance. Make 3 circles (galettes)
on each baking sheet. Season only with pepper; do not salt
the galettes before baking.

4. Place the cookie sheets, one at a time, in the center of the
oven and bake for 12 to 15 minutes, or until the potatoes are
nicely browned and crisp, turning once during baking. Season
with coarse salt and serve warm.

SERVES 6

WINTER GREENS

MY MOTHER USED TO CALL WINTER GREENS "APRON GREENS" BECAUSE it was customary for a farmer's wife to pick greens from the garden or backyard and carry them back to the kitchen in her apron. The greens were destined for the day's meal either by themselves or added to soups, stews, or legume and egg dishes for flavor, color, and texture. Even today these boldly flavored greens remain an important part of peasant cookery in countries where they are not grown commercially. Here, regional favorites like collards, kale, and turnip and mustard greens were rarely available beyond the southern states until a few years ago. Things are looking up now that produce markets all over the country are carrying a good variety of fresh seasonal greens during the autumn and winter. Due to this availability both chefs and home cooks are beginning to explore the creative possibilities of winter greens. Once I discovered the range and diversity of these greens the cold months started to offer greater culinary interest for me—indeed they now seem to offer as much variety and choice as summer and fall. One of the most appealing aspects of winter greens is that they marry beautifully with other winter dishes like stews, soups, and hearty roasts. Not only do they add color but, unlike the delicate greens of spring, they hold their own in a robust ragout. They are also delightful as a quick side dish, simply wilted in a skillet with some fruity olive oil and a sliced clove of garlic.

Escarole

Escarole is the only winter green that can also be used as a salad green. Perhaps because it has been so widely available for such a long time, few recognize the versatility of this slightly bitter but delicious green. Escarole is wonderful in soups, stir-fried, or tossed in a warm dressing with diced, sautéed bacon. A new blanched variety can be found in gourmet produce markets and some supermarkets; it has a less bitter flavor and is delicious mixed with other greens. Escarole has become a basic ingredient in the skillet salads so much in vogue now because it has enough substance to stand up to warm ingredients like seared chicken breast, tuna steak, or sautéed shrimp.

GARDENING

I count back ten weeks from the time of the first fall frost to determine the sowing time for escarole. Escarole likes a moisture-retentive, rich soil and, if the weather is dry when I sow the seed, I water the furrow first. Sow the seeds evenly and thinly and keep the soil moist to prevent bolting. Batavian is the standard variety, but Nuvol is the less bitter new variety and Sinco is a fine French variety worth trying. Harvest before hard frost. In the South, grow escarole as a winter crop.

Kale

Beautiful, curly, blue-green kale is becoming one of the most popular winter greens. It possesses a unique texture, firm but not tough when properly cooked, and a delicious, earthy flavor with just a hint of bitterness that I find very refreshing. And it is also just about the most nutritious green you can eat, rich in vitamins and fiber. Kale is a green I grew up with. My mother made a wonderful light soup based on clam broth to which she added cut-up kale, potatoes, and a generous amount of garlic. When the soup was almost done, she added spicy chorizo sausage and continued to cook it until the potatoes were almost falling apart. Although the kale was a little overdone, the memory of this delicious soup spurred me to include this robust green in my first vegetable garden. Now, excellent fresh kale is available in markets throughout the winter and deserves to be in every cook's winter repertoire.

Collards

My introduction to collards was hardly a case of love at first bite. Several years ago I was the guest of a charming Southern lady who was eager to introduce me to all kinds of regional delicacies, including her seventy-five-year-old aunt's legendary fried chicken. Aunt Mave preferred an early dinner so we sat down at four P.M. to a feast of crispy fried chicken, mouthwatering fluffy biscuits, and a most peculiar overcooked green vegetable that turned out to be collards. I was immediately curious to find out what collards were like in a less-than-overcooked state, but to my disappointment I couldn't find them in my market. Now that they are no longer exclusive to Southern markets and are widely available fresh in the winter months, this lovely cabbage-like green with the large smooth leaves has become one of my favorite vegetables. Collards have a softer, smoother taste than either mustard or turnip greens and, skillet-braised in homemade chicken, they are superb. They are also tasty braised in commercial beef broth which has been doctored with carrots, onions, celery, and a piece of smoked pork butt. In fact, this full-flavored stock is useful for braising any of the winter greens. Serve cooked collards as a side dish with roast pork or roast or fried chicken or add them raw to bean or root vegetable soup. Store them in the coldest part of the refrigerator only for a day or two because they tend to wilt quickly.

GARDENING

Both collards and kale, with their handsome big leaves, make a wonderful sight in the garden. They're both easy to grow for fall crops, can stand heavy frost, and have similar growing requirements. Sow the seeds in rich soil in midsummer about twelve weeks before frost. I've learned that keeping the soil moist after sowing keeps soil from crusting and aids germination. Collards will do well in even poor soil but both vegetables respond to a side dressing of fertilizer when the seedlings are well established. Both plants need plenty of room, so thin them to stand about two and a half feet apart. Georgia is a collard variety that produces juicy, blue-green leaves. Vates is the most popular kale variety, but Cottagers is an English heirloom variety worth trying and Lacinato is an Italian heirloom variety that is a unique dark blue-green and is very tender and mild.

HARVESTING

Harvest leaves of both vegetables as soon as the leaves are reasonably large. You don't need to harvest the whole plant. Both vegetables are very cold tolerant and frost sweetens their flavor. Be sure to leave a few kale plants in the garden for fresh greens all winter.

Mustard Greens

Although mustard greens are a spring crop in many parts of the country, I consider them more of a winter green. You can also find mustard greens in many markets during the winter months, and they're well worth including in the season's menus. I think mustard greens are at their best quickly sautéed with sliced garlic cloves in virgin olive oil until just wilted. They also make a delicious addition to linguine cooked with clams or sausage. Another favorite of mine is to serve them wilted with steamed red potatoes and a touch of garlic-flavored yogurt. Sometimes I like to enhance a natural bite of the greens with a little hot chili pepper in a stir-fry served on a bed of braised white beans or sautéed medallions of pork. When buying mustard greens, be sure to get them very young and fresh or their taste will be far too assertive.

GARDENING

Because mustard greens bolt quickly in warm weather, I wait until mid-August or roughly three weeks before the first fall frost to sow mine for a late fall crop. They grow fast and like an organically enriched, moisture-retentive soil. Fordhook Fancy is a good variety and Giant Red is a beautiful red Japanese kind.

HARVESTING

I think frost improves the flavor of mustard greens to I wait until there's been a frost before I start picking the leaves.

Broccoli Rabe (Broccoli di Rape)

Relatively new to the winter green scene, this vegetable is widely grown in Italy, where it is a popular addition to pasta and legume dishes. It has edible stems and small bud clusters similar to broccoli but much looser. The distinctive, robust, medium-sharp flavor has a great affinity to garlic and sweet or hot peppers. Although it is available in markets, broccoli rabe, fresh from the garden, is milder and does not need blanching. Wherever you get it, it is a wonderful winter green that is quick to prepare and is a delicious and interesting accompaniment to seafood, veal, chicken, and pork.

STORAGE

Pat the broccoli rabe dry and cut off an inch from the bottom of the stalks. Place in a perforated plastic bag with a paper towel to absorb any excess moisture and refrigerate. It will keep for three to five days.

GARDENING

This is a fast-growing vegetable that thrives in cool weather. Sow the seed in late summer in fertile soil and thin the plants so they are eight inches apart. Keep the plants well watered at all times so they make steady rapid growth.

HARVESTING

I cut both leaves and stems as soon as the stems emerge from the leaves, because broccoli rabe must be eaten when it is young and tender.

Linguine with Broccoli Rabe and Spicy Shrimp

Salt

1 pound broccoli rabe, trimmed of all but 2 inches of stem

7 tablespoons olive oil

3 large garlic cloves, peeled and thinly sliced

Freshly ground black pepper

¾ pound imported dried linguine

1 small dry red chili pepper, broken in half

1 pound medium shrimp, peeled

6 flat anchovy fillets, drained and finely minced

2 large garlic cloves, peeled and finely minced

½ cup finely minced fresh parsley

Broccoli rabe is now quite easy to come by, even if you don't grow your own. But if you cannot get it, you can substitute 1 medium head of escarole cut into 1-inch pieces or 2 to 3 cups small broccoli florets that have been steamed.

1. Bring plenty of salted water to a boil in a large casserole, add the broccoli rabe, and cook for 30 seconds. Immediately drain well and set aside.

2. Add 4 tablespoons of the oil to the casserole. Place over medium low heat, add the garlic and the broccoli rabe, and sauté for 1 minute, stirring constantly. Season with salt and pepper, transfer to a side dish, and reserve.

3. Bring more salted water to a boil in the casserole. Add the linguine and cook for 6 to 8 minutes, or until just tender "al dente."

4. While the pasta is cooking, heat the remaining 3 tablespoons of oil in a large cast-iron skillet over high heat. Add the chili pepper and cook until dark. Remove with a slotted spoon and discard. Add the shrimp and sauté for 1 to 2 minutes, or until bright pink. Do not overcook. Remove with a slotted spoon to a side dish and reserve.

5. Reduce the heat to low, add the anchovies, minced garlic, and parsley, and simmer until the anchovies have melted.

6. When the pasta is done, immediately add 2 cups cold water to the casserole to stop further cooking. Drain well and add to the skillet containing the anchovy mixture together with the shrimp and broccoli rabe. Toss gently over medium low heat until just heated through. Taste and correct the seasoning, adding a large grinding of black pepper. Serve hot directly from the skillet.

SERVES 4

Sauté of Broccoli Rabe Italienne (with Cremini Mushrooms and Smoked Ham)

Once it is blanched, broccoli rabe becomes quite mellow, and it marries well with a variety of mushrooms. The addition of diced smoked ham turns this side dish into a light starter. You may substitute diced smoked chicken or turkey for the ham if you prefer. As a side dish, serve with veal scaloppine, sautéed chicken breasts, or roasted Cornish hens.

Salt
1 pound trimmed broccoli rabe, trimmed of all but 2 inches of stalk
6 tablespoons olive oil
½ pound cremini or all-purpose mushrooms, trimmed, wiped, and cut into ¼-inch slices
½ cup finely diced smoked ham
Freshly ground black pepper

1. Bring plenty of salted water to a boil in a large casserole. Add the broccoli rabe and cook for 30 seconds. Drain immediately and reserve.

2. In a large heavy skillet, heat the olive oil over medium high heat. Add the mushrooms and sauté until nicely browned. Reduce the heat, add the ham and broccoli rabe, and cook for 1 to 2 minutes or until just heated through. Season with salt and pepper and serve at once.

SERVES 4 TO 6

Orecchiette with Broccoli Rabe and Fennel Sausage

Salt

1 pound broccoli rabe, trimmed of all but 2 inches of stem

6 tablespoons extra-virgin olive oil

¾ pound sweet Italian fennel sausage

1 medium onion, peeled and finely minced

2 large garlic clove, peeled and finely minced

Freshly ground black pepper

½ pound imported dried orecchiette

GARNISH

½ cup freshly grated Parmesan cheese

*I*t may take some looking to find orecchiette—a small disc-shaped pasta—but do make the effort. The somewhat chewy texture of this pasta works well with the robust sausage and the slightly bitter broccoli rabe. I usually serve this dish as a main course following the Belgian Endive and Stilton Cheese Salad (page 272) and end the meal with a winter fruit dessert.

1. Bring plenty of salted water to a boil in a large casserole. Add the broccoli rabe and cook for 30 seconds. Drain immediately and set aside.

2. In a heavy 10-inch skillet, heat 2 tablespoons of the olive oil over medium high heat. Add the fennel sausage and cook, partially covered, until nicely browned on all sides but still pink in the center. Transfer to a cutting board and cut crosswise into ¼-inch slices. Reserve.

3. Remove all but 3 tablespoons of fat from the skillet, reduce the heat, and add the onion and garlic. Cook until the onion is soft and nicely browned.

4. Add the remaining 4 tablespoons of oil to the skillet together with the broccoli rabe and sliced sausage, toss well with the onion mixture, and just heat through. Season with salt and a large grinding of black pepper and keep warm.

5. Bring plenty of salted water again to a boil in a large casserole, add the pasta, and cook until just tender "al dente." Immediately add 2 cups cold water to the pot to stop further cooking. Drain well and return the orecchiette to the casserole. Add the broccoli rabe mixture and toss well with the pasta. Correct the seasoning, transfer to a serving bowl, and sprinkle with half of the Parmesan. Serve hot with the remaining Parmesan on the side.

SERVES 4

Sautéed Escarole with Capers, Anchovies, and Gaeta Olives

Escarole is a super basic green, one that you can find in markets throughout the country. Widely used in Italian cooking, this lively green has not been given the credit it deserves. When combined with pine nuts, anchovies, and black olives, the result is an earthy side dish that is a welcome accompaniment to pan-seared lamb chops, a sauté of chicken, or a roast loin of pork.

1. Trim the escarole, separate into leaves, and wash thoroughly in several rinses of warm water. Drain and dry well in a salad spinner. Tear into 1½-inch pieces and set aside.

2. In a large heavy skillet, heat 3 tablespoons of the oil over medium high heat. Add half of the escarole and cook, tossing in the oil, until the leaves have just wilted. Remove with a slotted spoon to a side dish, season with salt and pepper, and reserve.

3. Add another 3 tablespoons of oil to the skillet and when hot, add the remaining escarole. Cook, tossing in the hot oil, until the leaves have just wilted. Transfer to the dish containing the first batch, season with salt and pepper, and reserve.

4. Reduce the heat to low and add the remaining 2 tablespoons oil to the skillet. Add the pine nuts and sauté, stirring constantly, until lightly browned. Remove with a slotted spoon to a side dish and reserve.

5. Add the garlic and anchovies to the skillet and cook, stirring constantly, until the anchovies have just melted. Return the escarole to the skillet together with the pine nuts, capers, and olives and toss gently to just heat through. Taste and correct the seasoning, adding a large grinding of black pepper. Serve hot.

S E R V E S   4

2 medium heads of escarole
8 tablespoons olive oil
Salt and freshly ground black
 pepper
3 tablespoons pine nuts
2 medium garlic cloves, peeled
 and finely minced
6 flat anchovy fillets, drained
 and finely minced
2 tablespoons tiny capers,
 drained, preferably nonpareil
12 Gaeta olives or other small
 oil-cured black olives

Escarole, Prosciutto, and Pine Nut Pizza with Smoked Mozzarella

Although I do not have the right oven or know much about the art of making pizza, I still like my own every bit as much as those served in most restaurants. To me the topping is what counts, and this full-flavored one is hard to beat. If good prosciutto is hard to come by, you can use fennel sausage or capocollo instead. Double the topping recipe and serve any leftover greens as a side dish to roast chicken or lamb chops.

4 tablespoons plus 1 teaspoon extra-virgin olive oil

4 medium garlic cloves, peeled and thinly sliced

1 pound escarole, separated into leaves, washed, and cut into 1½-inch pieces

Salt and freshly ground black pepper

2 tablespoons pine nuts

Coarse yellow cornmeal for sprinkling on pizza pan

½ recipe Quick Pizza Dough (page 359)

2 ounces thinly sliced prosciutto, cut into fine julienne

1 cup smoked mozzarella, coarsely grated (see Note)

1. In a large casserole, heat 3 tablespoons of the oil over medium heat. Add the garlic and escarole and cook, stirring constantly, until the escarole has just wilted. Season with salt and pepper and reserve.

2. Wipe out the skillet and heat another tablespoon of oil. Add the pine nuts and sauté until golden, about 4 minutes. Set aside.

3. Preheat the oven to 425°F. Brush a black 12-inch pizza pan with the remaining teaspoon of oil and sprinkle lightly with cornmeal. Set aside.

4. Roll out the pizza dough on a lightly floured surface into a 9-inch circle. Transfer the dough to the prepared pizza pan and stretch gently from the center outward to the edge of the pan. If the dough becomes too elastic, let it rest for 5 minutes.

5. Spread the escarole evenly over the surface of the dough, leaving a half-inch border. Bake for 10 minutes. Sprinkle first with the prosciutto, then the pine nuts and mozzarella, and bake for an additional 2 to 5 minutes, or until the crust is nicely browned and the cheese has melted. Garnish the olives and Parmesan and serve hot, cut into wedges.

SERVES 4

NOTE: The smoked mozzarella will be easier to grate if you place it in the freezer until firm, about 20 to 30 minutes.

Bouillon of Littleneck Clams with Corn, Kale, and Lemongrass

Lemongrass gives a classic Portuguese soup a delicious "East-meets-West" flavor that is refreshingly unexpected. If you happen to see large cherrystone clams, then use them instead of littlenecks. Even though cherrystones are nice and meaty and work well in this soup, their broth is usually quite salty, so be extra careful when seasoning.

1. In a heavy 3-quart saucepan, bring the water to a boil. Add the clams, reduce the heat, and "steam," covered, until all the clams open; discard any that do not.

2. Transfer the clams with a slotted spoon to a side dish as they open. Remove them from their shells and discard the shells. Dice the clams and place in a bowl with ¼ cup of their steaming liquid. Set aside. Strain the remaining clam steaming liquid through a double layer of cheesecloth and reserve.

3. In a large heavy casserole, heat the olive oil over medium heat. Add 1 teaspoon of the jalapeño pepper, the shallots, lemongrass, and garlic and cook for 1 to 2 minutes without browning.

4. Add the bottled clam juice or chicken broth, Old Bay Seasoning, and reserved steaming liquid. Add the corn and simmer, partially covered, for 15 minutes. Skim the top of the soup if necessary.

5. Add the kale and cook for 15 to 20 minutes longer or until the kale is tender. Add the diced clams together with their juices and season with a large grinding of black pepper. If you would like the soup a little more spicy, add the remaining jalapeño pepper. Garnish with the cilantro and serve hot, accompanied by a crusty bread.

S E R V E S 6

NOTE: The clams will not all open at once, so it is best to remove each from the pot as it opens to prevent overcooking.

½ cup water
12 littleneck clams, scrubbed clean
3 tablespoons olive oil
1 to 2 teaspoons finely minced jalapeño pepper
⅓ cup thinly sliced shallots
1 tablespoon finely minced fresh lemongrass
3 medium garlic cloves, peeled and finely minced
4 cups bottled clam juice or chicken broth, preferably homemade (page 360)
¼ teaspoon Old Bay Seasoning
1½ cups fresh or canned corn kernels
¾ pound kale, stemmed, washed, and cut into 1-inch pieces
Freshly ground black pepper

GARNISH
Tiny leaves of fresh cilantro

Stir-Fry of Kale with Shiitake Mushrooms

6 tablespoons extra-virgin olive oil

5 fresh shiitake mushrooms, stemmed and caps thinly sliced

2 medium garlic cloves, peeled and finely minced

2 pounds kale, stemmed, washed and dried, and torn into 1½-inch pieces

Salt and freshly ground black pepper

I used to think of fresh kale, with its large unyielding leaves, as somewhat uninviting. But once blanched, kale is a terrific winter green with enough personality to stand up to bacon, sausage, or meaty mushrooms such as shiitake or portobello. Serve the sauté as a side dish to roasted or pan-seared pork tenderloins, grilled fennel sausage, or roasted Cornish hens.

1. In a large heavy skillet, heat 2 tablespoons of the olive oil over medium high heat. Add the shiitake mushrooms and toss in the hot oil for about 1 minute. Transfer to a side dish and reserve.

2. Add the remaining 4 tablespoons of oil to the skillet and when hot add the garlic. Immediately add half of the kale and toss quickly in the oil until it begins to wilt. Add the remaining kale to the skillet and toss together with the first batch until it has all completely wilted. Season with salt and pepper. Reduce the heat to low and cook for another 2 minutes, or until just tender. Add the reserved shiitake mushrooms, and just heat through. Serve hot.

SERVES 4 TO 5

Tortellini with Gorgonzola and Kale all'Alfredo

A *true Alfredo sauce made with a light brown butter, good sweet cream, excellent Parmesan, and a large grinding of fresh pepper is one of those great tastes that well deserves its lasting popularity. For a more contemporary touch, I like to add an interesting winter green such as kale and further intensify the flavor of the sauce with the sweet subtle taste of Gorgonzola dolce. The combination of flavors makes for a sublime pasta dish that is good for dinner, lunch, or anytime you feel like "pasta e basta."*

1. Bring water to a boil in a vegetable steamer, add the kale, and steam, covered, until completely wilted and tender. Remove from the steamer and when cool enough to handle, gently squeeze to remove excess moisture. Reserve.

2. Melt the butter in a heavy 10-inch skillet over medium low heat and whisk constantly until it turns a light hazelnut brown. Immediately whisk in the heavy cream and reduce by one third. Add the Gorgonzola, season with salt and pepper, and just heat through. Set aside.

3. Bring plenty of salted water to a boil in a large casserole, add the tortellini, and cook until just tender "al dente." Drain well. Add the reserved kale and the tortellini to the skillet of sauce and simmer for 1 to 2 minutes, or until the sauce has reduced and coats the pasta. Add the Parmesan and correct the seasoning. Serve at once with additional Parmesan on the side and a crusty loaf of Italian bread.

SERVES 4

¾ pound kale, trimmed and stemmed, washed and dried, and torn into 1-inch pieces
4 tablespoons (½ stick) unsalted butter
1¼ cups heavy cream
3 ounces sweet Gorgonzola or other mild blue cheese, crumbled
Salt and freshly ground white pepper
1 pound fresh tortellini or other small cheese-filled pasta
⅓ cup freshly grated Parmesan cheese

GARNISH
Bowl of freshly grated Parmesan cheese

Quick Sauté of Calamari and Spicy Greens

8 tablespoons extra-virgin
    olive oil
I small head of escarole, leaves
    washed and torn into
    1½-inch pieces
4 large garlic cloves, peeled
    and thinly sliced
Coarse salt and freshly ground
    black pepper
4 large Belgian endives, cut in
    half lengthwise, then
    crosswise into ½-inch slices
I large head of radicchio,
    leaves torn into 1½-inch
    pieces, discarding most of
    the white part
I small dry red chili pepper,
    broken in half
I pound cleaned medium-size
    calamari, cut into ¾-inch
    squares

Sometimes the simplest dish can be an inspiration for a recipe that becomes a year-round favorite. A sauté I was served recently in a little trattoria in Venice is that kind of dish. It takes mere minutes to prepare and when served with good crusty Italian or French bread is really a winter winner. The original was made with arugula, but I find that escarole works equally well.

1. In a 10-inch cast-iron skillet, heat 2 tablespoons of the oil over medium high heat. Add half of the escarole together with 1 sliced garlic clove and cook, stirring constantly, until the escarole has just wilted. Season with salt and pepper, transfer to a side dish, and reserve. Add another 2 tablespoons of oil to the skillet together with the remaining escarole and 1 sliced garlic clove. When wilted, season and add to the first batch. Reserve.

2. Add 2 more tablespoons of oil to the skillet, add the endives and radicchio together with 1 sliced garlic clove, and cook, stirring constantly, until the leaves have just wilted. Season with salt and pepper. Return the escarole to the skillet and toss with the radicchio and endive for 1 minute longer. Set aside.

3. Heat the remaining 2 tablespoons of oil in a 10-inch non-stick skillet over high heat. When very hot, add the chili pepper, the remaining garlic slices, and the calamari and cook, stirring constantly, for 30 seconds; do not overcook. Season with salt and pepper and combine with the sautéed greens. Reheat, if necessary, over very low heat and serve immediately, accompanied by a crusty bread.

S E R V E S   4

WINTER SQUASH

WHILE GROWING UP IN SPAIN, MY ONLY ACQUAINTANCE WITH WINTER squash was the European pumpkin, a variety that is used primarily as a flavoring for soups and stock. Flanking the entrance of our neighborhood market in Barcelona were two small stands where we bought our soup greens. The "Soup Lady," as I used to call her, would deftly tie together a couple of carrots, a leek, and a parsley root and then slice off a large chunk of brilliant orange pumpkin, completing the assortment. Imagine then my amazement when, during my first autumn in this country, my husband and I drove through the picture-perfect Amish farm country of Pennsylvania. Acres and acres of pumpkins, in all sizes and shapes, were strewn across the fields of that fertile farmland. Some farms displayed extraordinary-looking squashes in remarkable shapes and color combinations.

My mother-in-law introduced me to the culinary pleasures of winter squash. She baked acorn or buttercup squash whole until it was tender. Then she halved the squash, removed the seeds, mashed a piece of sweet butter into the pulp in the shell, added brown sugar, freshly grated nutmeg, salt, and pepper, and returned the halves to the oven to heat through. As a side dish to roast turkey or a roast loin of pork, it was sheer ambrosia. Since then, I have discovered and experimented with other varieties of winter squash, preparing them in less traditional ways. A recent autumn trip landed me in Montreal, where I visited the downtown farmer's market, a favorite of mine. There I stopped at one stand after another, buying every squash that struck my fancy. And then on the way home through New England, I managed to stash even more squashes into the trunk of my car. There seemed to be no end to the colors and shapes. I learned a lot about winter squash on that trip. Besides the ubiquitous acorn and butternut types, the adventurous cook can find Banana Squash, Turbans, Mammoth, Cushaw, Canada Crookneck, Winter Crookneck, Kabocha, and Sweet Dumpling. While not all of these are particularly noteworthy, I did discover a new favorite that is for me one of the highlights of the late fall, namely the apple-size edible pumpkins. Two varieties that I highly recommend are Jack-Be-Little and Munchkin. These are delicious baked whole, with the seeds then scooped out and the cavities filled with baked spaghetti squash (page 356) or a sweet potato and carrot puree. The difference in taste among the various winter squashes is rather subtle, but the variations in texture, moisture, and sweetness are worth exploring both for the gardener and the home cook.

BUYING

Because growing winter squash, especially the large varieties such as Hubbard, often requires more room than most home gardeners can spare, you may be best off seeking out the interesting kinds at local farm stands or even your supermarket. For cooking purposes, you can often substitute one winter squash for another unless the recipe calls for the squash to be cubed, retaining that shape, as in the fricassee of butternut squash and pears (page 354). Most squashes other than the butternut and acorn types are best used in purees and soups. When buying any kind of winter squash, look for hard, smooth, unblemished fruits. I prefer them unwaxed, although you may not always have a choice.

STORAGE

Hard-skinned squash, including pumpkins, can be stored for months in a cool, dry place. At high temperatures they will either dry out or rot. Those that have been used as an autumn decoration, either outdoors or indoors, are perfectly acceptable for cooking.

GARDENING

All winter squash and pumpkins are vulnerable to frost and do their best growing in the heat of summer. But because they take 90 to 125 days to mature, they are seldom ready to use before September. All varieties are easy to grow, their only requirements being well-prepared soil (they have extensive root systems) rich in organic matter; plenty of water, especially during dry spells; and some fertilizer when the fruit has formed. Modern breeding techniques have yielded several varieties that are compact, bush-type plants, such as Bush Acorn Table King or Burpee's Butterbush, and are therefore suitable for smaller gardens. Otherwise, expect to see vines ten to twelve feet long. I like to grow the vining types along the sides of the garden so the vines can sprawl over the edges, saving garden space. As the fruits develop, gently turn them once in a while so that they ripen evenly.

HARVESTING

Winter squash and pumpkins should be harvested before frost when the rinds cannot be pierced with your thumbnail. Use a sharp knife to cut the stems, leaving a two-inch stub on the fruit. If the stem is separated from the fruit, rot will occur. Let the squashes dry in the sun or a warm place for ten days to cure the rind, then store them in a dark, airy place.

Vanilla- and Citrus-Pickled Sugar Pumpkin

2 small sugar pumpkins, about
    1½ pounds each
3 cups water
1½ cups sugar
1 vanilla bean, split
¼ cup fresh peppermint leaves
Juice of 1½ large oranges
Juice of 1½ large lemons

Unlike other winter squash, the texture of pumpkin is excellent *for pickling. After several tests both sweet and savory, I decided on this sweet version, which can be served alongside a spicy curry or a roast duck or turkey. You may add a cinnamon stick, two or three allspice berries, and a few whole cloves to the pickling juice for an interesting variation.*

1. Cut each pumpkin in half. Scoop out and discard the seeds. Peel the halves with a sharp knife and then cut each in half again. Cut each pumpkin piece crosswise into ¼-inch slices and reserve.

2. In a large saucepan, combine the water, sugar, vanilla bean, mint leaves, orange juice, and lemon juice. Bring the mixture to a boil and simmer for 1 minute, or until the sugar has completely dissolved. Add the pumpkin and simmer, partially covered, for 20 minutes, or until tender.

3. Remove the pan from the heat and let the pumpkin cool in its poaching liquid. Pack the pumpkin pieces into 3 hot sterilized pint jars, pour the liquid over each, and process in a hot water bath (see page 168), or keep tightly covered in the refrigerator for up to 4 weeks.

MAKES 3 PINTS

Basque Pumpkin and Bean Soup

Whew! You can't get much earthier than this. It's my version of a classic Basque soup that is wonderfully hearty and flavor-packed. Although Mediterranean pumpkin is quite different from the American varieties, ours works perfectly in this cool-weather soup. Serve it as a one-dish meal with some crusty bread, followed by a seasonal salad and a nicely ripened piece of brie, Italian Taleggio, or young Parmesan.

1. In a heavy 3½-quart casserole, heat the oil over medium heat. Add the chili pepper to the casserole together with the onion and garlic and sauté the mixture over medium low heat until the onion is soft and lightly browned. Add the leek, celery, and carrots and continue sautéeing until the vegetables are soft. Season with salt and pepper.

2. Add the pork butt and broth and simmer, covered, for 25 minutes. Add the pumpkin or squash and continue to cook until tender.

3. Add the cooked beans and the sausage, if using, and simmer until just heated through. Taste the soup and correct the seasoning, adding a large grinding of black pepper. Serve the soup hot, accompanied by crusty bread.

S E R V E S   6

2 tablespoons olive oil
1 small dry red chili pepper, broken in half
1 large onion, peeled and finely diced
2 large garlic cloves, peeled and finely minced
1 large leek, all but 2 inches of greens removed, diced and well rinsed
2 large celery stalks, peeled and diced
2 large carrots, peeled and diced
Salt and freshly ground black pepper
½ pound smoked pork shoulder butt, cut into 1-inch pieces
8 to 10 cups beef broth
3 cups pumpkin or butternut squash, peeled and cut into ¾-inch cubes
1 cup dried Great Northern Beans, cooked (page 364)
Optional: 6 ounces chorizo or kielbasa

Tiny Pumpkins Filled with Brown Sugar–Glazed Apple Compote

I am a great fan of slightly savory winter fruit compotes, especially apples and pears; and the somewhat nutty-flavored Jack-Be-Little pumpkins make the perfect containers for these purees. Serve the baked pumpkins decoratively around a roast duck or crown roast of pork and be sure to make some extras, since they reheat beautifully in a low oven or the microwave.

8 Jack-Be-Little pumpkins
8 medium McIntosh apples, cored, seeded, and cut into eighths
½ cup sugar
½ teaspoon ground cinnamon
Large pinch of freshly grated nutmeg
2 tablespoons water
8 teaspoons unsalted butter
8 tablespoons dark brown sugar

1. Preheat the oven to 350°F.

2. Place the pumpkins on a baking sheet, stem end up, and bake for 30 to 35 minutes, or until easily pierced with a fork.

3. While the pumpkins are baking, prepare the filling: In a large skillet, combine the apples, sugar, cinnamon, nutmeg, and water. Place over medium low heat and cook for 15 to 20 minutes, or until a thick compote is formed; stir often and mash the apples with the back of a spoon as they soften. Remove from the heat and set aside.

4. Preheat the broiler.

5. Cut a ¼-inch slice off the top of each pumpkin to include the stem. Set these "caps" aside. With a grapefruit spoon, remove and discard all seeds and stringy membranes from inside the pumpkins.

6. Spoon 2 to 3 tablespoons of compote into each of the hollowed-out pumpkins. Top each with 1 teaspoon of butter and 1 tablespoon of brown sugar.

7. Place the filled pumpkins on a baking sheet and set in the broiler, 6 inches from the source of heat. Broil until the sugar melts and caramelizes, being careful not to let the pumpkins burn. Remove from the broiler, top each pumpkin with its "cap," and serve at once.

SERVES 8

Jack-Be-Little Pumpkins Filled with Onion and Potato Puree

For years I used sugar pumpkins for decorative purposes, never giving them much culinary consideration. But ever since a friend introduced me to their edible charm, I like to bake them whole, then scoop out the seedy center and fill them with a seasonal puree. Since even the smallest pumpkin seems rather large when placed on a standard-size dinner plate, it's best to arrange them decoratively on a serving platter around a roast such as a glazed ham or a mustard-rubbed turkey.

1. In a heavy 10-inch skillet, melt the butter together with the oil over medium low heat. Add the onions, sprinkle with the sugar, and cook for 5 minutes, stirring often, until the onions begin to soften. Add ¼ cup of the broth, season with salt and pepper, and simmer, partially covered, over low heat, until the onions are very soft but not browned. Add the remaining broth if the juices run dry.

2. While the onions are cooking, bring salted water to a boil in a small saucepan. Add the potato and cook until very tender, about 15 minutes. Drain well and pass through a food mill or potato ricer. (Do not use a food processor to puree the potatoes as the texture will be too gummy.) Reserve.

3. When the onions are done, transfer to a food processor, add the heavy cream, and process until smooth. Add to the reserved potato, season with salt and pepper, and mix well.

4. Preheat the broiler.

5. Spoon 2 to 3 tablespoons of onion–potato mixture into each pumpkin and top with 1 tablespoon of the brown sugar.

6. Place the filled pumpkins on a baking sheet and set in the broiler, 6 inches from the source of heat. Broil just until the sugar melts and caramelizes. Remove from the broiler, top each pumpkin with its "cap," and serve at once.

S E R V E S   6   T O   8

3 tablespoons unsalted butter
2 teaspoons olive oil
3 large onions, peeled, quartered, and thinly sliced, about 4 cups
1 teaspoon sugar
⅓ cup chicken broth, preferably homemade (page 360)
Salt and freshly ground black pepper
1 medium all-purpose potato, peeled and cubed
¼ cup heavy cream
6 to 8 Jack-Be-Little pumpkins, baked, seeds removed and caps reserved (see page 352)
6 to 8 tablespoons dark brown sugar

Roasted Butternut Squash and Pear Fricassee

1 large butternut squash

3 medium semi-ripe Bartlett or Bosc pears

3 tablespoons unsalted butter

Salt and freshly ground black pepper

Large pinch of freshly grated nutmeg

2 tablespoons dark brown sugar

½ cup chicken broth, preferably homemade (page 360)

I have to confess that of all the winter squashes, butternut and acorn are my favorites. Butternut in particular has the ability to stand on its own as an interesting vegetable but also likes the company of other cool-weather vegetables and many fruits. This lovely fricassee is good alongside a baked ham or roast duck, turkey, or pork.

1. Preheat the oven to 375°F. Peel the butternut squash and cut into ¾-inch cubes. Peel and core the pears. Cut into ¾-inch cubes and set aside.

2. In a rectangular flameproof baking dish, melt the butter over low heat. Add the pears and squash and season with salt, pepper, and nutmeg. Sprinkle with brown sugar, add ¼ cup of the broth, and bake for 1 hour or until tender, adding a little broth if the pan juices run dry. Serve hot or at room temperature.

SERVES 4 TO 5

NOTE: When choosing pears, avoid the often too-under-ripe Anjou pear or the Comice pear, which tends to fall apart in cooking and is essentially an eating pear. Bosc and Bartlett are the best choices here.

Acorn Squash, Apple, and Wild Mushroom Soup

Acorn squash is another superb winter squash that is good simply roasted and in many seasonal soups. I am especially fond of the earthy mushroom flavor, which adds an interesting smokiness to the otherwise mild-tasting soup. Be sure to use a rich, well-seasoned broth.

1. Preheat the oven to 400°F.

2. Place the whole acorn squash on a baking sheet and bake for 45 minutes to 1 hour, or until very tender when pierced with the tip of a sharp knife. Remove the squash from the oven and when cool enough to handle, cut in half, peel, and remove the seeds. Dice the pulp coarsely and set aside.

3. In a 10-inch cast-iron skillet, melt 2 tablespoons of the butter over medium high heat. Add the apples and sauté until lightly browned. Add the sugar and continue to sauté over fairly high heat until the apple slices are caramelized and very well browned. Remove from the heat and reserve.

4. In a 3½- or 4-quart casserole, melt 2 tablespoons of the butter over low heat. Add the onion and cook until soft and lightly browned. Add the brown sugar and spices and continue to sauté for 2 minutes without letting the sugar burn.

5. Immediately add the acorn squash and the broth and simmer the soup, partially covered, for 20 minutes. Add the apples and continue to simmer for another 15 minutes. Cool the soup slightly. Transfer the soup to a food processor and process until smooth. Return the soup to the casserole, season with salt and pepper, and set aside.

6. Melt the remaining 2 tablespoons of butter in a small skillet over medium high heat. Add the mushrooms and sauté quickly for 1 to 2 minutes, or until lightly browned. Season with salt and pepper. Add the mushrooms to the soup, the cream, if using, and correct the seasoning.

SERVES 4 TO 5

2 medium acorn squash, about
 1 pound each
5 tablespoons unsalted butter
3 Golden Delicious apples,
 peeled and cored
1 teaspoon sugar
1 large onion, peeled and finely
 minced
2 tablespoons dark brown sugar
½ teaspoon ground ginger
¼ teaspoon ground coriander
¼ teaspoon cardamom
Large pinch of freshly grated
 nutmeg
8 to 9 cups chicken broth,
 preferably homemade
 (page 360)
Salt and freshly ground white
 pepper
¼ pound fresh chanterelles or
 ¼ pound shiitake
 mushrooms, stemmed and
 sliced into ¼-inch slices
Optional: ⅓ cup heavy cream

Sweet and Spicy Sauté of Spaghetti Squash

1 medium spaghetti squash
3 tablespoons unsalted butter
1 tablespoon peanut oil
1 small dry red chili pepper, broken in half
3 large onions, peeled, quartered, and thinly sliced
2 large garlic cloves, peeled and minced
1 tablespoon finely minced fresh ginger
4 tablespoons dark brown sugar
Salt and freshly ground black pepper

*T*he biggest problem with spaghetti squash is its name; many people who are unfamiliar with the vegetable think that it should be treated like pasta, dousing it with tomato sauce—for which this mild squash has absolutely no affinity. On the other hand, maple sugar, brown sugar, and spices such as curry, cumin, and the myriad of Far Eastern spices all go well with spaghetti squash, so experiment. Serve with a well-seasoned roasted breast of turkey. Leftover squash can easily be reheated in the microwave. A cupful of spaghetti squash is also a good addition to the acorn squash soup on page 355.

1. Preheat the oven to 375°F.

2. Place the spaghetti squash, whole, on a baking sheet and bake for 45 to 50 minutes, or until easily pierced with a fork. Turn once during baking. Remove from the oven and let cool.

3. Cut the squash in half lengthwise. Scoop out the flesh with the tines of a fork to form spaghetti-like strands. Measure 4 cups of the strands and reserve. Save the remainder for another use.

4. In a large heavy skillet, melt 3 tablespoons of the butter together with the peanut oil over medium high heat. Add the chili pepper and cook until dark. Remove the chili pepper and discard.

5. Add the onions to the hot chili oil and cook, stirring often, until the onions begin to brown, about 10 minutes. Lower the heat and continue to cook the onions for 30 minutes, or until soft and nicely caramelized.

6. Add the garlic, ginger, and brown sugar, toss with the onions, and continue to cook until the sugar has melted. Add the reserved spaghetti squash, season with salt and pepper, and toss to coat well with the onion mixture. Just heat through and serve.

SERVES 4 TO 6

BASICS

Crème Fraîche

Clarified Butter

Quick Pizza Dough

Provençal Vinaigrette

Chicken Stock

Beurre Manié

Homemade Mayonnaise

Basic Tart Shell

Cooked White Beans

Fire-Roasted Red Bell Peppers

Crème Fraîche

3 tablespoons buttermilk
2 cups heavy cream, not
ultrapasteurized

Crème fraîche can take ten to twenty-four hours to sour and thicken. It depends mainly on the temperature of your kitchen. Be sure to keep it in a warm, draft-free place. Once done, stir it thoroughly, cover, and refrigerate. It will keep ten days to two weeks. It cannot be frozen.

1. Combine the buttermilk and cream in a glass jar and whisk until well blended. Cover the jar loosely and set aside in a warm place until the cream becomes very thick.

2. Chill until ready to use.

MAKES ABOUT 2 CUPS

Clarified Butter

At least 8 ounces unsalted
butter

Clarifying butter is a simple technique that removes the milky residue and impurities that make butter burn quickly. It works best when done with at least eight ounces of butter. Once it is clarified, the butter can be refrigerated in a tightly sealed jar for at least two weeks or frozen for several months. Clarified butter is used for sautéing delicate foods, such as fish fillets, fritters, or anything that is breaded, and you can use it in any recipe that calls for regular butter for sautéing.

Melt the desired amount of unsalted butter in a heavy saucepan over low heat. As soon as the butter is melted and very foamy, remove from the heat and carefully skim off the foam and discard. Pour the clear yellow liquid through a fine sieve, leaving the milky residue on the bottom of the pan. Store the clarified butter in a covered jar in the refrigerator.

MAKES ABOUT 4 TO 5 OUNCES

Quick Pizza Dough

Pizza dough freezes quite well, so you can always have a ball ready for your own impromptu topping mixtures.

1. In a small bowl, combine the warm water, yeast, and sugar. Stir until well blended and set aside for 10 minutes, or until the mixture is bubbly.

2. Combine the flour and salt in a food processor and, with the machine running, add the yeast mixture, oil, and cold water in a slow, steady stream. Process for 1 minute. The dough will be slightly sticky.

3. Transfer the dough to a lightly floured surface and knead for about 2 minutes with lightly floured hands. Divide in half, place in plastic bags with room for expansion, and refrigerate for 1 hour. The dough is now ready to be used.

MAKES TWO 12-INCH PIZZAS

¼ cup warm water
1 teaspoon dry yeast,
 preferably not rapid rise
½ teaspoon sugar
2¾ cups all-purpose flour
1½ teaspoons salt
3 tablespoons olive oil
¾ cup cold water

Provençal Vinaigrette

This is the most basic of all vinaigrettes, an accommodating base for the addition of your favorite herbs, vegetable purees, or other flavorings.

Combine the vinegar, mustard, and garlic in a small bowl and whisk until well blended. Slowly add the oil, whisking constantly, until creamy and smooth. Season with salt and pepper.

SERVES 6

2 tablespoons red wine vinegar
2 teaspoons Dijon mustard
1 medium garlic clove, peeled
 and mashed
6 to 8 tablespoons olive oil
Salt and freshly ground black
 pepper

Chicken Stock

Homemade stock improves the flavor of most soups immeasurably, and some dishes, such as risotto, simply cannot be made without it. Fortunately it is simple to make and freezes beautifully, so there is no reason to be dependent on canned broths.

1 whole chicken, about 3 pounds, quartered
10 to 14 chicken wings or 2 pounds chicken necks and gizzards
2 large carrots, peeled and cut in half
2 large stalks celery, cut in half
1 parsley root, peeled, or 2 large sprigs of fresh parsley
1 large sprig of fresh thyme
1 large leek, well rinsed, or 1 large onion, peeled and stuck with a clove
Large pinch of salt
6 to 8 whole black peppercorns

1. Combine all the stock ingredients in a large casserole and cover with water by 2 inches. Bring to a boil slowly and carefully skim the surface from time to time.

2. Reduce the heat and simmer, partially covered, for 1 hour and 30 minutes to 2 hours. When done, remove the stock from the heat and cool uncovered.

3. Strain the stock and when completely cool, refrigerate uncovered overnight.

4. The next day discard the fat that has solidified on the surface. Transfer the degreased stock to a casserole, bring to a boil, and transfer the hot stock to 1-quart containers. Again cool the stock, uncovered, and when completely cool, cover and refrigerate or freeze.

MAKES 2 TO 2 1/2 QUARTS

NOTE: All stock must be cooled uncovered to prevent it from turning sour. If the stock is stored in the refrigerator, bring it back to a boil every 3 to 4 days to prevent it from souring. The stock can be frozen successfully for 6 to 8 weeks.

Beurre Manié

8 tablespoons unsalted butter, slightly softened

8 tablespoons all-purpose flour

A beurre manié is a flour and butter paste that is used in both classical and peasant cooking to thicken sauces. It can be formed into tablespoon-size balls and held successfully for several weeks. You will rarely need an entire beurre manié in any recipe in this book, since it is preferable to reduce the sauce naturally before thickening it so as to intensify the flavor.

1. Combine the butter and flour in a food processor and process until smooth.

2. Refrigerate the mixture until it is just firm enough to shape into balls with your hands. Divide the mixture into 8 equal parts and roll quickly between your palms.

3. Place the balls in a tightly covered jar and refrigerate until needed. The beurre manié can also be frozen for 2 to 3 months.

MAKES 8 BEURRE MANIÉ

Homemade Mayonnaise

1 extra-large egg
1 extra-large egg yolk
1 tablespoon fresh lemon juice
   or sherry vinegar
Salt and freshly ground white
   pepper
¾ cup peanut or corn oil

Despite the convenience of the food processor or the all-purpose blender, many cooks still shy away from making their own mayonnaise. This is unfortunate since the texture and taste of homemade mayonnaise is so much better than bottled. Not only can you modify its flavor by using different oils, vinegars, or citrus juices, but you can also control the texture of the mayonnaise according to your needs. Personally I much prefer making it in an old-fashioned blender rather than a food processor since it requires much less oil. Homemade mayonnaise will keep in the refrigerator for up to 10 days.

1. Combine the egg, egg yolk, and lemon juice or vinegar in a blender and season highly with salt and pepper. With the machine running at top speed, add the oil by droplets until the mixture begins to thicken. Then add the remaining oil in a slow, steady stream until all has been added.

2. Store in a tightly covered jar in the refrigerator.

MAKES ABOUT 1 1/4 CUPS

Basic Tart Shell

This is a very easily assembled tart dough, but if time is short, do what I often do and use a purchased dough sheet. The quality of the pre-rolled refrigerator crust is actually so good it hardly seems like a compromise.

1. Combine the flour, salt, and butter in a food processor and pulse on and off until the mixture resembles oatmeal. Add 3 tablespoons of the ice water and pulse quickly just until the mixture begins to come together.

2. Transfer to a bowl and gather into a ball, adding a bit more water if too crumbly. Flatten the ball into a disk, wrap in foil, and chill for 30 minutes or until firm enough to roll.

3. On a lightly floured surface, roll the dough into a circle about ⅛ inch thick. Transfer to a 9- or 10-inch tart pan and press into the bottom and sides of the pan, being careful not to stretch the dough. Fold the overhang into the pan and press it firmly against the sides. Alternatively, roll a circle of ready-made dough to a thickness of ⅛ inch and proceed as above.

4. Prick the bottom of the shell with a fork, cover with aluminum foil, and place in the freezer for 4 to 6 hours or overnight. At this point the tart shell can be kept frozen for up to 2 weeks. The shell is now referred to as *unbaked.*

5. Preheat the oven to 425°F.

6. Line the frozen shell with parchment paper. Fill with large dried beans and place on a cookie sheet. Place in the center of the oven and bake for 12 minutes, or until the sides are set.

7. Remove the paper and beans and continue to bake for 4 to 6 minutes longer, until the dough is set but not browned. Remove from the oven and place the pan on a wire rack to cool until needed. The tart shell is now *partially baked* and is ready for your desired filling. (For a *prebaked shell,* bake an additional 10 to 12 minutes, or until golden brown.)

MAKES TWO 9- OR ONE 11-INCH TART SHELL

2 cups all-purpose unbleached flour

¼ to ½ teaspoon salt

12 tablespoons unsalted butter, cut into 12 pieces and chilled

3 to 6 tablespoons ice water

OR

1 sheet of ready-made pie dough

Cooked White Beans

1 pound dried white beans,
    preferably Great Northern
Water
1 small onion, unpeeled
1 large sprig of fresh thyme
1 large sprig of fresh parsley
6 whole black peppercorns
½ pound smoked pork
    shoulder butt, quartered
Salt

You can cook beans by either of two methods: presoaking overnight and then oven-braising until tender, or quick-soaking the same day you plan to cook them.

METHOD ONE

1. Place the dried beans in a large bowl with plenty of water to cover. Soak overnight at room temperature.

2. The next day, preheat the oven to 325°F.

3. Drain the beans and place in a large, heavy flameproof casserole with a tight-fitting lid. Cover with water by 2 inches and add the onion, thyme, parsley, peppercorns, and pork butt.

4. Bring to a boil on top of the stove and cook for exactly 1 minute. Immediately cover tightly and place the casserole in the center of the oven. Cook the beans for 1 hour to 1 hour and 15 minutes, or until just tender. Do not overcook, and do not add salt until the beans are almost done. Remove the casserole from the oven and let the beans cool in their cooking liquid.

5. Discard the onion and herbs. Store the beans in their liquid for up to 5 days in the refrigerator. You will need both the cooked beans as well as the bean cooking liquid in most recipes.

METHOD TWO

1. Do not soak the beans at all. Instead place them in a large, heavy flameproof casserole with a tight-fitting lid. Cover with water by 2 inches and add the onion, thyme, parsley, peppercorns, and pork butt.

2. Bring to a boil on top of the stove and cook for exactly 1 minute. Immediately remove the casserole from the heat, cover, and set aside for 2 hours at room temperature. Drain the beans, add fresh water to cover by 2 inches, and continue to braise the beans in the oven as in Method One.

MAKES ABOUT 6 CUPS

Also use either of these two methods to cook red kidney beans, black turtle beans, pinto beans, cranberry beans, navy pea beans, cow peas, pigeon peas, and flageolets. Cooking times will vary with each bean. For chickpeas, add ½ teaspoon baking soda to the soaking water before soaking overnight.

Fire-Roasted Red Bell Peppers

Red bell peppers

*R*oasted peppers will keep for several days in the refrigerator, covered with olive oil, in a tightly covered jar. You may also roast green bell peppers or any other variety—jalapeños, serranos, yellow and orange— fresh tomatoes can be prepared in the same manner. They do not need to be wrapped in a damp towel after roasting; just set them aside to cool before peeling.

1. If charring the peppers outdoors, prepare the charcoal grill.

2. When the coals are red hot, place the peppers directly on top of the coals and grill, turning when necessary, until the skins are blackened and somewhat charred on all sides. As soon as the peppers are done, remove them from the grill and wrap each one in a damp paper towel. Set aside to cool completely.

3. When cool enough to handle, peel off the charred skin, core, and remove all seeds.

4. To char the peppers indoors, you may use either an electric or a gas stove. For an electric stove, place the peppers directly on the coils of the burner over medium high heat to char on all sides. For a gas stove, pierce the peppers onto the tines of a long fork through the stem end. Hold over a medium high flame and char on all sides. Remove from the burner, wrap in a damp paper towel, let cool, and peel.

INDEX

CONVERSION CHART

Equivalent Imperial and Metric Measurements

American cooks use standard containers, the 8-ounce cup and a tablespoon that takes exactly 16 level fillings to fill that cup level. Measuring by cup makes it very difficult to give weight equivalents, as a cup of densely packed butter will weigh considerably more than a cup of flour. The easiest way therefore to deal with cup measurements in recipes is to take the amount by volume rather than by weight. Thus the equation reads: *1 cup = 240 ml = 8 fl. oz. $^1/_2$ cup = 120 ml = 4 fl. oz.*

It is possible to buy a set of American cup measures in major stores around the world.

In the States, butter is often measured in sticks. One stick is the equivalent of 8 tablespoons. One tablespoon of butter is therefore the equivalent to ½ ounce/15 grams.

SOLID MEASURES

U.S. and Imperial Measures		Metric Measures	
ounces	pounds	grams	kilos
1		28	
2		56	
3½		100	
4	¼	112	
5		140	
6		168	
8	½	225	
9		250	¼
12	¾	340	
16	1	450	
18		500	½
20	1¼	560	
24	1½	675	
27		750	¾
28	1¾	780	
32	2	900	
36	2¼	1000	1
40	2½	1100	
48	3	1350	
54		1500	1½
64	4	1800	
72	4½	2000	2
80	5	2250	2¼
90		2500	2½
100	6	2800	2¾

LIQUID MEASURES

Fluid ounces	U.S.	Imperial	Milliliters
	1 teaspoon	1 teaspoon	5
¼	2 teaspoons	1 dessertspoon	10
½	1 tablespoon	1 tablespoon	14
1	2 tablespoons	2 tablespoons	28
2	¼ cup	4 tablespoons	56
4	½ cup		110
5		¼ pint or 1 gill	140
6	¾ cup		170
8	1 cup		225
9			250
10	1¼ cups	½ pint	280
12	1½ cups		340
15		¾ pint	420
16	2 cups		450
18	2¼ cups		500
20	2½ cups	1 pint	560
24	3 cups		675
25		1¼ pints	700
27	3½ cups		750
30	3¾ cups	1½ pints	840
32	4 cups or 1 quart		900
35		1¾ pints	980
36	4½ cups		1000
40	5 cups	2 pints or 1 quart	1120
48	6 cups		1350
50		2½ pints	1400
60	7½ cups	3 pints	1680
64	8 cups or 2 quarts		1800
72	9 cups		2000

OVEN TEMPERATURE EQUIVALENTS

Fahrenheit	Celsius	Gas Mark	Description
225	110	¼	Cool
250	130	½	
275	140	1	Very Slow
300	150	2	
325	170	3	Slow
350	180	4	Moderate
375	190	5	
400	200	6	Moderately Hot
425	220	7	Fairly Hot
450	230	8	Hot
475	240	9	Very Hot
500	250	10	Extremely Hot

EQUIVALENTS FOR INGREDIENTS

all-purpose flour—plain flour
arugula—rocket
confectioners' sugar—icing sugar
cornstarch—cornflour
eggplant—aubergine

granulated sugar—castor sugar
half and half—12% fat milk
lima beans—broad beans
scallion—spring onion
shortening—white fat

unbleached flour—strong, white flour
vanilla bean—vanilla pod
zest—rind
zucchini—courgettes or marrow